Wishing Well

Wishing Well

Making Your Every
Wish Come True

Paul Pearsall, Ph.D.

HYPERION
NEW YORK

Important Note to Reader

The material in this book is intended to provide an overview of the research,
theories, and cultural concepts related to the process of wishing. The material has
been extensively researched and is intended for readers wishing to pursue further
inquiries and study. Every effort has been made to provide the most accurate and
dependable information. However, the reader should be aware that professionals
may have differing opinions about the implications of this research. Any
suggestions for techniques, treatments, or life-style changes referred to or implied
in this book should be undertaken only with consultation with a licensed
physician, therapist, or health-care professional.

LIBRARY OF CONGRESS CATALOGING-IN-PUBLICATION DATA

ISBN: 0-7868-6561-X

Book design by Richard Oriolo

FIRST EDITION

10 9 8 7 6 5 4 3 2 1

With well wishes for:
my mother, Carol, for
peace, happiness, healing, and health now and forever;

my deceased father, Frank, that
you know you are always in my heart;

my sons, Roger and Scott, that
your lives flourish in safety and loving joy;

my miracle-making wife, Celest, that
your wishes be granted as you've granted mine

Acknowledgments

···················· ✍ ····················

A book is a wish come true. It is a wish made by an author but granted by the warm hearts, open minds, and hard work of hundreds—and in the case of this book, thousands—of persons willing to share the wish and help make it wisely and well. My wish would never have come true without the courage, trust, and loving heart of my editor, Gretchen Young. She is a true wish master. Without her unwavering support, my wish would never have been given wings. She showed faith when others doubted, hope in the face of others' cynicism, and tenacity when others resisted the idea that something as simple as a wish could have such immense power. Another wish granted at Hyperion was Jennifer Morgan. Mahalo for your 3 Ps essential in the making of any good book or wise wish—persistence, patience, and pleasantness.

I owe an immense debt to the many scientists, researchers, and authors whose work is included in this book. The careful and diligent researchers at the Princeton Engineering Anomalies Research program are founders of the scientific study of processes related to what I have called wishing. Dr. Marilyn Schlitz has been an inspiration to me in all of my work and this book would not have been possible without her pioneering studies on the subtle but significant role of intent in our lives. Dr. Larry Dossey's courage and creativity have been pivotal in guiding us all into a new era in medicine. As many others have, I quote his words and refer to his wisdom throughout this book. I express my most sincere appreciation to these and the many other giants upon whose shoulders I have stood to take a peek at the mysteries of wish making. I apologize and take full responsibility for any distortions or over-statements of what they are learning and teaching and for any errors or exaggerations of their careful work that may stem from my Hawaiian overeagerness to shout the magnificent news that our ancestors were right! Our intentions are creative acts of consciousness that transcend time and space.

I express heartfelt mahalo to my dear friends, teachers, and new 'ohana Drs. Gary E. R. Schwartz and Linda G. S. Russek. The "grit" of their sound and careful research combined with the grace of their loving hearts guides my canoe in waters still overwhelming to me. I sometimes think I have an inkling of where I'm going in the waters of my home culture of Hawai'i, but they are much more experienced paddlers in the oceans of the world. My special mahalo nui to Dr. William Tiller, whose brilliantly creative mind and warm Hawaiian heart shine through all of his work and in his words in his much appreciated foreword. Mahalo to Kahuna Frank Kawaikapuokalani Hewett for his foreword. He has long been my kuma—my most wise teacher, gentle guide, and loving friend in perpetuating the culture of Hawaiians, a people who have always known and profoundly respected the power of our infinite connection with everyone and every thing.

My own 'ohana have always been my wish partners, and I quite literally owe them my life. My love is beyond words for my wife, Celest. She is the wisest and most powerful well wisher I have ever know. My aloha to my sons, Roger and Scott, my mother, Carol, my brother, Dennis, and my father, Frank. Mahalo to our extended 'ohana Aunty Betty and Uncle Jack, Tutu Mama, all of the kupuna (elders) of Hawai'i who have shared their wisdom of wishing, and to the hundreds of men, women, and children who shared their wishes for this book. I wish, as all of you have all done for me, that your every wish comes true.

PAUL KAʻIKENA PEARSALL, PH.D.
Honolulu, Hawai'i
October 1999

Contents

PART TWO

Practicing Wishcraft

Let Your Wishes Fly

I ka ʻōlelo ke ola, i ka ʻōlelo ka make.
Words give life, words give death.

Dr. Pearsall's book comes just in time. We are entering a period when the influence of a mysterious invisible force that the Western world often fears and mocks will no longer be denied. This subtle but splendid invisible energy that dictates our destiny is becoming more manifest every day. It is like the wind. It cannot be seen, but it moves our soul. More people are becoming sensitive to this force now, and for the first time in written form, Dr. Pearsall presents the cultural and scientific evidence for the positive and negative aspects of one of our oldest rituals for dealing with this force—the simple but powerful process of making a wish.

As they always do, our wishes are coming true, yet we must ask ourselves what they have wrought. Have our granted wishes made us feel calmer, safer, and more deeply connected with others? Has the granting of our wish for high tech led to us feeling more in touch with one another? Has it made our hearts calmer, warmer, and more connected with other hearts? Have the timesaving devices we wished for really given us more time? Is the world we have wished upon ourselves the one our ancestors would have wished for us? As a healer (kahuna) trained in the sacred ancient wishing traditions of one of the oldest cultures in the world, I answer these questions with a resounding "no." Dr. Pearsall's book comes just in time because it can teach us how to wish well now, as we confront the results of our unwise wishing. It comes in time for us and our children so that we will be able to answer "yes" to these questions for the new millennium.

The violence, upheaval, and hostility in the world and the earth's climatic writhing and quivers that tumble our homes seem evidence that we have not always been wishing well. This book will likely find critics among those whose sixth sense is blind and who think only with their brain and not their heart, but it is precisely what we need now to learn to wish more wisely. It is a prescription for more reflective, careful, caring wishing in harmony with the *'āina* (land), the *'ohana* (family), and *ke Akua* (God or the higher power). It is a like a canoe that can carry us back and forth between Western science and ancient spiritual teachings. Those who refuse to get into the canoe and cling to one side or the other may find themselves alone and isolated. I beckon them to venture forth into the world of wishing that Dr. Pearsall describes.

Dr. Pearsall's many tests, assignments, teaching tricks, and stories about wishes help us venture safely and joyfully in our canoe. We can most easily learn about what makes us uncomfortable by having some fun doing so. The Hawaiian teaching style of fun, review, and teaching tricks offered in this book will be new to some, but it reflects the true nature of wish making.

Even though this book contains the latest "head-oriented" research on the components of wishing and what Western science calls intentionality, intuition, healing at a distance, subtle energy, resonation, and psi phenomena, Dr. Pearsall is not afraid to speak openly about the spiritual forces most of us have long sensed in our hearts. As a Hawaiian, he thinks "and" rather than "or" and "to" rather than "is." His is oceanic logic that flows easily between the hardness of science and the softness of spirituality, the occult, and mysticism. To learn to wish well, you will have to flow with this book too and do as Dr. Pearsall does. You will have to be willing to go beyond your continental, rock-style logic of boundaries, borders, and single definitions and explanations.

This book comes just in time because it offers many proofs and examples of the lessons I teach every day as kahuna. Wishing is asking, not telling. Because wishing is a request instead of a demand and humble instead of assertive, it represents a less aggressive and controlling way of being in and with the world. It is a way of acknowledging our connection with the world instead of trying to master and use it. Dr. Pearsall shows how wishing's gentle nature honors the ancient lessons of modest respect, ultimate responsibility, and undeniable belonging, from which many of our young people turn away in the hurried cynicism of their daily lives. He shows how wishing is fun, a way of playing nicely with the supernatural forces rather than fighting hard to overcome them. He shows how wishing is asking for just enough rather than trying to have it all. We have long needed a Western book that serves as a link between the peaceful ancient heart and the hurried modern mind. Dr. Pearsall warns with his science and research what I as a healer was taught by my ancestors: that our wishes can bring life but also death. To fail to wish well is to bring terrible consequences upon ourselves, others, and the world. This is why we need the lessons in this book now more than ever.

Dr. Pearsall shows us how we can more wisely learn to use our ancestral gift of wishing and embrace one of the most powerful ancient ways of living in harmony and sympathy with our world. He shows that wishing well is falling into forgiving sympathy, something his science calls sympathetic resonance, with the sacred truths of life. He shows that wishing well is wishing for the truth more than wishing that all our wishes come true. He shows us how we can learn to wish from our heart to connect more with the world instead of wishing from our head to try to control it. He shows us with cultural lessons, research, tests, and fascinating stories what my ancestors taught me as kahuna—to cherish the source of our being. If we are willing to go against our brain's wishes, Dr. Pearsall offers us a heart path to the way to harness the power of wishing for a more harmonious, balanced, peaceful, joyful life. In doing so, we wish upon ourselves and others a more sacred world.

Every point Dr. Pearsall makes about wishing was long known to my ancient ancestors and taught to me in my traditional Hawaiian home. I have never seen these lessons of wishing written about before. I was orally taught the lessons of wishing you will read about in these pages. I was taught that wishing well is expressing the sacred wisdom of all of those who went before and not our own selfish needs.

Dr. Pearsall writes about the importance of taking a deep breath, focusing on the heart, and then giving voice to our intentions. This is the power of the sacred breath (*hā*) and the *mana ka leo* (power of the voice). I was taught that our words have immense power. A stated wish has extreme spiritual potency. Dr. Pearsall writes of the space-free and boundless nature of a wish. Our most revered Hawaiian ancestors warned that when we make a wish, we *lele ka pule* (flight of the prayer). This means that we send our wishes resounding forever everywhere like a drum beating everywhere all at once. Dr. Pearsall writes of the timelessness of wishing. Kahuna know that we may think we are wishing in the present, but our wishes are timeless and forever. They work backward as well as forward, and they help or hurt everyone then, now, and to come. We may make our wish as if it were in the present, but once we put it into words, it becomes infinite and vibrates forever with *mana*, the ancestral authority and energy of our forebears.

Dr. Pearsall and his scientist friends call all of these principles of wishing "nonlocality," but I call it passing on the cultural collective memories of our ancestors. As Dr. Pearsall writes and our ancestors taught, wishing well is using our intention to make a possibility a reality. If our wish "passes on" loving energy left within us from our ancestors rather than petitioning for more things for ourselves, we wish well.

When Dr. Pearsall writes of wicked wishing, he expresses my deepest concern as kahuna about the danger of wishing. A selfish "head-oriented" wish attempting to get more power, control, and material things for the wisher rather than passing on the wisdom of the ancestors can be a deadly wish. He emphasizes wishing from our hearts instead of our heads, and this is perhaps the most important lesson of wishing well. It is in our hearts that our memories of paradise are stored. When we wish from there, we wish for and from paradise. Our Hawaiian ancestors taught that we must always wish gently and in unity and connection with the sacred spirit of all of those who have gone before us. Dr. Pearsall says that we must wish so that our wishes resonate with truth, not just to make them come to our own version of the truth. He says we must be careful to wish with reverence for the basic truths and knowledge of love of our ancestral spirits, a lesson every kahuna teaches and treasures.

Dr. Pearsall writes of the subtle but most magnificent power of a wish to do good but also to do harm when we wish wickedly. This is a wishing lesson I was also taught. He writes of "power wishing" or wishing together in harmony as a very powerful process, and my ancestors also spoke to me of this unity of spirit in making our wishes. Dr. Pearsall writes of the power of a wish's energy to enter into people and objects. This is also one of my ancient ancestral lessons. Even rocks contain our wishes, although we may have lost our ear to hear their language. We can hear them again if we wish to.

I have always been taught that we imprint objects with our wishes—the food we cook, the seeds we plant, and the things we make when we work. Dr. Pearsall calls this the "talisman effect," and I, too, know that we give people and things *mana* with our wishes as we spiritually saturate them with the divine energetic authority of our ancestors. Our intentions make our realities.

Dr. Pearsall's wish star is the perfect guide to wishing. It also reflects ancient Hawai'i of thousands of years ago and the teachings of wishing I have observed in my visits to other shamans around the world. When I am asked as kahuna what I wish for, I answer for life, for guidance from my ancestors to the path of peace, for protection and security for my family, for spiritual guidance from my ancestors, and to share aloha or love with others and the world. These turn out to be the same five realms of Dr. Pearsall's wish star. I wish many will read this book because we need millions of well wishes in these domains of the wish star if we are to return to balance and harmony in our lives.

Dr. Pearsall writes of the importance of patience in our wishing. This is also a most important lesson of ancient wishing we call *ho'omanawanui* (much time) and *ahonui* (great breath). If you cannot wait, do not wish. Our wishes are not granted in our brain's frame of time. Dr. Pearsall writes of wishing with respect for others' wishes, and I teach this, too. We must remember when we wish that everything we wish for or away must come from someone and go somewhere. Ultimately, our wishes always come true in some way and our wishes—angry or loving—always come back to us. This was the ultimate and terrible danger of the Hawaiian death prayer we call *ana ana*. To check to see if you have wished well for someone else, ask yourself, "Do I want this same wish to come true for me?"

Dr. Pearsall could have used the Hawaiian words for wishing well—*Mālama Pono* (honor the natural order)—for the title of this book. As in all things Hawaiian, and in wishing itself, the phrase *mālama pono* has many inclusive meanings. It means to always wish with respect for and to maintain the balance in life. It means to wish for "the way" rather than "our way." It means to be *mihi,* or forgiving, in our wishing rather than hostile, demanding, or controlling. It means to honor the *'ike,* or the divine knowledge and revelation of the sacred ancestors, as we make our wish. It means to wish with sympathy and to try to resonate with the world instead of trying to master it. It means to be constantly aware of those things we cannot see or touch and their importance in our life, the *mana* or subtle energy that is the representation of our ancestors' sacred knowledge. It means to wish with awareness of our connection with all that is and ever was and as if our ancestors were listening to and judging our every wish for its heart content. All of these and many more are lessons about wishing that you will read about in this book.

One day many, many years ago, I became angry. A friend had become mean, dishonest, and unfair and had done many things that hurt me deeply. I wanted to wish him evil. I went to my aunt who was one of my teachers as I trained to be kahuna, a protector and teacher of the "secret" of the power of wishing and healing. "What should I do, Auntie?" I asked. "I want to wish him the same pain I am suffering from his actions." My aunt smiled and pointed to her heart. "Wish him well, my son, wish him well," she said. "Wish as you think your ancestors would want you to wish. When you wish well, you become well." So I wished with forgiveness and for love in his life, and for the first time in my young life I felt the immense power of a wish made well. Our friendship eventually was healed, I was freed of my anger, and I felt in *pono,* or balance, with the way my ancestors would have wanted me to live and love. I had helped to make their wishes come true.

Dr. Pearsall's work is a book I have long been wishing for. It is my wish that you will read it slowly and contemplate its many messages. Most of all, I wish you well in your reading so you may learn to wish well in your own life.

Kahuna Kawaikapuokalani Kākoʻomaioʻloonalaninuiamamao Hewett
May 1999
Kāneʻohe, Hawaiʻi

Conscious Acts of Creation

··· ❧ ···

In Support of Wishing

This is a wonderful and timely book of great benefit for humanity. It contains abundant old and new wisdom combined with many very lucid questionnaires that allow readers to learn about their own "wish-ability." Its essence details and expands on the great Hawaiian healing tradition of establishing and maintaining a sympathetic harmony with nature and the miracles that happen when we wish with such unity and connectedness. By providing a sturdy bridge between the oldest cultural ideas and the newest scientific concepts about the ways our intentions change the world, this book extends the ancient wisdom of one of the most important processes in the universe—the remarkable power of making a wish.

In reflecting upon how I might most meaningfully contribute to Paul Pearsall's important book, it seemed that some detailed buttressing of its already strong scientific component might be in order. I offer it to help Dr. Pearsall convince the strongest skeptic that wishing works and human intentions robustly influence physical reality. This book is written for everyone who wants to learn to wish well. It is highly accessible, user-friendly, and fun to read. Dr. Pearsall clearly articulates for the layperson how to wish well and how wishing works. My foreword summarizes some of my own and my research teams' most recent experimental results and theoretical perspectives on the power behind what Dr. Pearsall calls the skill of "wishing well."

A Challenge to Five-Sense Science

In our laboratory, we have shown that the power of a wish, when intentionally embedded in simple electronic devices, significantly alters them. Dr. Pearsall calls this phenomenon the "talisman effect," or imbuing objects with the power of the energy of our wishes. As much as such an idea flies in the face of establishment science, our own findings are fully and completely consistent with Dr. Pearsall's research and the material he presents about wishing. They support what Dr. Pearsall's own work with 2,166 wishers for almost ten years reveals—we all make wishes because we know on some level that they come true. Nonetheless, it is likely that what Dr. Pearsall and we have found will be challenged by those unaware of the current research on the power of a wish. It is for this reason that I add our own most current research to his array of proof of the power of wishing.

Extensive research already exists on what Dr. Pearsall calls the anomalies and sixth-sense psi processes and the demonstrable effects of our wishes on various systems. However, many people still find it difficult to understand how the invisible energy of a wish can change the way the world works. Based upon the prevailing scientific paradigm, the conventional viewpoint is that humans cannot meaningfully interact solely via their wishes with any specific target experiment. Even more strongly, this traditional viewpoint would state that our wishes cannot possibly be captured in a simple electronic device and then cause that device to meaningfully and measurably interact with another device some time in the future—in other words, transpose, contain, and transmit a wish across time and space. However, in complete opposition to this prevailing paradigm and these predictions emanating from what Dr. Pearsall calls "five-sense science," we have documented in our laboratory three very different experiments that help prove Dr. Pearsall's hypotheses about how wishing works.

Wish-Imprinted Devices

We have worked with what we call IIEDs (Intention Imprinted Electronic Devices). These are similar to what Dr. Pearsall calls "wish objects" and what some might refer to as "lucky charms" that seem to carry with them the good wishes left within them. We have found robust interaction between the wish-imprinted device and another device with which that wish-imbued apparatus later comes in contact. The power of a wish seems to be maintained in the object even when we send the object coast to coast by overnight mail. We have shown in our research what Dr. Pearsall explains so clearly in his book: wishing literally alters the physics we have come to accept as set rules. When we make a wish, we go out of our "bio-suit" and employ our consciousness to travel in a world free of the limits of what we have come to accept as reality.

Three wish experiments that we have extensively explored, published, and will soon publish more about have shown that the power of a wish can alter the pH of water, the aging of a fruit fly, and the way the human liver works. Although the technical aspects of our research cannot be presented here, our work has clearly shown that wishing can have significant and lasting effects on a variety of systems.

The Making of Sacred Places

Dr. Pearsall presents many clear examples and fascinating stories of how wishing influences our lives and the lives of others. Our own complex theoretical model for understanding our wishing results are explained in detail in my book *Science and Human Transformation*. There is not space here for the complex details and mathematical formulas of my evolving scientific hypotheses regarding the underlying energetic system of wishing. My working hypothesis, however, is that human intention or a wish, imposed on the mind domain from the level of the spirit (or as Dr. Pearsall suggests from a heart in balanced resonation with the brain), is capable of casting or bringing forth an infinite variety of relative universes. It is our *collective* thoughts, attitudes, and actions that ultimately create what we experience as our universe. In other words, the world we are living in is the one we have wished upon ourselves. The good news is that by wishing well, we can constantly wish various possible worlds into existence. Wishing is the ultimate creative act.

Dr. Pearsall writes that we should be careful what we wish for and how we wish because our wishes create a kind of "wishing ecology." Our research shows that one consequence of repeatedly making wishes is that the environment becomes "wish potentiated." When we continuously run our IIEDs or wish-imbued devices in particular physical locations, these locales gradually undergo a unique type of "conditioning" to the energy of wishing. The location seems to become a wish-friendly place as the simple act of wishing creates a "wish world" locale that appears to become what we call "more coherent" and Dr. Pearsall calls "sympathetically resonated." As Dr. Pearsall suggests, it is possible that wishing well can make our home and work and healing places much more wish-friendly and thereby more loving places. This wish-ecology effect may be due to the influence of the subtle wish energy Dr. Pearsall calls a "fifth force"—"L," or love energy. In effect, when we leave devices imbued with wish energy running for a long period of time at a specific location, that place transforms from a secular to a more sacred place.

Coming to Our Sixth Sense

To those who say that Dr. Pearsall's claims about the power of wishing are impossible, I point out that we and other scientists are beginning to observe in our research phenomena that are categorically impossible based upon the science Dr. Pearsall calls "conventional." As they reflect on the emerging research on wishing and the transcendent power of human intent, even the most doubting scientists are now beginning to respect the power of a simple wish and are more willing to study what Dr. Pearsall refers to as "sixth-sense processes" such as making a wish.

Because of our research and other ongoing work, I totally agree with Dr. Pearsall when he speaks of the vital importance of "wishing well" in our life. In fact, I suspect that wishing well will become a major personal, social, and spiritual responsibility in the new millennium. As Dr. Pearsall describes in his chapter titled "How Wishers Are Made," teaching our children to wish well will be one of our most significant parental challenges in this millennium. I agree with him when he writes that wishing can "tilt" the probabilities concerning our future, a process Dr. Pearsall calls "nudging the cosmos." I was fascinated with his application of psychological theories to the concept of wishing, his blend of culture, psychology, medicine, and physics to show how wishing works, and his description and examples of the relationship between wishing and loving. He offers us the first curriculum for the development of what I call conscious acts of creation.

Inner-Self-Management

If I disagree with Dr. Pearsall at all, it is that I do not believe he has gone nearly far enough in his assertions about the power of wishing. I do not believe that the consequences of wishing need to be as small as Dr. Pearsall describes. I understand that he is taking a major risk in even writing about this topic and I respect his scientific caution and humbleness, but our research indicates that under some circumstances, the power of wishing can be incredibly large indeed. I further believe that as we humans become more "inner-self-managed," or as Dr. Pearsall puts it, learn to "wish from the heart," we can become more coherent and fall into what he calls "sympathetic resonance" with others and the world. By doing so, we make a major transition beyond our present level of "PAT," or our "Psychological Absorption Test" score, discussed by Dr. Pearsall in Chapter 4 of this book. We can learn to perform "CAC," or Conscious Acts of Creation, that boggle our present imagination. We can move to a stage of human development where all or at least most of us can become well wishers and our wishing can have robust consequences for manifesting a new physics and a new physical reality.

Dr. Pearsall's combination of a subjective and objective approach to wishing can be expected to usher in a new scientific paradigm that I believe will be deeply explored with great consequences for humans during the twenty-first century. It is for this reason that I say this book is of immense importance for humanity and that I feel it comes to us just in time.

Exposing the Power of Wishing

Before I close, it is perhaps important to ask what is so special about my experiments with wishing that caused them to lead to such robust or significant and measurable results. Why have our wishing devices generated objectively strong results where, again as Dr. Pearsall correctly points out, many other research approaches to "sixth sense" or "psi" phenomena have tended to yield relatively small effects? Why did wishing work so well and so powerfully in our laboratories? The answer rests in Dr. Pearsall's own speculations about the power of wishing.

One reason we noted such strong wish power is that most humans have wishes or intentions that vary widely and reactively over time. We make so many little wishes so often and so automatically that we may not even notice that we are wishing. We tend to wish casually and spontaneously. Dr. Pearsall's book is important because he draws our attention to our wishing. Not having read this book, most of us do not yet wish proactively around the wish star Dr. Pearsall has created for us, nor do we always wish well, in accordance with the principles he draws from ancient cultural lessons and modern science, or in harmony with the spiritual principles he presents in the following pages. The result is that the time-averaged effect of a wish and scattered wishes over weeks to months usually seems to be of a small magnitude. Researchers on wishing often have to work hard to draw the results of a wish from their vast array of data. Sometimes our lack of what Dr. Pearsall calls "wish sensitivity" and "intuition" causes us to fail to detect the robust nature of wishing's effects. In our work, we focus the wishing, control as many variables as we can, and measure and record the effects of wishing. By doing so, we may be more directly exposing the range of a wish's power than may be apparent in everyday wishful thinking.

As researchers, we call wishing "precipitating a specific intention into a device during a strongly focused session." Dr. Pearsall refers to this same process of wishing as "sympathetically resonating from the heart." Whatever the name of the process, we can help eliminate much of the noise of the more common four forces of energy and reduce the vacillation and negative effects of wishing by doing as Dr. Pearsall suggests. We can help our wishes come true by focusing more on making them and intentionally trying to "fall into sync" with other wishers and the world.

Power Wishing

It is well known that the effective output of a cooperative group effort depends on the number of units contributing to the group, the strength of each unit, and the degree of internal coherence of this group. Our IIED or wish imprint device effect appears to be much more aligned than what might be produced by just a few persons making their own individual wishes. When it comes to wishing, our research shows that some group effect happens. To account for our robust results, I conclude that the "unseen" cooperative subtle forces that Dr. Pearsall calls subtle L or love energy resonate within a cooperative and mutually caring group sharing a wish—what Dr. Pearsall calls the "power wishing effect." This has important implications for the reader who wishes to have more harmonious relationships with others, within the family, or at work.

From our research, it seems clear then that human consciousness can meaningfully influence physical reality, that the details of that reality are adaptable to our wishing, and that strongly held, focused, and sustained (Dr. Pearsall's "resonating") intentions have real, measurable, cumulative, and profound consequences. This is why Dr.

Pearsall's book is so empowering. By learning to wish well, you the reader are potentially much more powerful than you have ever realized or may have even imagined until you read this book. As Dr. Pearsall points out, you have the capacity to be a wizard skilled in wishcraft. If you learn the lessons and follow the steps in this book, you can become just what those who love you and the world need most, a loving wizard who wishes well for and with the world.

WILLIAM A. TILLER, PH.D.
Professor Emeritus, Department of Material Science and Engineering
—Stanford University

I

The Art and Science of
Wishcraft

Take kindly the counsel of the years.
Nurture strength of spirit to shield you
in sudden misfortune.
But do not distress yourself with imaginings.

—DESIDERATA

One

Mastering the Wizardry of Wishing

"Did you make that song up?"
"Well, I sort of made it up," said Pooh. "It isn't Brain . . .
but it comes to me sometimes."
"Ah," said Rabbit, who never let things come to him,
but always went and fetched them.

—A. A. MILNE, *THE HOUSE AT POOH CORNER*

A Penchant for Wishing

Have you made a wish today? Have you ever made a wish as you gently sent a ladybug flying, while blowing on a dandelion, or while pulling the petals of a flower one by one in hopes the last petal would grant your wish for love? Are the words "I wish" a regular part of your self or public dialogue? Would you say you have a wisher's disposition and make wishes almost every day? Are you like Pooh who trusts in his heart in processes such as wishing that allow things to "just come to him" or like Rabbit who is constantly going after them? Are you driven by your brain to work hard to have it all or by your heart to be able to cherish all you have? To help you begin the process of learning to wish well, determine your wishing tendencies by taking the following Wish Propensity Test.

Wish Propensity Test

4 = ABSOLUTELY 3 = PROBABLY 2 = ON MANY OCCASIONS
1 = ON A VERY RARE OCCASION 0 = ABSOLUTELY NEVER

1. _____ Would you toss a coin into a fountain or make a wish on a star?

2. _____ Do you tend to take things very personally and go over and over them in your mind?

3. _____ Have you ever sensed someone looking at you, turned around to look, and discovered you were right?

4. _____ Do you feel like you have a "sixth sense" about people and things?

5. _____ Do you enjoy reading self-help books and/or attend motivational, inspirational seminars?

6. _____ Did your parents or grandparents believe in rituals such as making wishes?

7. _____ Do you ever feel "jinxed" or that other people lead "charmed" lives?

8. _____ Do you ever talk out loud to yourself?

9. _____ Do you seem to have a good feel for people and sense "good" or "bad" vibes coming from them?

10. _____ Do you "go with your gut" and make decisions purely on instinct or feel?

11. _____ Do you have feelings of déjà vu?

12. _____ Do you or someone you know seem to be "psychic" and able to forecast the future?

13. _____ If you found what looked like a magic lamp, would you rub it?

14. _____ Do you consider yourself superstitious?

15. _____ Do think that the spirits or "energy" of deceased loved ones lingers in some form after their passing?

16. _____ Do you think there is life on other planets?

17. _____ Do you have a good imagination?

18. _____ Do you think it is at least possible that flying saucers exist?

19. _____ Do you think a deceased family pet goes to a form of "animal heaven"?

20. _____ Do you think claims of so-called abduction by aliens have any credibility?

21. _____ Do you carry a charm or other lucky object you think brings you good luck?

22. _____ Would those who know you best say you are open-minded?

23. _____ Do you cry and laugh easily and vigorously?

24. _____ Even if you don't put much faith in it, do you read your horoscope?

25. _____ Do you believe in some form of reincarnation?

_____TOTAL SCORE

Here's a scale to help you place yourself on the wish scale.

80–100 = SERIOUS WISHER   60–79 = FREQUENT WISHER   40–59 = BORDERLINE WISHER

20–39 = WISH SKEPTIC   0–19 = WISH CYNIC

For the last ten years, I have been testing and interviewing 2,166 men, women, and children regarding the role of wishing in their lives. The results of this research are shared throughout this book. The Wish Propensity Test was one of the many tests I gave this group. Eighty-five percent (787 men and 1,045 women) of our wish-research sample scored above 80 on this test. The "wish skeptic" 15 percent (334 nonwishers, including 227 men and 107 women) in our 2,166-person sample scored below 30. This cross section of persons presented a preliminary portrait of a regular wisher. Financial situation, social status, or occupation did not predict who made wishes. Our data showed that a well wisher tends to be someone who values interdependence over independence, is more concerned about enjoying life than trying to control it, has a very low threshold for being emotionally engaged with others and the world in general, is very sensitive to the slightest change in the social or psychological environment, often feels insecure and uncertain, and easily trusts in things that cannot be seen or touched. Like Pooh, those who wish regularly see life not as a Brain thing but as a matter of the heart and trust in the humble, simple processes such as wishing.

If we look at the very different characteristics of the wisher skeptic, we can see why it is that wishing can be such an important survival skill. The nonwishers' scores on this test and the tests you will read in subsequent chapters indicate that they tended to be egocentric, self-assured, quick-tempered, cynical and judgmental, rejecting of the supernatural, and distrusting of their sixth or "psychic" sense. They were convinced that if something was going to be done right, they would have do it themselves and not just sit there wishing for something to come to them. This same cluster of characteristics appears in those people who are considered to be the most likely to suffer or die young from heart disease and other ailments.[1] Making wishes is making health.

Wizards, Sorcerers, and the Occult

We are all wizards dealing in the occult. The first definition of the word "wizard" in *Webster's Third New International Dictionary* is someone "of wisdom and knowledge." All of us have been taught to wish and, as you will learn, have the innate wisdom, knowledge, and tendency to trust in the mysterious energy and magic of the power of a wish. The first definition of the word "occult" in this same dictionary is "to be hidden from sight," and most of us sense that much of our life is experienced on levels beyond the see-and-touch world. Each of us is capable of tapping into the unseen world of the wish and using our innate knowledge of wishing to cast a spell over our own and others' lives simply by making a wish, the focusing of our intent to make possibilities into realities. Just by our intentions, we can alter the destiny of persons, places, events, and things.

I learned about the power of wishing personally when I nearly died of cancer ten years ago. I learned about its influence as a scientist from my own research and interviews with hundreds of women, men, and children around the world from various cultures. I learned about wishing's power from the irrefutable scientific evidence collected by researchers demonstrating that our every wish is a command and our every intention is an act of creation. Science has proven that everything and everyone is profoundly affected by our good or bad intentions, what and how we wish, and the subtle way our intentions transform events across time and space.[2] The question no longer is does wishing work, but how can we learn to do it well so that we can be loving wizards instead of devious sorcerers?

More than 500 research articles have shown that our wishing is a proactive process in the establishment of reality. At the Princeton Engineering Anomalies Research laboratory, more than 50 million "little wishes" have been tested and converted to 3 billion bits of binary information for statistical analysis. These studies showed that conscious intention slightly but significantly altered the behavior of electrical, mechanical, optical, acoustical, and biological systems. The odds that the PEAR results could have occurred by chance alone are less than one in a trillion![3] All of this evidence shows that our consciousness is not just a reactive process that senses and classifies things; it is also a proactive process capable of causing measurable changes in things and events. There is no longer any doubt that wishing has the power to alter the course of our personal and collective history.[4] It works in wondrous, subtle, and often paradoxical ways, but it works.[5]

Proof of the Existence of UFOs

When Hawaiians first saw the white sails of Captain Cook's ships on the horizon, they were UFOs, "unexplained floating objects." In terms of the science of their day, these ships were what modern science calls "anomalies." These sailing UFOs turned out to be all too real, for contact with the Euro-American mind led to major changes in one of the world's oldest cultures and its indigenous subjective science. Today's science sees wishing's effects as "anomalies." They do not fit the established models of explanation. Like cells that cannot be detected with the naked eye yet are present in the sample under a high-powered microscope, they are "occult." They are presently beyond most of our established tools of measurement, yet some researchers are beginning to measure them in creative ways. They keep popping up everywhere to mess up the most carefully designed experiments and confound science's oldest theories. As the researchers at PEAR point out, however, good science cannot turn away from anomalies such as wishing's power because anomalies have always been science's most precious resource.[6] However unrefined, peculiar, weird, and even eerie anomalies like a wish's power seem in comparison to what is often called the "real" world, they are the stuff from which all the great discoveries of science have ultimately come.

As you prepare to hone your own wishing skill, consider the following anomalous findings about the power of a wish. If these findings seem extreme, it's because they are. They are way out of the bias band and beyond the unnecessarily narrow limits within which establishment science tends to operate. I've chosen the following few examples of wishing's influence because they illustrate the findings of researchers who embrace the true meaning of the word science as it derives from the Latin verb *scire,* meaning to know or to understand. These are the men and women willing to study things like wishing, which contemporary closed minds are currently calling "woo woo" and used to call "New Age" or "just too goofy and strange." They are dabbling in what some historical closed minds called heresy. They are challenging the established views of our place in and relationship to the cosmos in the same ways that got their predecessors like Copernicus and Galileo imprisoned, excommunicated, hung, or burned at the stake. Nonetheless, they are all respected by establishment science, their work has been published in prestigious and peer-reviewed professional journals, and they have shared their results at major scientific meetings.

◆ **Healing at a Distance**: Biofeedback, the process of using our intent to alter our own body systems previously thought to be beyond our control, is a well-established practice. It is well known now that detectable changes in our physiology are possible just by wishing for them; it is a researched way of "wishing ourselves well." Research on the new field of alleo-biofeedback shows that others can literally wish us well at a distance. A person sitting several rooms away from us can wish for our heartbeat and blood pressure to lower and our immune system to strengthen.[7]

✦ The Power of Intuition: Our sense of a wish in progress, what we call intuition, is not only strong enough to detect whether someone behind us is gazing at the back of our head or our lower back, but can also determine where the gazer is wishing to look, even while the gazer's eyes are closed and that person is just making a wish as to where he or she will look.[8]

✦ The Talisman Effect: A tiny electromagnetic device can be shown to be affected by our wishes. Much as an object is engraved with occult powers, tiny electrical devices can become "wish imprinted" and have their electromagnetic properties altered by the focus of our intent upon them. Called IIEDs or Intention-Imprinted Energy Devices, these tiny electromechanical structures can be imbued with our intent, mailed overnight across the country, and still be shown by science's own measuring devices to contain the power of our original wish and its energy.[9] Even more surprising to modern science, that same object can act as a talisman and transfer our wish to other objects with the influence of the original wish.

✦ Creating Sacred Spaces: The IIEDs or "wish-imprinted devices" just mentioned have another effect that defies prevailing scientific thought and principles. Leaving one of these wish objects "running" or placed in an environment results in a kind of "wish consciousness conditioning" of that environment, what scientist Dr. William Tiller calls a "sacred space." These places with a wish-imprinted "talisman" seem to become more "coherent," and data on the impact of a wish becomes more pronounced. The "wishing space" created by the presence of a wish-imbued device is categorically impossible based on the conventional physics paradigm.[10]

✦ Our Wish Antennae: New research has shown that human DNA, blood samples, the pH or acidic/alkaline balance of water, and liver enzymes have all been altered by the simple act of making a wish.[11] The slightest change in DNA, pH level, and blood and hormonal levels can radically affect our health, so science has shown that a wish can cure and even kill. Our basic genetic stuff, our DNA, has been shown to act as toroidal antennae for the reception of the subtle energy of a wish. Toroid means a spiraling coil folding back on itself. It's a shape that resembles the mushroom-cloud shape of an atomic bomb blast. Because of this unique shape, DNA may act as one possible receptor for the subtle energy sent by our intent.[12]

◆ **Wish Imprints**: Research shows that what a camera photographs can be influenced by the wishes with which that camera has been imbued by its owner. When a man wished to be able to "reveal God's universe" with his camera, his and only his camera recorded unusual (anomalous) ethereal energetic images undetected by cameras not containing his wishes. The reporters of this data described strange images on the film of the wish camera that seemed to emanate around "spiritual rock concerts, spiritual shrines, and highly spiritual lectures on metaphysics and the meaning of death."[13] Careful repeated studies placed the wish-imbued camera next to a non-wish-imprinted camera to record exactly the same event at the same time and showed the "ethereal detection effect" only with the wish-intention-filled camera. Kodak's laboratory personnel were shown the two sets of films and noted what they called unexplainable differences between the images on the two rolls that were "not within the range of any possible defects" and that they "had never seen before on any film." The film's processors did, however, report seeing on the wish camera's film the semitransparent portions of bodies at concerts, some type of "stuff" transferring between people and things at shrines, and amazing banners of light coming from the light wells during a metaphysical lecture by psychiatrist Elisabeth Kübler-Ross on death and dying. They did not say what caused them other than that the film used was not flawed in any way known to them. The startled researchers who reported these findings stated, "Indeed, this expression of God's universe shows us that there are many more levels of manifestation in nature than our science has thus far uncovered."[14]

◆ **Lifesaving Wishes**: It used to be standard practice to push relatives out of the emergency room or intensive care unit while the medical team frantically tried to save their loved one. Now, in the prestigious and conservative medical journal *Lancet,* researchers report that the presence of those wishing you well can help bring you back to life. *Lancet* reports that patients who had their relatives present and wishing in their respective ways for their loved one's survival during resuscitation had a nearly 25 percent better chance of recovering than those whose family members were forced to wait outside.[15] Even if they stood quietly in the background and just wished over the shoulders of the doctors and nurses for the survival of their family member, wishing's energy seemed to be increased by proximity to the wish target. This is preliminary evidence that even at the most traumatic and hectic times it may be wise to make room for wishing rather than send people to waiting rooms.

You will read many other amazing examples of the documented power of a wish and how our intention is an act of creation. The challenge I've set myself in this book, however, is to start with the assumption that wishes come true. The task now is to learn more about how wishing works and how to put it to work more constructively in our own lives. To learn to wish well, you have to become more aware that you are always wishing and changing the world with your intentions. You have to learn to recognize how you are doing it and how to wish carefully with clear knowledge of the delicate balance between the positive and negative effects of making a wish. Your challenge is to learn how to be a wishing wizard rather than a sorcerer by putting the power of wishing to work constructively in your daily living, loving, and working. Whether we like it or not, we are living in the world we wished for. If we want a better world, we need to be wiser wishers.

A sorcerer is someone who deals with and tries to manipulate black magic and evil spirits. A wizard is someone endowed with a special skill to accomplish things that many people think impossible. We all have the special skill to wish. We are prewired to wish and sense wishes being made. By learning to recognize and be sensitive to that skill, we can all become wishing wizards. Unless we try to make it so through our own bad intentions, the occult with which wishing deals is not wicked, diabolical, or sinister. Occult refers to those aspects of our life that demand more than ordinary perception and knowledge and those facets of living that are beyond our current means of measurement. There are many aspects of our life that are, by this definition, occult. We were given our innate ability to wish to allow us to negotiate lovingly through this strange but wonderful world of the supernatural.

A Little Wish Wary

Most of us are aware and even a little afraid of the power of the daily spells we cast with our wishes. Anthropologist Francis Huxley observes, "Even the most blasé of us will experience a twinge of guilt if we lose our temper with someone and damn him, and he then goes off and breaks his neck. We try to take the sting out of this coincidence by various forms of rationalization, such as the use of statistics, but even so the fit between a wish and an event may well bring an apprehensive shudder."[16] The delight and dilemma of wishing is that whether we are conscious of it or not, we are not just living in the world; we are constantly wishing it into existence.

With hundreds of carefully designed studies, respected scientists around the world are now confirming our innate sense that our wishes come true. Studies of the power of a wish to alter all sorts of microorganisms, bacteria, human body and cancer cells, immune cells, fungi, yeast, and other "nonthinking" organisms have rendered invalid the criticism that thoughts, emotions, and expectations are at the root of the power of intent to alter any system.[17] Unless we assume that bacteria and fungi think, research on changes in such organisms caused by wishing shows that it works whether or not the target of the wish is aware of the intentions of the wisher. When prestigious scientists such as Nobel physicist Erwin Schrödinger, Sir Arthur Eddington, and Sir James Jeans acknowledge the reality of the power of our individual intentions to influence the entire world system regardless of time and space, it is time to move away from questions about whether or not wishing works and focus instead on learning to wish wisely and well.[18]

Self-Hexing

Sometimes our wishing seems to backfire on us. We sense that we have "hexed ourselves" by some wrongful self-sorcery. Wishing unwisely by being insensitive to what we wish *away* whenever we wish *for* something and what we may lose when we wish something away, we end up wishing disappointment and regret upon ourselves. We may even end up wishing that we had never wished at all. By being unaware of how and how much our own wish may affect the lives of others, our wishing may stir up trouble in our family, social, love, and work life. By disregarding the fact that what we wish away must by nature's own rules inevitably fall upon someone or something else somewhere and sometime, we can suffer a wishing remorse and vague and nagging guilt for having harmed someone.

Our ability to wish can be a curse and a blessing. Something deep within us tells us that because we have a magical power to alter people, events, and things with our intentions, we should be very careful what we wish for. Learning to wish well is learning to recognize that we are wishing all the time. Even if we are not consciously aware that we are "making a wish," our intentions are still affecting all of the systems around us. Like a television on mute, our wishful-thinking signals are still being broadcast even when we think we are not making wishes. We sometimes say we feel "bad vibes" because we can sense the energy of another person's wishes even when they say they are not wishing. Wishing well is acknowledging and taking responsibility for our innate sorcery by focusing on our wish and making it carefully and sensitively by the scientific, mythological, and cultural rules you will read about in this book.

Wish Wars

One example of the prevalence of our belief in the power of wishing can be seen at sporting events. Such gatherings often become wish wars between supporters of competing teams. Many of us become so involved with our team that we go beyond "rooting" for them to wishing for them and against their opponent. Michael Murphy, the founder of California's Esalen Institute where processes related to wishing were often studied, discusses the power of "wishful rooting." He writes, ". . . it is no wonder that during certain contests balls take funny bounces and athletes jump higher than ever or stumble inexplicably. Many of us have sensed the uncanny at sports events, when an innocent game suddenly becomes a theater of the occult."[19] In effect, rooting is a form of loud collective wishing through which all sorts of chants and incantations are used to make our wish victorious over other wishes.

An example of the power of "wishful rooting" was shared by one of the subjects in the wish study you will be reading about in this book. A mother was cheering and rooting for her daughter during a water polo match. No matter how vigorously she rooted, her daughter could not send the ball into the goal. The goalie was highly skilled and turned away every shot her daughter made. The frustrated mother finally sat down from her screaming and cheering, closed her eyes and crossed her fingers, and whispered her wish that the goalie would "just disappear." A few minutes later, the game was suddenly whistled to a halt as the referee noticed the goalie was drowning. She had fainted in the pool and slipped under the water. Paramedics were summoned and revived her.

Wishing well requires remembering that any wish for victory is a wish for someone else's defeat. It involves constant vigilance for the fact that there can be dire consequences when we wish against someone. Wishing to do our very best is one thing, but wishing that others do their worst can be dangerous and can lead to serious negative consequences we did not anticipate. Wishing well is wishing cautiously and never against someone or something. It's wishing for harmony and balance more than success and triumph.

Why Wishing Works

Wishing works because we are all profoundly and deeply connected. To a slight but important degree, our every personal intention jiggles the entire system of which we are an integral and inseparable part. Like molecules of water, we all quiver when the smallest pebble is tossed into the pond. Research supports that we are connected with one another and the world in such a way that no matter how slight, our every intent reverberates through everyone and everything. Dr. Marilyn J. Schlitz, director of research at the Institute of Noetic Sciences, which studies science's anomalies, writes, "I think the data support the idea that we are interconnected at a level that has yet to be fully recognized by Western science and that is very far from being integrated into our worldview. If my intentions can influence the physiology of a distant person, if your thoughts can be incorporated into mine, . . . it requires that we be more thoughtful and responsible not only for our actions but for the ways in which we think about and interact with other people."[20]

Reluctant to use such a romantic word as wishing, researchers often prefer to use the phrase "distant intentionality." They mean that what we wish has effects beyond the physical limits of space and time and resonates within the whole system of which we are all a part. They have shown that wishing is not sending energy as much as logging on to the consciousness Internet that we all share and keep creating and recreating. The evidence documents the power of wishing and that we have a common consciousness with everyone that is not limited to our own brain or body.

Just as scientists have shown that our brain is not only in our head but is found as psychochemical brain bits throughout our body, they have also shown that our consciousness is not confined to the cerebrum.[21] When we make a wish, our shared consciousness is affected by it instantaneously. Evidence of these facts has now been thoroughly presented in several sources.[22] Although some of this research will be reviewed here, my purpose is to show you how to put what we already know about wishing to work for you. It's to show you how to wish well and how to make wishing a regular safe, healthy, balanced part of your own life. You're doing it all the time anyway, so you might as well learn to do it well.

Wishing's Necessary Dark Side

You're wishing all the time. Like the wish-imbued device described earlier that was left running, you are constantly filling your environment with the power and nature of your wishes. Even if you're not aware of it, you're doing it right now as you read these words. Even this book will to some extent ultimately become for you what you wish it to be. I will show you how to be more alert and aware of your wishing and how to identify and pass through the right "wish launch window" so that your wishes bring you and everyone a safe, healthy, balanced way of living. I will show you how to avoid what another of our wish-research subjects referred to as "slipping into sorcery," the danger of unwise wishing. As Dr. Schlitz warns, "If a person can influence the physiology of another person at a distance, it is clearly possible that influence may not always be positive."[23]

A wish can not only have negative consequences, it must. When we wish for recovery from illness, the wish comes true only when the germs causing the illness are wished to death. Any wish for healing is also a wish for death, the killing of whatever systems are causing our suffering. If our wish did not have negative or lethal effects, it could not work its miracles. Wishing works because it also has a dark side and the potential to kill as well as cure and hurt as well as heal. It is because of wishing's lethal dark side that wishing should never be taken lightly.

Only one letter distinguishes the word curing from the word cursing. Wishing's negative power served our ancestors well as a means of self-preservation. Wishing's power to harm may have allowed those who mastered that power to survive. Even if wishing does not have the power scientists and shamans say it does, at the very least our ancestors' primitive belief in wishing's lethal power must have given them a sense of confidence and control in a chaotic and frightening world.

Our ancestors' fear and even repulsion of the possibility that they could kill with their wishes may account for our modern uneasiness with the capacity of our intentions to do great damage. In our eagerness to deny culpability for wishes' impacts on others, we often diminish or even ridicule the idea that wishing is anything more than just a childish tradition or silly superstition. Nonetheless, we know on some level that wishing must have negative consequences if it is to have its positive effects. Just as the same power that allows heat to save us from freezing can also cook us, wishing needs its dark side or it becomes powerless. Wishing well is learning to harness, control, and channel our wishing to diminish its serious toxic side effects.

Mild Magic

Wishing is a form of everyday magic practiced by the common person. Author Richard Cavendish refers to high and low magic.[24] "High magic" is a way to transcend our human limitations and become superhuman or even divine. It's mysticism on a large scale. The magic of wishing or directing our intentionality is low magic designed to gain some worldly advantage in our daily working, living, loving, and playing. Wishing is not an attempt to change the rules of the cosmos; it's an attempt to get them to work out a little more our way.[25]

Wishing as the practice of minimalist magic to try to cause a slight shifting of the odds reflects exactly the nature of wishing as revealed in the thousands of experiments on the effects of our intentions on various systems. The research on intentionality altering events always shows the effect to be small and subtle rather than a big psychic show.

Researchers sometimes call wishing a "psi" or psychic skill, a sixth-sense "super-sensitive" way of connecting with those aspects of our existence that are beyond our basic physical senses.[26] In fact, most of what's going on around us is far beyond the detection of our eyes, ears, and sense of touch. Studies show, however, that the magical effect of our intentionality is not the exotic trait possessed by a gifted few Michael Jordans of the psychic world. Although there are such wishing superstars, the data show that all of us have been given the power of wishing as a basic survival skill and an innate inherited ability to be developed as we see fit. Dr. Richard S. Broughton, director of the Rhine Research Center in Durham, North Carolina, writes, "The purpose of psi ability [wishing] is survival."[27] Just as our innate ability to throw a spear evolved to being able to throw a ball, we all have the skill to throw, but few of us will pitch in the major leagues.

One reason wishing has received much less attention than such concepts as prayer, positive thinking, willing, and other mind-over-matter ideas is that wishing is seen as no big deal. It's a very mild, easy, slight, secular, and invisible thing that we do almost all the time. In fact, it's exactly the subtle nature of wishing that has given it its evolutionary and adaptive significance. Minimal "soft" spells cast by the everyday wisher have strong survival value because the larger-scale psychic superskills such as telepathy and clairvoyance have often led to disaster and even death for those who were bold or brash enough to show them off. Millions have been burned at the stake for such blatant shows of a power we all have. It's much more socially acceptable and adaptable to go unnoticed and modestly and lovingly keep making a little wish now and then than it is to bend a spoon.

Dr. Broughton states that subtle psychic skills such as wishing evolved ". . . to be deliberately self-obscuring because it works best when it is unhampered and un-noticed by the individual it is serving."[28] In other words, we wish best when we do not try too hard. The more gently, carefully, modestly, and selflessly we wish and the less we try to impose our idea of how things should work out, the more likely our wish is to come true. The less we tamper with our natural wishing ability and learn to just "go with it," the more likely it is that our wishes will turn out right not only for us but for everyone.

A Preview of the Way to Wish Well

You will be reading about the cultural and scientific lessons that lead to a set of specific steps in making a wise wish. Chapter 8 presents these steps in detail, but so that you don't have to wait to start wishing well and can begin to avoid some of wishing's dark side right away, here's a brief preview of the key steps in making wishes that bring you and those around you the happiness, hardiness, and health your heart desires. You will be reading about the reasons for these steps later, but for now use the following wish-making primer.

Steps in Wise Wishing

1. **W—Wait.** Have the persistent patience to sit down, be quiet, and take a deep breath. A rushed wish is usually an unwise wish likely to have a negative rebound effect. As you formulate your wish, remember that it may not come true exactly how and when you wish it to. As one of my Hawaiian neighbors who took part in our wish research pointed out, "Wishing well is like surfing. You don't always take the first wave you see. You have to be patient, wait, and take the time to wish for the wave that is meant for you. Once you've wished, it's like the wave has taken you, so wait to wish or your wish could cause you to wipe out."

2. **I—Imagine.** Be creative in visualizing all the many ways a wish might come true. Before you make your wish, imagine the impact of your wish on your own and others' lives. Remember that wishing has a negative dark side. Not imagining all the mysterious, metaphorical, and spiritually instructive ways wishes are granted can result in wishing that you never made your wish in the first place. Particularly if you find yourself wishing things away, remember that negativistic wishing often results in the paradox of getting precisely what you wished you would never have. It is usually your heart that knows what your soul needs, so ask your heart what it really needs.

3. **S—Sensitivity.** Be aware of the fact that what you wish away always goes somewhere to affect someone and what you wish for must come from somewhere, something, or someone. When you formulate your wish, do it slowly with a willingness to wait for the wish to crystallize, imagine how a granted wish might affect you and others, and remember that a single wish can have very big consequences. An insensitive wish is a wicked wish. One of our wish-project participants pointed out the importance of wishing sympathetically when she said, "I think of making a wish as throwing a stone at a huge glass window. I don't want to break the window. I just want to tap on it to get someone's or something's attention."

4. **H—Heart.** As you formulate your wish, ask yourself if it's coming from your heart or your head. Are you wishing for what your heart and the hearts of others need in the long run or what your brain wants now? State your wish in a few words; about eight seems to be a good number. Too many words cause your wish

to lack focus and thus be more vulnerable to unwanted side effects. Make sure your wish expresses your heart's desires and not your brain's demands. To help you focus on your heart, place your left hand over your chest, push gently against it with your right, and ask your heart, "Is this wish good for my heart and for others'?"

As you begin your reading of this book, keep the above W-I-S-H steps in mind. They will help protect you against wrongful wishing until you have learned all the lessons of wishing well.

The Dangers of Wish Tampering

An example of the dangers of tampering with the natural magic of wishing and failing to take wishing for what it is rather than what we want or need it to be is reported by Apollo 14 astronaut Edgar Mitchell. He founded the Institute of Noetic Science, an organization dedicated to studying the mysteries of processes such as wishing. He reports the story of his mother, who suffered from severe vision loss due to her worsening glaucoma. She was legally blind without her very thick glasses. During a conference, Mitchell met a shaman whom he introduced to his mother to try to "wish away" her glaucoma. Early the next morning, Mitchell's mother ran into his room screaming, "Son, I can see, I can see!" She dropped her thick glasses to the floor, ground the thick lenses into dust with her heel, and read out loud from her Bible. She drove herself home from the conference, a distance of several hundred miles without her glasses. This seemed clearly to be a Michael Jordanesque example of the power of wishing.

Weeks later, Mitchell's mother called to inquire if the shaman who had wished her vision to return was a Christian. When Mitchell said no, he reports that he could hear his mother's disappointment in her voice. He writes, "Hours later, the gift slipped away and thick new glasses were required."[29] Although we all have the innate capacity to wish, we do not have the ability to control the mysterious ways in which wishing seems to operate. Whatever it is that is involved when wishes come true, we are not the ones who make the rules. Making a wish is like pulling the handle on a slot machine. It doesn't matter how hard we pull. Learning to wish well is not learning to wish hard. It is learning to nudge the odds to work out a little more in our favor. Our wish is only one among millions contributing to the collective consciousness pot. As one of my wish-project subjects said, "If you want to learn to wish well, you have to follow the rule of the three S's—wish simply, selflessly, and 'in sync' with others and the world."

In a way, Mitchell's mother tampered with the "three S's" of a well-made wish. She complicated and restricted her wish with her religiosity, imposed her personal view on the way a wish should work and who should be allowed to make one, and fell "out of sync" with the gentle energetic flow of wishing. She imposed too many conditions on her wish and the nature of the wisher. Her reluctance to go with the flow and her effort to impose her own standards and views on the wish and the wisher canceled out their effect. The lesson is to wish gently and go with "the way" instead of demanding "our way."

The Physics of Wishing

Wishing is based on what physician Larry Dossey called in 1989 the "nonlocal" mind.[30] To physicists, "nonlocal" means "not just here." According to this well-documented view, our consciousness cannot be localized or limited to the here and now or this place and time. Nonlocality is a manifestation of the fact discussed earlier that we are all connected without regard for time and space. Wishing works because of the concept of nonlocality and the possibility that our intentions have influence without regard to the seeing and touching world's limitations.

We live in a world that is what historian Edward Tenner calls "tightly coupled."[31] He means that because we interact so interdependently and profoundly with everything and everyone, the slightest alteration within any "tightly coupled" system alters the entire system. A wish is such an alteration. Every wish we make stirs things up in the entire system in which we live. Tenner writes, ". . . tight coupling spreads problems once they begin."[32] Tight coupling is why a positive or negative wish spreads so far and wide through our own and others' lives.

Consciousness Conservation

Physicists accept the law of conservation, meaning that matter and energy cannot be created or destroyed. Both just "are." They never disappear; they only change form. When it comes to learning to wish well, we must remember that whenever we make a wish, we are tampering with the "tight coupling" that is the nature of our life. When we make a wish, we displace but do not eradicate the nature of whatever it is we are wishing about. When we wish for something, we may be causing problems for someone else because the evil we may be trying to wish away cannot go away; it has to go somewhere.

Misfortune is always conserved. If you try to wish it away, someone else always gets it. The same is true for good fortune. Evil always "goes" somewhere, but fortunately so does love. Another of the basic rules of wishing well is that a wish sent to or for someone who does not deserve the gift of that wish will come back to the wisher. If a person does not deserve a negative energy you wish for him, look out. Sometime, when you least expect it, it will come resonating right back to you. If a person does not deserve the love you wish for her, that love will come humming right back into your own heart.

As you begin your reading of this book, remember that your wishes are coming true right now. The nature of your life, your love, and your work are manifestations of your own and others' wishes come true. In fact, you yourself are a wish come true, the granting of someone else's wish and to some degree a figment of that person's imagination or wishful thinking. You are both wisher and wish, the space where nature has expressed her own awareness and imagination.

As you learn to wish well, look carefully to the lessons from wishes that may have already been granted in your life and how you are fulfilling the wishes of others. The art of wishing well is based on the wisdom to avoid wishing too selfishly and too strongly for what you might already have. The wisest wish of all may not be for things but for another way to look at things. The most well-made wish may be one for the patience, harmony, pleasantness, humbleness, and loving-kindness to be able to fully recognize and relish the gifts of wishes already granted.

—✦—

Two

Rediscovering the Miracle of Wishing

Please do not wish in our wells or throw coins in our fountains.

—SIGN OVER COIN-FILLED FOUNTAINS FOR
SALE AT A LANDSCAPING STORE

My Death Wish

Since the beginning of time, our ancestors have reached out to the mysterious forces of nature for a magical touchstone that could make their wishes come true. They relied heavily on their intuition, their sense for "something that kept telling them," and they made their wishes accordingly. Ten years ago when something told me I was dying of cancer, I too reached out for a touchstone. I sensed my cancer, but my doctors ignored my subjective and sixth-sense-oriented pleas. They said my fear was "all in my head," but they were deadly wrong. It seemed to be my heart that was telling me that I was dying, and it was right. As most of the light and sound spectrum is beyond our physical senses, my distress was beyond the range of my doctors' five senses.

As I lay dying, I experienced my first adult instinct to make a wish and take it seriously. Although I'm not precisely sure of all the reasons why, something made me wish. I am sure now that wishing contributed to the miracle of my survival. A decade after my illness, and after the decade of research I conducted on wishing since my "deaths," I am convinced that wishing works. I am convinced that no matter what we may do, our intentions alone can alter our own and others' lives regardless of time and space.

Half-Prayers

I prayed a lot when I was dying, and my family and friends prayed with me. We also wished. As you will read in Chapter 5, wishing falls somewhere between our capacity to reason our way through the secular and our power to pray our way to the sacred. It's one of our innate faculties for dealing with problems and forces that still remain beyond the reach of rigorous logic and blind faith. It seems to function as a kind of auxiliary "half-prayer" for those times when personal rationalizing or theology don't seem quite enough or somehow inappropriate for the challenge at hand. It's what we do when we feel the need to enlist the help of something that transcends all the known forms of energy yet feel, at least at that moment, that we really shouldn't bother God about it. Wishing is for those times when we feel we don't want to trust completely in technology or draw on our sacred resources.

A positive attitude works well for our secular survival, emotional intelligence works well for our social survival, and we pray to save our soul. Wishing, however, is a process very seldom discussed by psychologists. It's a way of meeting our spiritual needs at times we can't physically force, mentally figure out, or emotionally feel or work our way through a problem yet don't quite feel we have to or should be praying about it. It's temporarily allowing ourselves to go out a little on a spiritual limb, quieting our brain and opening our heart. It's entering what one of my wish-research subjects called her "brief ritualistic reverie." Wishing is how we act in terms of our superstitious heritage to deal with issues that have remained imperceptible, incomprehensible, and primarily the business of our sixth sense.

A Call from the Past

After my bone marrow transplant for a lymphoma that was eating away my hips, I reflected on how wishing may have played a role in my miracle. I was physically exhausted from modern science's manipulations of my body, bored and fatigued from my months of imagery and visualization, and weary of trying to maintain and often fake the positive attitude popular psychology insists is necessary for healing. Late one night while lying in the semidarkness of the intensive care unit and wondering if I would live until the doctors came the next morning, it happened. I made a wish. I suddenly remembered and felt those times as a child when I had simply closed my eyes, taken a deep breath, and made a wish. At the end of this chapter, I will share the miracle-making wish I made that night.

My years of professional education and clinical and scientific training had been firmly five-sense-oriented. It barely tolerated the role of the mind in health and healing. The idea that an abstract spiritual concept such as wishing might play a role in our destiny was never seriously considered. My fellow students and I often spoke of such processes in private, but intentionally trying to connect with a Love or Universal energy or our collective consciousness was something still often privately and secretly we all did at one time or another for our suffering patients and family. As I spent months of my life battling cancer, I lived with dozens of persons fighting for their lives. They, too, were regular wishers.

In a play on the World War II saying "there are no atheists in foxholes," there do not seem to be too many skeptics in intensive care units. Those of us unfortunate enough to end up there are willing to believe in anything "just in case." The terror of facing my death seemed to cause me to override my academic training and resonate directly with my ancestral past. More accurately, something about my ancestral past seemed to resonate within me.

One miraculous night, I realized that the act of wishing might hold remarkable healing properties that could contribute to my recovery. I am convinced now that by briefly entering a wishful state, I somehow brought all the power of my ancestors' mythological wisdom to bear on my problem and tapped into a consciousness I shared with every living person and everyone who had ever lived. I also know that simply through the process of entering a wishful state, I comforted my body and soothed my soul. In combination with excellent modern medical intervention, the power of prayer, and good luck, the result of my wishing was a healing miracle.

Make a Wish

If you could have just one wish, any wish, what would it be? Think carefully about your answer, because wishes have a unique power and most of them, somehow and at some time, come true. Take a moment before reading on not only to think about the wish you would make but also how your own, others', and the world's life might change if your wish came true. Write your wish on an index card and use the card as a bookmark as you read the following chapters. Refer to your wish as you read and reflect on it again as you complete your reading of each chapter and again when you finish this book. See how your wish and wishing style may have changed after you have learned the scientific, mythological, and cultural lessons of wishing.

Wishes are sixth-sense suggestions. They go beyond what author Gary Zukav calls our "five-sense personality" to draw from our innate ability to insinuate ourselves into processes that transcend what we can see, touch, smell, hear, and physically feel.[1] They are our built-in way of helping to create rather than just react to "the forces that be"; they enable us to become consciously creative rather than just re-actively logical. Wishes are consciousness expressed in such a way that it brings events into being without us actually doing anything. They do so by altering, however slightly, the workings of the invisible but pervasive subtle energy that is the universe. As impossible as it may seem at first glance, every wish we make subtly but certainly starts a cosmic chain reaction that can cause nature to change her tune. Whether you are the beneficiary or the victim of wishing's power depends on how willing you are to learn to deal with its immense positive and negative power.

In its simplest form, wishing well is having good intentions and knowing that our intentions literally change things even when we don't actually take physical action. A shaman in Costa Rica told me, "Wishing well is being spiritually polite." Unlike techniques that teach us how to cope with the stress of the hyperculture our brain has created for us, wishing can be a way to soothe the spiritual suffering often at the core of that stress.[2] It is an elemental, slow, patient, sometimes meandering "thought form" through which we use our consciousness to intentionally shape the subtle energy referred to by some of the world's most revered scientists, engineers, poets, and priests as Universal, Light, Love, Life, and Spiritual Energy.[3]

Stepping Back to Go Forward

Making a wish is taking an enlightened step backward to our sixth-sense heritage by at least temporarily employing it as our first sense. It allows us to continue or to get going again in our spiritual evolution by using one of our most ancient ways of connecting with the world. We have focused so much on our physical evolution and on the "survival of the fittest" that we sometimes forget the more mystical and magical ways of coping and survival that were so important to our ancestors. We have become such modern go-getters that we have ignored our innate skill simply to sit and wish for things "to just come to us." In fact, people who do so may be seen as lazy, passive, lacking in motivation, and "just playing around." In fact, wishing is powerful playing and a way to be non-goal-driven enough to allow wishes to come true.

For those of us who are willing to be sensitive to and open our hearts, something keeps trying to teach us that the most highly evolved among us are those who are also the most sixth-sense sophisticated. These willing wishers tend to be the same ones who are the most selfless and totally absorbed in the enchanted nature of life. They're the ones who seem so charmingly strange and at ease with the supernatural, those aspects of life that seem unnatural to the sixth-sense impaired. They are the ones to whom great new ideas seem to come most often and those to whom we may turn as role models when we need more magic or even a miracle in our lives.

The characteristics of the wisher may seem at odds with the purely physical self-survival interpretation of evolution we were taught in school. Nonetheless, the ancestors who gave birth to us were those who wished well, dealt effectively with the magical and invisible, and lived in balance with the enchanted nature of life. Although Charles Darwin is often credited with a competitive view of survival of the individual, he actually proposed a theory called "inclusive fitness."[4] He asserted that there was great survival value in being able to consistently "go along with," connect, and adapt to other people and the ways of the community. Thousands of years ago, inclusive fitness meant being able to connect with the magical, subtle energy and mystical ways of the times. Survival of the "wishing-est" seems to have been the evolutionary rule.

Wishing for Something More

Despite our pride in our technical accomplishments, there seems to be an increasing awareness emerging that we were created for much more than connecting on an exclusively five-sense level. Our information processing and communications systems have led to an explosion in the speed and amount of information processed every day. If you have ever thrown away a greeting card with a microchip that plays Happy Birthday when you open it, you threw away a piece of technology that represented the total amount of computer knowledge developed by the early 1950s. Your home computer processes more information faster than the largest computers of the government and big business just ten years ago. We can now talk on tiny phones to anyone around the world and be electronically connected with almost anyone anywhere in a matter of seconds. Push a button in your car and someone a thousand miles away can call you in seconds and tell you where you are and ask you what you need. We sort through and log on to thousands of images on an invisible Internet and send invisible mail to people we will never see or touch. Despite all of this electronic connection, we often feel more disconnected than ever before. Our inherited need to connect beyond the five senses and to communicate our intentions beyond electronic representations has been neglected. With all of our electronic marvels, we seem to have found more means to communicate yet less meaning in doing so. Learning to wish again can help meet our need for meaning and enable us to connect on a level that no computer chip will ever match.

Wishing well by intentionally trying to bring more bliss and balance into our own and others' lives is the next challenge of connection and the next phase of our human consciousness development. Author John White calls this next evolutionary phase "Homo Noeticus"—another way of knowing the world in its more mystical and energetic terms.[5] Like all enduring cultural ceremonies, wishing is a personally practiced mystical ritual through which we attempt to make contact with and alter forces beyond our seeing and touching world. As one of the subjects in my wish research said, "You either believe the world is as much magic as machine or you don't. If you do, you need wishing. If you don't, someday you may just wish you did."

A Needed Boost

Wishing's optimistic nature, sixth-sense orientation, and is as historical foundations are perfectly designed to offer some sense of comfort and perspective in our increasingly competitive, rushed, and cynical society. Although science and religion offer their own unique ways of dealing with the mysteries of life, we can fall back on our wishing instinct when squabbling between these two systems leaves us frustrated or when we require the spiritual boost of a well-made wish.

Wishing, then, is much more than a charming custom; it's one of our most valuable ancestral gifts, every bit as valuable as our evolving intellect. Its effects are much slower than those usually obtained by the fast-thinking brain, but it is also often much more spiritually profound. Unfortunately, wishing's innocent gentleness has been overwhelmed by modern psychology's emphasis on willpower, affirmations, visualization, the latest set of life "rules," and the importance of having a positive attitude.[6] Despite the current popularity of these mind-over-matter approaches, our predisposition for wishing has remained strong. It was passed on to us through the centuries for a reason; it works.

Wired to Wish

We seem prewired for wishing. Herbert Benson, a research cardiologist at Harvard Medical School, proposes that our conviction that there is something invisible and powerful that controls our life has always been essential to our survival.[7] He reviews years of research showing that those who hold such beliefs are less vulnerable to serious illness and more prone to healing than those who do not. Such persons are more likely than nonbelievers to maintain their intimate relationships, another key factor in health and longevity. There seems to be a kind of natural spiritual hardiness that derives from believing in what many scientists still call the "supernatural." Because of their willingness to become very absorbed in every aspect of life, these believers tend to be rewarded with more immunity to life's trials and tribulations.

Research shows that acts such as wishing translate to emotional and physical strength.[8] Since believers in some supernatural force tend to be "the fittest," they are more likely to survive and pass on their DNA than nonbelievers. Because wishing is such a long-tested way of relating to the supernatural, its spiritual seniority indicates that its survival value is well established. Our evolutionary directive is not only to become stronger willed, technically more proficient, and electronically more connected. As we enter the period of Homo Noeticus, we can also learn that in the new millennium, knowing the world with only five keen senses may not be enough. If we wish to live long and well, we cannot allow the fast and furious devices our brain has created to connect with other brains to numb the way our heart connects with other hearts. If we are going to be able to live well, we had better also learn to wish well.

Six Side Effects of Wishing

Imagine there was a new fitness craze offered to you today that was guaranteed to boost your immune system, give you a healthy high with no post-high crash, free you from much of the stress of your life, make you feel more forgiving of others, give you a new way to deal with severe challenges in your life, and make you feel more connected and loving. When you wish, research shows that these benefits come to you free of charge and with great enjoyment.

Whether or not you believe that wishes come true, there is no doubt that the simple act of making a wish has very beneficial side effects. Each of these effects has been documented by the most careful modern research, but our ancestors knew these truths long ago.

The Wish Boost

Even when I was dying, I remembered that wishing is at the very least good fun. In fact, I was so weak that wishing was one of the few happy, joyful things I could do. Research now shows that a state of joy, no matter how temporary, can produce positive changes in our physiology that last for hours.[9] Whenever I made a wish, I felt less stressed and tense. Something about wishing brought back the childish joy and optimism stored somewhere in my soul. My sense of relaxation even when facing death was likely due to the lowering of the levels of the stress hormones in my system that accompanies less animated states such as wishing. I know now that one of my own stress hormones, serum cortisol, dipped severely when I made a wish. I felt a little stronger when I wished and my record shows that I also became less vulnerable to infection after making my wishes. This was due in part to another research-supported benefit of wishing well, the increase in the levels of the hormone that helps fight off infection, colds, and flu called IgA (immunoglobulin A).[10]

During my long stay in the hospital, I noticed that my blood tests revealed that my immune system always seemed to get a postwish boost. Although not enough to impress my doctors or the computer's criterion, I noticed that my three-times-a-day blood tests revealed a wish-related increase in the number and activity of my T lymphocytes, the natural killer cells that protect us against infections and cancer. I felt much calmer and restful after wishing, a condition related to the fact that acts such as wishing have been shown to lower heart and breathing rate.[11] All these salutary effects resulted from the few seconds involved in making a wish. If there were a pill that could do all these things, it would quickly overtake the sales of the impotence drug Viagra.

In an increasingly stressful world that often lacks simple blissful joy and one so cynical that being told that "it's just your imagination" has become a criticism, wishing can be good spiritual practice. It's a relatively simple way of staying spiritually fit. It's a completely safe and free way of finding balance when illness or other stress challenges our equilibrium. At the very least, wishing can augment any benefits derived from visualization, imaging, and trying to "think positively." It can even bring a badly needed smile to your own and others' faces just when you need it the most. Instead of blaming your inner child, wishing is a way you can let her safely out to play. Having fun wishing is making an energy deposit in the body's health maintenance organization.

High on Wishing

In addition to the immune boost that seems to result from the simply joy of making a wish, wishing seems capable of strengthening the entire body system. It does so because it can be a way of engaging in one of the most profound acts of well-being, altruism. One of the most frustrating aspects of my months on the bone marrow transplant unit was that all of us there were so sick that we were constantly in a state of needy dependence. Things were constantly being done to and for us. It seemed that there was nothing we could do or offer to be of help to others. I found that wishing is a very nice way to keep giving and be active even when a crisis thrusts you into passive role of being a taker.

Altruistic acts such as making wishes for others have been shown to reduce chances of early death and make you less prone to stress, depression, and other symptoms.[12] In fact, research on altruism shows wishing well to be one of the healthiest forms of helping. It's usually done in the spirit of hope rather than demanded results. By its very nature, wishing is more a matter of casting out a line than expecting to always catch a fish. It's usually an expression of aspiration more than expectation. Well wishers don't blame the target of a wish for its failure. Researchers on altruism have shown that the healthiest helpers are those who expect no gratitude, success, or reward. They relish the simple dignity of a relationship in which one person wishes well for another.[13]

I learned that wishing for others during the lowest time of my life resulted in what researcher Alan Luks calls "the helper's high." As sick as I was, wishing always gave me that feeling that runners sometimes get. I experienced the euphoric kick of a warm rush associated with the endorphins released when one does nice things like wishing another person well. I noticed a slight but much appreciated postwish diminishing of my pain. Unlike other highs I had experienced in my life, I did not feel the fatigue, sluggishness, or torpor I remembered having after an intense exercise rush. This finding is in keeping with the research on altruism showing that repeated, ritualistic acts of giving result in long-lasting tranquillity, enhanced self-esteem, fewer symptoms of distress or depression, a sense of optimism, and no post-high crash.[14] Wishing seems to offer all the benefits of a psychochemical high without any of the negative side effects.

Wishing as Letting Go

A third side effect derived purely from the act of making a wish is the way it helps us surrender our illusion of control. It's a way of trying to get something to happen by not actually doing anything other than expressing a wish. It is a wonderful way to relax and still accomplish something. In so doing, we achieve a psychophysiological balance that enhances immunity and helps protect the cardiovascular system. Wishing is a way we cease trying to control life and realize that we are forever an inseparable part of it.

To say that we are all immersed in the subtle energy of life is scientific fact, not mystical jargon, but some of us seem less aware of or less willing to acknowledge our absorption in it than others. Wishing is something that those who are aware of this energy come to rely upon. They are ready and willing to assume the psycho-physiological reflexive state that results when we achieve what researchers describe as "passive volition," doing well without trying too hard. By its very nature, wishing is an acquiescent state through which we acknowledge that we are a part of and not masters of our world.

Passive volition is a mental orientation that allows the body to be free of its sometimes lethal alliance with its ever-driving brain. Unlike trying to "will" something to happen, well wishing is "inviting" subtle forces to allow it to happen. It's a personal announcement that one is available for a miracle. A gentle process that is an expression of hope more than demand, it allows connections to occur with whatever intangible forces that might be available. It's a way we stop trying too hard and enter a state of being rather than doing and being more open-minded than hard-headed. Wishing's passive volition results in the body's "going with the flow." As a result, all the body's systems fall back into their natural balanced synchronization.[15]

Wishing as Forgiveness

There is an important and unique fourth way that wishing well contributes to miracles. It's an excellent way of achieving what researchers are just discovering to be an extremely healthy condition, the physiological state that results from acts of benevolent forgiveness.[16] I learned that wishing well is not only a splendid whimsical way of trying to get things to go our way but also a strategy for dealing more peacefully with those who constantly seem to be getting in our way. As difficult as it may be to learn to do, wishing well for those who constantly aggravate and pester us is a powerful health-enhancing act.

Even if you do not believe that wishes come true, wishing can still serve as an excellent anger management technique. It tells your brain and body that it's okay to give up their readiness to fight or seek revenge. One of our wish-project participants said, "Whenever I feel myself start looking for a fight, I start looking for a wish instead." Wishing reduces and often replaces the feelings of lingering resentment that seriously impair our immunity and cause our arteries to clog. Wishing is a way we can reverse our psychosclerosis, the hardening of our attitudes. At least briefly and just when we need it the most, it can reduce the toxic prodding of the anger hormones. It can cause the release of a psychochemical antidote against the devastating bodily effects of hostility and can provide a transitory sense of benevolent peace just when you are ready to go to war.

Wishing well for those who hurt us acts as a heart protector because it seems to provide us with something to do when we feel helpless in what seem to be an unrelenting series of aggravations.[17] Since it is not other people but our own physiological reaction to our perceptions that "makes us mad," wishing is a way to break the ultimately destructive "cynicism—hostility—anger—aggression" cycle. Wishing well when frustrated by a "bliss blocker" acts like an immediate spiritual sedative stronger than any tranquilizer. I've learned that wishing is a remarkably effective way of asking for mercy from otherworldly forces while granting mercy in this one.

Wishing as Another Way

In addition to the significant physiological benefits derived from well wishing's side effects of joy, altruism, forgiveness, passive volition, and frustration relief, there is a unique fifth benefit from the act of wishing. It can offer us another way to be when how we are and what we are doing with our five senses doesn't seem to be working well. It provides us with a sixth-sense emergency alternative escape hatch for stressful times.

If we are willing to exercise our opportunity to be totally absorbed in life, we need several unique alternative ways out when we come to feel absorbed "by" instead of "in" it. Psychiatrist Robert J. Lifton suggests that people should learn from the character from Greek mythology named Proteus, the old man of the sea who could escape his captors by assuming all sorts of shapes.[18] By wishing, we can temporarily take on our magician's personality instead of relying exclusively on our logical self to always carry us through. One of our wish-project respondents summed up this sidestepping benefit of wishing by saying, "In a way, I have multiple personalities. I have the thinking and rational me, the feeling me, and my magical side. When nothing seems to work, I get more into my magical me and start wishing. When I can't work it out, I can always wish it out."

While clinicians know that we need one central and consistent self-image to center our life and coordinate a set of coping skills, we can also benefit from electively having alternative states of consciousness beyond the one we use the most. I found that wishing was a side of me, a mystical personality I had seldom used. When I felt trapped by my cancer, wishing became one optional way for me to "be" without losing track of who I really was. For those of us who, voluntarily or involuntarily, become so totally absorbed in life that we feel helpless, wishing provides a way to feel some sense of effectiveness when things seem completely overwhelming. A man suffering from prostrate cancer was one of our wish-project participants. He illustrated the sense of control wishing can provide in dire circumstances when he said, "When things get really bad, I can read a book about it by the light of a lamp to find an answer, throw the lamp, turn the light off and give up, or rub it and make a wish. I've done all of these things, and wishing works as well or better than the other ways."

Psychologist Patricia Linville at Duke University has researched the physiological and psychological benefits and affective resilience related to having "many selves" under the rubric of one certain and central self. Author Henry Dreher describes this unique "diversified self" factor as one of many characteristics of what he calls "the immune power personality." He refers to Greek legend in his description of our Hydra-like capacity to utilize our "other selves" when we need to.[19] No matter how intellectual or spiritual we may be, being open to making wishes may not be our usual "self." It can, however, offer another way of coping.[20] Like the monster called Hydra that kept growing new heads when Hercules managed to cut off one of its original nine, we can turn to wishing when we feel ourselves "cut off" from a safe and joyful life. Like the mythological Hydra, we can still keep our one central "head" or identity and at the same time be a willing wisher when the situation seems to call for it.

Wishing to Belong

I found the sixth benefit of wishing to be the most important wishing side effect for me as I was dying. There is nothing more potentially isolating than to be dying of cancer. The treatments can be horrendous and the pain unbearable. The desire to hide under the covers is strong. Because of their own fear, discomfort, and not knowing how to help, many people pull away from us. Ironically, those who seemed to have cared most about us before we faced death can be those who seem to disappear just when we need them the most. Their flight may be due to the fact that their sincere and profound caring made them feel helpless in the face of our plight. However, even when I did hide under the covers, I could still use wishing to stay connected to those I loved.

I learned that wishing gave me another way to feel connected that I may never have used when I was healthy. It became my simple way to communicate my feelings and desires to and for those I loved on a spiritual level I would not have considered had I not become ill. I wished for my friends and family more when I was dying of cancer than I ever did when I could rely more on five-sense interaction with them. Wishing became an empowering act that allowed me to feel connected with the mysterious and unique "whole," an essence we often call a person's "vibes" or "energy" that bonds everyone and everything together. It became a way I could connect with all those who were wishing for me and with the energy imprint of all those who had ever made a wish.

I know now that research supports what I instinctively felt about the connective component of wishing.[21] I know that wishing has the power to help us feel emotionally and spiritually connected even when we are physically so alone. Research by psychologist David McClelland and others has documented this physiological and psychological benefit of wishing. They call it "the affiliative motive."[22]

McClelland also writes about the immune-depleting effects of what he calls the "inhibited power syndrome" (IPS), the frustration of craving but not having enough control. A kind of inhibited power syndrome is precisely the state in which we cancer patients and other sufferers often find ourselves. McClelland's work points out that IPS can be countered by its exact opposite, the "relaxed affiliative syndrome (RAS)." RAS is the feeling that one is in a nonthreatening and loving relationship. Isolated in the intensive care unit, I could still feel a part of loving relationships by closing my eyes and making a wish for those I loved.

The six characteristics of wishing just discussed indicate that even if the exact wishes we make would never come true, the very act of wishing itself has the capacity to enhance and even save our life. It gives us a little joy and hope when disease or another crisis threatens to rob us of both. It helps protect us against disease, strengthens our heart, enhances and broadens our coping capacity, and helps us keep connected and loving even when we are hurting. These are some of the miracle-making traits of wishing.

Handle with Care

My personal journey through cancer and the regular wishing I did then also taught me that not all wishing is as healing, healthy, and helpful as the well wishing just described. There is an essential shadow of every wish, a mirror image of an unwise or "wicked" wish that makes our wish for serenity bring us turmoil, our wish for delight turn to disillusionment, our wish for purpose leave us feeling stagnant and trapped, our wish for meaning leading only to despair, and our wish for compassion leaving us feeling alone and isolated.

The power of a wish rests not only with its loving energy but also with its capacity to cancel out and even kill those things that threaten our survival. Truly wicked wishes, however, are not just related to the negative power of a wish. They are selfishly made wishes that we ourselves imbue with negativity. We need the dark side of wishing to work its magic against challenges to our welfare, but wicked wishing derives from our own shortsightedness and psychic blindness to the subtle energy that stimulates our sixth sense.

Wicked wishing can have devastating effects on the wisher and the wish object. Perhaps that's one reason we have abandoned our wishing ways. In the tradition of "once burned, twice warned," the malevolent consequences of our brain's selfish, impulsive, and therefore more wicked wishing may have frightened us away. We may have seen what damage we can cause when we use wishing wrongly. Wishes necessarily carry with them a forceful negative power designed to deal with the toxic aspects of our existence. This negative power may be misdirected or overflow when we wish selfishly, impulsively, and carelessly.

Heartfelt Wishes

New research supports the contention that the heart is a thinking, feeling, communicating organ that serves far more purposes than just pumping.[23] In fact, the heart may actually be less a pump than an energetic, rhythmic swing that shoves or "wishes" tiny blood packets along as they come passing through.[24] In a way, every beat of our heart is a miniwish that circulates and communicates the nature of our own subtle energy and our heartfelt intentions. One of the questions you can ask yourself about the wish you wrote on your bookmark card is, "Does this wish seem to come from my head or my heart?" If you find patience, harmony, pleasantness, humbleness, and gentle kindness in your written wish, your heart probably made it. If you find urgency, competition, cantankerousness, selfishness, and anger within the words of your wish, your brain was probably making it.

Unfortunately, our brain too often takes primary control of our wishing life. Its five-sense wishes tend to be more oriented toward the brain's imperatives of self-survival and personal enhancement. These wishes are prone to unleashing the dark side of wishing. They tend to be warrior more than lover wishes. These kinds of wishes may have been necessary for our primitive survival, but they have outlived most of the adaptiveness in a world crying out for connection and meaning.

Brain-based wishes arise from an agenda of "me first," and the result can be a lonely victory. The brain's wishes are more likely to become wicked wishes because they tend to lack balance between loving and personal survival. They are based more on what the brain thinks its body requires than what "something tells us" our heart really wants and our soul desperately needs.

When I was dying, I learned that wishing well is much more than a childish process. It involves the employment of a certain distinctive wisdom of the heart that differs from the rational brilliance of the brain. It is connective rather than competitive and caring more than clever. Wishing well is based on a kind of intelligence that our brain finds quite uncomfortable and even embarrassing. It's wishful thinking that we moderns have been taught to trust only at our own peril. "That's just wishful thinking" is a statement that reflects our brain's bias against what it sees as our softhearted silliness.

In addition to a blend of brilliant medicine, strong loving support, hundreds of prayers, genetic good fortune, and a huge dose of good luck and other unknowns, I remain convinced that I owe my life to wishing well and that the impact of others' wishes helped save my life. Learning to know how to wish judiciously and to recognize and understand the often puzzling and surprising ways our wishes come true was essential to my recovery. Because it saved my life and because of the findings in my own and others' wish research, wishing has become a more frequent part of my professional and personal life. It's always been fun, but since that fateful night in intensive care, I will forever take wishing much more seriously.

The Language of Wishing

As you begin your journey through the world of wishing, I offer a word of caution about reading this book. Wishing is an enchanted process. Becoming re-enchanted with life refers to being able to endow our lives with simple pleasure by seeking the charm in the ordinary. It's looking for the soul in nature that our ancestors so easily found. As author Thomas Moore writes, it's the ". . . appreciation of the sacred and the holy in every aspect of life: nature, work, home, business, and public affairs. I call this 'natural religion.' "[25] I will be combining spiritual, scientific, superstitious, and magical concepts as I explain the nature of wishing. I will move freely back and forth across what your brain sees as permanent boundaries between these realms. I ask that you be patient with your brain and give it time to adjust to a world without walls.

You may not be accustomed to reading about fairy tales and physics in the same sentence. Making a wish (focusing your intention) and being sensitive to the wishes of others (focusing your intuition) are based on both science and cultural mythology, so you will have to think "and" more than "or" as you read on. To grasp many of the lessons about wishing, you will have to be willing to allow them to "come to you" by wishing them to rather than just trying to figure them out or rationally trying to fit them into your current five-sense version of the world. Because wishes are usually incantations expressed in the form of a few words repeated over and over again and are designed to move rather than convince, much of what you will be reading is purposefully written in the incantational style of wishing. Parts may seem more chant than description and several acronyms are used as teaching guides to forming and making your wishes. As with most magical processes, there are many alliterations, lists, codes, and intentionally ritualistic repetitions. There are many catchphrases that your cynical brain may try to reject and mock. The heart thinks wisely but more slowly than your brain, so you will have to teach your brain to calm down.

Your brain is designed to try to "see through" the mystical rather than embrace it as a well wisher must do. Although your heart may be comfortable with this mystical style, your brain may find it annoying at first. If you give yourself time and allow yourself to become absorbed in the ways that wishing works, your heart will be able to get your brain's attention. I've used this combination of whimsy and reason as a means of illustrating and teaching the wizardry of wishing and of trying to speak more in the language of the center of every well wish, your heart. It's my wish that as it did me as I was dying, "something will tell you" to take a fresh new look at wishing in your own life.

I am not completely sure the cultural stories, myths, and research about wishing fully or even adequately explain how and why wishing has stayed with us so long and why so many of our wishes are in exactly the same form as they existed centuries ago. I suspect, however, that such a long-surviving practice must have some significant value for our ultimate well-being beyond the occasional good morning or good night wishes built into our daily behavior. Even if I don't manage to persuade you to take a fresh look at wishing as a means for making your dreams come true, it's my wish that you will at least become re-enchanted with the process of wishing and its health-enhancing side effects. In a world too often influenced by wicked wishing against instead of well wishing for, now more than ever we need to learn to wish more wisely, lovingly, and well. If we all learn to wish well together and for one another, perhaps our new century will herald our transition from the millennium of mechanisms to the millennium of the magical.

Without diminishing its gentle, magical glow, my intent in these pages is to bring wishing out of the soft light of the wishing candles on the birthday cake to help make every day a day we wished for. To believe again in the power of wishing, it helps to pay attention to the words of author Herman Melville: "The intensist light of reason can not shed blazonings upon the deeper truths of man." In the continued absence of the degree of certainty and comfort about life that both science and religion promised us, there is nothing wrong with a little wishful thinking.

The Wish That Helped Save My Life

I promised that I would share the wish I made as I was dying in the intensive care unit. I present it here as a preview of the nature of well wishing and the steps in wishing you will read about later.

When I was dying and spending what everyone thought would be my last night alive in the intensive care unit, I saw a shooting star. Although I was highly medicated, I was alert enough to know that a star was not likely to be falling into my hospital bed. I looked again and I thought I saw another one. Each star seemed to be a bright point darting across a black sky. I know now that what I saw was the point of light coming from the tiny flashlight nurses use to check a patient's status late at night. For me, however, it was a shooting star.

I was struggling to breathe. I was afraid to go to sleep for fear I would never wake up. The oxygen level in my blood had dropped to levels that had my doctors wondering why I was still alive. During the day, everything was shrouded in a gray mist. At night, everything appeared dark even when my eyes were wide open. A nurse had come to my bed and shined her light in my eyes to check my pupil response. I could not see her, but her tiny light seemed to dance in the night sky of my oxygen-deprived blindness. I remember thinking, "Here's my chance. Here's a star to make a wish on."

My hands were tied loosely to the bed so that if I panicked, I would not try to tear the breathing tube from my throat. As if drawn there by some magnetic force and despite the loose cloth ties, my left hand stretched toward my chest. My right moved slowly up and pressed my left hand softly against my heart. I closed my eyes, took a deep breath, and without any preplanning, let the wish come out. I could not speak because of the tube in my throat, but it seemed as if I could actually hear my words.

I had to wait for the machine that was breathing for me to allow me to exhale. When it did, eight words—one per beat—came from my heart. As the light shot past my eyes one more time, this is the wish I made. "Dad, Grandma, Grandpa, please be with me now." All of these persons had died several years ago. I don't know why I thought of them at that moment. I don't even know if they were my wish or if it is possible that I was theirs. I now think it was more likely ours. Somehow, they all seemed summoned to my bedside by a wish. I didn't physically see them. All of my five senses had been numbed by medication or damaged by cancer. I could, however, feel their presence. It seemed that I had not only made a wish; a wish had made me. In the safety and loving comfort of the loving energy of my deceased relatives, and for the first time in weeks in intensive care, I fell peacefully asleep.

As often happens in hospitals, I was awakened in what seemed like moments after I had finally fallen asleep. I heard the clanking of tubes and bottles. The nurse had left her desk and come to my bedside with a medical student. It was morning and I could see more clearly than I had for weeks. I remembered a phrase from a song and felt like singing "I can see clearly now, the gray clouds are gone."

"Did you hear him say something last night?" asked the nurse incredulously. "I swear he was talking to me or someone. I was shining my pen light in his eyes last night and I swear I heard him speak. He said something to someone."

"No way," answered the student. "He's intubated. [A tube was placed down my throat to keep me breathing and it prevented me from me talking.] It can't happen. You've been working this night shift too long."

The nurse seemed agitated and even a little frightened. She hurriedly double-checked the web of tubes and lines around me and said, "Well, I could have sworn I heard him talking to someone last night. I guess I was just hearing things."

Satisfied that the tubes she had checked earlier in the evening were exactly as she had left them, the nurse looked down at me in mock disgust. I could see her face clearly for the first time. She touched my shoulder, and winked. She said with a smile, "Keep it down over here, Doc. Patients are trying to sleep. And no secret visitors past midnight." She gave me a quick "thumbs-up" and walked away.

Later that day, all of the indicators of my health had improved. My profoundly low blood oxygen level had gone up and my blood tests showed small but noticeable improvement. For reasons I think will become clear as you read the following chapters, something very strange happened. An unfinished song appeared within me much as an advertising jingle you can't get out of your mind. The words were, "The old gray mare, she ain't what she used to be, ain't what she used to be, ain't what she used to be. . . ." The words repeated over and over again and while I could not speak, I felt I was singing them. There is a last phrase to the complete version of the song, but that last phrase wasn't left with me that fateful night. Every day for the rest of my stay in intensive care, that song played within me.

Some months after my miracle cure from cancer, I asked my mother about the "Old Gray Mare" song. She seemed startled and on the verge of tears. "Your dad used to sing that song to you over and over again when you were a baby. How did you remember that silly song?" To this day, I have no explanation for the appearance of the song after my night visitors' appearance. Perhaps the medicine, my lack of oxygen, my emotional state, or some set of five-sense factors explain why a song I had heard from my father's lips almost fifty years ago as a baby had suddenly appeared in my life. Perhaps it was a gift, a wish imprint left that night in intensive care, an unfinished melody signaling me that my life was not finished.

I remember silently singing the gray mare song as I waited for the doctors to decide if I could be taken off life support and returned to the cancer unit to heal. I had sung it to myself as a way of wishing as the doctors discussed their wonder about my sudden turnaround and I remembered what had happened the night before when I had wished on a star. When I heard one doctor say, "This is a miracle. Remove the tube. He's not finished yet," I became a born-again wisher. It's my most sincere wish that what you are about to read will convince you to give wishing a try.

Three

Harnessing the Power of a Little Boom

*The intelligent man finds almost everything ridiculous,
the sensible man hardly anything.*

—GOETHE

Getting into the Swing

Imagine yourself being pushed on a playground swing. Try to remember the sensations of being gently pulled back, suspended for a brief tantalizing moment, and—with a gleeful "whee!"—sent off into space. You may even be able to remember adding to the fun by giving a little kick with your legs at the very top of your swing. If you relive your childhood swinging, you have a sense of the physics involved with wishing.

Physicists know that the tiniest vibration can eventually be enough to bring down the largest bridge.[1] Theoretically, with sufficient patience and enough time, a child pushing over and over again against the side of the Sears Tower could cause it to begin to shake ever so slightly. If that child could somehow feel or "sympathize with" the structure's minuscule vibration and then kick her legs as she might at the top of the arch of her swinging and push again just as the building swung back, the building's memory of the first shove would combine with the next, and so on. Eventually, the amassed pushes could become enough to cause the tower to collapse. Though the time involved would make tipping a building with tiny pushes a practical impossibility, such an occurrence is theoretically possible. Through an act of extraordinarily tedious terrorism, an enemy of our government standing at the side of the Washington Monument could give it little pushes every day and night for years and years. If no other forces intervened, eventually the effort would be effective. So it is with wishing.

The best way to understand how a wish works is to think of it as a tiny spurt of energy. Like everything in the universe, our thoughts or intentions are also forms of energy. When we focus our intentions by making a wish, we are creating a tiny energetic shove within the system of which we are all an inseparable part. Because of the power of intentions to be nonlocal, to transcend time and space, they ever so slightly move the cosmos. This is why one simple wish can help swing things a little more our way.

Sympathetic Resonations

The potential of a little force to eventually become an immense power derives from the principle physicists call "sympathetic" resonation. This same law is the fundamental principle behind a wish's power.[2] An example of a little suggestion having immense power is found in one of the most common wishes we all make, the sending of a get-well card. I received hundreds of get-well cards when I was dying of cancer, and each one seemed to be an expressed wish that made me feel that there were many people I would never see willing to wish for me. These cards were often silly and contained simple, brief, "sympathetic" phrases that helped me resonate with people who cared about me, and they seemed to send little healing vibrations through my body every time I received one of them.[3] They were helpful precisely because they were innocently hopeful, nondemanding, and compassionate. Those who learn to wish well always seem to have one key personal characteristic above all else: they are first and foremost sympathetic in their wishes.

As Einstein pointed out, everything is energy. What looks like a stone is really a tightly wrapped bundle of potential rock power. Stones, stars, and thoughts are all energy. These and all systems are capable of doing work, the basic defining characteristic and definition of energy. They are also capable of storing energy. When a little energy is applied to any system, it remains in that system. Since energy cannot be created or destroyed, the energy we give to something stays within that something. It retains it, remembers it, and combines it. There are no exceptions to these fundamental principles of physics, so our thoughts, intentions, and wishes must work the same way.

No matter how slight, making a wish is one way we use our intentionality to give an energetic push that literally reverberates through the universe. Wishing is how we use our consciousness to try to become the cause of a positive effect and to get things moving more harmoniously in our life. We don't wish in order to knock over a building, but we do wish to get our life to vibrate in a more pleasing and less stressful manner. When I asked a high school science teacher who was one of our wish-research subjects to define a wish based on the physics principles presented here, she responded, "A wish is just a little mental shove that moves things slightly more your way."

Cumulative Effects

In the fairy tale "The Three Little Pigs," even the little pig's brick house could eventually have been blown over by a resolute wolf physically acting out his wish to blow the house down. He wouldn't have had to "huff and puff." He would only have needed to blow just hard enough to extinguish the candles on a birthday cake. If he did so over and over again for a very, very long time, the masonry pig's house would eventually suffer the fate of his two friends' houses. Patience, persistence, and subtleness are the ways of physics' sympathetic resonation and the best strategy for wishing well.

The immense power of sympathetic resonation stems from its cumulative energetic effects. It works on any and all systems. Over time, physics tells us that one little energetic shove of any kind—the wind, the rain, a thought, or a wish—reverberates within a brick, cell, plant, or person. Since the "energetic memory" of the first shove is stored in any object, energy system, or person being pushed, the first little push eventually joins forces with all the other pushes.

Lessons from a Skeptic's Nose

When I speak to scientific audiences about my theories and research concerning wishing as a process intentionally inducing sympathetic resonation, I expect disbelief and skepticism. Even though these theories are well established by all scientific standards and research verifying them is published in major journals, mainstream scientists seldom deal with them in their daily work. Most of their work is in the five-sense realm, so they often say, "We just can't accept it. It's too far out. You're asking us to believe in something we can't see or touch." In an attempt to persuade them to start from a point of trying to understand rather than an unwillingness to accept, I often use a simple demonstration. Holding a glass test tube above my head, I open my fingers and let it crash to the floor. "What caused that?" I ask. The answer is always, "Gravity, of course." I ask, "Have any of you actually ever seen or touched gravity?" Typically, no one answers. "Then I assume we can begin with the fact that, even as scientists, all of you already believe in something you can't see or touch." From that point, my discussion of the nature of wishing as a way of patiently, persistently, calmly, and gently trying to consciously induce sympathetic resonation in an invisible subtle energy system proceeds with my audience's increased skepticism of their skepticism.

Sometimes even my broken test tube demonstration does not lessen the resistance to such ideas as a subtle life energy modifiable by the act of wishing. There are always those who think that an open mind requires having a hole in one's head. At a recent scientific meeting, I shared some of my data about wishing. As I spoke about the unique energy that seems to be associated with wishing, one very well-known scientist was sitting in the front row. The television camera filming my presentation caught him fidgeting nervously and rolling his eyes not unlike an adolescent girl who feels she must helplessly endure her parent's hopeless out-of-it-ness. His disgust was flashed on the large television screens at both sides of the lecture hall for all to see.

I diverted from my presentation to ask the very uncomfortable researcher, "Is anything wrong?" He responded, "Well, yes, in fact, there is. I'm afraid you've lost me. Wishing is a very nice quaint thing for children to do, but it has no place at a scientific meeting. We deal with facts, not fiction. To propose that there is a magical process anyone can use to set the universe shaking is ludicrous. To suggest that by making a wish we are somehow tapping into a subtle energy that none of us can see or measure seems more like *Star Trek* than good science. Science is based on the rejection or confirmation of testable assertions, and this is just too far out. No one here could possibly accept or believe it. In fact, it's outlandish."

I had encountered resistance to my theories about wishing before, but never on television screens suspended over the heads of 500 of my colleagues. I had great respect for my critic. We had done some research together in the past and he had become a good friend. I knew he had a sense of humor. I decided to do an even more drastic demonstration about the pervasive belief almost all of us—scientist or saint—have in wishing.

"So you do not at all believe in the power of wishing?" I asked. "You don't think human consciousness can transcend time and space and cause a little energetic ripple that can alter events in ways beyond our measurement techniques?"

"Certainly not," he answered. "I unequivocally do not believe in wishing other than as a silly superstition. Objective scientists don't deal in superstitions." The audience seemed restless. Scientists usually don't confront each other publicly. We're more likely to reserve our intellectual disputes for snide and sarcastic letters to journals.

"Could we try a little Hawaiian experiment to test the hypothesis you just offered about scientists' beliefs?" I asked. He had visited my office in Hawai'i and was well aware of the role of mythology in my culture. "What do you mean?" he responded with a smile.

"Where I live, we have believed for centuries that there is an invisible but powerful energy beyond that which science can measure. We call it *mana* and we believe that we are made of, influenced by, and can influence that energy through our intentions. Through our chants and dance, we make wishes every day. It's how we insinuate ourselves into the *mana,* or subtle energy flow. We believe that the only way to reverse a wish is to use countermagic. You have to rub your nose vigorously in a counterclockwise direction for at least one full minute. [I made up the nose-rubbing technique. There is no such nose-rubbing practice in Hawaiian wishing tradition.] Since you don't believe in wishing or that it can set in motion certain subtle energetic changes, would you object if I made a wish right now that you would die tonight?"

The audience gasped, but my critic seemed unmoved. "I see what you're doing. Go ahead. But I assure everyone here that I'll see them at breakfast tomorrow," he laughed. I had depended on our friendship to help us both through this awkward moment. "Go ahead and take your best shot. Wish away!" he laughed as he stood up to make himself a better wish target. I told the group that I was making what Hawaiians call an *ana ana,* a wish for death used by some ancient kahuna as a subtle energy weapon against their enemies.[4] Of course, I was faking it. I would never make such a wish. Besides, Hawaiian wishing is based on the swinging principle outlined earlier. We believe that pushing too aggressively ultimately swings back to hit the pusher. Hawaiian healers, or kahuna, taught that any wish sent to a person undeserving of that wish bounces right back to the wisher. As a born-again wisher myself, I certainly wasn't going to take any chances. As a firm believer in the power of wishing, I certainly wasn't going to put my friend in jeopardy even humorously.

I noticed that the audience, either because they believed on some level in wishing or because they simply thought the whole idea was ridiculous, had become more uncomfortable. I closed my eyes, made up a few vague and silly gestures with my hands, and pretended to make a wish. I reminded my friend again that all he had to do was use a little wishing countermagic by rubbing his nose counterclockwise and the wicked wish would be canceled. He chuckled again and sat down. "Go on with your lecture," he said.

About ten minutes after I was back into my discussion of how gravity and strong nuclear energy, two of science's well-accepted invisible energies, are also only reasonable guesses about the mysteries of the world, the entire audience broke out in laughter. I was sure I had, as my friend had warned, finally completely destroyed my scientific reputation. I searched the audience for clues as to what was going on. One of the doctors was laughing so hard that tears were rolling down his cheeks. He couldn't talk, but he directed my eyes to one of the TV screens. A handheld camera had caught my critic bent over in an attempt to mask his very energetic counterclockwise rubbing of his nose. The video technician was repeatedly replaying my friend's nose rubbing. When my critic looked up to see his hand on his nose displayed for all to see, he quickly buried his reddened face in his hands. Either from relief or (I hoped) from acknowledgment of the possibility of the impact of wishing, the audience stood and applauded.

Placebo and Nocebo

Although many scientists may be highly skeptical of the possibility that human intention can alter reality, they actually deal with wishing's effects in every one of their experiments. They refer to its influence as the placebo effect. Even as scientists try to structure their experiments in order to diminish the effect of their own and others' wishes about the results of their research, they persist in denying its reality. Ask a scientist if she believes that wishing works and she will probably say no; ask her if she believes in the placebo effect and she will certainly say yes, yet they are one and the same process.

Any good researcher employs double-blind studies precisely for the purpose of keeping the power of a researcher's and a subject's own wishes out of experiments. Even with researchers' best wish-screening efforts, a large portion of the effects of the thousands of drugs listed in the *Physicians' Desk Reference* are due, to varying degrees, to the effects of the wishes of the researcher or the subject.

There are dozens of experiments showing the power of a patient's wishes on the course of treatment of various diseases. Dr. J. W. L. Gielding in the Department of Surgery at Queen Elizabeth Hospital in Birmingham, England, informed 411 patients that they could expect hair loss as a consequence of chemotherapy. Thirty percent of the patients received placebos instead of chemotherapy and suffered hair loss despite the fact that the pills they were taking contained no medication.[5] Many so-called drug effects are not due to pharmacological actions of the drug but to some subtle wish expressed by the patient regarding the drug.[6] There is something about our intentions that goes beyond the five senses.

It is not only the patient's wishes that may alter the energy of a healing event. Double-blind means that neither the subject nor researcher nor patient nor doctor knows if a placebo or a "real" drug is being given. Such studies are conducted to block the effects of both the patient's and doctor's wishes. Despite the most carefully conceived double-blind experiment, the physician's or researcher's own personal wishes also shape the outcome of therapy. Even in the most five-sense-blinded study, the sixth-sense suggestion of the researcher manages to peek through.

An example of a sixth-sense suggestion breaking through is seen in three double-blind studies of the use of vitamin E in treating chest pains. The "E skeptical" and "E believing" doctors involved were blind as to which group of their patients was receiving a placebo and which was receiving vitamin E. The doctors who "believed" in vitamin E had their wish come true. Vitamin E relieved the pain of their patients. In the patients of doctors skeptical of vitamin E's effects, no benefit was reported. Neither the believers nor the skeptics had any way of knowing who received only a placebo and who received the vitamin. They did nothing different on a five-sense level for either group of patients, yet their sixth-sense suggestion caused the same vitamin to have differing actions.[7]

Similar findings regarding the power of suggestion were found in the study of meprobamate, one of the earliest best-selling tranquilizers with the trade names Miltown and Equanil. In the late 1950s, there were conflicting reports as to whether meprobamate really had sedative qualities. Double-blind studies showed again that meprobamate had much more of a sedative effect than a placebo pill, but only for the patients of doctors who believed in it. There was no drug effect for the patients of the skeptical physicians.[8] Researcher Jerry Solfvin concluded, ". . . a wide variety of treatments have conclusively affirmed that the administering physician or researcher is not independent of the results in double-blind treatment effectiveness studies."[9] "Not independent of the results" means that wishing and the little push it seems to give to subtle energy works its way into even the most rigidly controlled settings.

Nocebo refers to the negative effects of a wish. If a positive intention filters into an experiment, it can have favorable effects on the drug or treatment being studied. If a negative intention, a nocebo, filters through, this same drug or treatment may be reduced in effectiveness. Wishing well is a placebo, a positive way of conveying our intentions. Wishing wickedly can be a nocebo, a negative approach that can result in unfavorable outcomes.

A Well Wisher's Healing Place

The effects of wishing as manifested in the benefits of the placebo and risks of the nocebo effects related to it were recognized by the developer of the heart pacemaker and many other mechanical devices used in medical treatments, Dr. Earl Bakken. He noticed that the very same apparatus put in place by exactly the same procedures had differing effects depending on the surgeon's "wishes" or intentions. He reports that those surgeons who seemed sensitive to the subtle and immeasurable energy involved in healing, who worked in harmony with the apparatus and surgical team, and interacted kindly, sensitively, and with the best wishes for their patient had much more positive outcomes than those who seemed, whether they knew it or not, to convey more nocebo or negative wish energy. In other words, well-wishing doctors had the most success with the same equipment.

Based on his experiences, Dr. Bakken helped design, build, and is now president of an innovative hospital in Hawai'i designed entirely around a staff and environment that convey good wishes—a placebo rather than nocebo place to heal.[10] This hospital serves as a wonderful example of the practical application of the seemingly far-out and impractical concept of L energy and how wishing well can condition or convert a secular place into a sacred one where wishes more easily come true.

After my lecture on wishing at a meeting sponsored by his hospital, I walked with Dr. Bakken through one of the first well-wishing healing hospitals in the world. He showed me how the hospital rooms each have a large glass door to the outside so the patients could "connect with nature," an element that seems key to wishing well. Natural light flows in through strategically placed skylights, gentle music plays throughout the hospital, and natural scenes play for hours on the televisions without repetition of relaxing scenes. Patient family rooms are provided so patients are never too far from well wishers. My wife said to me as we walked the halls of this wonderful place, "You can feel the sympathy here."

As we toured this unique wishing world, a happy and radiant young woman approached us. She is director of food services at the hospital. She greeted us by saying, "You know, our food is so good the general community comes to eat here. It's good because we wish the food well as we prepare it. Every patient gets food that carries our best wishes. We actually make a wish with each meal." Dr. Bakken nodded and smiled as he added, "You know, we work very hard to make this place energy-friendly. I don't just mean the energy most people talk about. I mean the kind of energy you talked about at our meeting today. We've tried to make this a place where wishes can be made easily and usually come true. We have the best hardware money can buy, of course, but we employ it with our best wishes. In fact, this hospital is built on a sacred healing land where kahuna practiced healing, a place where people came to heal hundreds of years ago. A lot of wishes came true here."

Dr. Bakken's hospital seems to represent the "sacred space" or "wish-conducive environment" described by researcher Dr. William Tiller of Stanford. Dr. Tiller's research shows that a place and people who wish well seem to convert any place to a sacred place highly conducive and hospitable to the energy of wishing. The well wishes constantly being made in this healing place seem to "condition" its staff, patients, and equipment for more well wishes to come true.

Green and Black Thumbs

Recently, other open-minded scientists like Dr. Bakken who are unafraid to deal with L energy and the power of wishing have been willing to look seriously at the fifth force of wishing that keeps popping up in homes, hospitals, and laboratories. Because their own work has taught them that most of what "is" is still invisible and beyond the reaches of our five senses, they have acknowledged that there is indeed an enchanted and enchanting "fifth force" involved in wishing the sixth-sense way.[11] It is the same energy that causes us to feel instantly attracted to some people yet repelled by others, makes a tumor shrink after a laying on of hands, and makes plants grow better for those who wish them well.[12] It's what we feel when we sense that someone is looking at us or when someone seems to instantly attract us from across a crowded room. It's the raw material of intuition and what we experience as good or bad vibes or a sense of impending doom or delight. It's the energy we sense coming from our children no matter where they are and from our grandparents even if they are no longer alive.

Researchers dealing with plants have noticed the power of sixth-sense suggestion and a subtle energy connection between persons and vegetation. Most of us have heard about persons who have a "green thumb" and to whom plants seem to respond well. There are studies documenting that some people seem to wish well with their plants whereas others suffer from "black thumb" and have plants that seem to refuse to cooperate.[13] Plant researcher Luther Burbank seemed to have the green thumb wishing skill, as evidenced by his growth of more than 800 new varieties of plants. He was a careful scientist and was convinced about the subtle fifth-force vibes connecting plants and people. He wrote, "Plants are as responsive to thought as children."[14]

Looking for Energy

Gravity, electromagnetism, and strong and weak nuclear energy, the four invisible forces scientists are willing to acknowledge, are every bit as mysterious and unseen as the subtle "L" energy of the wish. No one has ever seen gravity or knows where it comes from. Even the explanation of one of physics' newest accepted forms of invisible energy called subatomic "strong" energy sounds at least as implausible and mystical as the subtle fifth force related to wishing. There is no commonly agreed upon explanation for the behavior of the tightly packed clump of charged photons that make up the nucleus of an atom. In fact, the atom itself is an example of one of science's prior "impossibilities." Because of science's own law that like charges repel, the clustered photons ought to shove away from one another and cause the matter they make up to completely disintegrate. Since scientists cannot really explain exactly how or why matter can continue to hold together against their own "rules of physics," they called this invisible fourth force "strong nuclear energy."

Scientists' description of "strong nuclear energy" sounds very much like the fifth force I am proposing as the stuff of wishing. They declared that only in the nucleus of atoms and nowhere else does there seem to be a secret invisible force that breaks every one of their own scientific or "natural" laws. They've never seen it, no scientist has literally "discovered it," so scientists made up a set of rules that explained what the invisible fourth force did. Science could not explain something that seemed impossible, so they constructed a way to explain it. The subtle, pervasive fifth force of wishing plays by these same scientific rules. The fifth force is no more or less "supernatural" than the fourth.

Apart from their own experimental apparatus used to measure it, scientists have not been able to explain the nature of light. Since the apparatus is constructed by the scientist observer, what light "is" depends on what the scientist wishes to use to look at it. We have one mechanism to measure light in its wave form. We have another to measure light in its particle form. There is no gadget yet that can measure light in both of its forms simultaneously, so light is what the researcher wishes for.

The light energy reflecting on this page is but a tiny speck on the full and infinite light spectrum. It is that tiny part that our eyes can detect. There's an entire invisible world around you right now that you will never see with your five senses. Both ends of the light spectrum from ultraviolet to infrared light extend into infinity. What we consider "the" world is a tiny slice of the universe. So it is with the energy of wishing.

New Science Explores Ancient Wisdom

Despite their mystical sound, the concepts of a "fifth force" or "distant mental influence" are now being studied in various departments at several major universities such as Stanford, Duke, Princeton, and the University of Arizona.[15] This subtle force accessed by wishing is beyond our current apparatus and our usual means of physical or mechanical control. It seems to function as the "unrefined material" of the spirit that can help make the unseen real, the hoped for happen, and the feared prevented. Researchers are now devising creative ways to study how wishing functions as a sixth-sense suggestion that transcends time and space and influences people, places, and things.

Just as our eyes are attuned to a very narrow band of light energy and our ears to a restricted range of the energy of sound, our heart seems particularly attuned to the subtle energy involved in wishing. Our heart is capable of sensing our Oneness, the bonding subtle energy beyond the brain's sensitivity, and it helps us become synchronized with and, if we really put our heart in it, able to influence that energy. As you have read, this subtle energy has been named by some of the most skeptical and careful scientists who been willing to study it. They've called it Universal, Light, or "L" or love energy.[16] It seems to be the energy that is our spirit and the force we feel when we say things like "heartfelt" and "knowing in our heart."

In 1979, Robert G. Jahn, Ph.D., established the Princeton Engineering Anomalies Laboratory.[17] Its purpose was to pursue the rigorous scientific study of the interaction of human consciousness with sensitive physical devices, systems, and processes, in other words to see if and how wishing works. Volunteers, called operators, were asked to sit down near a machine designed to continually generate random numbers. This means that over time, the very large set of zeros and ones printed out should show no trend toward zero or one. Essentially, PEAR's random number generating machine was an automatic coin flipper. Over time and with enough "flips" of ones and zeros, it's the perfect 50/50 chance machine.

The operators trying to influence the 50/50 machine away from its ultimate pattern could be seen as making wishes. They were asked to consciously attempt to alter the machine's energy by simply "wishing" it to go toward more zeros or more ones. Beyond any reasonable scientific doubt and over millions of trials, the Princeton Engineering Anomalies Research (PEAR) researchers documented small but statistically significant differences in the way the machine "behaved" in terms of the numbers it generated. A conscious intent or little wish in the form of a sixth-sense suggestion was capable of resonating with and altering the subtle energy of the machine. Its random or "50/50 way" was wished away.

The PEAR "operators" had the same mild but verifiable wishing or "conscious intent" effect on other devices that they had on the machines. By making a wish, they altered the random swinging of a pendulum placed in a vacuum, affected the growth rate of plants, modified the random beating of a native drum, and altered computer-generated images. They were even able to "wish" a random number machine made to resemble a little froglike creature to come to them simply by wishing it to do so. Not unexpectedly, the open-mindedness of children rendered them the most successful random-frog callers.

In their millions of replications, the PEAR team reports that the odds of chance explaining this wish power are 1 in 1 billion.[18] Even more surprising was the fact that time didn't seem to matter. The wishes could be made days before the machine was turned on and the wishes still worked. The "intentions" or wishes could also be made after the numbers were generated and still seemed to affect the machine's past. The number generators could be left on and running for days at a time with no wishing. After the machines were turned off and the data stored, wishes were made in the "one" or "zero" direction of the numbers already generated and stored. When the records were opened after the wishing, the numbers fell in the direction of the wishes. As impossible at it seems to our five senses, wishing transcends time and space.

The PEAR researchers proved that however slightly and mysteriously, a very delicate and gentle conscious attempt to nudge the subtle energy of an object alters the behavior of that object. The milder the nudge, the more profound the ultimate effect. Much as a mother reading a book may gently and almost unwittingly rock her child in the carriage with her foot, wishing seems to be a way we delicately focus our own "L" or subtle life/love energy to make changes in our world.

The PWD: Personal Wish Detector

The PEAR studies have resulted in the granting of a U.S. patent for what might be called the first "wish detector."[19] About the size of a pack of cigarettes, this tiny black box has a set of red and green lights that flash specific patterns when the apparatus "senses" the subtle energy of the wishes of people around it. The red lights go off and the green lights begin to sparkle a series of green patterns when the apparatus detects a wish being made.

The wish detector is particularly sensitive to a well-made wish, one that is unselfish, caring, and gentle in nature and that reflects a wishing connection between those around it. When this kind of wish energy causes the random numbers being generated within the machine to fall outside the range of chance probabilities, its lights turn to green, the machine registers and stores the data, and then it digitally records the impact of a wish. A kind of "wish graph" is generated that shows when wishing is in progress. When one "tries hard," selfishly, impatiently, and with "brain-power" to make the machine respond, the red lights remain on. When one relaxes, connects lovingly and wishes with others, is patient, and wishes from the heart rather than the brain, the green lights go on and spurt up and down almost as if the little machine is glad to sense the well wishing.

I first encountered this wish detector following my lecture on wishing to several hundred business leaders and scientists meeting in San Francisco. The CEOs of the major Internet and technology companies were all in attendance to discuss the topic of "high tech," the latest computer and Internet advances and their implications for the next millennium. I was there to address the "high touch" side of the issue. I spoke on nonelectromagnetic connection and the documented power of wishing that creates its own subtle energy Internet into which we can all log on—a wish web to which we can all contribute. Following my address, I was asked to dinner by Bill Higgins, who wanted to show me his wish detector machine.

Bill is a graduate of the Naval Academy, retired Navy captain, and former FBI agent. He is now a highly successful real estate agent in New York. He is a brilliant, creative man who adores the careful rigor of good science. He has been involved as a supporter of the research at PEAR for several years. After dinner, Bill shyly reached into his pocket and placed his wish detector in the middle of the table between himself, his daughter who works for an Internet corporation, my wife who holds several academic degrees, and me. He explained that this device can sense "consciousness-related anomalies in random physical systems," a technical way of saying that it responds, measures, and records the energy of wishing. He handed me a lengthy technical research report about the wish detector and a copy of the U. S. patent it had received containing forty-three documented research claims about its wish sensitivity and twenty-four highly technical schematic drawings showing how its internal mechanism worked.

For almost two hours, four scientifically trained people played with the wish detector. The little wish meter's lights jumped every time we felt that we had "fallen into sync" with the apparatus and with one another. When we stopped trying, re-laxed, and felt connected as one group and forgot the machine was turned on, the machine drew our attention by blinking its acknowledgment that we had spontane-ously fallen into a wish synchronization with one another. When we became en-grossed in our conversation about the implications of wishing well, the machine again flashed its green lights. If we tried too hard or began to speak cynically and hopelessly about our wish that such a machine could be in every home, work, and healing place, the machine "calmed down" and its red lights stuck on like a traffic stoplight. Much as a puppy wags its tail in gleeful delight when it senses its owner's love, the little machine flashed its green lights wildly only when we seemed to be in a state of unconditional loving or kind resonance with it and one another.

The implications of this wish detector are profound. Bill Higgins reports that it can now be reduced to the size of a computer chip. It can serve as a well-wishing tutor by being placed in toys to teach children to be more gentle, graceful, cooperative wishers. It can be connected to a computer and be used to play wishing games instead of war games. It can be used to make handheld games in the shape of wishing wells that children, adults, and patients could use to reinforce the habit of wishing well. The effects of wishing can be graphically projected at a business meeting or to monitor the wishes of a surgical team hovering over their patient. It can be made small enough to be worn on the wrist as a "wish watch" to tell us how well we are wishing during the day. Because the wish detector responds so strongly to the components of a well-made wish (waiting, imagination, selfless sensitivity, and heartfelt energy flowing between persons), it could become a new PCC—a "personal consciousness caring" device for the new millennium. It could serve as a "wicked wish alarm," a "beeper" that buzzes annoyingly when we are wishing unwisely and plays a pleasing song when we are wishing well. Similar to a biofeedback machine, it could serve as a cardiofeedback apparatus that tells us when we are wishing from our heart rather than our head. It could even serve as a device to assist in the development of a "couple consciousness" to help lovers wed their wishes for more intimacy and lasting love. Once imbued with well wishes, the wish meter could be left running in a room much as an air freshener or ionizer to make that room a "sacred wish place" conducive and responsive to the subtle power of a wish.

As unbelievable and difficult to understand on a five-sense level as this wish meter may seem, it is nonetheless real and available today for further development. It measures at least one small aspect of what Stanford professor and wish researcher William Tiller calls our "conscious acts of creation." There is sufficient research to convince the most serious scientists and the technical staff at the U.S. Patent Office that it is reliable as a wish-sensitive instrument.[20]

The waiters in the restaurant watched with skepticism as we played with the wish detector. At first they laughed and mocked our efforts, but they soon gathered around in stunned awe. "I can't see how that thing can do that. It makes no sense at all. How does it know you're making a wish? What does it sense?" asked one waiter. "I don't know how it works, but we should put one in the kitchen. We need some better wishing in there." A waitress said, "I wished I would have had this thing to use with my first husband. He said he would take a lie detector, but I wish we could have tried this wish detector together. Maybe we could have got our wishes instead of him just getting his."

ISES's and Wishes

The PEAR researchers are careful, scientific researchers who don't shy away from terms such as "wishing." Nonetheless, they write of a subtle fifth force as "L" or love energy. L energy is not a weird, far-out concept but an increasingly documented force in all of our lives. It's the "something more" we can't seem to put our finger on but know and sense has influence in our life. When they encounter persons who feel uncomfortable with the concept of L or love energy, PEAR's term for wishing's sixth-sense suggestion becomes "an engineering anomaly."

Whether you prefer to use the term L or love energy, or engineering anomaly, conscious intent, or making a wish, PEAR's research has described a unique wishing effect each person seems to have as an "individual subtle energy signature" (ISES) that serves as his or her "intention profile." In over 3 million trials still going on at PEAR today, every wisher or "operator" tested seems to have her or his own unique energetic fingerprint. There is no scientific doubt that ISES's "come true." They change things. They are the closest thing yet to a laboratory confirmation of wish power and proof of the existence of our individual wish profile, which may manifest itself as a green or black thumb.

It was Dr. Jahn himself, a professor of engineering and director of the PEAR program, who coined the word "L" or love energy for this still mysterious sympathetic force of wishing. He writes, "Love! Even by the most rigorous scientific experimentation and analytical logic, it appears that we have come upon nothing less than the driving force of life and the physical universe: Love, with a capital L—the same overarching force of creative existence long recognized in virtually every other scholarly discipline and in every other cultural age."[21]

Wishing's Fifth Currency

If wishing is a catalyst for miracles, what Dr. Jahn has called L energy or, for those who prefer a less romantic description, an "energetic engineering anomaly" is the fuel. It's the universal currency of life that Dr. Bakken tries to nurture and generate at North Hawai'i Hospital. What light energy is for our eyes and sound energy is to our ears, L energy is to our sixth sense. Ultimately, because well wishing is a gentle, tender, connective act, it is an act of love. Its energy is easily masked by the intensity of the other four energies, but its subtle nature can be extremely powerful. It is the same force heralded by philosopher Rollo May, who wrote, "For in every act of love and will—and in the long run they are both present in each genuine act—we mold ourselves and our world simultaneously."[22]

Rediscovering the power of wishing is essential to our survival. Exclusive dependence on the brain over the heart, on the brain's unchecked five-sense lethal alliance with its body, and on its preference for intensity over subtlety will eventually consume us. Wishing is a way we can harness and direct the power of love. Theologian Pierre Teilhard de Chardin described the potential of wishing's L energy when he wrote, "Someday, after we have mastered the winds, the waves, the tides and gravity, we shall harness for God the energies of love. Then for the second time in the history of the world, man will have discovered fire."[23]

Super Wishing

Combining ISES's or wish profiles by making shared wishes in a loving bond results in an even stronger wish power. Those who of us who wished with the wish detector at dinner noticed this effect. In the PEAR lab, two men or women or a man and woman working as a wish team tended to have a stronger energy influence on the machines than single wishers. The strongest "intent" or wish effect took place in what the PEAR group called a "loving bond," two persons willing to share an intimate wish. The PEAR researchers write that the recipe for the strongest wish effect and generation of L energy through ISES or wishing ". . . is also the recipe for any form of love; the surrender of self-centered interest of the partners in favor of the pair."[24]

The physics of a "blended wishing" is illustrated by the way in which massive buildings are demolished. Relatively small charges of explosives are placed at strategic locations in the condemned structure. None of them in and of themselves could do much damage. However, when their collective little booms become a sufficiently big bang, the accumulated vibrations resonate through the entire structure. Within seconds, the building implodes and collapses upon itself.

Shared or blended wishing can have an even more significant and rapid effect than individual wishing. So long as the wishes are spiritually compatible, each wisher knows exactly what the other is wishing, and they share the same positive wish, they create a "super wishing." However, because one wish can also work against another, there can also be a cancellation of each partner's wish. A collection of selfish wishes expressed at the same time results in a confused agitation of L energy without direction and shared purpose. To "super wish," we have to be pushing together in the same direction.

Romantic Resonation

When we make a wish, we can use L energy to tickle molecules into wiggling, humming, and rearranging themselves in a kind of cellular sex that biologists call "binding." Binding is a unique form of cellular resonation. It's a "molecular mounting" that happens when ligands or other natural or man-made substances selectively mount molecular "receptors" on cell walls. This union causes each ligand partner to have the cellular equivalent of an orgasm and to literally vibrate with an invisible energy that makes them behave in new ways. The new cellular bond resonates in a unique way that is different from its component parts.

Mutual resonation is a widespread feature in the universe. All manner of systems resonate with one another, including mechanical, electromagnetic, fluid dynamic, quantum mechanical, nuclear, human, and cosmic systems. Musical instruments, radio and television circuitry, atomic components of molecules, all immerse us in what scientists call "sympathetic resonance" from which strikingly different properties of any thing or anyone emerge from those that characterized their original components.

Wishing well results in a loving echo that can resound through the universe. The word "sympathetic" derives from the Greek *sympatheia* meaning to "feel together," and "resonate" derives from the Latin *resonantia* meaning "an echo." Sympathetic resonance, then, is a scientific description of the way we "fall into sync" when we need to be connected with something beyond the brain's sense of its here and now. When two of us resonate together, the combined surge of sympathy or L energy can be immensely positive.

How Wishing Feels

Unlike the prayerful "high awe" of the sacred feelings we have when we feel the presence of God, wishing is the "lower awe" of the warm feelings we have when we meet a cherished old friend. All four of us felt the warmth of well wishing at that dinner when the wish detector gave us the green lights to keep wishing and the meter seemed to jump with joy as we "fell into sync" with each other. The state of wishing just seemed "to come to us" in more of a Pooh Bear than a Rabbit way of being. It's something that happens to us when we are willing to go beyond keeping "our eyes wide open" and "on top of things" to being willing to close our eyes, take a deep and calming breath, and become more absorbed in things.

Deep breathing is an important part of well wishing. You can't focus your intention to wish well unless you can calm down and pay attention to the place where your best wishes are made, your resonating heart. Deep breath helps bring our entire body into a state of coherence or balanced resonance, shifts the biogears of our body from drive to neutral, and allows the heart to resonate its loving energy throughout the entire body's system. It's a form of spiritual connection, because with each sacred breath of life, we are taking in exactly the same molecules of oxygen breathed by our grandparents, great-grandparents, and all who have lived before us. It helps us go back again in our heart to the rocking chair in which our wishing skills were learned and to intentionally surrender our self-centered interests in getting "our way" in favor of flowing with the infinitely puzzling grandeur of "the way."

When we make a wish, we feel young and comforted by our sense that we can affect the invisible forces that influence our life. We feel what one of our wish project participants called a "wish resonance reverie." This young lawyer described her feelings when she was wishing well by saying, "When I wish, I feel young again. It's kind of like blowing bubbles when I was a kid. If you blow too hard, the bubble bursts before it has a chance to grow. If you are very gentle and patient, you can blow a big bubble. If you are careful, you can hold it for a while in the palm of your hand. I have a little bottle of bubble-blowing soap and a bubble ring in my desk. When I wish, I blow bubbles. It helps me remember how to be patient, careful, and gentle."

Comfortably Bewildered

So far, you have read that wishing is a culturally tested and scientifically researched process through which we can resonate with L energy to cause changes. You have read that loving partners can combine to do "super wishing." Another component of how wishing works is the state of amazement with life it engenders. Persons unwilling to be amazed, astonished, and even flabbergasted by the mysteries of life are not very good at making wise wishes. The ritual of wishing requires the kind of awe Goethe described as ". . . the finest portion of mankind; However scarce the world may make sense—In awe one feels profoundly the immense."

Like children gleefully presenting their wish list to Santa Claus, well wishers enter into their wishing with a profound respect of the L energy involved. Well wishing is less a way of trying to "get" something than a way of allowing ourselves to trust innocently in and become overwhelmed for a moment by the poignant enormity of being alive. It is pausing to live less "for" than "in" the moment, and as one of the respondents in our wish-research program stated, it's being able to calm down enough to feel the subtle stimulation of our sixth sense.

Cosmic Coaching

We are not wishing well when we attempt to control the seemingly fickle energy that permeates every aspect of our life. The various pop psychology self-help strategies alone are not well suited for dealing with the frustratingly erratic and sometimes surprisingly dreadful ways subtle L energy behaves. They are ways of doing and not being. They are ways of imposing instead of proposing. They don't fit well with the whimsically clever, chaotic, and curiously subtle energy that so exasperates, tantalizes, and thrills us. Such action-oriented or "just-do-it" approaches work better in the world of our five senses than in the mysterious world of the invisible. They are less effective than learning the first step to well wishing—to "SDASU"—sit down and shut up.

Well wishing's gentle nudge of L energy is a process of "passive volition" and quietly and gently letting wishes work in their way and in their own sweet time. One of our research subjects called wishing "cosmic coaxing." Like a person who thinks she is drowning until "something tells her" to stick out her legs to touch the shallow bottom just beneath her, wishing is less a wish coming true for the strong-willed than the truth coming to the person calm and connected enough on a sixth-sense level to receive it.

Although stressful times in our life often compel us into being more dependent on and keenly aware of the role of wishing, some of our best wishing is done when we are very tired. When we have finally exhausted our five senses, our sixth sense is free to make its own suggestions as to how we might live. When we feel compelled to just sit down, shut up, breathe deeply, and look wistfully out the window, we can allow ourselves to lapse into a melancholy state of "passive volition" in which our best wishes are made. We may begin such wishes by sighing the words, "I really wish . . . ," and then, when the phone rings, be drawn back to "reality," reluctantly yielding our wishing response to the more intense and demanding energies of life.

The Power of Passive Volition

Scientists have finally discovered how the well-established practice of biofeedback actually works. They have discovered that it "clicks in" when, mysteriously and suddenly, the subject's blood pressure reduces, heartbeat and breathing slows and becomes more regular, and stress hormones and the immune system fall into balance. They now know that active effort to "try hard to relax" in order to alter the readings on the biofeedback machine only delays and often prevents progress. Like the Princeton wishers, hard effort is counterproductive to well wishing. Allowing the resonation response called wishing to occur is what also makes the effects of biofeedback take place.

It's now clear that biofeedback works best when the patients wish well and connect gently with the calming subtle energy that leads their body into a relaxed state. Persons successful at biofeedback don't try to operate or direct the machine; they try to connect and work with it. One of my own patients described her biofeedback approach as "trying to be good friends with the machine." A physician, another one of my patients who was suffering from serious heart disease and on whom I tried biofeedback to lower his blood pressure, reported, "I don't know when or how, but when I stopped trying, sat back, and just made a little wish, I connected with the machine somehow and became totally relaxed. Then, when I saw the change, I tried harder to get even more of an effect and the effect went away. It took awhile, but I took a deep breath, stopped being my usual strong-willed self, and just made a little wish that things should go as they should. I just let go and I felt everything become calm again. The main thing I learned from biofeedback was how to recognize that very subtle time when you feel calmly connected. You can't do it or make it happen, you have to sort of suggest that it happen."

Suspending Your Animation

If only for a moment during the making of our wish, we move out of the brain's natural default mode of vigilance and deliberation to a state of just letting things come to mind. In this case, mind means a coherent or balanced resonation between the brain and the heart. We fall into an "internal sync" that allows us to resonate better and fall into sync with the outside world. We enter a relaxed state that is a naturally healthy way for the body to function. Even if wishing didn't work as well as it does, you now know from our earlier discussion that the act of wishing alone is one of the healthiest things we can do for ourselves. We are practicing good preventive medicine when we wish. The increasingly rare state of "passive volition" induces a state of balance that benefits every body system.

The scientific description of passive volition is a perfect definition of well wishing. Science says passive volition is the "voluntary" control of the "involuntary" nervous system that allows the body to work naturally rather than in constant response to what the brain wants. Through this "wishing" state of acceptance, attunement, and alignment, significant measurable changes in "real" life occur. One does volitionally make the choice to try biofeedback, but those who benefit from that choice do not try to make or will physiological balance to occur. As with any sixth-sense suggestion, it must be wished and then waited for.

Researchers in processes such as biofeedback, imagery, and visualization refer to the state of making a wish at the base of these processes as operating by the principle of "the paradox of doing by not doing and achieving success by not striving." Wrongful wishing interrupts and blocks these processes because, like blowing too hard to make a bubble, trying hard to achieve them only makes them more illusive. Unwise wishing is trying to be strong-willed rather than peacefully wishful. Well wishing takes place when we realize that reality can, in fact, be modestly shaped by our own consciousness when we are able and willing to go into "reverse gear." To wish well, we have to cease our constant going forward and trying to will things to happen fast. We have to step back and gear down to our ancestral gift of gentle wishing.

Until 1933, no Rolls-Royce was equipped with a reverse gear. Sir Henry Royce did not want his cars to have what he considered an undignified mode of progression. Many still consider the concepts mentioned earlier such as passive volition, resonating with subtle L energy, and making minimiracles by "letting" rather than "doing" to be somehow unbecoming, silly, or "scientifically undignified." These mystical-sounding wishing guidelines are really no more implausible than our most popular scientific explanations for why we are and how we got here.

Going in reverse is still going. Perhaps the best metaphor for what my research subjects reported when they were in the wishing state of passive volition is that "in-between" time of suspended animation when we are switching gears between forward and reverse and not really going in either direction. That's why well-made wishes are best expressed by verbally timing them for the brief moment between heartbeats and the stillness between systole and diastole. One of my research subjects said, "You know, I never noticed it until we started talking in the wish project about the life-neutral times like that brief moment between each heartbeat. It's like the N or neutral position on the gearshift. I can't remember ever using it. I'm either in forward, reverse, or park."

Avoiding Wishing's "Decline Effect"

The physics of wishing well involves yet another principle researchers in the field of parapsychology call the "decline effect." If subjects are attempting to perform what researchers call a "psi" or psychic task such as wishing or to convey or acquire information from a distant individual or location through purely mental means, they are often highly successful—initially. The "success rate" of these psi efforts quickly declines to chance levels when the subjects try harder to do better. The more they "do" instead of "let," the less significant the effects of their psychic effort and the shorter-lived their initially high psychic spurt. This same decline effect was regularly recorded in the PEAR studies. Well wishers know that their natural wishing ability seems to work best when they are at ease in the world. It is clear to those who wish easily and wisely that nature welcomes our humble participation and sixth-sense suggestiveness but strongly resists our psychic pushiness.

Overcoming Jocularity Deficiency

I've seldom seen one of our wish-research subjects make a wish without also having a smile. Eighteenth-century author Arthur Collins suggested, "It would never have occurred to anyone to doubt God's [i.e., unseen power's] existence if theologians had not tried so hard to prove it." To be a well wisher, keep learning, searching, and doubting, and believing in God, but also lighten up once in a while. Make a wish just for the fun of it and try to get in the swing of things. If you follow the principles of well wishing presented in the following chapters, it can't hurt.

Paraphrasing a statement made by author G. K. Chesterton, it is a test of good religion and good science if you can make a joke about it.[25] Both science and religion tend to suffer from jocularity deficiency when it comes to their turf wars. Approaching wishing with a sense of humor can help both the skeptic and the fanatic realize the comfort wishing offers. Five-sense science often takes itself too seriously to deal with something as subtle and vague as wishing. Religion tends to take itself too sacredly to be open to a secular ritual such as wishing. It has its own ways of dealing with the supernatural and is not much interested in very human processes such as wishing that are the more ordinary, nonsacred ways of trying to express our spirituality. Some scientists still consider processes such as wishing to be borderline lunacy. Some religionists consider it to be borderline blasphemy. I suggest that both explanatory systems could benefit from lightening up a little and having some fun wishing well. As Dostoyevsky wrote, "If you wish to glimpse inside a man's soul and get to know a man, just watch him laugh."

Stupid or Silly

Wishful thinking falls between the rational and the ridiculous. It's the perfect thing to do when we tire of science's killjoy orientation and religion's often hypocritical sanctimony. It can help us remember that there are many things about this life that will always seem preposterous and that neither our brain nor our soul may ever be able to grasp on its own. For dealing with these mysteries, and until they are dismissed through discoveries derived from what science calls the "final unifying theory" or the coming of religion's conclusive miracle, we are wise to hedge our bets and keep wishing.

Another way to look at wishing in a way inoffensive to science and religion is to view it as just a little good-natured joshing with the universe. Wishing is being silly. The word "silly" derives from the Old English *gesaelig* meaning to be blessed. As you read this book about wishing and become tempted to say "this is stupid," take note of your brain's intolerance of the heart's blissful ways. Based on what you have read about the science of wishing to this point, it seems clear that wishing is not stupid, but it is silly. It's a blessing that is very good for you. When life gets rough, doing something silly like making a wish can be a good coping technique. It may not be the brain's way of taking the bull by the horns, but it's a good way to follow W. C. Fields's suggestion when he said, "There comes a time when we must grab the bull by the tail and face the situation."

Sometimes, to soften a serious request or mask our urgent need for something, we may teasingly ask for it in jest by saying, "Oh, I was only joking." Wishing can be done in this same innocently suggestive way. In keeping with the long tradition of the trickster myths and court jesters, we can harmlessly try to tease a little more out of life. Until something much better comes along from science or religion, we can be wishful thinkers who know how to be a little silly and turn to one of our oldest cultural and mythological traditions. As Shakespeare said, it may be better to be a witless fool than a foolish wit. You may not be able to get the big bang out of life that your brain wants, but you can at least experience the little booms or blooms that the heart desires. Within wishing's silliness rests some very good spiritual and scientific common sense.

Four

Becoming Totally Absorbed

*I do not ask how the wounded one feels.
I, myself, become the wounded one.*

—WALT WHITMAN, *LEAVES OF GRASS*

How Absorbed Are You?

A re you totally absorbed in living? People who wish well tend to be those who are the most engrossed in the glorious opportunity to be alive. They relish every aspect of daily living, particularly those things that a busier brain is often too distracted to bother with. They resonate with life energy and with all the energy around them, and because they are such willing and full participators in life, they frequently indulge in one of its most enjoyable and wonderful aspects. They wish freely, often, and well.

To assess the role of psychological absorption as it relates to wishing, we asked family members of our 2,166 wish-survey respondents about the life orientation of their relatives. Based on the psychological research on the characteristic of life absorption, we asked the following questions. We wanted to learn more about the world view of those people who tended to wish frequently versus that of people who wished infrequently and how those who wished regularly might be different from those who did not. Since my own and others' research shows that those who wish well are less likely to become ill and die prematurely, and more likely to lead healthy, challenging, and enjoyable lives, we wanted to see if there might be some beneficial cluster of life-view traits all of us could learn from frequent and wise wishers.[1] We wanted to get some sense of how others saw our respondents, so we began by asking a family member of our respondents the following questions.

- Does this person get really excited with little things?
- Can you hear the excitement in this person's voice and see it in her or his face?
- Can you easily see this person's face "just drop" when they are sad and "light up" when they are happy?
- Does almost every little thing that happens seem to "sink in" and cause this person prolonged concern?
- Does this person have trouble "just dropping it" and stopping himself from thinking over and over again about the same thing?
- Do most people seem to take things less personally than this person?
- Do other people seem much less sensitive than this person?
- Do others seem better able to let things "roll off their back" than this person does?
- Does this person seem like an "emotional sponge," taking every little comment to heart?
- Do you have to tell this person to just "chill out" or "calm down" or "take it easy"?
- Do you tell this person that he or she is "too serious" and "overreacts"?
- Does this person consider almost any new finding, news story, or book about mental, relationship, or physical health to apply to them?
- Is this person a "worrywart"?
- Does this person seem to be "spiritually hypersensitive," often asking questions such as, "What does it all mean?" and "What is it all for anyway?" and "Is this all there is?"
- Are this person's feelings easily hurt?
- Would you say this person feels "pretty upset" at least once a day?
- Can this person seem to "sense" the energy of other people and places?

The more "yes" answers to these questions, the more likely the person in question is high on the characteristic psychologists have long studied called "life absorption." As you learn to wish well, you must consider increasing the degree to which you are willing to become more fully absorbed in life. You have to consider being a little more like Pooh Bear and diving right in to search for the honey. You have to let yourself become excited again with the thrill of being alive and be willing to use wishing as one means to absorb yourself in living.

Wishing and Loving

Wishing well is like loving well. It is allowing yourself to become a human IIED— what researchers in wishing call an intention-imprinted energy "device" willing to become fully absorbed in the subtle energy of life. It requires the same total absorption in life that lovers feel when they become totally and completely immersed in and sympathetic for each other's lives. A loving bond happens when each partner seems to know what the other is thinking and feeling and is sensitive and reactive to cues that those outside the bond may never see. When we fall in lust, we experience a strong five-sense attraction, but when we fall in love, we connect so profoundly on a sixth-sense level that we feel absorbed in and with our partner and an inseparable part of our lover. A loving bond is a microcosmic and more "localized" representation and deeply personal experiencing of the "nonlocal" or total timeless consciousness connection that is the basis of wishing's power. Wishing works much like loving and has similar thrills, pains, and challenges.

Loving is a process of allowing ourselves to risk surrendering the self to become fully absorbed in another person's life energy. We eventually become so totally connected that we no longer love our partner because he or she is so much like us but because our partner seems to become us and we become them. Wishing is a similar process through which we allow ourselves to give up self-control in favor of being at least momentarily absorbed in our connection with everyone and everything. To learn to wish well you have to learn to love totally and allow yourself to become totally absorbed in all of the subtle connective energy of life that respected scientists call L or love energy.

A primary attribute of frequent wishers is their tendency to allow themselves to become so deeply involved in life that they are fully present in and reactive to every moment of it. Lovers find love in their life, but wishers are those who are genuinely in love with life. As one of our wish-research subjects put it, "I'm like Oliver Hardy. I'm always in another fine mess. I'm not leading my life, I'm in it. It's a very fine mess and I'm glad I'm in it. I hope, I pray, I meditate, and I wish. I need all the help I can get, so I'll try anything. Wishing is one of those things."

In our current emphasis on staying alive longer, we sometimes forget to be fully alive before we die. We work hard not to have to wish, thinking that we can ultimately achieve enough control that we will no longer have to be a wishful thinker. The frequent wishers we interviewed, however, had no intention of outgrowing their wishing. They were so ensconced and reactive to the ups and downs of living that wishing had become an indispensable part of their way of life. "Why would I want to give up wishing?" said one of our most frequent wishers. "That would be like giving up seeing or smelling. It's one of the main ways of dealing with things."

The Death Wish

When I was dying of cancer, I noticed something about wishing that left an indelible mark upon my soul. One of the clearest signs that death was imminent for patients on my cancer unit was when a person began working on making a last wish. This often occurred days or months before their death. It was not a form of surrender but an indication of a willingness to stay absorbed in all of life's manifestations and transitions. It seemed to reveal an ease and comfort with death that those who could not make the death wish seldom experienced. One fellow patient said to me the night before he died, "I'm not afraid of death anymore. In fact, I've developed a deep sympathy for it and for those who lead their lives wishing that they'll never die."

I learned about the "death wish" during my late-night meetings with my fellow bone marrow transplant patients. We all knew that many of us would die soon and often spoke together in private about our fears and the mysteries of death and dying. I would often roll my wheelchair into one of my fellow cancer patients' rooms and spend the lonely late hours of the night until the sun rose talking with him or her. I had become highly aware of change in my own wishing. I was extremely sick and in terrible pain, but I was strangely more absorbed in life and wishing more than ever before in my life. I noticed, however, that some patients I spoke with were at a different stage in their wishing.

I spent several nights talking with a woman in the room next to mine. Like all of us, she was suffering terribly and on the verge of death. We had often spoken about our wishes until, early one morning as the sun fell across her white bedcover, my friend said, "I think that's it. I don't have any more wishes to make other than my last one. I feel like pulling out of life now and not being so damned absorbed in trying to cling to it. I don't want to be so consumed with life and living anymore. I feel like I'm missing out on one of the most important times of my life; my death. I have only one more wish left. I wish my that death will be gentle for me and my family."

I immediately began to try to comfort, coax, and plead that she not give up. "Keep on wishing," I said. "Don't give up."

"I am wishing," she laughed. "You're just bothered because I'm working on my last one. I'm ready to go. You know, the doctors know, the nurses sense I know, and my family knows there is nothing more to do and that I will die soon. I don't want to wish anymore. I don't need to wish anymore. My one last wish is that my death is gentle for me and my family. What's wrong with that wish?"

I was crying, but she wasn't. "Come on, now," she said. "You aren't going to become a wish censor on me, are you? Do you think only one version of wishing is the right version? My death wish is every bit as valid and healing to me as any wish to live is. I'm just wishing to be strong enough to say the five things I learned from the hospice nurse. She said they were the hospice philosophy of death, and I want to share them with my own family. That's my wish. They are beautiful things. I wish to be strong enough to ask them to forgive me, say I forgive them, say thank you, say I love you, and then say good-bye, I'll see you later. I think that's as wonderful a wish as your wishing to stay so absorbed in living is, don't you?"

I learned from this and other death-wishing patients that wishing well is not only being highly absorbed in celebrating being alive but also being so fully absorbed in all of the transitional processes of life that we can make a wise last death wish. Wishing well is not only wishing to live fully but also wishing to die gracefully. It's not only being comfortable being near death but being able to embrace death itself.

The Science of "Perivitalology"

About twenty-five years ago research interest began in "perithanatology," the study of near-death experiences (NDEs).[2] One in twenty Americans say they have had an NDE.[3] There is no data on what percentage of Americans are having a fully absorbed NLE—near-life experience—but the frequent wishers in our study seemed to be having them on a regular basis. To the highly skeptical five-sense-dominated person, wishers seem weird precisely because they seem so "into" things. One benefit of learning to wish well is that it allows you to be much more connected with the vital life energy in and around you and aware of its transitions. Wishers are less concerned with immortality than with being what one of our subjects jokingly called ". . . mort-ified, that is, fully mortal now." As this patient illustrated, wishing to be fully alive is also wishing to be fully absorbed in the sacred nature of our mortality.

Woody Allen represented our quest for an immortal self when he quipped, "I don't want to gain immortality through my work; I want to gain immortality through not dying." Our study of wishing and of those absorbed enough in life to engage in wishful thinking reveals that the primary characteristic of those who wish well is that they are capable of being fully absorbed in all that life offers, including its gifts and crises and beginnings and endings.

The study of those who are not as immersed in living as frequent wishers might be is called "perivitalology," or the science of the less absorbed who are led by life but not leading it and have occasional near-life experiences. The less absorbed see their protected and controlling self as above such a silly thing as wishing. Wishers, however, must wish. It's one of their favorite ways of dealing with the mysteries of life they so profoundly sense. One of our nonwishers summarized the contrast between the subtle energy sensitive and those less wish energy aware when he said, "Every one of these guys who is wishing a lot is a little out there. I mean, they're strange or something. If you're going to go through life wishing, you're not going to be in control of your own destiny. I don't wish, I work."

NDEs and NLEs

When the less absorbed occasionally come "near" (peri) the vital energy of life's many transitions and manifestations, they don't truly experience them to their fullest extent. They don't pay enough attention to celebrating the often excruciating wonder and vitality of being temporarily mortal. If they're lucky, they may end up having a series of near-life experiences, or NLEs, tantalizing brushes with some sense of the supernatural that breaks through their high sixth-sense threshold. It's usually something about nature's magnificent beauty and power that causes these NLEs; perhaps a gorgeous sunset, an arching rainbow, a shooting star, the birth of a child, or the passing of a loved one.

During our interviews of the wishers and nonwishers, a strange pattern emerged. There were nine of our frequent wishers who reported having experienced an NDE. None of our infrequent wishers had an NDE, or if they did, they were not sufficiently absorbed in it to remember. The highly absorbed who had gone through an NDE spoke of it with a sense of fondness and described its serene, balanced, sacred nature, the same kind of descriptions provided by the nonwishers speaking of their NLE. They were almost disappointed that they had been brought back to the five-sense world and said they had experienced some reluctance to do so. Those nonwishers who talked about a brief NLE such as a surprisingly beautiful moonlit summer night often spoke of it as a pleasant distraction but welcomed and were relieved with their return to the comfort of their five-sense world.

Both of these groups had glimpses of the forces beyond the five senses, but the frequent-wishing and highly absorbed group embraced them whereas the less absorbed tended to see them as spiritual food too rich for their soul. Of course, these are not the words they would use for their feelings. As one of our sixth-sense phobics said, "It was great seeing those sunsets in Hawai'i. I really got into them. But that's not real life. You can't let yourself get lost in that kind of thing forever or you wouldn't get anything done."

A frequent wish reported in our surveys was stated in various ways, but its message was common. "I want to be fully and really alive before I die."[4] One of our research subjects expressed her life-absorption wish in these words: "I don't wish to become immortalized before I become fully mortalized."

The Psychology of Absorption

The feeling of being immersed in life that so characterizes frequent wishers is a personal characteristic psychologists call absorption. It's a trait of those who tend to connect with the world more with their heart than their head. Almost everything seems to "get to" them. They are much more sensitive than cynical and have a tendency to wonder at and feel affected by everything and everyone around us. They trust in their sixth sense and easily believe in those forces to which the less absorbed seem numb. They are highly responsive to the point of seeming allergic to the L energy of life and feel completely immersed in it. They are on the lookout for any invisible means of support available, and that includes processes such as wishing.

Absorbed people jump right into life and, as with the patient with the death wish, are able to be immersed in and fully sense life's transition into another state. They easily make leaps of faith. They struggle with the consequences of—but accept the truth in—author Graham Greene's statement, "When we are not sure, we are alive."[5] They are both bothered and fascinated by the intangible and invisible and, as a result, often employ wishing as one of their ways to cope with life. Another of our wish-research subjects said, "I can easily tell someone you call absorbed. They're much more likely to cross their fingers than make a fist."

Mystified Persons and Right Men

Absorbed persons are the exact opposite of what science fiction writer A. E. Van Vogt and British writer Colin Wilson called the "Right Man Syndrome."[6] This term describes someone, almost always a male, who feels quite certain about his world view. I showed some of my own Right Man tendencies when I struggled with my fellow patient's death wish. The Right Man is typically brain- rather than heart-driven, and his need to be right is primary. He feels his world view and explanatory system is the one correct explanation against which all others are compared. Maintaining his feeling of "rightness" assumes such supreme importance in his working, loving, and playing that he immediately attacks anyone who creates any cognitive dissonance that might put a crack in his wall of certainty. A Right Man would not acknowledge wishing for luck and would be more likely to say, "You make your own luck."

Absorbed persons, in contrast, are characterized by what may be called the "Mystified Person Syndrome." Almost everything that happens to an absorbed person goes directly to his or her heart. An absorbed person is never quite sure of anything but is able to flow and adjust to whatever comes along. Right Men call this kind of person "flighty" or "too soft-hearted." Where Right Men say "I'm sure" and "You're just plain wrong," absorbed persons are more likely to say "I'm not sure" or ask "Are you sure?"

Absorbed persons' wishing propensity is related to their tendency to feel as if they're living in a state of awe bordering on fear of the magnitude of life. They are not at all as convinced as Right Men that they can rely on their five physical senses and reason alone to get them through their working, loving, and living. They talk a lot about sensing good and bad vibes, and because they think with their sixth-sense-sensing heart, that's where they feel almost everything. They respond with emotion and physiological intensity to the same elusive and invisible forces that reverberate around all of us. One of our highly absorbed patients said, "It feels like I'm energy allergic. It's like life is a big hand at the top of a chalkboard and I'm always waiting to see if its fingernails are going to scratch down it. It seems like I'm the one waiting to react to things and forces that don't seem to bother other people much. Everything seems to get me right here (gesturing to her heart)."

Because they are never too self-confident, feel totally connected and affected by everyone and everything around them, and never feel completely in control, wishing is a good way for the highly absorbed to deal with life. They rely on their imagination, superstitions, and wishful thinking as important ways of helping them through the day. Right Men circle the edges of life, analyzing and doubting it. Mystified or absorbed people are always in the midst of it.

Research on Absorption

Although it hasn't often found its way into popular psychology, the trait of absorption has been a subject of research psychologists for years. Their technical definition of "absorption" is a characteristic of the individual that involves an openness to experiencing emotional and cognitive alterations across a variety of situations."[7] In simple words, absorption means you let things get to you quickly and often.[8] It's a trait that is normally distributed in the general population, tends to remain stable throughout life, and is a temperament or orientation toward life that might be called "extremely soft-hearted." Studies of monozygotic or identical twins reared apart indicate that being an easily "absorbed" person may have a genetic basis.[9]

To learn more about how absorption and wishing were related, I combined the current research on absorption as a consistent personality trait with the family member responses to the questions listed earlier. The correlation between the two tests was .93, meaning that each test predicted the other's results more than 80 percent of the time. I constructed a quiz, the Psychological Absorption Test (PAT), to administer to the 2,166 members of our wish study. Listed next in test form are the research-documented characteristics of persons prone to being highly absorbed in and by their daily life. They present a portrait of someone who makes a lot of wishes.

Psychological Absorption Test

Answer yes or no to the following ten questions:

1. _____ Do you feel "edgy," jump when the phone or doorbell rings, or become easily startled when someone enters a room? Highly absorbed persons have been shown to react very strongly to sudden loud noises and to be hypersensitive and overreactive to the slightest changes in their social and physical environment.[10]

2. _____ Are you highly suggestible and influenced when someone says she feels warm or cold, thirsty or hungry? Because of the ease with which they allow others to influence them, persons high on the absorportion scale also tend to make the best subjects for hypnotism.[11] This may explain why frequent wishers easily and willingly lapse into the state of "wish reverie" of closed eyes and deep breathing that goes with making wishes.

3. _____ Do you believe in ESP, fortune-tellers, certain "signs" of impending events, and hidden meanings in your dreams? High absorbers tend to be "sixth sensors" and those most likely to report mystical or paranormal experiences[12]

4. _____ Do you sometimes seem to "drift away" or feel like you are "in a trance"? Highly absorbed people tend to be more likely to report experiencing altered states of consciousness.[13]

5. _____ Does your heart sometimes seem to skip a beat, race, or pound in your chest? Highly absorbed people tend to be very "cardioreactive" and experience marked variations in heart rhythm.[14]

6. _____ Do you tend to "tense up" quickly and feel that your blood pressure is going up? High absorbers are prone to significant variations in blood pressure. In a syndrome called "white coat hypertension," they often measure as having higher blood pressure when it is taken by a nurse or physician.[15]

7. _____ Is it very easy for you to picture things in your mind and to be influenced by a soothing voice presenting a lovely image? High absorbers are very responsive to imagery, visualization, relaxation, meditation, and biofeedback techniques.[16]

8. _____ Do you tend to fall in love easily, be very sensitive to whether others like you, to be very deeply and chronically hurt by an ended love relationship, and to blame yourself for love failures? High absorbers tend to be prone to lovesickness, to be devastated and distracted by relationship problems, and to take love failures personally, pervasively, and permanently.[17]

9. _____ Do leaky faucets, squeaky doors, and other noises that only annoy others seem to drive you crazy? High absorbers are constantly "on the lookout" for signs of trouble and asking themselves "what's wrong?" and "what next?" For them, many things are like fingernails dragged along a chalkboard.[18]

10. _____ Are you constantly "coming down with something," feeling like you "might" be getting sick, or bothered by repeated nagging physical problems? High absorbers are world-class hypochondriacs well aware of the most deadly interpretation of the slightest symptom. They tend to fall prey to "stress-related disorders" such as digestive or bowel upset, night-

mares, difficulty sleeping or getting back to sleep once awakened, somatic complaints, and migraine or cluster headaches.[19]

Score 10 points for every "yes" answer. The higher your PAT score, the more likely you are to be highly "absorbent" and therefore probably a wishful thinker. You probably rely more than many others on any process that can help get you through the night and day, and wishing is one of those ways. If you know people who would score very low on the absorption test, they probably are doubtful of wishing and see the persistent wishful thinking of someone highly absorbed as a sign of their emotional instability or intellectual weakness. They may even regard your purchase of a book about wishing as silly and, not knowing the difference between "nonsense" and the "sixth sense," perhaps stupid.

In our 2,166-person wish study, those who said they wished regularly (85 percent of the group, or 787 men and 1,045 women) scored 40 points or more on the absorption test. Those who said they did not wish regularly (15 percent, or 227 men and 107 women) scored 30 and below. The "low absorbers" tended to place most of their trust in their brain, not their heart. They worked hard to remain in control. One frequent wisher told her much less absorbed husband, "You'd better learn to lighten up and live before you tighten up so much I'll leave."

Beyond Descartes' Error

Most of us have been raised in a world that emphasizes being right over being vulnerable and being in control of life rather than absorbed in it. Even though the most common sense may be our sixth one, we have been told to trust in reason more than enchantment. Coming "to our senses" means using our five physical senses and not relying on a sixth-sense process such as wishing. We "believe our eyes," have confidence in the visible, and think that seeing is believing. We are still suffering the cultural fallout of what author Antonio R. Damasio called "Descartes' Error."[20] When Descartes asserted that rational thinking and awareness of thinking are the substrates of the essence of our being, the value of a sixth sense—imagination, fantasy, and our cultural and mythological legacy of trusting what we sensed in our heart—fell into disrepute.

Wishing is a cultural leftover of the sixth-sense kind of logic the ancients employed. It's how we flex our imagination and get right in to the flow of subtle energy. It's what we do when reason seems to be failing us or when we seek to supplement it with our innate sense that a little more imagination is what is called for. It's how we stop thinking about how to make the world right and try to resonate more with it. To learn to wish well, you have to avoid Descartes' mistake that our rational view of the world is that world. You have to be willing to question the premise that we "think therefore we are" in favor of "we are therefore we wish." Wishing well requires that we learn to think and feel with our heart and trust in our imagination as another way of being.

Lessons from a Four-Leaf Clover

To be a good wisher fully immersed in life, you have to learn to trust in what author William Faulkner called the "old verities and truths of the heart, the old universal truths lacking which any story is ephemeral and doomed."[21] The old universal truths are contained in much of the strange logic of wishful thinking, superstition, and the wishes we make that are based on these processes. They are encoded in our centuries-old ways of wishing because our ancestors had little choice but to feel absorbed in their life. Their five-sense tool world had not evolved to the level that allowed the arrogance of certainty we suffer from today. They were forever on the prowl for ways to connect even more with the subtle cues and signs of nature's energy.

As an example of a wishfully absorbed life, consider an ancestral wish favorite, the four-leaf clover. A misfit, freakish plant derived on rare occasion from the three-leaf clover herb, its legendary role as a wish object extends back hundreds of years. Something in our heart seems to tell us that it's a perfect wish object. Although we don't usually remember where and how, most of us seem to sense that finding a four-leaf clover offers an opportunity to end up "in the clover." While the less absorbed would step on one, anyone totally absorbed in life would never miss the chance to pick it up and wish upon it.

A surgeon in Detroit attended one of my lectures. She approached me after my talk and said she was a "hopeful doubter" about the process of wishing. I noticed a green four-leaf clover pin on her lapel. She said, "I'm Jewish, not Irish. I wear this four-leaf clover just for luck. I just wanted to give you this note. I thought you'd get a kick out of it." She handed me a small piece of paper containing the following words:

One leaf for fame,
One leaf for wealth,
And one leaf for a faithful lover,

And one leaf to bring glorious health,
Are all in a four-leaf clover.

I showed the note to a medical student standing next to me. "Oh, I know that one. That's what you're supposed to say when you find a four-leaf clover."

"Where did you learn that?" I asked.

"Oh, I don't remember." She blushed as she placed her hands to her chest. "I've just always known it."

No one knows for sure where such mystical incantations as the wishful clover chant actually came from, but theories abound. One is that Eve took a four-leaf clover with her when she was cast out of the Garden of Eden. The Druids of England believed the four-leaf clover to have magical powers. Chances are that if you scored relatively high on the PAT, you may have picked up a four-leaf clover yourself. Even if you didn't know the clover chant, you may have made a private wish in one of the four areas referred to in the clover chant.

Do You Believe in Luck?

Do you consider yourself lucky? Do you talk about "lucky streaks" and try to avoid symbols of bad luck? Perhaps, like Right Men, you believe that "people make their own luck," but highly absorbed people are ever alert for signs of good or bad luck. They watch for four-leaf clovers and any other of nature's energetic invitations. If you talk about luck and feel that it is not just a result of hard work, you're probably very absorbed in the L energy of life. You probably believe in forces like L or subtle love energy that you can't explain rationally but can sense affecting your life. In other words, you're a natural born wisher.

Luck is invisible. It has no real scientific explanation beyond statistical estimates of chance. Unless you've fallen completely for the brain's propaganda that you and you alone are in sole charge of making all of your own luck and determining your fortunes and misfortunes, you probably make wishes. Because wishing is a conative process, meaning that it deals with such things as luck, jinxes, and other processes, it goes well beyond our physical, cognitive, and affective ways of dealing with life.

There is something within those of us who feel totally immersed in life that causes us to be instinctively driven to make wishes in order to stay afloat. It's a process that persists no matter what our level of intelligence, economic status, or religion. None of these factors differentiated our regular wishers from the nonwishers in our survey. Wishing is ingrained in some form in every culture and is at the core of some of our most instructive fairy tales. It plays a major role in the mythology of every society and is an essential part of many of our oldest family rituals such as birthday parties and Thanksgiving dinner. It causes us to wish complete strangers gesundheit and results in the clogging of many fountains with wishfully tossed coins. Despite our brain's best efforts to create a reasoned world, there's something about wishing that still seems to fall within our personal realm of reasonable doubt.

The Spoiled Brain

Since Descartes, we have assumed that the ultimate state of evolution is a purely reasoned state. As a result, processes such as wishing have been largely ignored or have remained in the pages of children's books. My recent search of the literature about wishing revealed a brief developmental history of the wish. Of the 997 books published in the past ten years with the word "wishing" or "wish" in the title, 573 were children's books, 111 were adolescent or young adult books, and the rest were romantic novels. The major encyclopedias do not reference wishing. Unless under the category of "conscious intent," or "healing at a distance," when it is occasionally written about in professional journals, it is usually in the context of dreams as wishes or depicted as pathological or delusional. Literature shows that wishing is safe in childhood literature, weakens with age, and disappears in the glare of adult reason. We might remember, however, that it is the brain itself that does much of the writing and publishing. It is the brain that has edited out wishing.

We've overindulged our brain, and as a result, it can spoil our life. Like an undisciplined child, we have allowed our brain to think it has lordship over everything and is deserving of our unbridled deference. It mocks processes like wishing for which it is poorly equipped to deal. The brain has taken center stage because we humans have spoiled it. We have capitulated to its selfish demands for attention at the expense of our much shier heart. Scientists and the society that so idolizes the brain cling to a cerebral-centrism that Descartes would adore. But has the brain created a world we can really put our heart into, that we really wish for, and with which we feel a compatible, peaceful component?

Myth Power

Late-nineteenth-century English anthropologist James Frazer's book *The Golden Bough* chronicled archaic mythology.[22] He writes that our cultural history is divided into three developmental phases: mythological ignorance, religious faith, and a utopian third stage of "pure reason." He wrote, "The human race is slowly crawling out of the magic mode up to and through the religious, and will finally emerge in the sunlight of science and rationality."[23] Our society has bought into this cerebral agenda, embracing this head hierarchy and valuing above all our rational sense. Behind closed doors, however, there is revolution going on. Even the brightest and most scientifically skeptical are beginning to say things like, "There must be more than this," and "If we're so smart, why aren't we happier?" and "Isn't there some safe spiritual middle ground in the squabble between the secular and the sacred?" There are dozens of professional conferences a year meeting all over the world that deal with the supernatural, paranormal, subtle energy, and our potential to know life beyond our five senses. Many are beginning to ask, "The brain's way is a great way, but is it the only way?"

Publicly, we often frown on those who speak too freely about such things as myth, prayer, or their deepest religious convictions. Talking seriously about wishing leads to the same misgivings. We reward the hard-nosed more than the soft-hearted and commend those who are brilliantly manipulative and able to outsmart others. We glorify the accomplishments of the brain's tool world. Nonetheless, the data you will read about in this book indicates that there are millions of closet wishers out there who, while trusting in the head, are still bonded to their spirit and the processes such as wishing that are related to it.

Degrees of Implausibility

The protests of some of my scientific colleagues that wishing is the stuff of magic, voodoo, or misguided New Age mysticism are similar to those I often heard when I first lectured about how the immune system actually responds to our emotional states,[24] how many studies of prayer show clearly that it works,[25] and how the heart is more than just a pump.[26] "Believing that wishing works is scientifically implausible," say the skeptics. I respond by pointing out that nothing would seem to be as extravagantly implausible as what science says about a process that sounds every bit as strange and purely metaphorical as making wishes, the Big Bang.

When I attend scientific meetings to discuss the process of wishing, I'm told that I should be more careful to distinguish between faith and reason. "Wishing is pure faith," I'm told. "Science is pure reason." Things spiritual, such as wishing, are seen as dreamlike, implausible ideation, whereas "sound reasoning" and emotional distance rather than personal immersion is viewed as dealing only with "hard objective data."

A close look at the language and concepts of science itself calls this assumption of objective distance into question.

Author Gregg Easterbrook points out that the distinction between reason and belief drawn by science may be artificial. He writes, "Today's rational, skeptical scientists believe a range of things that can sound notably less plausible than a sacred tree in a perfect Garden."[27] Scientists have no trouble speaking freely about "black holes" that swallow everything and turn it into nothing. They tell of superstrings of energy "folded" into "probability structures" millions of times smaller than a single atom. They teach their students that our bodies are made from elements of stars that exploded eons ago and that we will be able to clone ourselves into identical matched images. They lecture about such "facts" as strong and weak nuclear energy, invisible subatomic particles, quantum foam, and a range of "forces" and "invisible fields" that seem to emerge out of nothing. They tell us that energy and matter are the same thing and that light is either particle or wave depending on what we decide to look for. They even say that time is relative and astronauts age more slowly than us terrestrialites. Despite this arcane array of scientific "fact," many scientists still balk at the idea that wishing might be a plausible way to make a sixth-sense suggestion.

A Cosmic Fairy Tale

Commenting on the selective mysticism of science, Easterbrook writes, "Modern thought finds supernatural circumstances [such as wishing] acceptable when claimed in the name of science but unacceptable when claimed in the name of the spirit." Consider, for example, the following scientifically accepted yet still speculative tall tale, the cosmic fairy tale of the Big Bang.

Once upon a time when there was no time, there was a very Big Bang. From a tiny point much smaller than the period at the end of this sentence, there was a stupendous explosion of light and energy that became everything. We called this everything "the universe." Suddenly, for no reason, and spontaneously out of nothing, came everything. From this everything came billions of galaxies including our own. We can see stars from these galaxies now, but they really aren't there anymore. They were born and died billions of years ago. The galaxies were sent spinning out by some force we cannot see or measure. They are still propelling away from each other at millions of miles per hour. We ourselves are moving that fast right now. Although no one knows how, why, or perhaps by Whom, motion, matter, and eventually plants, animals, and we ourselves seem to have been "wished" into creation by something or some One.

What a story! Most scientists believe it and pass it on much as a mother tells her child to be careful what he wishes, to wish on a four-leaf clover, not to tell anyone what he wished, and how to wish on a star. As theoretical astrophysicist Abraham Loef says, "Suddenly, the universe lit up like a Christmas tree."[28] As Genesis suggested and science agrees, everything everywhere originated "ex nihilo," meaning that it somehow became everywhere starting from nothing nowhere. Talking about making a simple wish and believing it actually might come true sounds like mild stuff compared to the astronomical wizardry offered by "hard" science's own factual fables. It often appears that the only thing "hard" about modern science is its heart.

More Evidence of the Power of a Little Boom

Wishing causes the "little boom" or spurt of energy that can result in significant energy changes. It sends ripples of "sympathetic resonation" or slight vibrations remembered and combined within the system or "wish target." The significance of the most minute change in any system is revealed in science's own Big Bang fairy tale. It's a scientifically documented fact that even the most minor tinkering with the way things were originally set in motion would mess up everything. It would have even made everything that exploded in the first bang explode back upon itself and disappear. For example, the tiniest change in the value of the fundamental forces initiated at the exact time of the Big Bang would have resulted in a universe made exclusively of helium. There could then have been no protons or atoms. That would mean there would have been no stars and, ultimately, no us. Any single slight change in the beginning would have resulted in the First Wish not coming true. We would have ended up with a brief shooting star universe that exploded back upon itself in a kind of cosmic backfire.[29]

If you're completely absorbed in life and not bossed around by your brain, you are free to concoct your own blend of mythologies. Science offers a magnificently beautiful world view, religion offers a grand sacred model of the soul, and wishing offers a cultural/mythological view that crosses over into both realms. The challenge for each of us in this life is not to decide which system is right but what combination of mythologies ultimately brings us and the world the most peace, joy, and love.

Science's Best Guesses

The randomness that science prefers to use to explain its Big Bang is only one possible explanation—a hypothesis. Like the hypothesis that wishing works, the Big Bang theory is based on an assumption no more valid than supposing that "supernatural forces" are at work in the universe and that wishing can help us connect with them. When we do things like wishing, we are not choosing to reject randomness but to add to its explanatory power. Wishing is based on the hypothesis that there is something more and beyond what numbers can measure.

When we make a wish, we contribute our own little boom to the universal energy pool. We don't deny the plausibility of a Big Bang or the creation of everything by a supreme being. We try our luck at doing what our ancestors did to play a part in the drama of the evolving cosmos. Wishing is a way our ancestors taught us we can try to connect with the subtle energy that exploded us into existence or saved us from our impulsive, wicked five-sense wishing in the Garden. It is one way we the created can become more fully absorbed with the energy of the Creator.

Wishing provides a culturally established way to create a postsecular synthesis that does not deny what science thinks it knows while still believing and trying to connect with what it may never know. Its innocent, joyful, but powerful way allows us to blend modern scientific findings about the mystical forces of the Big Bang and other astrophysical "realities" with the insights and teachings of the wisdom of those who experimented with wishing. It's one means of living more safely and happily on one tiny piece of shrapnel left over from the Big Bang, a way to remain absorbed in life without becoming drowned by it.

Necessary Illusions

Another of the Right Men's criticisms of wishful thinking is that a wish's effects are only illusions. Even if that were true, however, psychologists now know that certain kinds of illusions are very healthy and even essential to our survival. Even if the process of wishing is merely a fantasy and illusion of some control of and connection with the subtle forces of the universe (and you will read that it probably is not), it's a grand illusion. At a time of spiritual searching and confusion, wishing can serve us very well. All optimism requires some silly (but not stupid) fooling of ourselves, and wishing is the ultimate act of optimism. It is a way of saying that we can enter into at least some level and kind of personal relationship with "the forces that be" and ask for their blessing.

Psychologist Martin Seligman's research shows that the illusion of having some sense of control of one's destiny is as, if not more, important than actually having that control. If the absorbed person's illusion is his doubt of one reality, the Right Man's illusion is that he has found that reality. Wishing is good for you whether it really works or not. If we are going to allow ourselves to become totally absorbed in life, we need some sense of control to prevent feeling consumed by it.[30]

There are five primary ways in addition to wishing through which we try to connect with the invisible life energy of the universe. Needing, wanting, hoping, willing, and praying all work to varying degrees and in their own way. Right Men remain essentially in the domains of needing, wanting, and willing. Wishers work from the same perspectives from which hoping and praying emerged. We tend to become most aware of which of these processes we trust when things aren't going too well, but they are important ways in which we lead our everyday life. Each of them constitutes a method through which we try to influence our own destiny. Until I was confronted with my own death and felt the burning pain of cancer cells squeezing the life from my body, I never thought much about wishing. When I did, it was as an auxiliary backup process that I didn't take too seriously. The information you will read about in this book taught me to never make that mistake again. I never felt more absorbed in life than when I was dying. Perhaps that's what brought my wishing to my heart.

A Wish Wave

Recuperating from huge doses of poisonous chemotherapy and whole body radiation, I found my lungs were failing. As I gasped desperately for air and looked at my family crying around me, it seemed as if a thin black shroud were being draped over the entire room. The sad family voices that were my lifeline began to sound like vague echoes and I began to sob in the unique dread of the dying that even though everyone was losing me, I was losing all of them. I was in the process of losing all of them. I was rushed by a "crash team" for emergency lung surgery, and as my stretcher was slammed hurriedly into the elevator, I could barely see the shadows of my wife and sons. I could, however, intensely feel my family's presence and could see that they were holding up their hands in our secret "wish wave."

All cultures have their own unique wish signs. High absorbers use them all the time. From crossed or snapping fingers, shaking a rattle, joining little fingers, or making the sign of the cross, there have always been physical manifestations and signs that go along with wishing. New research reveals that when we gesture, we are often struggling to express abstract and very personal thoughts in a concrete way. When we feel very absorbed in life, we start flailing away to express feelings for which our five senses have no language. Experiments show that we gesture more when we are trying to speak of such concepts as "love" or "evil" and about such ultimately complex physics concepts such as "near or far" and "past and present." It also appears that gesturing is something that helps us retrieve ancient ideas, concepts, and behaviors from our paleomammalian memory bank.[31]

Children blind from birth gesture just as much as sighted children and use gestures when communicating together. There's something in our genes that causes our body to try to say what our brain cannot express. Various movements and signs have long been associated with making wishes. My family's wish gesture is a modified thumbs-up sign with the thumb pointing up, little finger pointing down, and the remaining three fingers curled inward to point to our heart. It's our modification of the "shaka" or "hang loose" gesture often used in our Hawaiian home. It's also similar to the sign deaf persons use for love and is the same wish wave we had used through many prior crises whenever one of us seemed too immersed in life to verbally express our state of heart. As the elevator doors slowly closed, I somehow managed to lift my hand and send the wish wave back.

May the Best Wish Win

As my body shook with the rattling of the cart, I could feel the power of that special wish I had just received and I felt strengthened and comforted by it. But then, something went even more terribly wrong. As the nurse changed the oxygen mask from the small clear-plastic version dangling from the tank on the cart to the large, black one used in the operating room, I felt myself being absorbed by another manifestation of L energy. I was dying, but I could hear a young resident I had trained whisper, "After all this poor man and his family have been through with the cancer and transplant, I sort of wish he'd die while he's under and end all of this for them."

Two days later and squinting against the bright lights in intensive care, I could make out the shadow of my wife's face. I knew then that our well wish had won out over the doctor's unintentionally wicked wish. Our well wishing had kept me absorbed in physical life and managed to work a countermagic against the unintentionally wicked or at least untimely wish made by my resident. Our collective power wishing had overwhelmed his solitary wish and made the subtle energy of our wish for my survival into a miracle. I had "died" three times in the last several hours, but somehow I felt more absorbed in living than I had ever felt in my life. I know that loving support, prayer, modern medicine, and a vast array of unknowns helped save me, but I also know that wishing played a role in the making of our miracle.

As we celebrated our wish come true, we were all crying. Chemotherapy had long ago damaged my tear ducts and no tears would flow. My wife's warm tears fell into my eyes as she looked down at me, and she gave our wish wave again. My hands were tied down to prevent me from pulling the respirator tube from my throat and speaking was impossible. Morphine was causing me to drift in and out of awareness, but my wife says she saw my hand return a weak but clear wish wave.

An Invitation from the Queen and King

If you have trouble believing what you have read so far, or think that wishing and its subtle L energy is immeasurable and therefore must be nonexistent, I ask you to consider the advice from the Queen of Wonderland and the king of physics. First, the Queen said to the incredulous Alice, "Why, my dear, I've already believed in ten impossible things before breakfast." Albert Einstein said to his critics who doubted the invisible, relative, timeless, totally connected and boundary-free world of the wish he had discovered, "Not everything that counts can be counted and not everything that can be counted, counts. Imagination is more important than knowledge."

Five

Learning a Sixth Way
to Get Your Way

In order to be a realist you must believe in miracles.
—DAVID BEN-GURION

A Spontaneous Star-Wishing Seminar

All around the world, the wishers came out in droves. My family and I were among them as we sat with dozens of our friends on the beach behind our home in Hawai'i. Just like our prehistoric ancestors, ancient navigators, Chinese emperors, and astrophysicists, we had come to wish upon a star. One of my colleagues, an oncologist, was holding her daughter on her lap. She was the first to notice dozens of the brightest shooting stars I had ever seen. They darted all over the sky and were sometimes so bright they reflected in the ocean.

"Look, sweetie," said the doctor excitedly to her child. "Quick, make a wish!"

"Mommy," answered her daughter. "The stars are playing hide and seek with us. They go behind the clouds and come out when you're not looking." The Hawaiian evening sky is usually blotted with dull white clouds with seas of star-speckled black between them. As soon as a star appeared, it seemed to hide behind a cloud.

"Make a wish when you see one come out," said her mother. Without taking his eyes from the sky, a local grocery store owner sitting nearby said, "That's right, young lady. You say, 'Star light, star bright, first star I've seen tonight. I wish I may, I wish I might, have the wish I wish tonight.' " His words came in the form of a rhythmic chant and everyone around him joined in for the final few words.

A teacher contributed her wishing wisdom. She added, "But you have to look at the star when you say it. Don't say anything more until you see another star and your wish is more likely to come true."

"You've got to say it quick, too," added a young Hawaiian who operated a charter boat service. "If you can make the wish before the star disappears, your wish will probably come true."

"And if you can count seven shooting stars tonight, you can be double sure you'll get your wish," added a police officer standing near his car.

With these contributions of wishing philosophies, the spontaneous star seminar fell silent, waited, and watched. Every time a star flashed across the sky, one of the stargazers would shout, "Look, over there, make a wish!"

The Temptation of Temple-Tuttle

More than 10,000 "shooting stars" were appearing per hour, so this evening was a wisher's delight. We had hundreds of wish targets to choose from. It was one of the largest astronomical displays in decades and millions of tiny dust particles burned into the earth's atmosphere. The result was a fabulous display of sparkling white trails of light crisscrossing the night sky. The shooting stars were, of course, not stars at all. They were actually tiny bits of cosmic clutter shed from the long tail of Comet Temple-Tuttle. At our wish jubilee, however, no one was quibbling about the scientific details that might spoil our wishing fun.[1]

Named the Leonid meteor storm because ancient observers thought the meteors came from the constellation Leo, this fiery litter occurs every November with little fanfare. These same astronomical tidbits probably served as wish targets for our ancestors. Every thirty-three years, however, the comet speeds through the inner solar system and sheds particularly large swarms of particles as it nears the Sun. The fragments are snatched from space by the invisible force of Earth's gravity, and like almost all natural phenomena, the display was a catalyst for our cosmic ceremony. It gave proof that wishful thinking is still going strong.

Six Ways We Try to Get Our Way

Most open-minded scientists acknowledge the validity of the research that illustrates the way in which wishing works. The data usually convince them that we are all connected beyond the here and now, that there is a fifth force or subtle L or love energy that connects all of us, and that our individual intentions can create mini-shock waves through the entire system of which we are an inseparable part. The next question they ask is how wishing is different from the five other ways humans try to cope with this characteristic of our existence. To understand the nature of a wish and distinguish it from our other psychospiritual resources, I've included a chart comparing and contrasting the processes of needing, wanting, willing, hoping, wishing, and praying (see the chart on page 86). It shows how needing, wanting, willing, hoping, wishing, and praying compare in terms of how they are experienced, where they come from, and how they seem to work.

The simplest way to distinguish a wish from the other five ways we try to influence our destiny is to ask yourself how you feel when you make a wish. Our research subjects typically answered that they felt as if they were softly and ritualistically expressing a small request of some vague power to alter things in their favor. They distinguished that feeling from a need, which they felt as a more basic and physical impulse; a want, which they experienced as more of a drive or motivation; willing, which they experienced as concentration or being mentally focused; hoping, which they experienced as a more passive emotional state; and a prayer, which they experienced as a sacred and reverent act. Wishing, they said, was a simple personal ceremony to try to get things to go better for them or to avoid things going the wrong way.

A Wish Come True

I asked one of our wish research subjects to help clarify "the sixth way" as opposed to the other five ways we deal with life. She is a dancer on a major show now appearing on Broadway and struggles as a single mother to balance an extremely demanding career with raising an eight-year-old daughter. She said, "I felt a need to have children. Saying I had the need didn't do anything to meet it, but I really felt the need within me. Then I became motivated to have a child. I thought about it almost every moment and I set out to find someone to have children with. I just couldn't find someone. Then I tried artificial insemination. It failed for months and

The Six Ways

Secular ——————————— Social ——————————— Sacred

Personal ——————————— Metaphysical

Physical	Emotional	Mental	Cultural	Ancestral	Spiritual
NEED	WANT	WILL	HOPE	WISH	PRAYER
Sensation	Motivation	Concentration	Visualization	Intuition	Devotion
Body	Lower Brain	Cerebral	Mind-Set	Heartfelt	Soul Directed
Reptilian Brain	Paleomammalian Brain	Neomammalian Left Brain	Neomammalian Right Brain	Brain/Body/Heart Triune Mind	From the Soul
Biophysical Signal	Goal Directed	Neurochemical Signals	Unconscious Signals	Heart Signals	Holy Spirit
Cellular Energy	Systemic Energy	Mental Effort	Consciousness Energy	Cellular Memories	Spiritual Imprints
Genetic	Emotional	Cognitive	Belief	Subtle "L" Energy	Spiritual Energy
Physical Impulse	Interpreted Impulses	Mental Intent	Conviction	Ancestral Imprint	To Higher Power
Reflex	Directed Response	Imagery	Fantasy	Habit	Worship
Narcissism	Rationalization	Intellectualization	Denial	Regression	Sacralization
Agitation	Attention	Focus	Distraction	Imagination	Petition to the Divine
Feel a Need	Experience a Want	Impose Will	Have Hope	Make a Wish	"Say" a Prayer
Darwin, Wilson	Maslow, Murray	Peel, Robins	Cousins, Siegel	Cultural and Mythological	Scripture, Religious

months, but then I willed it to work. The need was something physical. The want was something moving me to action. My will was my total mental focus to make it happen. To me, hope was just a bonus. It was like a general feeling state I had and worked to maintain. Of course, I prayed and prayed, and that was a very religious and spiritual thing that I know really worked. Now, when it comes to a wish, I did that all the time while I was doing all the other five things. It was my "sixth way" as you call it. I would say my wish for a child under my breath like a ritual. I made wishes even when I put on my costumes for my performances. I sort of kept my wishing to myself, but I told people what I needed, wanted, hoped for, prayed for, and was trying to will to happen. Wishing felt the most childish of all the six ways, but I wouldn't have gone without doing it. My daughter fulfills my needs to mother and she is all I could ever want. She represents what my willing and hoping could do and surely she is the answer to my prayers. But I am convinced that those hundreds of repeated little wishes moved things my way. My daughter is my wish come true."

Wishing as the "sixth way" seems to overlap all of the other five ways of trying to influence our destiny. Based on our interviews, it seems to be the most ritualistic, secretive, mythological, personal, and common of the six ways. It seems to be more habitual and automatic than the other five ways and a way of intentionally regressing to an earlier magical state in our life for a source of comfort and control.

The basic six ways we try to cope with the subtle and enigmatic energy of life can be seen as varying along a continuum from the purely secular to the profoundly sacred, from the personal through the sociocultural to the metaphysical, and from what we experience as "here" and sense as "heaven." Listed next are descriptions of each of the five basic life-coping ways as they contrast to wishing. All of these processes come to the surface in various ways and at various times when our life's circumstances seem to require a change in consciousness.

Needy People

Do you think others would describe you as a "needy person"? If so, they probably are referring to the fact that you tend toward immaturity, selfishness, and impulsive responsiveness to your most basic physical needs. You are often seeking relief rather than joy and may spend a lot of time feeling incomplete or out of balance. Your body may reflect your state of agitation as it tries to express its need for better physiological balance. The husband of one of our wish-survey members described his wife's neediness this way. "When she is needing, she shows it all over her body. She has a way of tilting her head, looking down to the left, and slouching her shoulders. If I ask her if she needs anything, she may say no. But I can see it. It drives me nuts. I call it her needy look."

Needy people can drive others away. Since needing is such a personal state and because we all have the same innate irritability that drives us in search of our needs, others' neediness can distract us and make us impatient. Very few persons are looking for a love partner they describe as needy. Needs exist as the most fundamental guidelines for our physical survival, not as ways to establish deeper connection with the world. When we say, "I feel the need," we mean we are trying to alleviate some physiological aggravation. Even if we say, "I feel the need to tell you" or "I need you to," these needs originally derived from some basic physical imbalance. When we say "I need you" to our lover, we are expressing our sense of incompleteness and that we "need" that person to gratify some physiologically based drive.

We are becoming an increasingly needy society. If we don't have enough needs, advertisers will teach us new ones. Therapists encourage us to make our needs known immediately and directly. Such advice seldom works, however, because although we may have wants and hopes, few of us have many real needs left to meet. What we say we need is often only epiphenomena, mere reflections or approximate images rather than real needs. We say we are hungry and need to eat, but we probably have never felt the real hunger and need for food of those who are starving. We say we are cold and need warmth, but few of us who say so have ever really experienced the bone-chilling cold of the homeless.

Another problem with the modern manifestation of neediness is that it is the nature of our needfulness that a met need is always immediately replaced by another need. Our brain is never satisfied. Its role is to be our "need monitor," but it is very literal in its interpretation of what constitutes a need. It is constantly scanning our system for imbalance that it expresses as a need. If it can't find a need, it draws on the body's and its own cellular memories of prior needs, ups the need ante, and bothers and disturbs us until we do something. If the body is not really hungry, the brain will express a need for food anyway. A bored brain often seeks to amuse itself by causing perturbations in its own body.[2]

Being in need signifies that we are out of balance and require something physical or at least a cultural representation of that physical need to reestablish our emotional or physical homeostasis. Because of the increasing distance between real needs and the cultural and societal symbols that represent them, it becomes difficult to feel that a need is truly satisfied. We don't really need a lot of money, but we may need what it can buy. When we get a lot of money, we seem to want more. Money is more a want than a need because its meaning comes from higher up in the brain's hierarchical structure. Signals of a need come like an alarm from the lowest and most primitive levels of our brain, known as the reptilian brain.[3] We feel them in our body as various levels of biophysical deficiency, and it's our brain's job to express them for us.

We can become quite emotional when our brain thinks one of our needs is not met. Author Daniel Goleman uses the term "emotional hijacking" to describe what happens when our needs are not immediately met in our way and by our own time standards.[4] When our needs aren't met to our brain's satisfaction, it feels threatened. It agitates our body by stirring up the psychochemicals that cause a "rage rush." We become so upset that we may be angry that our need is not being met but not even know exactly what the need was in the first place. The stress hormones called catacholomines are released and our fight-or-flight response kicks in.[5] Unless our perceived need is met, we become more and more frustrated. Frustration quickly turns to anger for the impatient brain. Feeling angry can turn to aggression, and since aggression is seldom an efficient way to meet a need, we often regress to tantrums, sulking, and self-pity. The frustration-aggression-regression cycle is not good for our own health or the well-being of those around us.

When we are needy, we are yielding to our brain's evolutionary preprogrammed egocentrism. Our brain and body are wired with an innate sense of what it takes to remain in sufficient balance to stay alive. Unfortunately, being needy can be experienced as a very vague and confusing state. Because needing is a fundamentally narcissistic and self-serving state of being, met needs seldom result in complete satisfaction. Even when we end up physically content, our heart can still feel unfilled. We may feel a post-need-fulfillment crash, especially if a rage rush accompanied our needfulness. As you will see, one benefit of well wishing is that it is usually free of the brain's selfish demands, the related anger, and the postneed downer.

Just "feeling or being needy" is, of course, never enough to meet a need. There's yet another need cycle involved. We respond with the "drive, cue, response, reward" sequence. First we feel a need. Then we look for something that might fulfill that need. Next, we do something to quickly quiet our need by getting it. Like the lizards whose archetypal brain is directing our neediness, we can become irritable "busy bodies" always alert to our cravings and scanning for the most immediate thing that our brain thinks will meet them.

"Needing" is on the far left of the secular–sacred axis because it is a state designed to start and motivate the process of getting us to do something that keeps us alive long enough to pass on our DNA. Zoologist Richard Dawkins of Oxford University theorizes that we ourselves are vehicles of our genes' needs and that we exist primarily as an expression of our genes' craving to make more of themselves. He writes, ". . . in a universe of selfish genes, blind physical forces and genetic replication, some people are going to get hurt, others are going to get lucky, and you won't find any rhythm or reason for it."[6] Of course, wishers would strongly disagree with Dawkins's genetic neediness theory. Where he finds no design, they see patterns in the sky that suggest otherwise. Where he sees indifference, they see paths to joining as an active participant in the L energy of the universe.

Biologist E. O. Wilson also emphasizes our sociobiological neediness as central to the human condition.[7] He suggests that even if we do experience an "emotional need," it still stems from our basic biophysiology. I'm often asked if wishing isn't really just "needing." I answer that wishing is a much more civilized, calm, connective sixth-sense process than just being needy and serving as a gene passer. Although there are wicked wishes based solely on physical needs and our interpretations of them, these needs are experienced on a five-sense level. Wishing is concerned less with trying to pass on who we are than trying to enhance how we're being in the world. Needing is a way our brain helps us stay alive, but wishing is one way our heart tries to bring a sense of meaning and connection to our life.

Sigmund Freud, Abraham Maslow, and many other psychologists have based their entire theories on the premise called "needs hierarchy."[8] Going from physiological to sexual to social and then to higher-level love and self-actualization needs is the premise of these approaches. Well wishing in the five realms of wishing we identified in our wish research (serenity, delight, purpose, meaning, and compassion) is more a matter of circularity than hierarchy. No wish is "lower" or "more advanced" than another wish. For example, a wish for serenity is not less important or more basic than a wish for meaning or compassion in one's life. What seems to be important in learning to wish well is to keep moving rather than focus on moving up.

You will be reading in the next chapter about what our research subjects called "the wish star." It represents the five realms of wishing. Continued progress around the star is necessary for wishing well. One does not "achieve" a state and then stay at that level. If we wish for serenity, we must wish in the future to find delight in our granted wish. If not, we may regress to wishing for compassion and understanding for the disappointment and turmoil we begin to experience when we fail to appreciate what we have. To wish well, we have to be aware of the nature of the wishing domain that lies behind and in front of our present wishing state. Wishing well is wishing proactively by moving from our concern for delight to a sense of purpose, and so on.

So long as we keep our wishing going in a clockwise or in the "right" direction through the five wishing domains of serenity, delight, purpose, meaning, and love, we are wishing well and our needs are more likely to be met (see the figure on page 103). If we wish regressively by going back to making wishes for love when we can't seem to find the serenity we wish for and wish for someone to bring us the peace we cannot find within ourselves, we become a wicked or five-sense-oriented wisher.

As you can see from the comparisons in the chart on page 86, needing and wishing are quite different processes on all counts. While we make, construct, and express a wish proactively as a sixth-sense suggestion, being needy is a more reactive personal state that is usually accompanied by urgent self-expression. When we say "I need," our brain is expressing a demand and trying to convince someone to meet our basically secular need. When we say "I wish," our heart is making a request and trying to move the L energy in the direction of its more spiritual aspirations.

Motivated People

Would people describe you as highly motivated? Motivation is related more to "wanting" than "needing." It's one step up the human coping ladder. When what we want matches what we need, and when we are clear and specific about the nature and degree of our need, we are more likely to make progress toward a sense of contented balance in our life. When there is a conflict between our needs and wants or when our brain has nothing better to do than bother us about escalating our needs, we tend to feel unfulfilled no matter how motivated we behave.

Motivation originates from a little higher up in the evolutionary archaeology of our brain in a part called the paleomammalian brain. It's more emotional than physical and involves interpreting needs and not just experiencing them. It is within our paleomammalian brain that our sense of direction for meeting our basic needs is processed. When we feel the thirst need, it is our want center that causes us to begin to look for something to drink. When a baby is needy, he may have no idea of what will meet that need. Maturity requires matching the right want with the right need in the right way at the right time. There is nothing more frustrating than living and loving with people who seem very needy yet are not clear about what they want.

When our lower brain tells us we're thirsty, its "want" center directs us to a water fountain and we take a refreshing drink. If our brain's want center mislearned how to appropriately and nondestructively meet our thirst or other agitated state by taking us to a bar for a drink of alcohol, we may become less thirsty but also increasingly less clear about the crucial need–want relationship. In the most drastic case, we can eventually become drunk or addicted if we try to quench our thirst need by wanting "just one more cocktail" or by mistaking a need for emotional sedation for "just one more drink." What we want isn't always what we need.

Needing alerts us, but motivation directs us. Motivation is the process of putting a label on a need. It's goal-directed behavior experienced as a gravity coming from a goal object. We are energized to "motor" (a root word of mot-ivated) to a need-fulfilling goal. A person in a coma needs food but doesn't "want" it. A conscious person may want a hamburger but not need one. One of the healthiest states is to want what we really need.

Needing is primarily a brain-expressed physical reflex. Wanting is an emotionally experienced drive. Our needs are only human, but our wants are primarily our own. They're our personalized experience of the same bodily needs everyone has. Essentially, we all need the same things, but we want a variety of different things. Because needs constantly regenerate within us, they will never be completely met. Wants are our brain's best current estimate of how we can engage in a commerce with the world to negotiate for the meeting of our perceived needs. Because the currency differs from society to society and from time to time, our wants also constantly change. One man's caviar is another man's pizza. One man's candlelight dinner is another man's small bowl of rice.

In my interviews about wishing conducted around the world, it seemed clear that needs were almost the same everywhere. It was wants that varied greatly and often seemed to result in competition and conflict. I also noticed that wishes were similar in every culture I visited. Perhaps because wishes tend to come from the heart, they are more closely associated with what we really need. From Aborigines to Laplanders, wishes were always for serenity, delight, purpose, meaning, and compassion.

Needing is impulsive. Wanting is more, but certainly not always entirely, rational. Needs aren't learned, but wants are. Psychologist Henry Murray described two basic wants of most persons. He suggested that in our need for personal security, we can want to achieve (nAch) or to affiliate (nAff) to meet that need. Psychologists now know that how we translate our basic needs to our wants drastically influences our emotional and physical well-being. Those who tend to translate their need for a sense of safety and security to a want for power, prestige, and success (nAch) more than to mutually caring social interactions and love (nAff) are also those who are more likely to become sick and die early.[9]

When we say we are "e-motion-al," we are usually describing the fact that we feel "set in motion" by our needs. We feel motivated to go in the direction of what our brain has been taught to think we want so that once it is obtained, we can get rid of our need. As pointed out by psychologist John Mayer, self-awareness is being aware of both our mood (need) and our thoughts about that mood (want).[10]

Wanting is different from wishing. It's a much more realistically and secularly based process. It tends to be a concrete lower-brain-driven state. As author Daniel Goleman points out, being emotionally intelligent is being sensitive to our needs while remaining smart enough to know what is motivating us and how our motives are affecting us and everyone else around us.[11] Wanting is moving farther along the scale from the purely physical to a more cerebral approach to life, but it is still far from the metaphysical or sacred.

Strong-Willed People

Would those who know you best say you are "strong-willed"? If so, they probably see you as very focused mentally. People often speak of being willing to make something happen. They believe in "mind over matter" and that thinking hard and long enough about something can make it happen. Needing is biophysical, wanting is emotional, and willing is a higher-level mental process of "positive thinking."

Willing is mediated by the most evolved part of our brain, which is called the neocortex. Beyond the primal sensations of our needs and the emotionality of our motivation, willing is a matter of intentionally mobilizing and trying to direct our mental energy. We tend to "feel" our needs and "express" our wants. Willing is a matter of focused thought. When things aren't working out in our commerce with our world, we may be told to "just concentrate," put our mind to it, and have more willpower.

Needs are our shared biophysical characteristics. Wants are our own unique translation and experience of these universal states. Willing is an expression of our own personal philosophy as to how our needs should be experienced and our wants actualized. It's the brain's bragging about what it alone can accomplish if we only use it by "thinking hard." It's a much more intellectual and focused process than needing and wanting. It involves more awareness and attention. Willing is how we try to impose our personal view of how we think life should be.

Persons with strong needs often become highly motivated. From there, they move on to trying to meet their needs and get what they want by being strong-willed. We are just coming out of the century of the cerebrum. The last several decades have highly valued the "power of positive thinking." Those who fail are seen as being "weak-willed" and not "mentally focused enough." In this view, successful people aren't lucky, they're strong-willed. Despite the Beatles' philosophy that "all we need is love," the central assumption of the last century has often seemed to be "the brain is all we need."

The emphasis on "willing" has led to the encouragement "Don't worry, be happy." The idea seems to be that we can accomplish anything if we will it. An entire industry of "willpower teachers" has emerged. They often call themselves trainers or motivationalists, and they regularly speak to Fortune 500 companies and offer their services as "personal motivational coaches." In his book *The Power of Positive Thinking*, willpower pioneer Norman Vincent Peale wrote, "The happiness habit is developed simply by practicing happy thinking."[12] The idea of willing almost anything by positive thinking was described by author Wendy Kaminer when she pointed out that before New Age there was "new thought." She defines this strategy as "an amorphous collection of beliefs about the power of the mind. . . ."[13] The mind in this case is the higher brain called the neomammalian brain, which is where our rational thinking is centered.

Wishing is the enemy of the positive thinker who prides herself on being so strong-willed that there is little need for mysticism or the equanimity of wishing. Wishing is much too passive, gentle, and humble for the needy and power-motivated brain. "Will it to happen and it shall be so" is the lesson taught by positive-thinking gurus. For example, one of the most popular motivationalists is Tony Robbins. His "unlimited power" concept has been embraced by celebrities, CEOs of major corporations, and President Bill Clinton and First Lady, Hillary Rodham Clinton. To prove the power of "will," Robbins and others encourage their students to walk barefoot on 800-degree coals. They quickly jog across the coals and are greeted by cheering fellow fire walkers. As any scientist knows, however, "willing" has nothing to do with their safe journey across the coals. The capacity of coals to conduct heat to your feet is extremely low. As long as you keep lifting one foot after another as you run, you won't get burned. That's why a cake in a 450-degree oven and the air around it doesn't burn the cook. Only the high-conducting pan can do that. Fire walking is more a matter of physics than mental fitness.

"Willing" approaches often involve pseudoscientific explanations such as Neuro-Linguistic Programming (NLP) to buttress their claims. NLP assumes that one can achieve anything by assessing the "willing" or perceptual style of highly successful people and then matching it with one's own style. Mirroring the body language of the strong-willed and believing that willing can make it so if we only set our mind to it are also tenets of NLP. There is little scientific evidence of the validity of such claims, but such inspiring yet misleading assertions persist in the motivational movement.[14] Putting a happy face on a suffering body does little to alleviate the real causes of the suffering.

Another downside to the willpower movement is the risk of blaming the victim. While explaining things away as socioeconomic inequities and unfairness can excuse us from the necessary self-responsibility to try to correct these conditions, blaming the victim can result in ignoring the serious problems of society that cause so many to suffer needlessly. The willpower movement can mock the notion and reality of social justice by denying the many degrees of injustice. Simply "willing" more self-esteem, just "knowing" we can do anything if we will it, and the idea that only the weak-willed suffer or fail to heal are dangerous premises that can obstruct a more tolerant and constructive balance between personal and societal responsibility and the facts of life.

Hopeful People

Would people say you are an optimistic person? If so, they probably think you rely a lot on hope. Beyond the physical nature of needing, the emotional nature of wanting, and the mental process of willing is altering our consciousness to maintain a state of optimism regardless of reality. Hope goes beyond positive thinking to trying to maintain a positive affective state no matter what we or anyone else really thinks. It's a strategy of selective awareness and intentionally deciding not to notice or face up to the implications of something the five-sense brain says is undeniable.[15]

Optimism can be a very constructive state of consciousness. However, it loses most of its value as a coping technique when it denies all reality or derives from insincere efforts of "trying" to appear optimistic rather than being truly hopeful. An old saying is that those who keep their head when everyone around them is losing theirs is crazy. More difficult than realizing that there are things we cannot change can be the actual surrender of some of our hope. To go from hope to wishing requires a trust in forces that go beyond the physical, emotional, and societal. We make some of our best wishes when they augment and are compatible with our hoping, calm our willing, and recognize the difference between what we need and what we want. Wishing isn't giving up hope; it's one way to employ its energy.

Unlike the body-oriented energy of needing, the brain/body systemic energy of wanting, and the higher cerebral energy of willing, hoping is based on a premise of at least temporary immunity from all of these sources of energy. It transcends the narcissism of needing, the rationalizations of what we say we want, and the intellectualization involved in trying to remain strong-willed; hoping relies heavily on selective denial.

Beyond being simply aware of a need, attentively motivated to meet a perceived need, or mentally focused in an attempt to impose one's will, hope is a matter of personal reflection. It is a process that moves closer to the metaphysical side of the personal coping continuum. We don't necessarily feel or experience hope. We try to "have it."

The personal experiences of author Norman Cousins in overcoming serious illness and the inspiring and comforting clinical work of cancer surgeon Bernie Siegel first introduced the research and concepts of the power of hope. Their key message was that in the absence of certainty, there is nothing wrong with hope.[16]

Wishing goes beyond "having hope." It's taking action when we are willing to give up just hoping; it is to start wishing for help from the mystical and magical. Wishing is more cultural than hope's more socially determined philosophies of life.

It's more actively ritualistic than the emotional and attitudinal nature of being in a state of hoping.

Prayerful Persons

Would those who know you well say you are a prayerful person? If so, they probably mean that you are a very spiritual individual who has moved far to the right on the coping continuum noted in the chart on page 86. When I present my research on wishing, the human coping technique I am most often asked about as contrasted to wishing is the process of prayer. I have three basic answers to that question.

First, wishing tends to be a cultural, metaphysical process, whereas praying is a more spiritual, sacred process. We pray to a higher power, but we wish to "the powers that be." Wishing is inclined toward the occult, those aspects of our life that we are pretty sure are there but that we cannot see or touch. Praying leans toward the orthodox, those aspects of our spiritual life that transcend the simply invisible and ascend to sacred certainty. Wishing deals in magic, fairy tales, cultural lessons, and family traditions. Prayer stems from personal religious beliefs or established doctrines.

Second, wishing comes from the heart and connects with life's subtle energy. Praying comes from the soul and connects with the sacred. That's not to say that our heart is not involved in praying, but it is more the expressor than the source of who and how we are. Praying comes from the soul, all that we were, are, and will be on the deepest level of our being. Wishing is our heart's way of making its soul's more earthly needs known. If our soul is the information and codes that constitute who we are beyond our physical body, it is our L energy–sensitive heart that conveys and expresses the energy that carries the soul's code.

Finally, wishing is an attempt to connect with an invisible power. Praying is a way we try to connect with the Creator of all power. Unlike prayer, our wishes are not typically made "to" someone. They are swung "out there" for help from the subtle energy of the universe. Wishing is a way we connect with some of the energy the Absolute created, but praying is how we try to talk to the source, the Creator.

Prayer is an act of worship, but wishing is magical thinking, an intentional act of regression to childish ways of asking for help from the subtle and invisible L energy. There is no "being" involved. It's based on a long-established and largely unwritten cultural code and mythology rather than scripture and sacred writings. Prayer is based on inspiration and a sacralized view of the world. Wishing is ritualistic tradition passed on over the Thanksgiving dinner table and birthday cake. Prayer is learned either in a church, mosque, or temple or based to varying personalized degrees on lessons learned there or as translated by relatives. There's no Sunday school for wishing. Grandparents, uncles, aunts, and parents are the tutors in wishing. Wishing is trying to get our way; praying is petitioning God or an Absolute for His, Her, or Its way.

Lessons from a Pope's Sneeze

I first realized the difference between praying and wishing when I saw the Pope sneeze. It was not just a tiny "a-choo" but a full-blown, shoulder-raising sneeze. Several families were gathered for a special audience with His Holiness, and we were standing nervously in a chamber near the Pope's offices in the Vatican. I had just lectured to the group that had arranged this rare privilege and had been invited to attend. As His Holiness entered the room, he smiled and gestured to all of us in that humble but magnificent way only the most spiritually powerful can. As the Pope was offering a prayer in Latin, he sneezed loudly. A father, mother, and their little girl standing next to me with heads bowed softly said in unison and without looking up, "gesundheit." Smiling and without looking up, the Pope stopped his prayer, said "thank you," and returned to praying.

In this most holy of places with this most saintly of persons, not one person seemed at all surprised at the interchange that had taken place. In fact, no one but me seemed to notice the simple and automatic familial wish of good health that was made for the Pope. At the luncheon with some of the Pope's staff, I asked one of the bishops about what had happened.

"Oh that," he said. "That was a just a simple little wish. It's only polite to wish someone good health when they sneeze. Don't you do that in Hawai'i?"

"Of course," I responded, "but I was just a little surprised that His Holiness seemed to be so accustomed to the wish, especially at a time when he was praying."

"There's nothing wrong with wishing," answered the bishop as if he were discussing the obvious, "just so long as one remembers the difference between a prayer and a wish."

What an opportunity! Here was my chance to conduct wish research in one of the most spiritual places in the world. "What do you think the difference between a prayer and a wish is?" I asked as I took out my pad and pencil to capture every word.

The bishop put down his soup spoon, patted his lips with his napkin, and leaned over to whisper in my ear. "Young man," he said, "praying is connecting your soul with God, and wishing is a way of connecting with the spiritual energy of the world He gave us to use in helping Him work His will. You have to be very sure you know that you are wishing and not praying and not mix up the two. Prayer is the expression of pure and sacred passion for the Supreme Being and the highest form of a child-to-parent reverence. Wishing is more like a simple earthly brother/sister love. It's based on respect, not veneration. Both are important. Wishing is one tool God gave us to use while we are here on earth, and just like any loving parent who has given something potentially dangerous to their child, He watches very carefully, and probably with not a little bemusement, to see how we use it. We are well advised to watch out, too, because our wishing is one way we demonstrate for God how we value and use His gifts; sort of like a divine test. Wishes can be very powerful things and can be misused, so you had better start praying if you make unwise wishes. You can't pray wrong because God always knows what you mean, but you can wish wrongly. If you do, God help you!"

Alfred North Whitehead wrote, "A clash of doctrines is not a disaster, it is an opportunity." There is nothing about wishing that in any way challenges the sacredness of praying, especially if what we wish for is compatible with what we pray about. As the bishop rose from his seat to make a toast to the assembled group, he smiled and winked at me. "My prayers are with you my son," he said, "and I do wish you a very loving day." From the day in Rome until today, I still use the term "Gesundheit Factor" to help me distinguish praying from wishing.

The Seven Wishes Test

Another one of the research instruments we used with our wish-study group is the Seven Wishes Test. We used it to promote group discussions among our participants as to how wishing played a role in their daily life and world view. The Seven Wishes Test is designed primarily as a facilitator for understanding more about the nature of our wishing and where it fits in our life. You may find it helpful to find a "wish partner" with whom you can discuss wishing.

The Seven Wishes Test

To better understand the role of wishing in your own life, write down your answers to the following questions. Take plenty of time to consider your answer before writing it.

1. _____ If you could have just one wish granted right now that would come precisely, literally, completely, and irreversibly true forever, what would that wish be? Write your one most precious, important wish. (In Chapter 2, I suggested that you write this wish on a card.)

2. _____ Using the same criterion as listed in item number 1, what wish would the person you love the most write for herself or himself?

3. _____ Write the one wish the person who knows you best would say *you* would make for yourself.

4. _____ Write a wish you have made that has come true in your life. (Make sure it was a wish and not a need, want, hope, will, or prayer.)

5. _____ Write the one wish you *now wish* you had never made.

6. _____ Write the one wish the person who knows you best would wish for or about you.

7. _____ Write the one wish you have made many, many times throughout your life that has never come true.

Ask yourself, reflect about, and discuss with someone who knows you well the following questions about the seven wishes just outlined. You may want to have your "wish partner" do the same exercise and make this assignment a mutual exploration of the nature of wishing as it affects not only your own life but your relationship. The following questions are only starting points for a discussion about your wishing ways.

1. _____ Is my wish (#1) a wish for me and my life? How does it compare to what you wrote for wish #3?

2. _____ Am I completely sure I want my wish (#1) to come true exactly as it is stated?

3. _____ How would my own life change if my wish (#1) literally and fully came true?

4. _____ How would the lives of those I care about change if my wish (#1) came true?

5. _____ How would the world be changed if my wish (#1) came true?

6. _____ What danger might there be in this wish (#1) or any of the other six wishes coming true?

7. _____ What would happen if the exact opposite of my wish (#1) or any of the other six wishes came true?

8. _____ Have you ever seen this wish (#1) come true for anyone else?

9. _____ What do think your wish (#1) says about how you view life in general?

10. _____ How similar is your wish (#1) to your partner's idea of your wish (#2)?

11. _____ What has been the long-term effect of your wish number 3?

12. _____ How similar is wish number 4 to wish number 1?

13. _____ What do you think your partner's wish for you (#6) says about changes you might need to make in your view and conduct of your life?

14. _____ Does my wish (#1) reflect hope or fear?

15. _____ What changes would you make in your wish number 1 after your discussion and reflections about all seven wishes?

The purpose of this test was to facilitate our discussions and interviews with the wish-study participants and to help them see how wishing had already played a role in their lives. Our group was familiar with the concepts of needing, wanting, willing, hoping, and praying, but they had talked much less about wishing. We spent hours talking about the issues raised in the Seven Wishes Test. To better understand the differences between wishing and the other human coping systems described earlier, I hope you will take the time to—as we say in Hawaii—"just talk story" about the role of wishing in your life.

Six

Wishing on a Star

Five Lessons from Wise Wishers

Peace, joy, direction, faith, and love. In our interviews of people around the world regarding their wishes, these five aspects of life were consistently at the foundation of their wishes. During my ten years of speaking with over 2,000 patients and persons from all walks of life, it became clear that no matter the exact words of the wish, almost every wisher expressed a desire that fell within one of these areas or described a failed wish related to these issues. It also became clear that there was an opposing dark side to each of these wish realms that contributed some of a wish's essential negative power.

Every wish contains an element of the negative and in some way expresses a need not only to get something but also to get rid of something in the process. A wish to get over a cold is also a wish to kill off the virus that causes it. When we wish selfishly, impulsively, reactively, and without awareness of the dark side of wishing, our wishing becomes unbalanced. When we allow our brain to do most of our wishing for us, the dark side of wishing can begin to dominate the nature of the wish and we may receive a granted wish that we end up regretting. The key to wishing well is to wish more from the heart and to wish gently and with awareness of the delicate balance between getting what we want and losing what we need.

The Wish Star

Nineteenth-century Polish poet Cyprian Norwid wrote, "To be what is called happy, one should have something to live on, something to live for, and something to die for. The lack of one of these results in drama. The lack of two results in tragedy."[1] When we reviewed our interviews and the results of the wish tests given to our 2,166 wish-research subjects, we consistently identified aspects of Norwid's three categories of happiness. In addition to something to live on (sufficient health and wealth for a sense of peace), to live for (sufficient balance and bliss to experience joy), and to die for (sufficient sense of challenge and commitment to feel a direction to and for life), we learned that our wishers also wished for something after their death (faith) and someone with whom to share the joy of their wishes made in the other four domains (love).

To help us establish consistency in our interviews about wishing, we sketched a five-pointed star that represented the five domains of what we and the research subjects came to call the "bright" and "dark" wishing star (see the figure on page 103). We were able to classify most wishes within these five light and dark realms. To encompass the range of the wishes we heard, we called the five bright-star wish realms serenity, delight, purpose, meaning, and compassion. We labeled the results of "dark wishing" turmoil, disillusionment, stagnation, despair, and loneliness.

Defining the Wish Star Domains

The wishes reported by our subjects could be classified into one of the five light or five opposing dark wish star domains as defined here. Those subjects who reported receiving the wish they made revealed a keen awareness of the lethal as well as the loving aspects of the five realms of the wish star.

Serenity: A wish for calmness. Wishes here relate to seeking a sense of consistent and predictable security and peace free of constant stress and worry over

Serenity

Something to Live On

Doing

Attending

Knowing What Can and Can Not Be Changed

"Health and Wealth"

Grateful

Compassion

TURMOIL

LONELINESS   DISILLUSIONMENT

Delight

Someone to Share Life

Loving

Connected

DARK STAR

Something to Live For

Being

Feeling

DESPAIR   STAGNATION

Knowing How to be Vulnerable

"Kind and Tender"

Adoring

Knowing What to do With Life

"Balance and Bliss"

Fulfilled

Meaning

Something After Life

Believing

Revering

Knowing What We Can't Know

"Faith and Coherence"

Devoted

Purpose

Something to Die For

Contributing

Accomplishing

Knowing What to do For A Living

"Challenge and Commitment"

Significant

one's own or another's safety, health, and economic survival. These are usually wishes related to feeling in control of one's life.

𝒯urmoil: A wish that brings agitation. Very little is accomplished in life unless we are willing to stir things up a bit. When we seek more control than nature allows, we risk losing any chance for the true serenity of going with the flow of life. Without the essential ups and downs, life becomes boring and spiritually and intellectually numbing. In our search for a super serenity, we miss out on the joy of life's natural surprises and the important spiritual lessons of life's chaos, which is what challenges and develops our soul. Wishing for complete serenity can be a wish for no life at all, or it can result in a state of chronic agitated searching for a peace and tranquillity that is always just beyond our present state. This in turn leads to feeling that things are constantly "screwing up" when we are really the ones wishing this state upon ourselves. We feel in constant fear about one or another's physical or financial well-being. Dark-side wishes here relate to trying to maintain control when the best strategy might be wishing to be able to give up control.

Delight: A wish for cheerfulness. Wishes here are for a sense of joy and happiness. These are wishes related to wanting to feel joyful almost all the time.

Disillusionment: A wish that results in feeling disappointed. The only truly negative emotion is a "stuck" or unrelenting emotion. The dark side of wishing in this domain relates to constantly expecting to be "up" and happy. Wishing for constant delight without unhappiness and suffering is unrealistic and can result in feeling that nothing can make us happy enough. People around us often come to feel that they are the cause of our unhappiness. Dark-side wishing here shows itself by an ever-rising threshold for pleasure.

Purpose: A wish to feel productive. Wishing here relates to seeking a sense of pride and self-respect from the daily work we do. Wishing well in this realm results in a sense of personal significance through acknowledged contributions. These are wishes related to feeling important.

Stagnation: Wishing that results in feeling useless. The dark side of wishing in this domain is represented by a sense of worthlessness at whatever constitutes one's daily work and being trapped in useless, unappreciated, or even destructive work that brings very little personal pride. Trying to wish away the dreary, thankless, and repetitive tasks that accompany all work is unrealistic and can lead to feeling disenchanted with our work and personally useless and unimportant.

Meaning: A wish to feel comforted. Wishing in this realm relates to spiritual confidence, a sense of coherence, and optimism regarding the meaning of life and death. Wishing here relates to having an adaptable and adequate explanatory system for the bad times in our lives that helps us understand and accept its apparent un-fairness. Or, as one of our wish-research subjects put it, "Life is fair, it just might not be our view of fairness." If wishes for serenity are related to feeling physically safe, wishing in this domain relates to feeling spiritually safe here and in the hereafter.

Despair: Wishing that leads to spiritual desperation and cynicism. The dark side of a wish for meaning in life is pessimism and lack of a dynamic explanatory system that promotes adjustment to transitional life crises. Wishing for spiritual guarantees meaning and complete answers to questions that cannot be fully answered can lead to the dark side of meaning represented by angry disbelief of anything other than what can be recognized in the five-sense world.

Compassion: A wish to feel adored. Wishing here relates to reciprocal love. It leads to a feeling of deep and enduring connection and being loved to the same extent one loves. Wishing well in this realm leads to feeling safely and permanently bonded to another person with whom we can share our passion for life as manifested in the first four wish domains.

Loneliness: Wishing that leads to feeling detached. The dark side of wishes in the compassion domain leads to a sense of isolation and separateness. It often comes from wishing for an unrealistic loving free of all conflict, pain, and anguish, and from wishing "for" rather than "to be" the right partner. Dark-side wishing for compassion leaves the wisher frustrated and the partner of the wisher baffled as to how to ever be the lover for which their partner constantly seems to be wishing.

As we interviewed our wish-study participants about their experiences with wishes in the bright and dark domains just discussed, we used the following scale to help them reflect on the results of their wishing and where on the wish star they were wishing well.

Wish Domain Scale

Circle the number that reflects best where you fall on the wish domain scale at this time in your life. Use the definitions just outlined to find your score.

Peace

1. My life now is characterized by a sense of:

   Turmoil 1 2 3 4 5 6 7 8 9 10 Serenity

Joy

2. My life now is mostly one of:

   Disillusionment 1 2 3 4 5 6 7 8 9 10 Delight

Direction

3. In terms of what I work at every day, I feel a sense of:

   Stagnation 1 2 3 4 5 6 7 8 9 10 Purpose

Faith

4. In my spiritual life, at this time in my life I find a sense of:
   Despair 1 2 3 4 5 6 7 8 9 10 Meaning

Love

5. In my love life now, I feel a deep sense of:
   Loneliness 1 2 3 4 5 6 7 8 9 10 Compassion

After reflecting on the scores in the five domains of the wish star, our wish subjects were usually able to identify which domain showed the most imbalance toward the dark side of wishing and required more immediate attention. Those subjects who wished well averaged a score of 7 on each of the domains. Those who reported frustration and disappointment with their wishing averaged a score of 3. Wishing for an unrealistic 10 in each domain is likely to result in a wish backlash toward the dark side as inevitable discouragement sets in.

After discussing the bright and dark side of the five domains of the wish star, we discussed lessons our subjects had learned from their wishing experience related to the five realms. We discussed the difference between what they felt to be their brain and heart-oriented wishes (see the figure on page 107). The lessons of wishing on this star are presented next.

Wishing for Serenity

Lesson from the Wish Project: "Wish for the wisdom to seek what your heart needs, not what your brain wants."

We all make wishes related to our need for something to live on. We wish for things and situations that will bring us a sense of peace and certainty in an increasingly fast-paced and unpredictable world. We wish for those things that make us feel more safe and secure and that help us achieve a state of assurance that we will be able to live in reasonable comfort and health.

It's not surprising that so many of our wishers expressed a desire for "a little peace and quiet." In just over sixty years, we have gone from the first speed limit in London of 20 miles per hour to Apollo 10's astronauts suspended from their spacecraft and moving at almost 25,000 miles per hour. Mistaking more speed for a better life, our brain is urging us to move faster and faster. The result is often hectic turmoil, a consumerist orientation to life, and a set of "hurry-illnesses" that includes hypertension and cardiovascular disease.

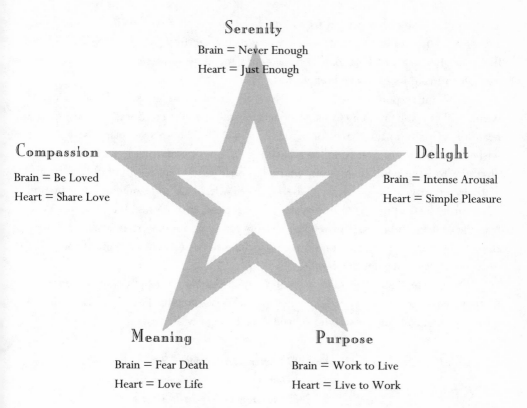

Serenity

Brain = Never Enough

Heart = Just Enough

Compassion

Brain = Be Loved

Heart = Share Love

Delight

Brain = Intense Arousal

Heart = Simple Pleasure

Meaning

Brain = Fear Death

Heart = Love Life

Purpose

Brain = Work to Live

Heart = Live to Work

Surveys show that almost three-fourths of Americans think time is moving too fast and wish that they "had the time" to slow down. One of my patients said, "My life is sure madness most of the time. We get up and go, keep going when we get home, and then collapse. I can't remember doing just one thing at a time." The twentieth century may be referred to in the future as "the hundred-year madness," a time when our own machines began to enslave their creators.[2] It began with horses and hours and ended with Maseratis and microseconds. Wishes in domain one (serenity) are attempts to overcome what one of our wish-research respondents called "Paige's Pace." He said, "Paige's Pace is based on baseball pitcher Satchel Paige's warning. Paige said, 'Don't look back. Something might be gaining on you.' That's sort of how I feel. I even get impatient waiting for a revolving door and feel that I have to keep going faster just to keep up."

The result of our ever-accelerating life tempo has been the failure of the one body organ most responsive to and responsible for our body's rhythm. Our hurried heart cannot keep pace with the rhythm the unsympathetic brain wishes upon it. The number of persons who die of heart disease in this country every day is equivalent to seven jumbo jets crashing daily with no survivors. Our dark-star wish to get more, and to get it faster, has caused us to hurry our hearts to death. Whether our brain and busy body know it or not, when we wish for serenity, our heart is asking our brain to give it a break before it breaks and to allow it to slow down and relax enough to make its own brighter wishes.

One of our respondents referred to serenity-domain wishes as "health and wealth" wishing. They sought things that would bring them more comfort, security, and a healthier velocity in their own or someone else's life. Those who made wise wishes wished for the gift of gratitude for what they had more than for the dark-side wishes of trying to have what their brain wanted. Those who were happy with the results of their serenity wishes seemed to be aware of what can be changed about life and what can't. Instead of trying to wish avoid all illness, they wished for the capacity to heal themselves and others. Instead of wishing for more money, they wished to enjoy the money they had. They seemed to be wishing for a sense of steering through life rather than being driven through it.

To illustrate wishing in each domain, I've listed sample bright-star wishes made by those subjects who scored 7 or higher on the Wish Domain Test. I've also included dark-side wishes from those who scored 3 or lower on the test.

Heart's Serenity Wishes: *"To never worry about money again."*
"That my cancer never comes back."
"That Grammy will be like she was again."

Brain's Turmoil Wishes: *"To win the lottery and be filthy rich."*
"To get promoted and have a corner office."
"To never die."

Wishing for Delight

Lesson from the Wish Project: "Wish to find the joy in what you already have and the appreciation for not having what you don't need, not for more, different, better, or bigger things and experiences."

Wishes in the delight realm of the wish star related to having something to live for and a sense of appreciation of the gift of life. Whereas wishes for serenity had to do with staying alive, wishes for delight had to do with feeling alive. They were wishes having to do with experiencing a sense of joyful balance and bliss in everyday life and to appreciate the gift of life more fully.[3]

Wishes in domain two (delight) were associated more with a state of being and feeling than domain one's being healthy enough to "do" and wealthy enough to be able to fully "attend" to the quality of life. Dark-side wishing in this domain often translated to the brain's addiction to stimulation and wishes for high arousal that mistook intensity for meaning.

The brain's wishes in the delight domain tended toward one's expressing the "more and me" philosophy. The dark side of wishes in this realm revealed a sense of disillusionment no matter how much stuff, how fast, and how much personal authority a person managed to achieve. Here are examples of heart and brain wishes in the delight domain.

Heart Wish: *"To enjoy my husband and be more fully with him."*
"To just sit down on the beach in Hawai'i and enjoy paradise."
"To have less soccer time and more spiritual time with my kids."

Brain Wish: *"Get a chance to bungee-jump out of a plane."*
"Climb Mount Everest."
"Drive a Porsche in the Indy 500."

Wishing for Purpose

Lesson from the Wish Project: "Wish to find meaningful work, not meaning through your work."

In consideration of the years of our life devoted to what we do for a living, wishes in the purpose domain of the wish star were related to having something worth dying for. Whereas serenity wishes related to a sense of gratefulness, and delight wishes related to having a sense of fulfillment, purpose wishes dealt with feeling significant. They were about finding a sense of challenge and commitment, primarily through one's job or major life tasks and responsibilities.

Domain one wishes were for joy, domain two wishes were for happiness, and domain three (purpose) wishes were for a sense of importance. It's not surprising that work-related wishes were so common in our research group. Work is second only to sleep in the number of occupied hours in our life. It consumes most of our life for the most important years of our life and is closely associated with our self-esteem.

Wishes in this domain were about feeling that one is making, has made, or will make a lasting impression through one's life's work. Work in this sense was not restricted to only "out of the home" or financially compensated tasks. Work in the third wish domain referred to the activity one engages in day in and day out.

Wishes in domain one focused on our body. Wishes in domain two focused on our feelings. Wishes in the third domain focused on putting our body productively to work as one expression of our soul. The wish domains seemed to rotate from a safe self to good feelings to an important mission.

Wishes in the serenity domain required wise wishful thinking about the physical and economical aspects of life. Wishes in the delight domain tended to be about being able to become more fully absorbed in the grandeur of the life we have. Wishes in the purpose domain related to feeling that one's life had significance and value to other lives. Instead of the kind of wishes that focused on what to live on and what to live for that characterized the first two wishing domains, wise wishful thinking in domain three related to doing something for a living that seemed to make the world more one for which we all wish.

The longer we spoke with our wish respondents, the more the wishes we discussed began to become existential in nature. The further clockwise around the wish star, the more wishing seemed to be associated with spiritual issues. For example, wishing in the purpose domain seemed to reveal a concern to move from an "instrumental" to a more "sacred" view of work.[4] There seemed to be a desire to move away from working as a means to earn income to being able to make a significant contribution. Wishes in the purpose domain were along the lines of author Elbert Hubbar's statement, "We work to become, not to acquire."[5]

Wise wishing for purpose de-emphasized the brain's wishes for power and prestige in favor of the heart's desires to do good work. Here are some verbatim examples of heart and brain wishes in the purpose domain.

Heart Wish: *"That I'd be remembered for what I contributed."*
"That people would say I made their world a better place."
"That I made a difference, a lasting contribution and legacy through my work."

Brain Wish: *"That I'd get more days off."*
"I wish I'd get the money I deserve for all the work I do."
"That I could make as much and have the power my boss does."

Wishing for Meaning

Lesson from the Wish Project: "Wish for the gratitude for the thrill of being alive and the spiritual insight that your essence is immortal, not to lengthen life to avoid death."

Author John Sutherland Bonnel wrote, "What a man believes about immortality will color his thinking in every area of life."[6] Wishing in domain four (meaning) usually dealt with the hope that there is more than just this life and that what we experience as our "self" does not vanish at our death. In one way or another, wishing in this domain dealt with concerns about the meaning of death and the implications of life's brevity. Wise wishes in this domain were based less on futile attempts to escape the death of the physical self and more on finding a sense of devotion to leaving one's loving energy imprint after one's physical passing. As one of our respondents joked, "I wish that my tombstone will list not how I died, but why I lived."

Wishes in this realm were concerned not with what to live on, live for, or die for but for some representation of the self after life. They were wishes to experience faith in the ultimate verification of our hopes and dreams that there is some kind of "more" left after we have physically disappeared. They were mediated by a wishful thinking comfortable in the knowledge that there is much about life and death that we will never know.

Wishes in domain four were about faith and a sense of coherence. Psychologist Aaron Antonovsky defines a sense of coherence as a combination of comprehensibility, manageability, and meaningfulness.[7] All three of these traits were present in wise wishes in domain four. They were wishes for a kind of spiritual hardiness that allowed room in a secular world for the possibility of the survival of some representation of the self in the next world.

Wishes in the meaning domain were attempts to avoid the despair of a spiritually pessimistic point of view. They had to do with having a conviction in the survival of the soul. In keeping with the subtle L energy concept presented in earlier pages of this book, Victorian scholar E. B. Tylor defined the soul we wish to survive. He wrote that the soul our ancestors wished to perpetuate was a ". . . thin insubstantial human image, in its nature a sort of vapour, film, or shadow . . . mostly impalpable and invisible, yet also manifesting physical power."[8] Wishes in the fourth domain were wishes for the survival after life of this intangible manifestation of our life.

Just as they were for our preindustrial or "primitive" ancestors, these kinds of wishes were ways of trying to avoid the despair of a "you live, you die, that's it" orientation. They included wishes about an afterlife or to make some form of contact with a deceased loved one. While the brain wishes to literally continue forever, the heart desires only that our loving template be left forever in others' hearts. Here are some examples.

Heart Wish: *"To be remembered as a loving person."*
"To see Grandpa again someday."
"To feel God in my heart."

Brain Wish: *"To feel personally fulfilled."*
"To realize my potential before it's too late."
"To have what I want while I can still enjoy it."

Wishing for Compassion

Lesson from Wish Project: "Wish to be the right partner, not to find the right partner."

The fifth domain of the wish star is the domain of loving wishes. Wishes here had to do with the desire to find someone with whom to share the necessary suffering of life in order to make living less miserable. While we often speak of love in physical or romantic terms, wishing well in the fifth domain was characterized by the need to find the missing component for a full life—a "soul mate" sensitive to our unique anguish and willing to help us alleviate it as we help soothe theirs. The wisest wishes in the compassion domain were those that expressed the hope of being the kind of lover we wished would love us.

Wishing realm five deals with trying to have the sensation that someone cares deeply enough about us to share (the root word "com" as in committed) our passions (passion referring to suffering). To suffer in this sense did not necessarily refer to agony but to endure the ups and downs of life with another person. This is the domain where we make wishes to find someone with whom to share the wishes of the first four domains.

Domain five love wishes are wishes to avoid one of our deepest fears: loneliness. It's where we wish to release ourselves from the constraints of wishing only for and by ourself and realize that the best wishes are those that are shared. Someone wishing in the love realm may wish to find a marital partner, but well-made wishes are more focused on finding a spiritual partner, an equal with whom to meet the needs of the sixth sense and not just the basic five senses. One of the most significant wishes we make is the wish to be adored by someone to the same extent we adore that person. Author Gary Zukav summarized the surrender of selfish wishing in this domain when he wrote, "As the consciousness of each of you becomes lighter, your partnership becomes richer."[9]

Wishing well in domain five of the wish star requires knowing how and being willing to give the most important loving gift of all, the gift of self. It's wishing to be able to be more vulnerable so that we can feel more connected and cared for. It's wishing to turn a life of "me" into a life of "us." Unlike wishing for something to live on, live for, die for, and live after, wishing in this domain focuses on finding someone with whom to share all of life's challenges and charms. Wishes in this realm are not just for love but for a lasting, reciprocal love.

A unique aspect of wishing in domain five is the "power wishing" phenomenon you read about earlier. Two persons who choose to wish together lovingly can exert a profound influence on the subtle energy of their relationship and the world. Sharing wishing may be one of the most neglected intimate relationship skills.

The dark side of wishing in this realm relates to the brain's mistaking lust for love and self-enhancement for mutual connection. A key question that might be asked before committing to any intimate relationship is, "Are we willing to make and share the same wishes?" Here are examples of heart and brain wishes in the compassion domain.

Heart Wish: *"To be loved by someone as much I love her."*
"To find someone to share all my life with."
"To feel totally and completely loved in every way."

Brain Wish: *"To find my dream lover, the perfect man for me."*
"To have a gorgeous woman worship me."
"To be made love to all night by three women."

Wishing in the Right Direction

Based on our research on wishing and an analysis of the various wishes made by our sample group, there seemed to be a kind of "positive pull" or gravity involved in wishing (see the figure on page 114). To obtain the most satisfying results from wishing for the long term, there seemed to be a "right track" to the well-wishing process. Those who made the healthiest wishes and the wishes that seemed to result in positive life outcomes wished progressively clockwise around the domains of wishing.

In this clockwise direction the wish star seemed to operate by a spiritual sequence.

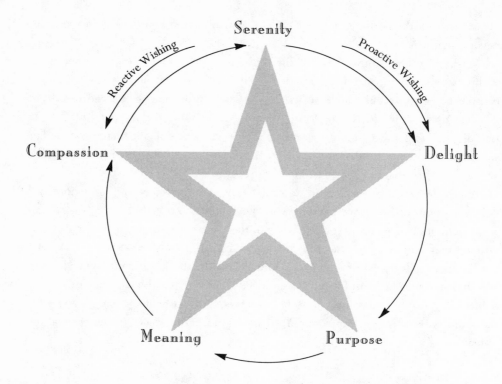

Serenity was enhanced by having found a compassionate partner. The chances of having a wish granted to find such a partner were improved if one had wished well for a sense of meaning in life. A wish for meaning was more likely to be granted if one had learned to wish well for a sense of purpose. Those who had their wishes fulfilled for delight had also wished for purpose, meaning, and compassion.

Two Forces of the Wish Star

There are two subtle energy principles of the wish star that seem to hold true in all wishing. First is the wishing sequence rule just described. This means that proactive wishing moving from serenity to delight, delight to purpose, and so on seemed to lead to the most constructive wishing and the greatest chance of healthy wishes coming true. Being frustrated with a failure of purpose and then regressing to go backward on the wish star to seek happiness by wishing for personal delight seldom led to fulfillment in either domain. A counterclockwise spinning backward along the wish domains often followed.

The second principle of the wish star's energy is that regressive wishing results in the wisher being "sucked in" to wishing's dark side. For example, if a wish for meaning seemed to have failed and the wisher sought to wish "backward" for purpose, the despair and stagnation of failed wishing in both domains seemed to follow. If the wisher was unable or unwilling to wish gently and wait in one domain, the dark-wish star drew the wisher under its influence. If a wish was made in the delight realm and the wisher unwisely became impatient and "pushed too hard" to cause the energy vibrations she hoped for, she might turn immediately to wishing in the serenity realm to soothe her disillusionment. By not waiting for her wish to work its magic and for the timeless nature of sympathetic resonance to "do its thing," the regressive nature of her wishing might lead her to wish for love to bring her the delight she failed to recognize and wait for and for the meaning she may have been too impatiently brain-driven and heartless to see. We found that most wishes come true. The challenge is to be patient, wise, and sixth-sense-sensitive enough to recognize it.

Here's a wishing catastrophe of wishing backward from one of our interviews. Wishing from his heart to find something worth living for, a man made a wish in the "delight" realm. He said, "I wish I could feel more fulfilled and content in my life." His heart was trying to get his brain to experience a contentment and gratitude for the blessings in life he already possessed. Instead of wishing and waiting for his sixth-sense suggestion to work its magic, the man's brain impatiently felt that his wish for contentment would never be granted. Wishes made in the spirit of speed are often those most likely to become wicked or unwise wishes. Not finding the peace and balance he thought his first wish should have granted on his time rather than on wishing subtle energy's relative time, he regressed on the wish star to make a wish in the realm of serenity.

"I wish I had more time to just enjoy life," he wished. When his life seemed to become even more hectic and his brain even less willing to wait for his first or second wish to come to fruition, he went wishing again. He wished for a person who might bring him the delight and serenity his heart desired but his brain was too rushed to see even if these wishes were being granted. "I wish I had a more loving wife who would understand me," became his counterclockwise wish in the compassion domain. He had become what we came to call a "wish shopper," making a wish and moving on before giving that wish the opportunity to coalesce. His impatient, brain-driven wishing sent him spinning further and further back on the wish star and spiraling faster and faster into the dark wish star's control. He desperately wished for meaning, stating, "I wish I could at least see some sign from Him that God really gives a damn about me."

The unwise wisher was now riding faster and faster in the wrong direction on the wish carousel. He wished for a better job, better friends, a better lover, a healthier body, and on and on. He ended up wishing again in the delight domain, but this time his wishing was even more brain-driven. He wished to be able to move to a desert island, to win the lottery, to have an extramarital love affair, to be granted tangible gifts from God, and for a more high-powered job. After spinning around in the wrong spiritual direction for months, he studied the wish star during one of our interviews. After taking some of the tests presented in this book, he finally changed his wishing ways and direction. He said he found the Seven Wish Test particularly helpful and talked about it with his wife for hours.

As I was writing this chapter, the man in this example called my office. He asked when the book about his and the other research subjects' wishes was going to be published. When I posed the question we usually ask of our subjects when they contact us, his response revealed a much wiser wisher. I asked, "How are you wishing?" He answered, "Fine. When I finally wished in the serenity realm that I would be more attentive to what I already had in life, I decided to wait a long time for that wish to come true. One night as I was sitting in my car in a traffic jam, I started to think about my serenity wish. Then it clicked. It had already been granted. I was sitting patiently and just watching the people on the streets. Before, I would have been seething. My wish had come true. I'm going to wait awhile, but my wife and I are talking about making a wish together about our purpose in life and our careers. We want my first wish to really set in first."

A Wishing Lesson from the Mount

Our research indicates that all of us, to varying degrees and in our own unique ways, make wishes in the five domains of the wish star. The brain's wishes are automatic and urgent. They stem from the physical and secular needs, wants, and willing coping styles of the brain. The heart's wishes fall somewhere between our most sincere emotions and our faith in the metaphysical and sacred. They take much more patience and sensitivity and are therefore often among the most difficult wishes to learn to make. Like true love, wishing's "little boom" effect cannot be hurried.

In the Sermon on the Mount, Jesus teaches, "For where our treasure is, there your heart will be also."[10] Well wishing is based on letting our heart do our wishing for us. It, not the brain, knows where the true riches lie. Whereas faith, hope, and prayer are ways to "store up for ourselves treasures in heaven," wishful thinking can be a way we ask for a slight alteration in the Absolute's L energy while we're here on earth without jeopardizing our chances for heaven.

Wishful thinking is an almost sacred way of trying to make life better. In the Sermon on the Mount, we are told to "Ask, and it will be given . . ." and to

". . . knock, and the door will be open for you." Wishful thinking is a humble and delicate tapping. It may not offer the immediate emotional solace of hope, or the sacred confidence of prayer. Wishful thinking, particularly if its wishes are made in harmony with the principles of the bright wish star and with awareness of the dangers of the dark wish star, does provide a kind of cosmic compromise between the two. Wishful thinking's culturally established way of dealing with the world is the topic of the next chapter.

Seven

·····❧·····

Recovering the Wisdom
of Wishful Thinking

So you hear them tell it and they mean if it works it's
good and if it don't it costs nothing."

—CARL SANDBURG, *THE PEOPLE, YES*

Safe Habits

Wishing's just superstition, nothing more," challenged the teacher as we walked from the meeting room. I had just completed my lecture on the importance of teaching wishful thinking to children of all ages. There were ladders and cables scattered throughout the room as the hotel staff took down the lights and sound system. "Wishful thinking is based on delusion," she continued. "It's not a form of intelligence like verbal or mathematical IQs. That's why kids go to school, to learn to be logical thinkers, not wishful ones."

Before I could respond, I noticed that we were walking straight for a high ladder opened directly in front of us. Without looking up, the teacher altered her path to avoid walking under the ladder. I stopped to look as she circled around it, stepped over boxes, and squeezed against the wall to avoid passing under it. When she saw me watching, she snapped, "It's simply habit, that's all, simply a habit."

The teacher was correct. Our wishful thinking and superstitions are habits that have been passed on to us, but that does not mean they are just or only habits. They are a form of what the science of memetics calls "memes," units of cultural instruction that persist over the centuries.[1] Memes are passed on from generation to generation as ways to automatically do things even when we may not be aware of what we're doing or why. Making a wish while blowing out the candles on a birthday cake and knocking on wood to avoid bad luck are also examples of well-established memes. The injunctions of the Ten Commandments and the multiplication tables are also memes. While not chemically coded in our chromosomes, memes are functionally equivalent to a gene. They contain cultural instructions decoded by the brain and heart.

The word "meme" is derived from the Greek for "imitation" (c.f., mime, mimetic). Our ancestors watched nature and mimicked their uniquely sensitive ways of connecting with it. Wishing evolved as a memetic process because it was an attempt to employ the "sixth sense" that all of nature's creatures seemed to have about nature's subtle energy.

Over the centuries, wishes became what author Richard Brodie calls "viruses of the mind."[2] Like advertising jingles or a phrase of a popular song, certain wishes seem to spontaneously "pop into our mind" and out of our mouth Once there, they act much like a computer virus that, whether we know it or not, can affect our entire life program. They can even cause a logical teacher to avoid walking under a ladder.

Thinking Wishfully

Wishful thinking is one of our many intelligences. It's a way we solve problems that go beyond the five senses. It's how we try to understand and then influence forces our brain is not designed to fathom but which our heart knows well. Wishful intelligence is thinking about the world as a place of wonderful potential eventualities that we can change into actual happenings simply through our individual intentions.[3] As one of our wish-research subjects put it, "Wishing is a way of helping nature make up her mind in our favor."

Wishful thinking is a relaxed cognition that leads to viewing the world optimistically and being able to discover connections that elude the brain's quick-judging nature. It's thinking that does not always trust fully in perception and values intuition as much as raw intellect. All well wishers engage in wishful thinking because they can think slowly when they have to. They can wait for an answer rather than quickly and urgently seeking one. Wishful thinkers know not only that there are supernatural forces that act upon us but that we can connect on some level with these subtle or "mystical forces." They think that by wishing we can even engage with and manipulate these forces in our favor. Wishful thinking is being aware that through our intentions we are creating our life. We need our various cognitive intelligences to deal with the five-sense world, and they have created magnificent miracles. However, our adaptive brilliance also requires knowing when to just make a wish rather than trying to rationalize a way to act.

Here's a chart summarizing the differences between rational and wishful thinking. Circle the word in the left or right column that best reflects your way of thinking.

RATIONAL THINKING	WISHFUL THINKING
Material	Mystical
Data	Stories
Objective	Subjective
New	Old
Analyze	Synthesize
Representative samples	Anecdotes
Reduction	Elaboration
Latest research	Oldest traditions
Clock	Calendar
Study and control nature	A part of and responsible for nature
Academic journals	Ancestral wisdom
Masculine	Feminine
Yin	Yang
Contractive	Expansive
Skeptical	Intuitive
See/touch/smell	Sense/feel
Suspect	Believe
Doubt	Trust
Wait	Act
Technical procedures	Song, dance, chant
Challenging	Accepting
Confrontation	Tolerance

Unbiased	Cultural/familial bias
Replication	Tradition
See it = believe it	Believe it = see it
Printed word	Imagination
Assertive	Humble
Serious	Humorous
Confident	Docile
Statistical predictions	Omens and signs
Control	Connect

The clear wishful thinker circles answers in both columns, reflecting a balance between rational and enchanted thinking. Psychologist Jean Piaget wrote about the importance of "the problem of the match."[4] If intelligence is adaptive thinking, true genius derives from being able to remain rationally aware of the seeing and touching world while being wishfully immersed in the realm of the invisible. Our modern curricula are designed to produce clear-thinking and highly rational adults who are good and fast with words and numbers, but we damage our children when we do not also teach them to think wishfully and how to know when this form of intelligence is called for. As the brilliant wishful thinker Buckminster Fuller wrote, "None of us are a genius. Some of us are just less damaged than most."

The Value of a Little Irrationality

The adaptive wishing ways our ancestors evolved to help them make sense of their world may seem whimsical, quaint, and charming remnants of a dumb way to see things, but their wishful thinking still has value for us today. Our modern mental default mode is that of a quick, rational, logical brain that dismisses wishful thinking as sluggishly dependent and not suited to immediate adaption and problem solving.[5] Our society has come to undervalue wishful thinking, yet it remains a key source of true wisdom and the understanding of connections that exist beyond the conventional fast-brain-oriented ways of seeing the world that author Guy Glaxton calls "hare-brained thinking." Glaxton says that we fail to tap into our creative spirit when we fail to remember that "To tap into the leisurely ways of knowing, one must dare to wait."[6] Enlightened wishful thinking is to be able to balance our rational, distrustful brain with our more willing and obliging heart.

Only a less rushed and open way of thinking can explain the often amazing power of the subtle energy connection that is at the core of our wish making. For example, many pet owners sense a unique connection with their dogs, cats, and other animals that goes beyond reasonable thought. There "just seems to be" a unique, irrational bond on a level that is difficult to explain logically. One has to be a "wishful thinker" and "with it" in terms of L energy to understand how a lost pet may travel hundreds of miles to find its family.

Consider the documented case of Bobbie, the collie that got lost on a family trip in Indiana. He managed to find his way to his family's home in Oregon, 3,000 miles away, after crossing the Rocky Mountains and ice-jammed rivers in the dead of winter.[7] This and many other documented cases of so-called animal psi trailing, or animals sensing their way back home, defy "realistic" thinking.[8] Only those wishful thinkers who are oriented to the subtle energy and have sufficient docility or "teachability" about the unseen are suited for dealing with such connections. Wishful thinkers would have no problem accepting the case of Bobbie. They easily use phrases such as "it's magic" or "there's just something that draws us together."

The Magical Hay Wagon

The rapid development of our ancestors' intellectual skills and the tools associated with them did not result in their abandonment of their docile or highly responsive and adaptive wishful thinking. No matter how smart they became or what religious systems they finally developed, they remained reliant on superstition and wishful thinking to get them through the day. No state dictate or religious threat could prevent them from secretly clinging to superstition and wishes.

An example of the blending of rational and wishful thinking can be seen in one of our ancestors' first "rational" developments, agriculture. In rural areas today, a farmer in Idaho sitting on the most modern, computerized tractor still makes a wish when he sees a load of hay. Ask him about it, and he might say it's just superstitious wishful thinking. Ask him more about his wish, and you will likely get an answer similar to the one I received in my interview of an agricultural wish maker as a part of my wish research.

"It's just a thing we always do and have always done," said the eighty-two-year-old Wisconsin dairy farmer. He was holding a computer-generated chart he said showed him his crop and irrigation patterns as fed back to him by satellite. It was a very hot and humid Sunday afternoon, and the old man fanned himself with his computer readout as he described his wishful thinking with dead seriousness.

"You always make a wish when you see a load of hay. You have to. And if the hay is baled, the wish you make won't come true until the bale has been broken."[9] He paused and then, looking at the crops sprawling out from where we sat on his porch, he continued.

"Now, if you happen to pass a hay wagon, you should count to thirteen and make a wish," he said. He spoke as if he were a college professor lecturing to a class on conation. "Then, you must turn away so as not to see that load of hay again. If you accidently look back and see it, the wish will not be granted. If you fail to make a wish when you see hay, it means that serious sickness or even death might ensue. None of us would risk that."

I wrote down this rural philosopher's every word. I thanked him and began to walk down the old wooden steps of the porch that wrapped around the entire farmhouse. "Hey," he said. "Write this down, too. If you see a load of hay pass and you make a wish, you must not say a word to anyone until someone asks you a question you can answer with the word yes. That sets the wish in and it will surely come true. You have to be patient, but it will."

Sympathetic Magic

I've since spoken with several other farmers around the country. Every one of them had a similar version of the hay wish. The peculiar logic of wishful thinking revealed in wishes like those made about hay is based on "sympathetic magic."

The fundamental physics of wishing indicates that "sympathetic resonation" and one little energetic nudge can eventually shake a massive object. Sympathetic magic is derived from this same principle and relates to the power of wishful thinking. As the farmer did when he wished on a bale of hay, tradition has it that making a wish while looking at or touching something associated with prosperity or other good fortune made our ancestors expect the realization of the wish. They were trying to feel "sympathy" for and gain "sympathy" from the positive nature of the hay. They believed, based on what they saw in nature, that "like brings like," and they wanted to "get into sync" with those things that symbolized safety and well-being.

When I first learned about wishful thinking's sympathetic magic, I called my farmer friend in Michigan to ask him about it. He said, "Oh yeah, that's true. That's why we wish on hay. Hay stands for a successful harvest, so if you connect with it somehow, you get some of that energy from it." In modern physics terms, my friend was saying that wishing was his way of falling into syncronized resonation with the subtle energy emanating from baled hay. In wishful thinking terms, wishing allowed him to bask in what even the most skeptical person often senses as "good vibes" coming from the hay.

Countermagic

In the wishful thinking lexicon, there is also "countermagic." This is the concept that doing something in reverse or saying something that was the exact opposite of what you really wished for might change bad luck to good luck. An example of counter-magic relates to saliva. When our ancestors first noted that saliva could change the nature of food in the mouth, they decided it had magical powers to "dissolve" almost anything, including bad luck. When I asked my rural consultant on wishful thinking about this salivary superstition, he had a ready explanation.

"Why do you think we spit so much?" he asked. "We don't spit because we chew tobacco, we chew tobacco so we can spit. Your spit is very powerful. It has your energy in it and can sort of digest any bad energy that might be floating around. Haven't you ever noticed how much more spitting baseball players do when the game is tight? You might say they're just showing signs of stress. I say that whether they know it or not, they're trying to dissolve any bad energy."

As a part of my wish research, I visited one of the wishful thinking centers of the world, Las Vegas, Nevada. I noticed gamblers at a craps table at a large Las Vegas hotel spitting on the dice. During a particularly big pot, saliva seemed to be flying everywhere. I noticed the well-known comedienne who was appearing on stage at the hotel. She was also a dice spitter and I asked her about it. She was awaiting her turn to role the dice, and without looking up from the game, she said, "Sure you spit on the dice. You cancel out any bad energy that way. Why do you think I call this place the 'expectoratorium'? It's the spitting capital of the world."

Feeble Minds or Sensitive Hearts?

A Nobel laureate crosses her fingers as she waits for the right chemical reaction to occur. The CEO of a Fortune 500 company knocks three times on the wood of the conference table after making a business prediction. A cynical teenager screams in horror when she drops and shatters her makeup mirror. A Tony Award–winning Broadway performer shudders when someone says "good luck" instead of "break a leg" just before his performance. A heart surgeon says "wish me luck" as she cuts open her patient's chest. I witnessed all of these events over the last several weeks.

When I asked each of these superstitious persons about their behavior, their responses seemed to reflect the essence of poet Carl Sandburg's quote at the beginning of this chapter. "I can't help myself," said one scientist. "Who knows? If it works, fine. If not, so what. It's free. It can't hurt."

Kings, queens, princes, Egyptian pharaohs, Greek politicians, dictators, heroes, philosophers, and Roman emperors were all wishful thinkers.[10] From the days of Mesopotamia forward, monarchs and leaders have relied heavily on superstition and the power of their own and others' wishful thinking. Winston Churchill was highly superstitious and regularly made wishes about his personal, political, and military life.[11] Napoleon Bonaparte believed firmly in superstition and in being exceedingly careful in what he wished for and worried about what others were wishing. John Blaine, secretary of state under three presidents, was a confirmed wishful thinker, as were Grover Cleveland, Ulysses Grant, Shakespeare, Lord Byron, Adolf Hitler, and Woodrow Wilson.[12] Einstein and many other brilliant scientists were also regular wishers whose greatest ideas about the connections between things and events just "came to them" while they were engaging in slow, gentle, patient wishful thinking.[13]

Attack on Wishful Thinking

The first formal attack on wishful thinking was launched by the London Thirteen Club. This was a group of doubting journalists and scientists in England in the 1880s. Wishing and other superstitious behaviors were becoming quite commonplace then. To rid society of this "mindless thinking," seventy-eight superstition skeptics met together for a dinner to "prove" just how silly wishful thinking and its related superstitions were. The group was sponsored by the major newspapers of the time. What took place resulted in public outrage.

Sitting thirteen to a table, the group met for dinner on Friday the thirteenth in January 1884. They were summoned to their tables by the loud smashing of a very large mirror, and the members paraded defiantly into the room, walking under a ladder. At the start of the meal, each member spilled salt on the table from a coffin-shaped shaker. Letters poured in from the readers of the *London Times*. They were outraged and worried. Superstitions, they wrote, should never be treated as a joke, and flouting of superstition was sure to bring misfortune. The meetings were eventually suspended due to a mutually agreed upon "lack of interest in the aims of the club."

In the United States, a similar wishful thinking debunkers club was formed on

Friday the thirteenth in 1946. The American Museum of Natural History in New York City held an exhibit of open umbrellas, a giant cake with thirteen candles, someone smashing mirror after mirror, and another person throwing rabbits' feet into trash cans. This display horrified many people and ultimately failed to have much effect on the extraordinary tenacity of the half-beliefs related to wishful thinking.

Many prominent people had been invited to join the London Thirteen Club, including writer Oscar Wilde. As most of those invited did, he declined. He said that he would have loved the company of the bright journalists but that he loved his superstitions more. He wrote, "Superstitions are the color element of thought and imagination. They are the opponents of common sense, which is the enemy of romance. . . . The aim of your society seems to be dreadful. Leave us some unreality. Don't make us too offensively sane." The role of wishful thinking and our superstitious ways is to prevent us from becoming too "offensively sane" and so cerebrally aloof that we can no longer be totally absorbed in living or trust our heart and its memories.

Old Ways for New Times

Superstition was defined by anthropologist Charles J. S. Thompson as the survival of old beliefs in the midst of a new order of things.[14] It's the superstitious thinking behind these old beliefs that can bring some of the old rituals into play to prevent the new order from dictating every moment of our life. The new order may be intensely stimulating, but it's our oldest beliefs that offer us the most established ways of maintaining some sense of the mystery of life.

Superstition is often defined as a useless but common habit stemming from a fear of the unknown.[15] Many psychologists say that superstitious behaviors and the wishful thinking that supports them may be symptoms rather than adaptive skills. They say wishful thinking is another name for fantasy. They see it as delusion and its superstitious behaviors as evidence of a morbid scrupulosity that reveals immaturity and even mental illness. I suggest, however, that superstition has persisted exactly because it is a way to keep our sanity. It's of value precisely because it is irrational, a way the mysterious can break through our brain's uncompromising defensiveness. Wishful thinking is not the way we should think about life, but it is one way. If we understand it, it augments rather than impairs rational thinking. Wishful thinking's open heart promotes a much more open and facile mind.

The Superstition Survey

Over the past ten years, I have administered my Superstition Survey around the world. I also gave it to our 2,166 wish-research subjects. Take the test yourself to see how you compare to others in terms of your wishful thinking tendency to be superstitious. Notice the memetic nature of the superstitions, their sympathetic and countermagic, and their reflection of our ancestors' docile "with-it-ness" in their connection with the forces of nature.

The Superstition Survey

For each item below, score yourself four points for every yes answer and zero for every no.

Have you ever said or thought to yourself:

1. _____ "It's a snap."

2. _____ "A little birdie told me."

3. _____ "What a lucky break" or "I got the short end of the stick."

4. _____ "Let's break bread together" or "Don't just throw me crumbs."

5. _____ "Things happen in threes."

6. _____ "A penny for your thoughts."

7. _____ "He or she got up on the wrong side of the bed."

8. _____ "This is getting us nowhere. We're just going around in circles."

9. _____ "Thumbs-up!"

10. _____ "Keep your fingers crossed."

11. _____ "It was love at first sight."

12. _____ "The family circle" or "the family tree."

13. _____ "Put your best foot forward" or "got off on the wrong foot."

14. _____ "The stork came."

15. _____ "It (or I) was turned down."

16. _____ "They tied the knot."

17. _____ "She or he is true blue."

18. _____ "She or he has a widow's peak."

19. _____ "I was double-crossed."

20. _____ "He or she just fell into it."

21. _____ "Seeing red."

22. _____ "Worth your salt."

23. _____ "Knock on wood."

24. _____ "That's nothing to sneeze at."

25. _____ "Swan song."

_____ Total Superstition Survey Score

Here's a summary of Superstition Survey scores of 2,166 men and women. The scores were collected from 1988 to 1998. As you have read, the group included highly successful owners of their own businesses who were usually the CEO, college professors, ministers, housewives, physicians, nurses, teachers, and various researchers and scientists. All were either patients in my clinic or had attended one of my lectures on wishing and taken the test during my presentation. All had at least four years of college education. There were more women tested because of my presentations to teachers' and nurses' professional organizations, which during the time of testing, still tended to be primarily composed of women. Where does your score fall compared to the wish-project group?

SCORE	MEN ($N = 996$)	WOMEN ($N = 1,170$)
88–100	527 (53%)	675 (58%)
68–84	208 (21%)	433 (37%)
48–64	102 (10%)	40 (3%)
28–44	81 (8%)	12 (approx.1%)
4–24	59 (6%)	8 (approx.1%)
0	19 (2%)	2 (less than 1%)

Eighty-four percent of the men tested and almost 98 percent of the women tested had used a majority of the superstitious phrases on the test. The 14 percentage-point difference in favor of women is consistent with my finding that women tend to be somewhat more prone to wishful thinking than men. This difference may be related to the fact that men are more prone to suffer from RMS (Right Man Syndrome) and many women tend to be more comfortable thinking with their heart and not just their head. No matter your gender, if you are like most people in terms of your wishful thinking, you probably scored high on the Superstition Survey.

To illustrate the long and stable history from which the comments on the test were derived and the ancient wisdom and wishful thinking behind the superstitious statements, here is the background of each comment. Note the diversity of times and cultural myths that found their way into the Western thinking and superstitions that persist today.

1. "It's a snap."

OLD WISHFUL THINKING: Our ancient ancestors would snap a stick to scare away evil spirits and bring good luck. Snapping and breaking sounds were mythologically supposed to ward off bad luck (another meaning for "lucky break"). The sound of snapping and breaking may have frightened off some predators.

MODERN APPLICATION: Snapping of the fingers is still a habit that many think brings good luck. Some persons crack their knuckles. Perhaps snapping the fingers is a "meme" or remnant of an ancient ritual that surfaces when, know it or not, we are looking for a little help from L energy.

2. "A little birdie told me."

OLD WISHFUL THINKING: In answer to "how did you find out?" the reply is often "a little birdie told me." This stems from the early observation that birds seemed to have a uniquely coded speech of their own and could bring information from mysterious sources. Both the Old Testament and Koran contain verses that indicate that birds were able to talk and give messages. Birds are natural ventriloquists. They seem to be able to "throw" their songs several feet from the listener. In ancient times, some shamans and healers would master this difficult trick and use it to mystify others and establish their credentials of divinity. This led to the idea that wise men could speak to and understand the language of birds. When they said, "a little bird told me," people thought they were dealing with subtle L energy and were impressed and readily believed them.

MODERN APPLICATION: We often sense things without actually seeing or hearing them. Saying "a little bird told me" may be a convenient, culturally tested way of explaining such a complex and mystical occurrence. The words also gently and humorously help protect promised confidentiality.

3. "Lucky break."

OLD WISHFUL THINKING: Circus people often referred to a good break in the weather at their next town as good for business, a "lucky break." Poor weather was a "bad break." More traditionally, two persons made a wish and then pulled the ends of a wishbone. The one for whom the wishbone broke "luckily" was rewarded with the larger piece and was more likely to have the wish come true. The clavicle or "wishbone" of the bird symbolically represented the "crotch" of the human body and the repository of life, thus possessing a magical energy containing answers to life's mysteries and able to "give birth" or life energy to a wish.

As early as 322 B.C., the Etruscans had a "hen oracle," the medium through which a special god could reveal hidden knowledge. Hens were killed and their collarbones were put in the sun to dry. A person seeking an answer for some life problem or decision wished on the bone, thus the name "wishbone." When two persons wished and snapped the hen's wishbone, the person with the larger piece got the "lucky break."

MODERN APPLICATION: Anyone who has engaged in the ritual of the wishbone with another person knows that gentle, patient tugging and allowing the other person to do the vigorous pulling usually results in getting "the lucky break." Connecting with the traditions of the past, particularly at holidays such as Thanksgiving with the turkey bone, combined with being gentle and patient and joining with another person in a wishing ceremony, can provide families with the comfort and assurance of tradition.

4. "Let's break bread together."

OLD WISHFUL THINKING: Bread has long been known as the "staff of life." A metaphorical mixture of water and grain merged by the catalyst of the soil of Mother Earth and the powerful sun, bread was a sacred gift. Wasting crumbs was considered unlucky and potentially harmful. Kings wore crowns of gold that seemed to crackle in the sun and give off sparks when the sun reflected off them, giving the monarch the appearance of having golden curly hair. Since the royalty were rich and could eat all the bread they wanted, curly hair also became associated with eating bread, particularly the crust. "Breaking bread" together was seen as a sacred act of respect and friendship, and later bread become part of the communion ceremony. In Greece, breaking cake over the bride's head was seen as lucky. Guests would gather the pieces from the floor and take them home, a precursor of taking home pieces of the wedding cake. The bride and groom cutting the wedding cake together is still one of their first mutual wishes.

MODERN APPLICATION: In our hyperculture, we too seldom take time to fully enjoy our meals together. Connecting with our ancient heritage of respect for the gifts of nature by reverently sharing our meals and ritualistically celebrating the meaning and source of the "staff of life" can be physically as well as emotionally and spiritually healthy.

5. "Things happen in threes."

OLD WISHFUL THINKING: Three has been a sacred number for centuries. Primitive man was fascinated and puzzled by the miracle of birth. Since birth required three people, the father, mother, and child, the number three came to signify life itself. Early man noted such trinities as body/mind/spirit, earth/sea/sky, and animal/vegetable/mineral. "Three" thinking is seen in Jonah's three days in the whale and Daniel's meeting with three lions. Macbeth's three witches also reflect this strong belief in triads.

MODERN APPLICATION: Our society has come to believe in "pure randomness" and that "stuff happens." Looking for and talking together about patterns and systemic nuances in life can serve as a means of comfort and connection. Of course, things also happen in fours and sixes, but just taking the time to talk and reflect about patterning and the history and future of events can promote a starting point for finding meaning in chaos. Superstitions or wishful thinking are safe so long as we remember Shakespeare's warning, "There is nothing either good or bad but thinking makes it so."

6. "A penny for your thoughts."

OLD WISHFUL THINKING: Since their existence, coins have been symbols of superstition. The silver dollar was seen as a symbol of the moon, which controls tides and therefore is supposed to be able to influence growth and prosperity. Placing a penny inside a new wallet is supposed to prevent poverty to the recipient, and finding a penny means luck will follow. If the bridegroom gives his bride a coin and she wears it in her shoe at the wedding, the marriage will be happy. Tossing a coin has a long history. "Heads you win, tails you lose" is the usual phrase. This is derived from the times of Julius Caesar when Caesar's head on one side was always the "right side."

MODERN APPLICATION: "A penny for your thoughts" seems a much nicer way of asking, "What are you thinking?" or "What's on your mind?" Again, the whimsy of superstition paves the way for social discourse about very personal things.

7. "He or she got up on the wrong side of the bed."

OLD WISHFUL THINKING: It has long been believed that the right side is the "good" side and the left the evil side. Climbing out of bed on the left side was seen to mean a bad day ahead. Hotel bedrooms were originally planned with this in mind and beds placed so that the visitor could not get up on the left side and become an ornery guest causing problems for management.

MODERN APPLICATION: Focusing attention on how one begins the day and starting off in the right state of mind can be a good way to begin our time-driven day. Telling someone they seem to have gotten up on the wrong side of the bed seems less confrontational than telling them they have a lousy attitude.

8. "This is getting us nowhere. We're just going in circles."

OLD WISHFUL THINKING: The circling sun has always played a key role in wishful thinking. The sun was an important part of the ancient divination system called "Gyromancy," the practice of a person moving around and around in circles until falling from dizziness. From the point of the fall, the gyromancer made prognostications. To protect their eyes, the first wishers wishing on the sun closed their eyes. A "meme" or cultural imprint of that eye-closing still accompanies how most of us make our wishes today.

Because of what they thought was the circling of the sun around the earth, circling of all kinds became important signs for our ancestors. A circle or ring about the finger is still a symbol of lasting love. Egyptian women rouged their lips not just for beauty but to emphasize the red circle formed by the mouth. Some anthropologists suggest that the mouth became an advertisement of the state of the vagina and that making the lips look fuller and flushed with blood was a way of signaling sexual readiness in the sexual circle formed by the labia. Since the mouth was believed to be the door of the body, circles there were supposed to keep the spirit or soul from exiting and bad spirits from entering. Going around in circles also reflects the innate circularity of life. Blindfolded persons tend to move their body in circles, and lost persons tend to wander and circle back to their starting point even though they are sure they were walking in a straight line. Something about L energy draws us around even when our brain tries to keep driving us straight ahead.

MODERN APPLICATION: Our hectic life often seems to lack rhythmicity. Sensing and reporting to someone else that we feel lost and helpless by saying we feel that we are going around in circles with them is less threatening than blaming someone for our confusion.

9. "Thumbs-up!"

OLD WISHFUL THINKING: The "rule of thumb" has been important since the days of Julius Caesar. Thumbs-up from Caesar meant a gladiator lived. In an ugly part of our own American history, the legal "rule of thumb" for determining if a man had "illegally" beat his wife was whether or not the weapon he used was thicker than his thumb. The position of thumbs at two important times in life have also played a role in our superstitious thinking about our thumbs. Babies usually are born with thumbs folded down in their hands. Each day, the finger of each hand releases the thumbs, hence "thumbs-up!" became a sign of life. When a person dies, his thumbs relax and seem to turn into the palms of the hands. So, to the Romans, thumbs-down meant death.

MODERN APPLICATION: Most families have their own version of a positive wish sign. Our modern world still has dozens of such gestures in the form of cultural "memes." There are vulgar gestures and gestures to convey hope. We often express our wishes for someone with our fingers. The middle finger may be raised in anger, but when it is joined by the index finger in a "V" shape (a meme from the end of World War I), the desire for peace rather than an aggressive sexually oriented threat is conveyed. When we give a thumbs-up, we are quickly showing faster than any words could express that everything is fine.

10. "Keep your fingers crossed."

OLD WISHFUL THINKING: Crossed fingers represented both the sympathetic and countermagic of wishful thinking. The gesture grew out of the belief that the cross was the symbol of perfect unity. A wish was supposed to be held safely tied in where two straight lines (or fingers) crossed and met. Uncross the fingers or untie the knot and the wish is set free.

MODERN APPLICATION: Without words, we can express a well wish to a complete stranger or a wicked wish to an enemy. Letting our fingers do the talking is a long-practiced means of social discourse and a rapid way of conveying a sense of faith and hope. Just by holding up crossed fingers, we can let someone know we are wishing very hard.

11. "It was love at first sight."

OLD WISHFUL THINKING: The Greeks assumed that originally every man and woman were one. A mysterious force severed this oneness into two beings challenged forever to seek their "better half" to be reunited in loving harmony. Love at first sight is the experience of suddenly discovering our other or "better" missing half and feeling complete and fulfilled.

MODERN APPLICATION: Although modern science suggests that love at first sight results from a brief psychochemical spurt causing lovesickness and blindness, the idea of considering love as a rebalancing through the reuniting of two spiritual halves can help promote a lasting and enduring love.

12. "The family circle" or "the family tree."

OLD WISHFUL THINKING: The family circle derived from the circularity of life valued by our ancestors and the ancient sun worshipers who saw the sun's apparent circling as a template for living. The sun kept the home fires burning by providing the loving energy that fueled the family's growth. The family tree refers to the ancient reverence for wood. Wood comes from trees and trees were thought to be the bodies of gods. Trees grew tall and strong and with deep roots, another symbol of hardy family life.

MODERN APPLICATION: The idea that the family is sacredly united, strong, and constantly growing is a healthy model for modern family living. In our modern world, too many families are uprooted before they have the chance to grow together. The symbol of an unbroken, consistent family circle remains a desirable model in today's society.

13. "Put your best foot forward."

OLD WISHFUL THINKING: The right side of the body has traditionally been seen as "the best side." Putting the best foot forward meant always stepping first with that foot. The Romans placed a guard at the entrance of public places to make sure people entered correctly, right foot first. "Come right on in" is another meme implying welcome and a wish for a pleasant visit.

MODERN APPLICATION: Attending to starting off right and cautiously by "watching our first step" can be a helpful orientation to daily life. Most indigenous cultures have long-established protocol for entering another person's home. Our modern-day "dropping by" and "stopping by" is not acceptable to them. Chanting to convey well wishes was the first "right step." Perhaps if we did more than just ring the doorbell and instead put more effort into the simple social graces when we visit, we would feel more connected and calm in our daily life.

14. "The stork came."

OLD WISHFUL THINKING: In A.D. 185, the philosopher Euphues wrote, "Constance is like unto the stork, who wheresoever she fly cometh in no nest but her own." Telling children that the stork brought the new baby related to the idea perpetuated in Hans Christian Anderson's fairy tales. Storks live to be seventy years old and nest in the same chimney year after year. They bond as two for life and, once losing their mate, never pair again. Thus, storks came to represent fertility and lasting love. Confucius recommended the stork's conduct as the perfect example of how to love forever.

MODERN APPLICATION: Uncomfortable parents at a loss to explain birth to their inquisitive children can still use the stork story. If they incorporate the real biological facts of life with the stork's committed loving and fidelity, the lessons their children learn from the arrival of a sibling can serve them well. If our teenagers behaved a little more like storks than rabbits, the tragedy of their out-of-wedlock pregnancy rate could be reduced.

15. "I was turned down."

OLD WISHFUL THINKING: As an example of the countermagic of wishful thinking, turning a photograph upside down was supposed to cause evil spirits to pour into the person in that picture. In colonial days, a suitor too bashful to propose would place a courting mirror face upward on a table near his lady. He would look into it before giving it to her so his likeness would remain in the glass. If his lover accepted him, she would leave the mirror upward. If not, she turned it down and the suitor was rejected.

MODERN APPLICATION: In a time when computer images dominate our existence, the idea of giving a mirror wishfully containing the image of another person as an act of love sounds strange indeed. However, the idea of having one's image "turned down" has more appeal than personally being "dumped."

16. "They tied the knot."

OLD WISHFUL THINKING: As you read earlier, wishes were thought to be contained in the knot at the junction of two crossing lines. Wedding ceremonies often involved the tying of ribbons. The characterization of the wedding ceremony as "tying the knot" refers to an ancient Babylonian custom in which a thread was taken from the clothing of both the bride and bridegroom and tied together to symbolize the union.

MODERN APPLICATION: As you will read in Chapter 15, conceiving of marriage as a commitment to join together to share common wishes and as a permanent knot in which two spirits are entwined is in keeping with chances for a lasting love. One of our wish research participants who had been divorced four times said, "I don't think I've ever tied the knot tightly enough. It came loose before I knew it. My vow was only for now."

17. "He or she is true blue."

OLD WISHFUL THINKING: The little blue flower called the bachelor button was seen by Asians to foretell a happy marriage. It was to be picked early in the morning and not looked at for twenty-four hours. If it remained fresh and "true blue," it meant that the young man had found the right wife. If it was withered and discolored, as it often was after an evening in a man's pocket, the man had the wrong woman. "True blue" has come to mean a faithful friend.

MODERN APPLICATION: Reading signs in nature, reflecting on their symbolism for lasting love, and taking time to reflect on romantic decisions based on natural time rather than hormonal passions can serve a useful purpose in solidifying intimate relationships.

18. "She or he has a widow's peak."

OLD WISHFUL THINKING: The ancient idea that a woman born with a V-shaped hairline will be a young widow has been around for centuries. Wearing black for mourning was traditional until it was discarded at the time of the emperors of China. White is still the customary mourning color for Chinese people. When Anne of Brittany wore black again at the death of her husband Charles VIII, she was apparently so attractive that Louis XII could not resist her and made her his wife. For the second time, she became the queen of France. Costume designers of the sixteenth century immediately returned to black mourning creations and created a modified V-shaped "widow's peak" like Anne's. They made a black and white bonnet to frame the face of mourning widows. The "widow's peak" derives from the front of the mourner's bonnet.

MODERN APPLICATION: Wishful thinking related to the mysteries of death is common. The myth of the widow's peak can convey the concept that "life and love goes on." An example of this is the story of the widow crying at her husband's gravestone. The minister approached her as she weeped, "Father, I had engraved on my dear husband's tombstone the words 'my light has gone out.' Now I've fallen in love again. What shall I do?" The clergyman winked and said, "Just have another phrase chiseled in that says 'I've struck another match.' "

19. "I was double-crossed."

OLD WISHFUL THINKING: The cross is unparalleled in its role in wishful thinking. It existed as a cultural symbol long before Christianity and has been found among the ruins of the oldest races that inhabited the earth. Since a wish was believed to be held at the point where two lines cross, "double-crossing" or undoing the cross is countermagic to release the wish or not live up to a promise.

MODERN APPLICATION: Knowing that the image of the cross transcends any one religion and that almost all religious symbols contain crossing symbolism helps us understand the universality of our shared faith in "something more." Crossed lines in the Star of David hold the same meaning.

20. "He or she just fell into it."

OLD WISHFUL THINKING: Stumbling at the beginning of the day has long been seen as a bad omen. (The farmer I interviewed about the hay wishes discussed this superstition.) Countermagic requires circling three times after the fall to cancel out the bad luck and give a person a fresh beginning. Tripping into one's own home, however, was seen as very good luck, thus the statement "He fell into it."

MODERN APPLICATION: The idea of being able to "do over" and have new beginnings can provide optimism and hope even when it seems we have gotten off to a terrible start. The idea that coming home offers safety and healing after a difficult day that has "brought us to our knees" can also add a sense of comfort.

21. "Seeing red."

OLD WISHFUL THINKING: Bullfighting is an ancient sport with foundations in early Greece and Rome and Latin America. The idea that the color red enraged the sacred bull persists today, even though all animals except man and monkey see only shades of gray. Our own nervous system, however, reacts quickly to the color red. The occipital lobe of the brain is highly activated by red, thus the expression "seeing red" refers to becoming agitated and angry.

MODERN APPLICATION: Researchers now know that anger has the potential to destroy our health. Knowing what makes us angry can help us stay healthy and avoid overreaction. Being aware that the anger and aggression of "seeing red" is a major health risk and being sensitive to those acts and people who seem to make you "see red" is a sound anger management technique. When we think we are "seeing red," we are well advised to consider it not as a yellow caution light but as a red stoplight.

22. "Worth your salt."

OLD WISHFUL THINKING: When we spill salt, we often throw some over our left shoulder to wish evil away. When our very distant ancestors lived in the sea, their bodies were adapted to their salty environment. Although we've been terrestrial for millions of years, we still need a constant replenishing of salt to maintain physiological balance in our body. We also need it to maintain the proper amount of water in our system. We need it to keep up the electrical potential that surges across our cell membranes, especially the cells in our heart that help keep its rhythm syncronized. When we spill salt, our heart may sense at least a minor threat to its salt supply.

Because salt can thaw snow but also freeze ice cream, its dual nature always impressed our ancestors. They saw animals licking it, assumed that it must have a special quality, and developed a taste for it. Because it seemed to have preservation qualities, ancients thought it also had human protective and preservation powers. Spilled salt meant that a guardian spirit was tipping off the spiller about pending disaster. Since good spirits lived around the right side of the body and the evil ones on the left, our ancestors threw salt over their left shoulder to bribe the evil spirits away. Since salt was also rare and precious, it was often used as a gift for a person's new home. Its scarcity resulted in it being used to pay Roman soldiers a "salarium," which derived from the word "salt." From this, we get the word "salary" and the idea of being worthy of reward and "worth our salt."

MODERN APPLICATION: We are the only animal that cries and sweats salt. Remembering that fact helps connect us with nature and question whether we are worthy of reward and worth our salt.

23. "Knock on wood."

OLD WISHFUL THINKING: As pointed out earlier, wood has always been seen as sacred. Its grain is a natural historical record and reflects the stresses and strains of life. Knocking on wood when we boast is sympathetic magical thinking in the hopes that "like produces like." Knocking on wood can also be a form of countermagic because the noise is supposed to distract any spirits resentful of our arrogant certainty and disrespect of their power. Ancients believed that any unseen spiritual being or forces would not serve as killjoys when they heard our expression of good news if we drowned out the bragging with the distracting noise of knocking on wood.

MODERN APPLICATION: Knocking on wood is one of our longest-lasting behaviors that has been motivated by wishful thinking. The proverb "He that talks much of happiness, summons grief" reflects our archetypal idea that our words have an invisible energetic power. Modern psychology has shown that no emotional state lasts, so being aware of the blessing of our good fortune without flaunting it is a good idea even today.

24. "That's nothing to sneeze at."

OLD WISHFUL THINKING: Saying "Gesundheit" or, in Italian, "Felicita" when someone sneezes is a common practice. Even Popes respect its meaning. In the Near and Far East, clasping of the hands and bowing toward the sneezer is still common. Since the ancients believed that the breath was sacred and resided in one's head, a sneeze might accidentally expel the spirit. This mythological wishful thinking imprint is one reason we still cover our mouth and excuse ourselves when we sneeze or yawn. Our spirit might be getting out for the whole world to see. Countermagic involved blowing the spirit of the sneezer back at him. So serious was the danger the sneezer's spirit might enter someone else's body that persons in the Middle Ages said certain situations were "nothing to be sneezed at."

MODERN APPLICATION: Awareness of our interdependence when it comes to health and well-being is conveyed by the ancient lesson of respect for the "ha" or breath of life we all share. Using a phrase such as "nothing to sneeze at" gently conveys the importance of an issue.

25. "Swan song."

OLD WISHFUL THINKING: "Swans a little before their death sing sweetly" wrote Pliny the Elder about A.D. 77. The Greek legend told of the soul of the god of music, Apollo, passing into a swan. It was thought that swans sang beautifully at their death because their aviary sixth sense told them that Apollo had wonderful things in store for them. The last work of a poet or musician today is still referred to as her swan song.

MODERN APPLICATION: Swans are hardly talented, mellow singers. Their loud sharp trumpeting sound can be heard almost two miles away. Some researchers report, however, that some dying swans do in fact produce sounds far different from their usual song, giving rise to them seeming to sing their best song just as they die. Since swans have anything but melodious, pleasing voices most of the time, the lesson is clear. It is indeed unfortunate to die without having sung one's best song or having never sung at all. Don't wait. Sing out now.

If you think the lessons contained in these sample superstitions still have something to teach you about coping and finding meaning in your life, that the humble regard for the magic of nature they reflect is a wise way to lead your life, that life is enchanted, and that sympathetic and countermagic have some relevance to today's world, you will find wishful thinking a welcome addition to your intelligences.

·············· ❧ ··············

Eight

Taking a Leap
of Faith

The modern mind is selectively skeptical. We have no problem believing the entire universe came out of a pinpoint, but if told 5,000 brunches once came out of a basket, we confidently exclaim, "That's impossible!"

—EDMUND ROSE JAMES, *ABIDE FOR ME MANY DAYS*

Willing to Be Weird

This chapter teaches you the steps in making a wise wish. To begin to wish well, you not only have to be willing to allow yourself to become fully absorbed in life and open to wishful thinking. You also have to be willing to be just a little weird, or at least to tolerate people less absorbed in life seeing you that way. You have to be willing to take "a leap of faith" in what your brain refuses to accept as possible. You have to be willing to trust in what your heart tells you about those aspects of life that go beyond the five-sense world. Like some of our greatest wishers, such as Darwin, Einstein, Copernicus, Galileo, and Sir Isaac Newton, you have to be willing to look at the world differently from the way your and other brains say you must. As these men did, you have to dive into what many consider to be impossible and even ridiculous.

Wishing well requires that you take the plunge and trust in the power of wishing. Some of our world's greatest minds were seen by doubters as taking too large a leap of faith or foolishly acting on their faith. At one time or another, they were willing to be seen as wishful thinkers out of touch with the only reality that really counts. To wish well, you have to act on your faith in wishing and regularly make wishes even before you are completely sure they work; you have to become what one of our wish-project members called a "romantic researcher." Like any good researcher, however, you will have to be courageous and patient and keep conducting your wishing experiments even when they seem to fail and others may mock or even criticize you. Galileo almost leaped to his death when his beliefs about the heavens caused the Catholic Church to consider him a heretic. In 1998, hundreds of years after his death, the Vatican formally and somewhat circuitously apologized for its persecution of Galileo's leap of faith. It can take a long time for the impossible to be seen as possible, so the slow and hopeful process of wishful thinking is essential in wishing well.

One of the most influential nineteenth-century thinkers regarding faith in the invisible was Søren Kierkegaard.[1] He originated the phrase "leap of faith." He wrote that one would have to be "quite literally a lunatic" to embrace any kind of belief in supernatural process. He assumed that constant doubt was the only intelligent way to think about life. He thought that only after many different levels, kinds, and degrees of terrible anxiety, dread, and anguish driven by incessant cynicism could one suddenly "leap" from doubt to faith. Even then, he wrote, the only advantage of taking such a leap was to ease the pain of sinking more deeply into wretchedness.

Wishing well takes the opposite approach. It suggests that we take the leap now and not wait for all the evidence to be in about the validity of what our sixth sense keeps telling us. It suggests that if wishing works, we shouldn't delay in benefiting from the miracles it can help create. We should go ahead and allow ourselves to feel the enchantment around us, live in accordance with it, and boldly relish it. Even if it turns out that wishing really doesn't work to the degree I assert that it does, the very least benefit you will gain by trying it is to have fun and enhance your physical health at the same time.

Would You Wish upon a Car?

You're more likely to wish on a star than a car. You might wish for a car but not likely on one. The modern mechanical marvels our brain has created for us make life more livable. Making life wonderful is more related to connecting with God-made rather than man-made things. A key step in wishing well is to be on the watch for nature's invitations to make a wish. For example, birthdays are often days where we are even expected to indulge ourselves in a little enchantment and be forgiven for some foolishness. They are times offered to us when we are allowed to take a little time away from daily hassles and are excused for being a little lazy and wistful. We are expected to make a birthday wish or two and be more alert to what really matters in life. The number of candles on our cake reminds us to make our wishes wisely while we can. Birthdays are days when silliness and whimsy, both key characteristics of a well wisher, are tolerated. We may receive funny birthday cards, surprise parties, and joke gifts. The "happy birthday" wish may be made by persons with whom you seldom speak. It is the one day of the year when you are likely to be spontaneously sung to by a group of strangers and the day that you feel in your heart that all the time we ever really have is now. It's the one day a year that almost everyone becomes a wisher and displays many of the traits of a wisher.

Events like birthdays, Thanksgiving, and Christmas seem to bring natural times for wish making. There is something natural, comforting, and fun about celebrating the cyclicity of time with those we love. Such days draw our attention to the brevity of our physical existence and the value of "something more." Perhaps so many well wishes have been made before at these special times that these days seem to have been "conditioned" to be perfect times to wish by those who came before us and left their wish imprint on these special times. They may have imbued such times with the subtle energy of wishing. It is at just such times that we seem to sense that the ecology is right for going beyond the seeing and touching world.

Nature's Five Wish Rousers

The well wisher's characteristics of being alert to opportunities to connect with the subtle energy of nature can be developed by trying to be more a part of than an observer of nature. Nature is constantly resonating invitations for us to join with her and to wish for and with her. Wishing well is realizing that because you yourself are one of nature's wishes come true, you are forever one with her. Practicing wishcraft requires being vigilant for signs from nature that indicate her willingness to offer us some comfort and sense of oneness with her. One of Buddha's "First Noble Truths" is that "life is suffering."[2] Even though we all must suffer, nature keeps sending us signs that we don't have to be miserable and alone. She made us as a manifestation of her imagination and created within us a way to be a creative part of her evolving system. She gave us awareness of our consciousness so we could use it to focus our intentions to be active participants in her infinite creation. To the experienced wishcrafter's watchful eye, there can be many signs from nature that invite us to make a wish.

Mystical Waters

Water has always invoked magical images. Essential for life, it is the only substance that is lighter when it is in its solid form. It's able to go from liquid to solid to gas and back again. This magical quality of water was duly noted by our ancestors and they engaged it in their wishful thinking's sympathetic magic of "like brings like."

Water is still an important wish elicitor today. Couples often honeymoon at Niagara Falls. They typically come with the sense of enchantment, sense of new adventure, whimsy, and open heart that makes them vigilant for any chance to make a wish. For more than a century, loving couples have tossed pennies into what is called the Bridal Veil Falls on the American side and the Horseshoe Falls on the Canadian side. They often join hands and hold the penny together. They close their eyes, make a wish, and throw the penny into the falls. When I saw a couple doing this, I asked them why. "It brings you good fortune for your whole married life," said the wife. "It makes your marriage lucky," said the groom. Local authorities at Niagara Falls report that the custom of throwing pennies is so common that they collect in heaps below and behind the flowing veil of the falls.

Water wells have been used as wishing places for centuries. Water drawn directly from the earth seems to be a better wish promoter than tossing a penny into your kitchen sink or bathtub. As if drawn there by some invisible hydrogravity, guests often cluster by the dozens around the tiniest swimming pool at a hotel or resort. We may be drawn there by the sympathetic magic of our 98 percent water-composed body seeking its kind.

By the Light of the Moon

Historically, wishing wells have also been places used to look into the future to see if a wish will come true. A girl hoping to marry would throw a coin into a well and wish to see the face of her future husband reflected in the water. So she could see her lover's face clearly, this was generally done under a full moon. The moon has always been another of nature's key wish solicitors.

Wishing by the light of the silvery moon was thought to be a lover's delight.

Being "moonstruck" refers to being a little goofy or awed, both states very conducive to the silliness (blessedness) of wishing. Singer Dean Martin's definition of love was associated with the moon hitting us in the eye "like a big pizza pie" to cause "amore" or love. Ask any emergency room nurse or doctor or any police officer about the power of a full moon. You will likely hear some very unusual stories. Taking advantage of a "blue moon," the cyclical occurrence of a second full moon in one month, is also a wishcrafter's delight.

Starry-Eyed

As popular as water and the moon have been for wishers across the ages, wishing on a star may have the longest wish history of all. As you read in Chapter 5, "falling" or shooting stars have always been associated with wishing. Shakespeare wrote, "Whenever a mortal falls in sin, tears fall from angel's eyes. And at these time there fall Bright stars from out the skies."

To some, falling or shooting stars still mean sadness or even death. Countermagic is needed in a wish to reverse the sign of doom. For most people, including the persons in my wish-research sample, shooting stars seem to spontaneously (mimetically) elicit sympathetic magical wishing. As an example of a countermagic wish on a star, one of my research subjects said, "If you see a falling star, repeat the word money. Say money, money, money. You have to cancel out the bad luck." An example of a sympathetic magic wish (and a power wish) was provided by another respondent: "If you're lucky enough to see a falling star, take the hand of someone you love and make a wish. Then you know it will come true."

Warm Love

Nature's fourth wishing solicitor has always been fire. Making a wish while blowing out the "fire" or candle flames on a birthday cake has been a family tradition for centuries. It stems from the idea that life is associated with warmth and from the Greek concept that a candle represented life. Each candle represents one year "burned." By blowing out every candle in one breath (the breath representing the spirit), you extinguish any past bad luck and set the stage for good luck in the year to come. Telling your wish means it is less likely to come true.

A "warm heart" and "being on fire with passion" are examples of our association of fire with our emotional state. One of my wish-research subjects gave an example of her association with fire. "I can still remember it. We used to sit around the campfire and tell story after story. There was something about the warmth of that fire that made us get very spiritual. We would tell ghost stories and often make a wish and throw something into the fire. We would even look into the fire for some sign that our wish would come true. Sometimes we would see a face in the flames. We could see all kinds of images."

The Exuvial Wish

A fifth of nature's wishing temptations is the exuvial wish. Anything shed from the body of man or animal was seen as containing the energy of that being. Using the sympathetic magic of "like brings like," making a wish on something associated with a lucky being means your wish is likely to come true.

When I asked my wish-research group about exuvial wishing, they were not sure what I meant. When I explained that it had to do with wishing on something that was once a living part of another being but no longer necessary to that creature, they understood. One woman said, "Oh, that's the eyelash wish. If you take the eyelash from someone you think is very lucky or nice, you place it on the back of your left hand, close your eyes, and make a wish. Then you hit the back of your left hand with your right. If you open your eyes and the eyelash is gone, it has been sent to make your wish come true. You have three chances. If after the third swat the eyelash is still on the left hand, the wish will not come true."

The five wish rousers just described are only a few of the hundreds of natural objects and events that elicit our wishing reflex. They are a small part of the cosmic menu available to those enchanted, willing, alert, whimsical, and loving enough to read them. Even the simple accident of two persons saying the same thing at the same time can lead to the spontaneous ritualistic sharing of a wish. One of my research group members described a spontaneous opportunity for a power wish when she explained, "When you say something at exactly the same time someone else does, you join little fingers with that person and make a wish."

Wishers Come True

Another step in making wise wishes is to wish with the knowledge that what often seems to come true is the "motive" of the wisher as much as the object or purpose of the wish itself. A person who wishes well tends to be "with it" when it comes to knowing how her motivational and emotional state influences others and how it affects her own destiny. Wishing seems to attract what the wisher's soul secretly harbors and not what the wisher says.

Based on what our wish-research subjects told us, it is wise to be extremely careful not only in "what" you wish for but also in how you "are" when you make your wish. Sympathetic magic applies to the wisher as well as to the wish. What you get depends as much on how and who you are as what you wish for. If you are impatient and wish for more time, you will likely receive more time with which to feel even more restless. If you are isolated and defensive and wish to feel more connected, you will likely end up surrounded by isolated and defensive people. If you are angry with your situation in life and wish for a lover to help decrease your anger, you might end up with an angry lover matched to your wishing state. If you are arrogant and selfish and wish for more acknowledgment and credit, you could receive more acknowledgment of your arrogant selfishness. If you are combative and harsh and wish for more of "what you deserve," you may end up living a life of constant hostility and confrontation. The lesson for wishing well is to pay as much attention to what's already in your heart as you do to the wishes you make on its behalf.

Nature's Immune System

Being willing to take your leap of faith and being enchanted with and alert to nature's invitations will help you wish well only if you make your wishes with full recognition that nature has her own wishes. Nature seems to have a system—like our own human immune system—that recoils and defends against changes. Nature's immune system tries to quickly reestablish its original way of being. That is why it's important to gently swing a wish outward rather than push it upon nature's energetic system. To wish well, think of your wish as a mild antigen, agitation, or gentle challenge to nature's system.

Mild anomalies such as altering nature's energy by wishing can elude nature's immune system or at least work in harmony with it. Wishing well allows the small miracles that can come with wishing to work their magic without making nature sick. Aggressive, demanding, hard-wishing effort and ill-willed wishes antagonize nature's immune system and act as spiritual antigens. Such selfish processes can lead to dark wish star wishing because they result in a severe metaphysical "allergic" reaction through which we become an infecting agent that is aggressively rejected by nature's built-in immunity.

When we try too hard to tell nature what to do, nature's immune system reacts against the intrusion. It vigorously defends against such spiritual tampering and may view our pushy and selfish efforts as vivid anomalies that it easily identifies as an antigen or challenge to its system. Much as our own immune system attacks a bacterium, it immediately begins to try to rid itself of the intruder. Like our own immune system, nature's defense system remembers the invasion and strengthens its resistance against similar attacks. In effect, nature can develop an immunity against us.

There is already some evidence that our reckless wishing is causing nature's immune system to kick in. Disease, famine, and climatic disasters may be immunoresponses against our brain's arrogant attempt to impose our will on nature's way. In effect, nature may be developing a resistance against wicked wishers. If we are not more careful in our wishing to stay within the realms of the bright wish star, we could end up the victims of the sixth in a series of catastrophic extinctions that nature's immunity may have already caused.[3]

Nails and Kingdoms

The best template for understanding how to make a heartfelt wish can be found in the words of the following reminder from folklore:

> *For want of a nail, the shoe was lost;*
> *For want of a shoe, the horse was lost;*
> *For want of a horse, the rider was lost;*
> *For want of a rider, the battle was lost;*
> *For want of a battle, the kingdom was lost!*

In the context of this ditty, a wish is the nail. When we wish, we ever so slightly set in motion forces that can eventually drastically alter the way things are and will be. The heart's gentle wishes are well suited to the subtle energy of the universe, so skilled wishcraft requires heartfelt wishing.

There is another "hard" science that illustrates the sympathetic resonation principle behind the power of a gentle wish made from the heart. It derives from the science called chaos theory.[4] This complex mathematical science seeks to explain the way order and patterns form amidst the constant turmoil of natural forces. It is the study of how even the most infinitesimal event can result in major natural changes. One key premise of this new science that relates to wishing is referred to as "the butterfly effect."[5] Meteorologist and mathematician Edward Lorenz showed that the minuscule amount of wind change generated by the flap of a butterfly's wings in Brazil could set off a tornado in Texas. Making a wish can have the same effect because it is our way of intentionally causing a tiny perturbation in the way things are that, sometime and somewhere, can turn out to have major consequences.

Lorenz's "Butterfly Effect" was eventually given the technical name "sensitive dependence on initial conditions." When we make a wish, we are establishing an "initial condition." Chaos theory helped us finally have one way to explain what our ancestors observed about their world. They knew that one little wish could create major events. That's why they tried to wish their way into and through the chaos.

Wishing Our Way through the Chaos

Lorenz and other scientists studied the fascinating idea that within puzzling chaos rests mysterious order. This offers another source for understanding how wishing might help contribute to the order of our life. First, we must realize that wishing is nothing with which to trifle. If chaos theory is correct, a peasant's wish can bring down a dictator, one nail can topple a kingdom, and one butterfly can cause a hurricane. Even when we make a wish for a nice day, we must remember that we are not only influencing the wishee's day, we are giving the cosmos a little tweak that could have universe-sized consequences.[6] Wishing was our ancestors' way, and if we choose, it can be our way of getting involved in the eerie order that rests just beneath the chaos.

As much as science and religion may assert their respective ideas of a "perfect order," they are unlikely to find it. There will always be nature's ultimate trickster in the form of the "chaos" factor waiting to challenge our view of perfection. As much as science points to pure randomness and disorder, splendid patterns will pop up seemingly out of nowhere to surprise it and mess up their statistical certainty. Scientists of chaos theory have shown that there is a wonderfully fascinating rhythm and vibratory nature to everything from coastlines to snowflakes to heartbeats. There seems to be a constant resonation and vibration to which we may be able to contribute our own personal butterfly effect simply by making a wish.

How to Make a Wise Wish

Integrating all the above suggestions just discussed for the practice of wishcraft, here are the "how to do it" steps of wishing. Each step is based on our wish research and the science, mythology, and cultural lessons you have read about so far. They are provided as guides for you to fashion your own wishing style. In its simplest form, a well-made wish is a leap of faith that comes from the energy of the heart and is expressed in words. To help silence your brain, first follow the sun wisher's technique of closing your eyes. Next, make a sympathetic magical association with some natural event, person, place, or thing that elicits and guides the wish impulse. Next, tune into your heart as the energetic center for gently swinging the wish outward.

Before practicing the specific steps in making a wise wish, you have to be sure you are wishing from your heart and not your head. Your heart's central location in the body's energy system makes it uniquely suited to dealing with and mediating the subtle L energy of wishing. Author Joseph Pearce writes, "Two closely bonded people often share information across time-space, to which we attach occultic labels of various sorts, while all the time it is only our true biology, the logic of our life system, the language of the heart."[7] To say that the heart mediates the subtle L energy of wishing is not to say that its electromagnetic manifestations alone are not powerful enough to exert the power of our intentions. Its energy can be measured almost twenty feet from your body, so a wish from the heart spills out over everyone around you.

The heart is our body's most electromagnetically energetic organ. It's forty times more electromagnetically powerful than the brain, and its energy can be measured anywhere on the body. New, extremely sensitive electromagnetic instruments being developed by the Federal Bureau of Investigation can detect a heart beating its energy through a cement wall at more than 1,500 feet away. By contrast, the brain's electromagnetic energy can only be measured less than an inch from the skull. When you wish from your heart, your "wishing field" resonates strongly. As you read these words, you are probably sitting in someone else's heart energy field and under the influence of their heart's wishes.[8] Combine this physical energy with the heart's billions of cells forming a quantum energy generator, and you have the place where our most powerful wishes are created and broadcast.

The Heart-Head Inventory was given to all of our wish-research subjects to help assess the degree of balance between their heart and their head orientation to the world. Take it yourself before trying the eight-step well-wishing program.

The H H I
Heart-Head Inventory

Who hath put wisdom in the inward parts?
or who hath given understanding to the heart?
—JOB 38:36

The brain that forgets to listen to its heart loses its mind. It can end up in a lethal alliance with its body, using it and its heart to do its selfish and spiritually undisciplined bidding. Unbalanced brain-dominated wishing can result in wishing your life away. When the brain's heartless wishes are granted, the result can be a bypassed and literally heavy, hardened heart. Physical illness, emotional distress, and spiritual suffering are symptoms of brain-biased wishing. The following inventory is designed to help you assess the degree of balance you have between the brilliance of your rational brain and the wisdom of your loving heart. Well wishes are made when the brain works with and for, not on, your heart.

Write the name of the person who knows you the best.

Score the items below in terms of how you think *the person you named* would score you. Circle the number along the 0 to 10 scale that best approximates how you think the person you have named would score you on each item. There is no value or weight to the numbers; they are used only to indicate how far and in which direction you tend to fall in each category.

1. Head-Oriented	0 1 2 3 4 5 6 7 8 9 10	Heart-Oriented
2. Rational	0 1 2 3 4 5 6 7 8 9 10	Intuitive
3. Objective	0 1 2 3 4 5 6 7 8 9 10	Subjective
4. Mentally Focused	0 1 2 3 4 5 6 7 8 9 10	Distracted
5. A Realist	0 1 2 3 4 5 6 7 8 9 10	A Dreamer
6. Punctual	0 1 2 3 4 5 6 7 8 9 10	Tardy
7. Controlling	0 1 2 3 4 5 6 7 8 9 10	Submissive
8. Organized	0 1 2 3 4 5 6 7 8 9 10	Disorganized
9. Impatient	0 1 2 3 4 5 6 7 8 9 10	Patient
10. Taker	0 1 2 3 4 5 6 7 8 9 10	Giver
11. Picky	0 1 2 3 4 5 6 7 8 9 10	Tolerant

12. Going/Doing	0 1 2 3 4 5 6 7 8 9 10	Sitting/Being
13. Talker	0 1 2 3 4 5 6 7 8 9 10	Listener
14. Happy Optimist	0 1 2 3 4 5 6 7 8 9 10	Sad Pessimist
15. Selfish	0 1 2 3 4 5 6 7 8 9 10	Sacrificing
16. Sex	0 1 2 3 4 5 6 7 8 9 10	Sensual
17. Cynical	0 1 2 3 4 5 6 7 8 9 10	Trusting
18. Critical	0 1 2 3 4 5 6 7 8 9 10	Complimentary
19. Judgmental	0 1 2 3 4 5 6 7 8 9 10	Accepting
20. Future-Oriented	0 1 2 3 4 5 6 7 8 9 10	Past Reflective
21. Intellectual	0 1 2 3 4 5 6 7 8 9 10	"Touchy-Feely"
22. Serious	0 1 2 3 4 5 6 7 8 9 10	Playful
23. Hot Reactor	0 1 2 3 4 5 6 7 8 9 10	Cool Reactor
24. Sound Sleeper	0 1 2 3 4 5 6 7 8 9 10	Agitated Sleeper
25. Doesn't Dance	0 1 2 3 4 5 6 7 8 9 10	Loves To Dance
26. Doesn't Sing	0 1 2 3 4 5 6 7 8 9 10	Loves To Sing
27. Dull Senses	0 1 2 3 4 5 6 7 8 9 10	Sharp Senses
28. Concrete	0 1 2 3 4 5 6 7 8 9 10	Abstract
29. Hostile	0 1 2 3 4 5 6 7 8 9 10	Amicable
30. Frowner	0 1 2 3 4 5 6 7 8 9 10	Smiler
31. Denier	0 1 2 3 4 5 6 7 8 9 10	Ruminator
32. "Normal"	0 1 2 3 4 5 6 7 8 9 10	"Nuts"
33. Independent	0 1 2 3 4 5 6 7 8 9 10	Interdependent
34. Serious	0 1 2 3 4 5 6 7 8 9 10	Silly
35. A Worker	0 1 2 3 4 5 6 7 8 9 10	A Lover
36. Private Crier	0 1 2 3 4 5 6 7 8 9 10	Social Crier
37. Chuckler	0 1 2 3 4 5 6 7 8 9 10	Guffawer
38. Swears/Cusses	0 1 2 3 4 5 6 7 8 9 10	Whines/Moans
39. Animals Avoid	0 1 2 3 4 5 6 7 8 9 10	Animals Love
40. Likes "Techno-Toys"	0 1 2 3 4 5 6 7 8 9 10	Loves Nature
41. Competitive	0 1 2 3 4 5 6 7 8 9 10	Collaborative
42. Kids Respect	0 1 2 3 4 5 6 7 8 9 10	Kids Love

43. Practical	0 1 2 3 4 5 6 7 8 9 10	Impractical
44. Pragmatic	0 1 2 3 4 5 6 7 8 9 10	Romantic
45. Sarcastic	0 1 2 3 4 5 6 7 8 9 10	Soothing
46. Analyzer	0 1 2 3 4 5 6 7 8 9 10	Synergizer
47. Uptight	0 1 2 3 4 5 6 7 8 9 10	"Loosey-Goosey"
48. Masculine	0 1 2 3 4 5 6 7 8 9 10	Feminine
49. Grit	0 1 2 3 4 5 6 7 8 9 10	Grace
50. "I-Me-Mine"	0 1 2 3 4 5 6 7 8 9 10	"Us-We-Ours"

Scoring

1. IGNORE THE ACTUAL VALUE OF THE NUMBERS.
2. IGNORE ALL OF THE "NUMBER 5" RESPONSES.
3. ADD UP THE NUMBER OF ITEMS CIRCLED *TO THE RIGHT OF "5."* _____
4. NEXT, ADD UP THE NUMBER OF ITEMS *TO THE LEFT OF "5."* _____
5. NOW, SUBTRACT LINE 4 FROM LINE 3. = H H I SCORE = _____

Interpreting Your Score

- ◆ An HHI score of "0" indicates a **perfectly balanced brain–heart wishing system.**
- ◆ A negative score toward the minus side of "0" indicates **an egotistical, dominating brain** that ignores the wishing wisdom of its heart.
- ◆ A positive score toward the plus side of "0" indicates a **hypersensitive heart** out of balance with its reasoning brain.

Look to the areas on the inventory where you were most off-center, or furthest from "5." These are the places in your personal, working, and family life that require better heart/head balance for making wise wishes. This inventory is designed to facilitate awareness of a more balanced approach to your wishing life. Wishing well requires more than the specific wishing techniques you will learn in this book. It also requires putting more heart into every aspect of your daily living. Well wishing is not only making wise wishes; it's also making difficult choices every day in order to live the life your heart, not just your brain, wishes for.

A word of warning about the HHI. If you've skimmed past it and not taken the time to take it, your brain was trying to protect its territory and make you keep moving. If you took this test too seriously, were critical of yourself, and feel badly that you are not "heart-oriented" enough, your heart may require a little rational nudge from your brain. If you laughed, shared, reflected, and considered the points presently, you are well on your way to "re-minding" your brain that it has a heart with which it can work together to make wonderful wishes come true.

As you prepare to design your personal wish-making style, remember the statement by Stephen Sondheim, "The Heart knows, the Thought denies, is there no other way?" Learning to wish well by following your heart more than your head can be another way.

Putting Your Heart into It

Well wishing is actually a form of "cardiocontemplation." It's a way of resonating your heart with your brain so that you fall into sympathetic vibration with the world around you rather than try to control it. It requires letting your heart have its way rather than allowing your brain to busy you with trying to get its way. As physicist William Tiller points out, "The cardiovascular system is the only known nerve input to the brain that will inhibit the activity of the brain's cortex which is usually regarded as the seat of higher brain function."[9] Unlike the other oscillating organs of the body, the heart is autorhythmic, meaning that it is the source of its own beating. It can get the entire body system, including the brain, to "think" or resonate "its way." Calming down, breathing deeply, falling into a state of meandering mentality or a relaxed cognition rather than hard thought, and connecting with the subtle energy that is everything is best accomplished by putting your heart into your wishes.

In Chapter 1, you read a brief summary of the steps in wishing well. Based now on the cultural and scientific material about wishing you have read and on what our research subjects said helped them make their best wishes, here is a summary of the steps used by many of the wish-project subjects to make wishes after they learned about the role of the heart in wishing well. Try to make your own wish following these steps.

How to Wish Well

1. SD-SU-CD—Sit Down, Shut Up, and Calm Down.
The heart has a gentle, melodic rhythm that helps get us into the swing of wishing well. To wish well, you first have to quiet your busy body so that your most L-energy-sensitive organ, your heart, can connect with that energy.

2. Pick a wish target.
Connect and resonate with nature by looking at something alive. If you can't get outside, look out the window at a tree or flower. Have a "wishing tree" or plant in your home or office. As our ancestors taught us, nature resonates with the energy of wishing, so feel a little "sympathy" for her so that you can establish the sympathetic vibrations that make your wishing intentions work their miracles.

3. Close your eyes.
Once you've got an image of the natural object, close your eyes. This decreases input to your occipital lobe, the major source of stimulation to the brain. It also promotes connection with the wishing style of the very first wishers who closed their eyes as they wished on the glaring sun.

4. Breathe deeply and abdominally.
To help quiet the brain and body and give the heart enough peace and quiet to have a chance to think, take deep, full breaths. The brain's style of breathing is just beneath itself and takes place in your upper lungs and chest. The heart's breathing is just beneath itself and is a deep breathing in the center of your body and abdomen. Think of your heart breathing with each beat. You should be able to see your abdomen going out when you breathe in. Remember, our ancestors considered the breath to be a manifestation of our spirit—the "ah" that comes out when we are most enraptured with our existence. Treat it gently.

5. Place your left hand over your heart.
Well wishing requires getting your brain to listen to what your heart has to say. Placing your left hand over your heart helps draw your brain's attention to a more L-energy-wise organ.

6. Press your right hand gently but firmly on your left hand.
Pushing your left hand more firmly against your chest enhances the brain/heart connection. You'll need your brain to speak for your heart and say the words of the wish. Since the brain is accustomed to using rather than listening and working for the heart, a little pressure on your chest helps focus your brain's attention to your wishing center. If you're making your wish at night in bed, be sure to lie on

your left side. This position brings the heart a little closer to the outside of your body.

7. *On exhaling, whisper your wish.* Say one word per every space between each heartbeat. The most restful, L-energy-sensitive state is between heart-beats.

8. *Use eight short words.* Try to keep your wish within the magical eight-word limit. There's a mythological basis for this limit. Here's the reasoning, as well as why we decided on eight steps for the wishing well process.

* Limiting the length of your softly stated wish helps keep it specific, focused, and more of a little push than a hard swing. It makes for a better meme.
* Eight words help you remember your wish. The number eight is the "recall" number. Psychologists know that a series of more than eight numbers exceeds our short-term immediate memory capacity. That's why phone numbers are usually seven basic digits, Snow White had only seven dwarfs, and Santa Claus had only eight reindeer (not counting Rudolph).
* The number eight turned on its side represents infinity.
* There were eight gifts of the yoga siddhis that free one from being trapped in one level of reality.
* In numerology, the number eight represents new life or a new beginning.
* In music composition, an octave is composed of eight notes, and every eighth note merges into unison and resonates with its counterpart.
* Shamans from many cultures suggest that while a man's body has seven orifices, a woman has a unique and sacred eighth opening through which we are born.
* Christians consider the number eight to be symbolic of life after death or rebirth.
* Finally, eight is the first cube ($2 \times 2 \times 2 = 8$) number and thus represents entry into a new dimension of mathematics.[10]

As with any endeavor and particularly with an art such as wishcraft, practice makes perfect. This may be a good time to consult the card on which you wrote your wish as you began your reading of this book. How does your "starter wish" compare to the wish you just made using the wishing well steps? Are there any of the wishing well steps that you think will help you make wiser wishes? Telling someone how to wish, even if that advice is based on the best science and cultural lessons, is like telling someone how to paint. You can give them a brush and canvas, but until they take brush in hand and start to make their wish come true on the canvas, they do not learn to paint.

I suggest you write another wish on the back of the wish card you created as you began reading. As you read along in this book, write a few more wishes when you feel like it. As you read, you will probably develop your own modifications of the steps of wishing well. The more you become fully absorbed in the wishing process, the more likely your heart will tell you what and how to wish.

·····························〜·····························

Nine

How Wishers Are Made

The dust of exploded beliefs may make a fine sunset.
—GEOFFREY MADAN, ENGLISH AUTHOR

Born to Wish

We are born irritable, with urgent wishes to make and no skill in making them. Whether we end up with a balanced life characterized primarily by the bright side of the wish star (serenity, delight, purpose, meaning, and compassion) or with a chronically stressed life reflecting the dark aspects of wishing (turmoil, disillusionment, stagnation, despair, and loneliness) depends in large measure on how we learn to wish. We often focus on making our children strong-willed and independent, but teaching them to wish well and in harmony with others is an equally important challenge.

Even if the birth process is a relatively peaceful one, it's not long before the newborn expresses her or his brain's inherent cantankerousness. God gave us a brain so we would get out there, get going, and start trying to assert and protect ourselves. We were also given a heart so we could enjoy the journey. When we are taught to make our wishes primarily from our brain, we end up with more of the dark side of wishing. If, however, we are fortunate enough to have parents who wish from their hearts and teach us to do the same, we have a much brighter wishing future.

From Being Testy to Being Tender

Every theory of child development is a sequential history of the attempt to move humans from being testy to being tender.[1] We come into the world as beings, but it's a parent's job to create human beings. Theories about how children develop may be seen as stories about how to help a child move beyond the brain's selfish concern for staying alive to the heart's loving ways for understanding why we were given life. Parenthood is the difficult challenge of trying to get out of one's own childhood long enough to help another being with hers. It's the task of continuing to wish well in your own life while dealing with the annoying aggravations and frustrations of trying to fulfill the wishes of a helpless being born without the skill of wise wishing. As a pediatrician who was one of our wish-research subjects put it when we discussed how teaching wishing was related to parenting, "I think being a parent requires the skill of making whiners into wishers. It takes patience to try to convert egotistical little whiners who make all kinds of crazy wishes into caring grown-ups who know how to wish well for themselves and others."

Psychologists have paid comparatively little attention to how we learn to wish and become wish granters.[2] The development of the power to use our intent and intuition has largely been ignored as a key element in human maturation. Most of psychology's attention has been focused on how to raise smart, fast-thinking, independent, and self-assertive children, not children who wish well by subtly, gently, slowly, interdependently, and selflessly trying to focus their intention to make possibilities realities. It has primarily concerned itself with behavioral modification and the development of the brain more than the heart. When it comes to problems such as how and whom should I love and how can I find and share the serenity, delight, purpose, meaning, and compassion of the wish star, psychology has largely failed. Psychologist Larry LeShan writes, ". . . psychology has so lost contact with real human experience that there would be no point in asking it to solve major human problems."[3]

When wishing has been addressed as a developmental task, it has typically been treated as a childhood artifact, a delightful but small and insignificant part of our mental and emotional development that must be overcome if we are to be adults. It has been seen as a kind of mental play that we must grow out of if we are to face and deal with reality. It has been dismissed as the stuff of fairy tales used to soothe us. Wishing is seen as taking place in the temporary wonderland shelter of a make-believe world that we must leave as soon as possible, an infantile stage that the brightest children are the quickest to outgrow.

Wishing is a form of mental play. Play is non-goal-directed behavior, and wishing well depends on wishes that are not related to specific goals or objectives. As author Joseph W. Meeker points out, we need about as much playful thought every day as we do REMs, the rapid eye movements that signal we are dreaming. If we do not dream enough, we become irritable, edgy, and even angry. So it is if we do not engage in playful things such as wishing.[4] So wishing is a basic human need, but it is much more than that. It's not something you have or get; it's something you do. It's a crucial life survival task that helps express needs from many levels of our being. Our prisons and mental institutions are full of adults who failed to learn how to wish well and lovingly and, as a result, took from others or lost themselves. Executive boardrooms have failed wishers sitting at the head of the conference table, their every need apparently met but their most cherished wishes unfulfilled.

The Birth of Irritability

About 2 billion years ago, irritability was born. Like the helpless fetus carried swaying along in the amniotic fluid inside his mother's uterus, the first one-celled animals called protozoa existed without the ability to move. They were simply bandied about from one place to another in the primeval sea. They lived and died by the principle of irritability. If an "irritating" food particle was sensed coming in contact with the surface of the protozoan's cell membrane, that irritation led to a protozoan response. Functioning like a whole-body mouth, it would absorb the food particle into its system. If the protozoan happened to float into a harmful substance, its membrane reacted with the first primal immune response. Sometimes it automatically became "thick-skinned" and, through some innate form of self-protection afforded by a re-active thickening of its membrane surface, prevented a toxin from entering. Other times, the protozoan emitted a protective secretion that rendered the invader harm-less. The first animal, then, was an irritable reactor without the ability to "wish" to avoid toxins and seek pleasures.

Like a newborn baby, the first animal could only react to the environment in immediate contact with its body. It functioned essentially as a tiny floating impulse system. It was one big primitive brain with no heart. For it, the world was indistin-guishable from the state of its own body. Just as a newborn, if it was going anywhere, it had to be carried; if it was going to live, it would either have to be kept safe by the carrier or some automatic response had to kick in. Not only could it not think or feel, it had no wishes and no system for making them. As a chronically hostile and aggressively defensive person may be in the modern world, it was a ball of peevish id, or a reactive instinctual system.

Developmental theorists have shown the importance of the evolution of the physical ability to locomote and carry one's self. When protozoa grew tiny paddlelike feet, they could go searching for food and sex on their own. As higher-evolved animals moved far beyond a purely "instinct-psyche" to a more cognitive and affective psyche, they also had the potential to tune into their wishing organ and develop their innate conative or wishing psyche.[5] As the brain's extensions of itself, the five physical senses, became more refined, the most basic wishing skills developed along with them.

When the first mammals appeared about 175 million years ago, they developed highly responsive and sophisticated physiological, emotional, and—to varying levels— cognitive mechanisms. While these capacities have received most of the anthropological attention, the evolution of the skill to make wishes has received far less attention. To the extent we have become more civilized, we have also developed our sixth sense and learned how to wish wisely for the right thing in the right way at the right time. To the extent we have failed in our wishing development, we have remained selfish, territorial, aggressive, and irritable.

Naughty or Nice

Being a "soccer mom or dad" may help produce skilled competitors in an increasingly harsh and hurried world, but being a "well-wishing mom or dad" by teaching our children how to be aware of the impact of their intentions, to have good ones, and to learn how to wish well will help them lead a more balanced and connected life. No matter how well they play soccer, how high they score on tests, or how emotionally intelligent they become, if our children are not alert to the profound impact of their intentions and how their wishes affect their own and others' lives, the quality of their life is diminished. If we only teach our children how to make their intentions known without also teaching them how to gently focus their intentions to try to subtly and lovingly influence their world, we end up with tough and successful adults who feel alone and without the life we wished for them. Transforming our children from the innate irritable temperament of the unrefined wisher to the loving temperament of the well wisher is one of the greatest gifts we can give them and our world.

Try a child psychology experiment of your own to see just how much wishing instruction is being provided by parents. Sit and observe families at the airport. Watch how the children behave. Do you see well-wishing behavior shown by patient, quiet, considerate wishes being made and reacted to? Do families seem to have the time to be connected heart to heart? Do the families you see seem to be emanating the subtle L or love energy that can convert a secular space into a sacred space conducive to everyone's wishing? Do you see parents and children showing good intuition through strong wish sensitivity for others' heartfelt needs and subtle good intentions? Do you see children "in sync" and "in sympathy" and resonating with the world around them? As you watch and conduct your field research on wishing development, ask yourself two simple questions, the answers to which reveal much about the development of wishing in our society: Do these people seem sympathetic? Do these people seem to have good hearts? Both of these questions are really about the well wisher's key distinguishing traits being nice.

The two words of parenting that most clearly convey the way to make well wishes are "be nice." Perhaps you remember your parents telling you to "be nice" or warning that something you did was "naughty." Being nice requires the skill of making wishes that come from the heart. It requires a way of wishing that does not encroach on others' wishes and helps promote their fulfillment.

When I was conducting one of my own wish development field observations at the Detroit Metropolitan Airport, I saw two examples of the "naughty–nice" continuum. The naughty example was a family of five whose plane was delayed. They had sprawled out on ten chairs. Their luggage was everywhere and two of the three children were chasing each other around the ticket podium. "I want that!" yelled the little girl chasing her brother. He laughed and threw whatever it was in the trash can. The girl began to cry, slapped her brother, and as if nothing had happened, stopped crying and walked to the refreshment stand. The father was working on his computer and talking loudly on his cellular phone. The mother was reading her book with her legs propped up on the chair next to her. Her other daughter was asking for a candy bar. She tried tugging at her mother and finally whining and hitting her. The mother seemed unaware of her daughter's actions as she munched on her own candy. When the announcement came that the flight was ready for boarding, the entire family rushed to the gate.

I saw another family of four standing against the wall. The rushing family knocked over some of their luggage as they passed. "I'm sorry," said the mother of the family of four. "I guess we left our bags in the aisle." No one from the rushing family acknowledged her comment. The quieter family had been unable to find a seat. The father was reading something aloud to his family and they had been discussing the story together. They seemed to unconsciously move as one group in order to readjust their position to accommodate passing passengers and gate personnel.

As I continued my observations, I noticed the more gentle family's little girl sitting quietly and with her eyes closed. Without looking up, I heard her mother say, "I think Genny wants a soda." The little girl smiled, jumped up, and clapped her hands gleefully. "That's exactly what I was wishing for," she said. He mother hugged her, took her hand, and guided her to grant her wish. "We'll be awhile," said the mother, "so let everyone else get on first. Stay off to the side so you're not in their way."

These two examples may seem like simple matters of politeness and discipline. Looking for the wish ways of these families, however, reveals that the second family in the example seemed to be alert and responsive to one another's wishes and were "being nice" to each other and everyone. The rushing family seemed oblivious to any wish but their own aggressively expressed individual wishes. The children were behaving "naughtily" and the parents showed little regard for their children's, each other's, or anyone else's wishes. I thought about how wishing was being taught by each respective family and what kind of wish teachers their children might be when they were parents.

Three Key Parenting Questions

If you're a parent, ask the following three key questions related to your child's wishing development and your parental wishing wisdom. Ask your child:

1. "What do you think my number one wish is for you?"

2. "What do you wish for me?"

3. "What do you think my number one wish is for myself?"

Do your child's answers reflect what you wish for them in your heart? Is your own heart warmed by their answers? Do the answers seem to come from a kind, "nice" heart by reflecting the five bright domains of the wish star not only for your child and yourself but for everyone? If you answer yes, you're likely to be doing a good job of teaching your child to wish well. Congratulations. You're developing a nice adult for a more congenial world.

Here are three sample answers from a seven-year-old son of a couple in our wish-research project (Child A) as contrasted with three answers from an eight-year-old daughter (Child B) of two executives I met at a recent business meeting. Although in childish terms, these answers illustrate the contrast between the heartfelt wishing and the more brain-oriented wishing taught and modeled to these two children.

1. What do you think my number wish is for you?
    Child A: That I be a very nice person.
    Child B: That I do better in school.

2. What do you wish for me?
    Child A: That you feel happy and don't cry much.
    Child B: That you get the job even though they don't appreciate you there.

3. What do you think my number one wish is for myself?
    Child A: That you be a good mommy.
    Child B: That you get enough money to not work anymore.

Avoiding Wish Abuse

Another challenge in the making of well wishers is to avoid parental wish abuse through wishing dominance. Unconsciously, and in the worst cases intentionally, parents' wishes can overshadow and inhibit the development of their child's own wishing skill. The child can become wish exploited, a vehicle for the parents' wishes and a means of fulfilling their present or past unfilled wishes. The parents can fail to nurture the free evolution of their child's own unique wishing skills because they are still working on their own childhood wishes.

Wish abuse can be extremely subtle. "I only wish the best for my children" is a common parental statement, but this statement sometimes masks the more selfish wishes of the parents, to which the child is very sensitive. The parents may be trying to fulfill their wishes for a perfect child rather than a child who wishes well for himself and others. "I want the best for you" can be translated by the child as "You'll be happiest if you fulfill my wishes for you." Parents who model strong brain-oriented wishes can unknowingly create an overwhelming wish gravity that draws their children into their own wish star rather than allowing them the freedom to wish their way from their own heart. Remembering to keep asking your children about their wishes, being tolerant of wishes much different from your own and patient for more mature wishes to develop, and promoting and being tolerant of a range of wishing and wishes are ways to avoid wish abuse or exploitation.

Another potential parental mistake in developing children's wishing skills is to prematurely grant their every wish. Overindulgence can be as dangerous to a developing wisher as neglect. A parent who anticipates her child's every wish and projects her own childhood wishes to her child is interfering with the development of that child's wish ability. Because wishing well is basically wishing "nicely," the model of wise-wishing parenthood is showing self-restraint and social awareness in our own wishes. It's subtly expressing our intentions rather than forcefully trying to impose them. It's not only knowing what and how to wish but knowing when and where not to and how to be sensitive to other persons' wishes. We can only be good wishing teachers if we ourselves have learned how to wish well and make the effort to show our children how to do it by the way we conduct our daily social discourse. In all that our children see us do, they are acting as our wish wizard's apprentice. Whenever you wish or discuss the process of wishing, think of the warning sign that reads, "Caution: Wishers Being Made Here." Ask yourself, "Do I really want my child wishing as and for what I am wishing?"

Teaching Heartfelt Wishing

Teaching the art of well wishing is showing that the best wishes should be sensed and expressed from the heart, not the body and brain. It's teaching that well wishes are made not only from one's own heart but with others' heartfelt wishes in mind. It's teaching the key wishing well skills of "waiting for the wish" rather than whining for it and knowing how to resist the urgings of the irritable brain. It's modeling well wishing by showing children that not all wishes should be made or expected to be granted in the time frame imposed by the brain. It's showing through how we lead our day-to-day family life how to fit in, care about, and make our wishes contingent upon the physical and social ecology and not just our own selfish psychology. It's teaching self-restraint instead of modeling self-gratification.[6]

Without our wishing skill, we can become stressed and discontented adults who know what we want but are insensitive to what we and others really need. We can end up feeling that we have everything we could think of but nothing we had hoped for. We may feel strangely unfulfilled even when our every need and want would appear to be satisfied. Needs and wants are the brain's motivational states. Because the heart is where our well wishes originate, our brain's best efforts to try to have it all leave us feeling that all we have is the trying. Wise conation is one of the skills that gives life its color and meaning. Without it, we can feel intensely and think brilliantly yet still suffer from our neonatal irritability and behave like a multicelled modern version of a protozoan.

Teaching Tales of the Third Wish

You have probably heard stories about a genie granting three wishes. In most of these mythical wish-teaching stories, unwise wicked wishing leads to using up all three wishes just to get back to where the wisher started in the first place. The lesson is never to wish impulsively, selfishly, and without regard for the impact of one's wishing.

Have you talked to your child about wishing? Teaching the self-restraint and altruism essential to healthy wishing requires conveying the lesson of the third wish to our children. It requires that we read to them, tell them stories, and encourage them to tell us stories about wishing and what happens when we make certain kinds of wishes. It involves asking our children questions such as, "What do you think happened next?" "And then what?" "How do you think he or she felt about that?" "What do you think he or she is wishing?" "Do you think that was a nice wish to make?" and "What do you think might have been a nicer wish?" It requires removing your cellular phone from your ear, taking the newspaper down from your face, and closing your laptop computer to take the time to talk with your children about theirs, yours, and others' wishes. It requires that parents use wishing tales to convey the lesson of "what if?" and the point of view of "looking around" rather than just "looking within."

The Six Stages of Well Wishing

As we were conducting our research on wishing, discussions with our subjects often turned to how children learned to wish and the implications of such learning for their own and the world's future. Many of them asked us to provide some guidance as to how to teach their children to wish well. To establish a starting point for discussing the development of conation, I turned to the research and theories of psychologist Lawrence Kohlberg, one of the notable exceptions to scientific psychology's lack of relevance to those things that really matter in life.

Kohlberg developed a comprehensive theory of cognitive and moral development.[7] His hypothesis is that we learn right from wrong in the same way and through the same stages in which we learn how to think. He says that our morals are based on how we learn to conceptualize our world and our relationship to others. How and what we wish also reflects our moral learning. It reflects how we see others and our interactions with and responsibilities to them.

Because in its simplest form, being a moral person is knowing and acting on the difference between naughty and nice and being aware of the impact of one's wishes on others, learning how to wish and learning how to think morally go hand and hand. One of the best ways we can raise moral children is to raise them to wish responsibly, maturely, and lovingly. The accompanying chart (see the chart on page 167) combines Kohlberg's six stages of cognitive moral development with the ways in which a child learns how to relate to the world—physically, cognitively, affectively, and through wishing. By studying the chart, you can track your child's and your own wishing development.

The Safety Wish

This primitive stage of wishing relates to Kohlberg's morality stage one called pre-conventional morality level one. During this first stage of moral development, children are human versions of the irritable protozoan. They wish wildly and without clear direction to reduce their natural state of irritability. They wish to avoid the "toxin" of punishment and pain. They try to enhance and protect the self at all costs. The irritable brain is in complete charge and focused exclusively on avoiding discomfort and seeking pleasure for its body. Its thinking is selfishly protective and the feelings are of immature dependence. "What will they do to me if I do this?" is the primary question.

At this stage of wishing, the child's wishes derive from bodily impulses and needs and are expressed to the primary caretaker. The wishes are to avoid punishment and the motive is primarily self-protection and physical self-preservation. Wishing is done defensively to avoid negative consequences for the physical self. Like the one-cell paramecium, the child is essentially a tiny ball of id or instinct, and his wishes reflect this primitive state. There may be remnants of the mother's own unfulfilled wishes far beyond the child's recognition that covertly aggravate the child's system. The result is that, even if a wish is granted, it may seem like the wrong wish came true.

In a primitive kind of countermagic, wishes are made to try to avoid negative consequences or to avoid the punishment of an impulsive act. The attempt is not to wish to be nice or even seen as nice but to be satisfied and safe. Here are some sample wishes from children at this stage. We collected these and the other sample wishes listed here from children of the persons in the 2,166-member wish study group and the children's wish focus group you will read about later in this chapter. Sample "safety" wishes were:

The Six Stages of Wishing

Body ——————————— Brain ——————————— Heart

Safety Wish	Reward Wish	Security Wish	Acceptance Wish	Esteem Wish	World Wish
Kohlberg's Stage One	Kohlberg's Stage Two	Kohlberg's Stage Three	Kohlberg's Stage Four	Kohlberg's Stage Five	Kohlberg's Stage Six
Preconventional Morality Level One	Preconventional Morality Level Two	Conventional Morality Level One	Conventional Morality Level Two	Postconventional Morality Level One	Postconventional Morality Level Two
To Avoid Negative Consequences	For Positive Consequences	To Go Along	To Get Along	To Be Seen as Nice	To Make the World Nice
For My Body	For My Feelings	For My Comfort	For My Popularity	For My Image	For My Soul
To Any Provider	To Parent Figure	To My Family	To Peers	To Society	With the Subtle Energy of the World
To Avoid Punishment	To Receive Reward	To Be Accepted by Family	To Be Accepted by School Social Group	To Be Accepted by Society	To Heal the Planet
Protection Motive	Negotiation Motive	Approval Motive	Belonging Motive	Respect Motive	Ethics Motive
Self-Preservation	Self-Enhancement	Self-Competence	Self-Recognition	Self-Pride	Self-Sacrifice
Defensiveness	Bargaining	Obedience	Discretion	Prudence	Altruism
Physical Help	Ego Enhancement	Protect Image	Develop Identity	Personal Values	Collective Morals
Physiological Dictates	Instrumental Rules	Family's Rules	Society's Rules and Laws	Personality	Character

- "to not get spanked"
- "to not get thrown away [bitter divorce] like David's parents did to him"
- "to not have to go and stay in my room"
- "that my sister will not tell on me"
- "that no monster gets me"

Reward Wish

This second stage of wishing development relates to Kohlberg's morality development stage two, which he called preconventional morality level two. During this stage, children wish more to receive rewards than avoid pain. They try to "cut a deal" with the world. As in the "punishment phase" of moral thinking, protecting one's physical body is the focus. The thinking is self-enhancing and the feelings become more emotionally manipulative. Trying to figure out ways to elicit pity or emotional attention characterizes the thought pattern. It is often manifested as pouting or brooding to get attention.

At the second stage of wishing, the child wishes for positive consequences rather than just the avoidance of negative ones. Wishes begin to be made more by affect or feelings than pure physiology. They are made to a parental figure rather than just any provider and are matters of negotiated enhancement rather than simply self-preservation. Conation evolves to ego rather than bodily enhancement and is a "If I do this, then you do that" type of thinking rather than the "just do it for" approach characteristic of stage one. Instead of wishing to be nice and make life nice, the child at this stage attempts to get her way by doing something nice. Sample "instrumental" wishes from children at this stage were:

- "to be good to get my list from Santa"
- "to stop hitting my brother so Daddy will give me a Nintendo"
- "the Good Fairy will give me big money for my tooth"
- "Aunty will give me more than a dollar for me kissing her"
- "make the Easter Bunny bring good stuff and not the junk like last year"

Security Wish

The third stage of wishing parallels Kohlberg's moral development stage three, called conventional morality level one. The child has gone from doing things to avoid outcomes through doing things for outcomes to this stage of doing things to go along with the family system. This is a stage during which the child wishes to fit into the family rather than wishing only to use it. There is an attempt to conform to what the child believes is necessary to be seen as a nice girl or boy. The child may feign cuteness to be seen as a good boy or girl deserving of love and may even try a little naughtiness to test loving limits. The thinking now is expectation of due reward for doing those things that result in family praise for conforming.

If only for selfish purposes, wishing becomes more concerned with how others feel and being seen as a nice person. The thinking goes, "If I say the magic word 'please,' that seems to make you happy. When you're happy, I seem to get more rewards or your criterion for reward giving is a little less." There is less concern for immediate reward and less fear of punishment.

The child at this stage of wishing begins to wish for approval and a sense of self-competence. If wishful thinking is developing well, the child becomes more obedient because she wishes to protect her self-image as a good little girl. Wishing by this time should be based less on the physiological and instrumental rules of life of the first two wishing stages and more on the family's routine, rules, and rituals.

- "for my sister to like me more"
- "that my mama would be happier"
- "that I wouldn't get Daddy so mad"
- "my mom would get to use the couch and have peace and quiet so she will feel like baking cookies"
- "for me to be the good one"

Acceptance Wish

This fourth stage of wishing development corresponds to Kohlberg's stage four morality, which is described as conventional morality level two. Wishing corresponds more with the wishes made by peers and fellow students and not just siblings. This fourth stage involves trying to obey the law and go along with social expectations. There is an effort to match one's wishes with the reality of the societal world. Being not just a nice son or daughter but a generally nice person begins to take on significance in the child's mental life. The thinking is more in tune with teachers and other authority figures' ideas of what constitutes good behavior. Affect is associated with reactions to what the child interprets as society's ultimate treatment of "good and bad" people.

Wishing evolves to more social wishes and concern for popularity and a sense of belonging. The child's wishes show more discretion and awareness of the lasting impact of those wishes. Also, the child's own unique wishing style begins to coalesce, in what researchers at the PEAR laboratory might call an "Individual Subtle Energy Signature." Sample "abiding style" wishes in this stage were:

- "to not ever get sent to the office like Jason does"
- "to be very good and do what Ms. Smith says you should do"
- "not get made fun of like Jerry always is"
- "to not be the one who ruins recess time again"
- "not to have to be sent out in the hall at Sunday school"

Esteem Wish

The fifth stage of wishing relates to Kohlberg's stage five of moral development, which he called postconventional morality level one. This is the stage at which the developing person is concerned with more abstract and universal rights such as life, liberty, and the pursuit of happiness. The thinking now leans more toward the Ten Commandments than personal, parental, teacher, peer, or even social rules. Wishes are associated with a developing sense of fairness and justice. This often results in paralegal debates with parents about what is fair and what is not and which wishes are good and which are bad.

Rather than operating in the egocentric and more independently physical way of the first four stages, the brain now merges more with signals coming from both the body and the heart. By now, the child has moved from a primarily reactive "irritable" orientation to a more good-natured way of dealing with the world. In other words, the child begins to be very nice and to have more heart.

In this phase, the child's wishing personality becomes more apparent. Her "Individual Subtle Energy Signature" becomes clearer and she focuses on establishing and acting in terms of persistent values rather than making reactive adjustments to avoid punishment, gain reward, or achieve social stature and acceptance. The personality or temperament begins to crystalize and some idea of the child's future adult wishing style emerges. Wishes begin to reflect a sense of personal and family pride and the legitimate wish to be seen as a genuinely nice person who makes nice wishes.

If the child is fortunate enough to have parents who are modeling and teaching wise heartfelt wishing, then wishing begins to involve concern for others' welfare and for things to work out right for everyone. All of the wishing stages are relatively independent of age, so a teenager, young adult, or even older adult may still be "fixated" at the safety, reward, security, or acceptance wish stages. By this time, however, one hopes the developing person has gone beyond wishing to get something and "fit in" to wishes expressing a concern for a reputation as a caring and helping person. Sample esteem wishes are:

- "I wish my dad would not be so mean to my mom."
- "I wish Mommy and Daddy would never yell at each other again."
- "I wish the good ones would not have to be hurt."
- "I wish nobody's parents would get divorced unless they had to."
- "I wish that no kid would get cancer like the ones in the movie."

World Wish

Kohlberg's morality stage six is called postconventional morality level two because it is a highly developed ethical stage. It's the highest morality level and involves thinking about self-responsibility for the state of the world more than how to use or benefit personally from it. Personality gives way to a developing character as lifelong, relatively permanent principles begin to solidify, displacing the more dynamic and situational-dependent values system. The child's feelings are less about "me" and even "us" than about "everyone everywhere." Thinking focuses on moral questions and not just society's laws. Sensitivity to sacrificing to help others develops now as concern for one's own physical state is pushed to the background in favor of the state of the world ecology. In essence, the child is now developing an ego the size of the world.[8]

Affect at this stage is attuned more to the suffering in the world than just the family or local society. Wishing evolves to the highest level of a well wish. It is a wishing based on the recognition that our needs are by their very nature insatiable and our wants are socially defined and therefore constantly changing. It is based on learning the lesson that the real source of a sense of well-being is wished for beyond the five senses. Wishes now come more from the heart and to the heart of others.

They are based on sufficiency and simplicity rather than consumerism and excess. Sample world wishes were:

- "I wish there would be no more war and killing people."
- "I wish the bombs would only hit the bad ones."
- "I wish that nobody would kill the fish by putting stuff in their home."
- "I wish the skinny kids that have flies on their face on TV would get food."
- "I wish that the bad men would not hit their family on *Cops*" [the cable television show].

Take a moment now to reflect on the status of your own and your family's wishing. Review the wishes you wrote on the cards. What is the stage of wishing in your life? At which stage do you think your family is making most of its wishes? How much time do you spend teaching, talking about, and making well wishes together as a family?

World or principled wishing goes beyond always changing personal values to an establishment and conformity to universal principles such as not killing or hurting people, not using or lying to people, and not abusing the earth. By learning and teaching about the six-stage wish cycle of safety, reward, security, acceptance, esteem, and the world wish, we and our children learn how to make the wisest and healthiest wishes of all—those made for the welfare not only of ourselves but of others and the world.

Childhood Wish Inventory

In our study of wishing, we asked parents to take the Childhood Wish Inventory (CWI). We wanted to get an idea of the degree to which parents nurtured and developed the wishful thinking intelligence of their children. Before reading about what children said about wishing, take the CWI to see how your child compares with the children of our sample group. Although many of the items in the inventory refer to Christian-based mythology, we found that many children from families of all of the religions represented in our research group (Jewish, Protestant, Catholic, Muslim, Buddhist, Agnostic, Atheist, Taoist) "borrowed" beliefs across the religious orientations identified by their parents.

Childhood Wish Inventory

4 = FOR A VERY LONG TIME 3 = FOR A WHILE 2 = VERY BRIEFLY
1 = JUST BARELY 0 = NEVER

Did your child:

1. _____ Truly believe in Santa Claus?

2. _____ Truly believe in the Easter Bunny?

3. _____ Leave a tooth under the pillow for the Tooth Fairy?

4. _____ Have an invisible, make-believe playmate?

5. _____ Believe in the "Boogie Man" or other "monster?"

6. _____ Enjoy being held, rocked, and hummed to?

7. _____ Play elaborate make-believe games?

8. _____ Play "fair" and go along with the fantasies of other children?

9. _____ Enjoy being sung to?

10. _____ Ask for a bedtime story?

11. _____ Make houses and forts out of boxes?

12. _____ Send a letter to Santa Claus?

13. _____ Leave cookies and milk for Santa Claus?

14. _____ Enjoy and want to help decorate for holidays?

15. _____ Get very excited about getting and giving gifts?

16. _____ Insist on and want to be part of family rituals?

17. _____ Seem very sensitive to others' moods?

18. _____ Enjoy drawing, painting, and making things?

19. _____ Enjoy dressing up for Halloween?

20. _____ Laugh easily at silly things and sounds?

21. _____ Enjoy playing hide-and-seek?

22. _____ Take wishing on the candles or cutting of the birthday cake seriously?

23. _____ Enjoy family meals and actively take part in discussions around the table?

24. _____ Enjoy and ask to look at family pictures?

25. _____ Have a favorite doll or toy?

_____ TOTAL CHILDHOOD WISH INVENTORY SCORE

The higher the score on the CWI, the more evolved your child's wishful thinking and the more likely she is progressing in her wishing ability as well as her cognitive, affective, and physical development. Although we did not collect medical data on our wish research group, we did note that the parents who recorded scores of over eighty for their children also reported the fewest medical, school, and emotional problems for them. This is in keeping with the finding that ritual and the ability to imagine and temporarily escape from the stressful realities of life are associated with overall well-being in children.[9]

Sixth Sense Parenting

Good parents know, honor, support, and praise the evolution of wishing and wishful thinking as much as they value physical, cognitive, and emotional development. They nurture the instinct to wish just as they try to promote physical, intellectual, and emotional health. Good, multidimensional parenting combines teaching about children's cognitive, affective, physical, and conative lives. The result of conative teaching can be less irritated, and therefore less irritating, people more skilled in wishing for a calmer, more pleasing world for everyone and everything.

Clearly reading and knowing the differences that exist between what one needs, wants, is motivated by, hopes for, and why and to whom or what one prays all involve varying degrees and aspects of conation. Much of our conscious life is taken up by focusing our intentions and consciously trying to make them real. Children who become able to tune into their own L energy or into the wish traces left by their parents are more likely to feel calmer in their wishing. Those who learn how to wish well in the context of loving parental wishes are also those who not only fulfill their wishes but may be able to help their parents fulfill theirs. As one of the parents in our wish project asked, "Isn't that what families are for?"

Parents who are teachers of wise wishing nurture their child's delightfully innocent wishful thinking. They model a wishing that is in harmony with the world's welfare and do not cynically and prematurely dismiss wish-fulfilling magical figures such as Santa Claus, the Easter Bunny, and the Tooth Fairy. They truly relish the not-quite-cooked eggs, too-cooked bacon, and messy kitchen that come with a child's wish for a Mother's or Father's Day surprise breakfast in bed. Even as they teach a rational approach to living, they model and teach a trust in the invisible. While not neglecting the nurturing and refinement of their children's five basic senses, they are also unrelentingly committed to sixth-sense parenting. They augment the school's head-oriented five-sense curriculum with their own modeling of and instruction in the heart's sixth-sense sensitivity.

Parents who know how to wish well show their children that they are "possibilities." They model that one can balance a thoughtful, reflective approach to daily life without surrendering a faith in an invisible L energy. They talk to their young children about pretend creatures and playmates. They spend regular dinnertimes sharing wishes and discussing their meaning and impact. They regularly tell their children stories and have their children make up pretend stories for them. They read them fairy tales and talk with them about the magical signs in nature such as shooting stars and magical hay wagons. They play make-believe games with the same eager and uninhibited joy they hope will continue throughout their child's life.

Rock and Read

Parents interested in developing their children's wishful thinking intelligence intentionally try to hone their children's natural instinct and reflex to resonate innocently and subjectively with the world. To do so, they perform one of the most effective wish-teaching rituals, rocking and reading. While in the comforting arms of a loving parent, eyes closed, breathing deeply and slowly, and being gently and rhythmically rocked to the heartbeat pentameter of a whispered fairy tale, children receive the lessons about good and bad wishes. It is in this way that the ability to enter into a wishful state is established within the cellular memories of the child. Perhaps this is why, when we wish as adults, we often do so in response to something that elicits a memory of our former infantile paradise.[10]

The wishing imprint may explain why, when we see a shooting star, we remember a grandparent's wishing instructions related to this wish rouser. When we see a white horse, we may instantly recall our mother or father turning to us in the car on a family country drive to tell us to make a wish. Our wish imprint may cause us to automatically make our own wish even when someone else blows out his birthday cake candles.

Why Families Who Wish Together Stay Together

Wish-wise parents also teach the process of wishing well by succumbing to their own natural resonance reflex. They let their children see them modeling a calm, gentle, trusting, hopeful, non-cynical connection with life and a faith in the impossible, unseen, and immeasurable. They blatantly and without shame wish together right in front of their children and make wishing a regular part of family rituals. They make sure that no one cuts the birthday cake without first making a wish, and they save the "wishing bone" from the turkey for a later wishing ceremony. They do not stifle their children's childish wishing by presenting them with only an "in-your-face reality" that robs them of the power of constructive denial, resourceful regression, and productive illusion.

Families who wish together share a common intentionality. By trying to connect together with subtle L energy, they strengthen their family bond. The quiet, restful, gentle nature of wishing elicits in the family system the same balance it produces in individuals who enter a wishful state. Looking at family conflicts in terms of incompatible wishing and trying to find ways to share wishing can be a helpful problem-solving technique. However, children wishing as many people dead as possible while playing against them in a video game are hardly learning how to wish well for others in the real world. The increasingly violent and realistic nature of video games is taking some of the fantasy and magic out of playing and making children wicked wishers.

Parents who help their children learn how to rationally solve the mysteries of life while still supporting their trust that they can connect with the mysteries of life are helping to produce adults with a better heart/head balance. By teaching their children not only to ask "why?" but also to freely exclaim "wow!" and not only to "wonder about" but also to "wonder at," these parents are producing the creative leaders of the new millennium. They help their children preserve the true identity of Santa Claus as the same mythological figure they themselves still believe in as the spirit of an extraordinary loving and giving wish granter. Even when it seems to come too soon, they gracefully help their children make the transition from a belief in a fat man living at the North Pole into an image not too different from a loving uncle or aunt who has a giving heart.

Wish-wise parents teach their children to be subtle energy donors as well as recipients. They spend at least as much time teaching their children how to enjoy fulfilling others' wishes as they do trying to fulfill their child's every wish. They know that the definition of a spoiled child (or a pampered adult) is someone who constantly makes wishes but seldom tries to grant them.

The Primal Wish Imprint

What was the one wish that seemed very important in your childhood? What wishes did you see and hear expressed by your parents? My own and others' research shows clearly that there is an answer to a very important question that predicts to some extent whether or not you will get cancer, develop heart disease, kill yourself, prematurely age, or die young.

We asked our wish-research group members, "What was your parents' single most important wish together about their life together?"[11] No matter what the objective specifics of the wish were, if the research subject's answer reflected a shared, caring, trusting, tender wishing between two loving parents for essentially the same kind of life and love, that subject was 200 to 500 times less likely to become sick, depressed, or die young than subjects who could not identify such a wish.[12] It is clear that, even before birth and early in childhood, the tradition of wishing noted between one's parents is forever imprinted in our brain, body, heart, and soul.

Entering the World of the Wish

In preparing to write this book, I wanted to talk to those still relatively safe from cynicism and who would most likely be totally honest about the role of wishing in their life. To do so, I conducted a "wish focus group" with ten six-year-old girls and boys from a kindergarten class in Michigan. Their parents, grandparents, and teacher were present but were asked not to actively participate. I later interviewed each parent and one grandparent of each child about what they had heard in their children's discussions. Some of the sample wishes you have read in this chapter came from the children in this group.

When I asked if any of the children made wishes, all but two said they "used to" but no longer did. One of the two girls who reported still making wishes said, "I do sometimes at night, but only if I can see my star." The other, the group's sole admitted believer in Santa Claus, said, "After I say my prayers, I look at her picture and make a wish that my grandma is happy in heaven." When I asked who in the group believed in Santa Claus, the Easter Bunny, or fairies, only that one little girl raised her hand. When I asked how many believed that wishes could come true, only the two girls said they did. As his mother nodded in agreement, a six- year-old boy responded, "My dad said wishing is silly and that if I want a bike I have to do a lot more than just wish for it. I have to work for it." Another little boy modified one of his mother's favorite wish-dismissing sayings that "if wishes were horses then beggars would ride" when he added, "You might not get a horse if you wish. My mom says that if a wish was a horse that beggars would have their own horses to ride around on instead of walking on the street downtown." Another boy added, "Sissies wish."

A girl who seemed to be teetering on the enchanted edge asked me, "Do you have to make noise when you wish? Is it a wish if you don't say it?" My Santa supporter placed her hand on one hip, rolled her eyes, looked upward to nowhere, and sighed, "You're not supposed to tell someone what you wish, stupid! You just say it to yourself. If you tell it to everybody, it won't come true. That's why you don't believe in wishes. That's why wishes don't work for you. You do it wrong."

It appeared from our discussions with our children's wish group that what we had assumed would be a pristine world of the wish had already been polluted by the cynical pessimism of modern life. The two little girls admitting their belief in wishing were ridiculed by what had become the reality majority. I also detected tolerant but patronizing smiles on the faces of the parents not only for the two wishing girls' naivete but in response to the delusional doctor who asked such ridiculous questions and seemed to take wishing so seriously. Nonetheless, when our wish group was over, and as the most cynical professionals do after every one of my scientific presentations, the teacher and almost every parent and grandparent were eager to talk one-on-one about wishing.

As if in a support group for Alcoholics Anonymous, eight of the children reluctantly admitted they had indeed been wishers in their brief fancifully dysfunctional former lives but were now in enchantment recovery. They reported in various ways how they had overcome their "wish addiction" and had become well-educated little cynics giving testimonials about what they now knew about the "real" world.

"You're stupid," responded the boy who had been chastised by the Santa supporter. "Wishing doesn't work and there ain't no Santa Claus. That's just a stupid fairy tale. Your parents buy the presents and they eat the cookies and drink the milk you leave out on Christmas Eve."

Another recovering wishaholic gave his testimony. "I wished I could see Santa's reindeer," he said, "but I got up and saw Daddy making little deer prints in the snow to make it look like a reindeer. Only Toys-R-Us can make all the toys, not Santa. He's just a guy paid by Sears to sell pictures of kids with him."

Another wish cynic who had already seen far too much in his young life in the ghetto added, "There probably was a Santa once, but he's dead now. He got shot in a drive-by shooting downtown. You can't carry all that stuff he carries around in the 'hood."

The contrawish momentum in our group was now in full swing. "My mom says rabbits carry all kinds of diseases," said one little girl. "You wouldn't want an Easter Bunny in your house anyway. He would poop all over." I am still saddened when I think about the little Santa supporter who, despite apparent courage in the face of wish cynicism, privately wiped away a tear as the group seemed to be convincing her that wishes are silly, fairies are for fools, and that Santa, like philosophical "shock jock" Friedrich Nietzsche's God, is dead. There is no doubt that wishing requires an act of faith, a willingness to give up our illusion of total individual and willful control of our destiny. It does not, as you have seen, require that we surrender our sanity to be just abnormal enough to believe in magic.

Beyond the Reality Principle

Psychologists know that developing from child to adult requires learning what they call the "reality principle." This is the idea that life is a constant struggle to survive in a cruelly indifferent world. They also believe that maturity requires giving up the "pleasure principle," the idea that life is influenced by magical mystical forces. The pleasure principle says that good things come to those who "wish," but the reality principle teaches that the best things come to those who "will."

The pleasure principle is concerned with what psychologists call the primary and subjective processes of life; with fantasy, wishing, and loving. The reality principle is concerned with the "secondary processes," or objective life realities such as rational, skeptical, manipulative ways of achieving one's goals. The pleasure principle focuses on now whereas the reality principle focuses on the future. By wishing well, we establish a delightful, enjoyable, comfortable balance between both of these life orientations.

An example of a healthy balance between the reality and pleasure principles is found in a story about two rabbis attending a boxing match. One of them notices one of the boxers' trainers crossing his fingers and making a wish. "You've been to many boxing matches," says the rabbi as he turns to the rabbi next to him. "Does wishing like that really help?" The boxing-smart and wish-wise rabbi answers, "It does if you're a very good trainer and have a very good boxer."

Romantic Regression

Although the word "ego" is often understood to mean "self," it really refers to "reality" and the ability to go from selfish impulse to socially responsible control. "Regression" is often seen as a weakness or even a symptom of psychopathology, as in regressing to behave childishly and exclusively by the pleasure and primary processes of life.

However, the clinical phrase "regressing in the service of the ego" refers to knowingly and intentionally suspending our illusion of total control of life when the situation calls for such action. It involves trying to connect with our vague inner sense that there is something more that influences our life than what our five-sense system can detect. It's knowingly making a wish to try to connect with L energy or "the forces that be."

Enlightened regression requires the willingness to move freely back and forth across the enchanted boundary between wishing and doing. It requires being just "abnormal" enough not to be too "well adjusted" to trust in what you cannot see or touch.

It's being willing to become energy-malleable enough to be at least as subjective about life as we are objective. We can learn to be secure enough in our adulthood to be just childish enough to take wishing seriously. We can become wish-wise enough to believe again in Santa Claus and still shop early to avoid the Christmas rush.

Five Characteristics of a Mature Wisher

Our research on the development of wishability—the skill of focusing and expressing one's intentions in order to influence the world—shows that clear wishful thinking and wishing well is characterized by five general daily life skills one of our wish-research participants called a "wishing personality." These five traits provide a model of the child raised well to wish well. I use this list when I observe the wishing behaviors of families in airports and other public places. You may want to refer to the two families I observed in the Detroit airport to see how their respective wishing personalities compare.

1. *Persistently patient.* To master the art of passive volition by quieting the urgings of the brain and "letting" things happen more than "doing" them. To use an analogy from fishing, the well wisher has learned to troll and cast as well as chase and spear. This skill helps make wishes in the serenity realm of the wish star come true.

2. *Harmoniously connected.* To be able to use the sixth sense to detect and connect with the subtle, quieter energy of life. A sense of harmony is key to the wishing personality because true and lasting enjoyment of any wish requires that others share in its fulfillment. Remember that power wishing requires two persons sharing the same wish and a sensitivity to nature's wish rousers so that you may be alert to nature's invitations to wish.

3. *Pleasantly agreeable.* To be able to get along, trust in the innate goodness of people and the world, and to maintain one's sense of purpose even when something or someone seems to interfere with our objectives. Because wishing well

requires being a generally nice person who maintains a sense of clear direction even when things aren't going well, this skill helps wishes in the purpose realm of the wish star come true.

4. *Modestly humble.* To accept the fact that no one tells the universe what to do and to realize that we are all the created, trying our best to timidly connect with our Creator or the Absolute. Because wishing well requires finding meaning beyond the self and the here and now, developing this skill helps wishes in the meaning domain of the wish star come true.

5. *Kindly tender.* To try to make others' wishes come true and share wishing with someone in a way that strengthens a loving bond. Because well wishing deals with L or love energy and being in a state of love creates a good wish-energy match, this skill helps wishes in the compassion realm of the wish star come true.

To a large extent, our children are granted wishes made from within a loving bond. Like talismans engraved by the energy of our own heart, our children are endowed and inspired by the nature of our own wishes to work their magic in the world. Ultimately, our children are expressions of how they have seen us making and sharing wishes in our own life. A purpose of a family is not only to raise children whose wishes come true but also to raise children who know how to wish in harmony with the fundamental truths of life. By modeling and incorporating instruction in well wishing through our parenting, we will benefit more than just our own children. By helping to raise wise wishers, we are helping to make the world more like the one we all wish for in our hearts.

Ten

························· ✦ ·························

How to Avoid the
Wicked Wish

*The vital force is not enclosed in man, but radiates around him
like a luminous sphere, and it may be made to act at a distance.
In these ethereal rays the imagination of a man may
produce health or morbid effects.*

—PARACELSUS

The Danger of Wishing's Dark Side

Musician Frank Zappa said, "In the fight between you and the world, back the world." He meant that always trying to get your way rather than learning to go along with "the way" is a fruitless task. In fact, wishing against the natural order of things is worse than wasted effort. It can lead to ultimately wicked wishes with serious, even deadly, consequences. There is an ancient proverb that says, "Every stick has two ends," and every wish has a bright and dark side and both positive and negative power.

Based on cultural mythology and the experiences of our wish-project participants, we have come up with seven warnings about the dark side of wishing and ways to minimize the wicked or unwise wishing that causes it to dominate. They are based on the idea that wishing's energy, like all energy and matter, cannot be created or destroyed. Its appearance and feel may change, but as one Alaskan Indian told me about wishing's nature, "Whatever it is about a wish, what it is . . . is. You might be able to help direct it a little and get it to slightly change form, but you can't destroy or create it. Much like when you write your name in the sand and the ocean comes to wash it away, wishing just temporarily rearranges and redistributes the way of nature. If you remember that, you will wish more wisely with nature instead of against her."

Caution! Wish with Care

Wishing would not be the wonderfully powerful act it is if it did not have its opposite negative side, the power to do damage as well as good and the capacity to work against things as well as for us. Like all powerful things, wishing must be handled with extreme caution. If, as research shows and mythology teaches, our mere intentions can help heal across time and space, surely they can also do harm. Good intentions have noble effects, but bad intentions can cause real trouble. As a review of the pitfalls of unwise wishing, here are the seven basic warnings about wishing I have collected from healers around the world. You have already read several versions of these warnings in the earlier chapters of this book, but I present them here in summary form so you can use them as a single "wisher's warning reminder list."

1. The "Come and Go" Rule: When you wish for something, remember that you are also wishing something away. A wish for wealth and success can result in the loss of the more simple and less stressful times you already had. One Sami healer I met in Norway told me, "When you make a wish, think of it as going fishing. You must use bait. Sometimes we use very tasty little fish to try to catch big ones. We often lose many of these just to catch one big fish. Sometimes the big fish we catch doesn't even taste good. We have to make sure what we give up is worth what we are trying to catch."

2. The "Go and Come" Rule: When you wish something away, remember you are also wishing for something. When you wish your life to be problem-free, you may be wishing upon yourself a dull and tedious existence. A Hopi Indian medicine man told me, "When you wish something out of your life, you create a vacuum. Something will pop in because nature does not tolerate vacuums well. She will fill it with something else. When you wish something away, make sure you remember that you have sent an invitation for something else to come and fill the void your wish created."

3. *The "Get and Take" Rule: When you wish for something, someone else loses something.* A Tongen healer told me, "There's only so much *mana* [energy]. If you take some, someone must give some. When you reach into the pot and take, there's less left there when someone else reaches in because you have it. You always take a little from everything whenever you take something." Wishing well requires constant awareness that we never make a wish that does not affect everyone and everything in some way.

4. *The "Go and Give" Rule: When you wish something away from you, someone ends up getting it.* Wishing never permanently eradicates anything, it only displaces it. A Maori shaman told me, "What you send out must go somewhere. You can't cast a stone in the pond without a ripple. You can't wish anything away without it landing in some way or form in someone else's life." Wishing well is wishing gently and lovingly so that we do not unknowingly hurt others.

5. *The Rebound Rule: An undeserved wish sent to another person always comes back to the wisher.* A monk in India said, "Buddha warned that a gift not deserved always returns to the sender. The same is true with wishing. Don't send a wish unless you're ready to take it back."

6. *The Respect Rule: If possible, ask permission before you wish for someone else.* A Navajo medicine man told me, "We can't assume we know what others wish for or even about. If we want to wish for them, we should ask them if at all possible if it's okay. A wish without asking permission is an invasion of spiritual privacy. We may be even imposing our own wish upon them or unknowingly using them in our wishing. Wishing is pretty powerful stuff when you come to think about it. Like any strong medicine, we should seek permission before prescribing it. We may think we have good intentions, but we can never be sure how they might work out in another person's life. To be safe, if you must wish without permission, just wish with and for love."[1]

7. *The Patience Rule: Wish and wait.* Never rush a wish. A Hawaiian healer told me, "You don't wish and run and then go on to the next wish. When you do that, everything can build up and you get a crazy mix of wishes all crashing together at once. You might not even know or remember your wish or be able to sort one from another." Think of making a wish as pushing the button to summon an elevator. One push is sufficient.

The five elements of the dark side of the wish star seem to emerge when these seven warnings are ignored and wishing is brain- rather than heart-based (see the

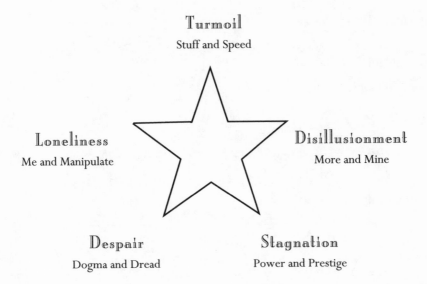

figure above). The inevitable result is turmoil, disillusionment, stagnation, despair, and loneliness. When we feel our wishing going wrong, we often begin to wish reactively, desperately, and regressively. For example, we might start to wish impulsively for loving compassion from another person as a substitute for our own unwillingness to wait for our wish for personal serenity to come true. As a result, we spiral further inward to the dark side of the wishing domains (see the figure on page 186).

A Wish's Toll

Since wishes almost always come true in some form at some time, it is important to be cautious in what we wish for; when we get it, we may wish we hadn't. Wishing well requires being fully and deeply aware of what we will have to do when we get what we wish for and what we will have to do without when our wish comes precisely and literally true.

There is a toll for every granted wish. More money may mean less freedom. More fame may mean less privacy. More attractiveness may mean less assurance that you are appreciated for who you are rather than what you look like. A longer life may mean giving up the advantage of a gentle, peaceful, and timely end to life. Sometimes the granted wish itself can result in getting much more than we bargained for.

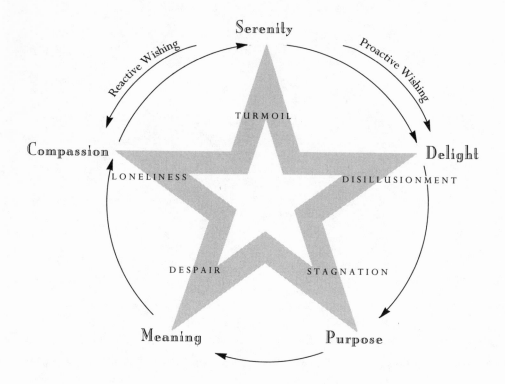

The Midas Factor

An example of a literally granted wish gone wrong is the "Midas Factor." This is a principle taught in many forms in many wish myths. In the Midas myth, the king had many wonderful things in his life. He had power and great wealth but felt that something was missing. Despite his good fortune, he found little peace in his life and always felt a lack of the joy he thought his status would bring him. As a result, he made a wish that violated almost every rule of wishing well.

Instead of being patient and wishing in the form of a mild suggestion, Midas wished big. Instead of wishing from his heart for "just enough," he was drawn into the dark wish star's "never enough." Because he wished from his selfish brain instead of his loving heart, his wish for more delight and serenity spun inward into the negative forces of wishing. Instead of wishing to experience more gratitude and appreciation for what he already had, he wished for greater wealth. Instead of tenderly swinging a little well wish outward, he wished very, very hard for everything in his life to turn to gold. He got his wish, but it eventually cost him his life.

Midas's wish was granted to the fullest. Everything and everyone around him turned instantly to solid, cold gold. Because he wished wrongly in the areas of delight and serenity, he ended up living in turmoil, loneliness, and despair. His granted wish was worthless because, like everything in life, gold has no value without other people to give it meaning. As a result of his wicked wish, the king was left with everything he thought he wanted but nothing his heart really needed. He died amidst his piles of gold a sad and lonely old man.

Midas is the poster child of wicked wishers. His unwise wishing included five elements of unwise wishful thinking that usually leave us wishing around the dark rather than the bright wish star. Here's a profile of the Midas mistakes stated as dangers to be avoided in wishing "for" something.

1. *The "Me" Mistake: Don't make selfish wishes.* They always end up leaving you feeling isolated. When you wish for something, think, "This wish is likely to come exactly and literally true." Then ask yourself two questions: "Is that what my heart tells me it really needs?" and "What will happen to other hearts if my wish comes true?"

2. *The "Stuff" Mistake: Don't wish for "things" or "more stuff."* The granting of such wishes eventually ends up stealing your life away. When you wish for something, ask yourself two questions: "Do I feel in my heart that I really need this?" and "Will I and others enjoy my life if I get what I wish for?"

3. *The "More" Mistake: Don't wish for more of what you already have.* All desires are insatiable and all desire states are transitory, so if you wish to try to have it all, all you will end up with is wishing and trying. Before you wish for something, ask yourself two questions: "Don't I really already have what this wish represents?" and "Should I wish first to be able to appreciate more what I already have instead of wishing for more of it?"

4. *The "Literal" Mistake: Don't take your brain's demands literally.* The heart expresses its needs in symbols and metaphors. Selfish wishes from the brain seem to be taken and dealt with literally by the L energy force that grants wishes. Before wishing for something, ask yourself two questions: "What if I get exactly what I wish for?" and "What if I can't change my wish or give it back?"

5. *"The "Wanting" Mistake: Don't mistake what your brain says you want for what your more docile heart hints is what your soul needs.* Before you wish for something, ask yourself two questions: "Where did this wish come from, my head or my heart?" and "Am I remembering that my brain is never satisfied?"

Beware of Self-Hexing

If you are not careful and very clear about what you are trying to wish away, you may end up hexing yourself. Consider this example from one of our wish-research subjects. One of the women in our group had lost her mother to breast cancer when she was three years old. Since that time, she had wished vigorously to "never be sick, ever." This is a wish in the serenity domain related to health and well-being, but it was made so powerfully and selfishly that it wished away other aspects of the woman's life. She became consumed with exercise, meditation, and eating healthy foods. Almost everything she did related to trying to avoid illness rather than fully experiencing the health she already had. She was in a constant state of fitness turmoil, never feeling confident that she had exactly the right diet or exercise program to protect her from early death. Instead of being fun, her exercise was a form of ransom to her health terrorism.

After several years of fixated wishing in the serenity domain, this young attorney never progressed along the realms of the wish star. Her lonely struggle to stay healthy caused her to eventually slip back to wishing in the compassion domain to fulfill her increasing loneliness. She quickly fell further back to wishing for some sense of meaning but experienced only despair as she fell under the dark star's spell. Her wish was literally granted. She became an extremely healthy but unhappy and lonely older woman. She had wasted much of her life trying to save it. She was a beautiful and fit woman for her age, but her fixated wishing focused only on her body, resulting in little time left to become interested in anyone else's.

For this bright young attorney, her unwise wishful thinking led her to make a wicked wish. Like Midas, her world turned lifeless and cold. She, too, made the "me mistake" by focusing on her own well-being. She made the "stuff" mistake of translating a good life to the quantity of years in life. She made the "more" mistake of thinking that a long life is necessarily a joyful and full life. As if wishing for the exhilaration of morning without its necessary opposite of night, she made the "literal" mistake of translating good health into never being sick. Finally, she made the "want" mistake by confusing her heartfelt need to feel serene and cherish the lessons of her mother's life with her brain's frightened demand to save its own life. Her wishing away of all illness brought her only loneliness and lack of fulfillment.

Both the greedy Midas and the frightened attorney failed to progress in their wishing development. Their wishes were not of and for the world but for their own safety, security, and reward. The higher stages of wishing for acceptance and esteem and wishing in balance with the world's welfare were never attained.

Wicked Wishing's Backdraft

There seems to be a backdraft to an evil-spirited wish that results in "retributive rebound." When it comes to wishing, the old principle of "what goes around comes around" is a fact of life. If what you wish either for or against someone is not deserved by the wishing target, the wish will come swinging back to you. If you wish love and well-being to someone who has not led a life deserving of that gift, it comes back to you. If, however, you wish evil for someone undeserving of such a wish, you have just wished yourself into serious trouble. Here's another example of wicked wishing from our wish group.

A young executive wished that he would eventually have the opportunity to take over his boss's position. He made a wish against his boss that he would ". . . somehow just go away or vanish so I could get his job." His wish came true as his supervisor was wished away, unexpectedly resigning with no stated reason. The young and ambitious executive was immediately promoted to the job for which he had wished so hard for so long. Several weeks after assuming his new position, he encountered his new immediate supervisor. He turned out to be extremely and unrealistically demanding. The wisher spent less and less time at home. His wife finally filed for divorce and received custody of his twin daughters. He was making a lot of money and had the prestige enjoyed by his former supervisor, but he longed for the delight and sense of purpose he had in his prior position. After more than two years of working six-day weeks of ten-hour days, he felt weak and sick. When he visited his doctor, he discovered that he had developed high blood pressure and ulcers. Tests revealed that four of the arteries leading to his heart had become clogged. Like Midas, his world and even his heart were becoming hardened and lifeless.

In this example of a wicked wish, the brain got its way. The young executive got exactly the position he coveted, but he also received a heavy dose of chronic stress, gained a difficult and mean-spirited boss with whom to work, and lost his wife and children. His heart had literally become hardened by neglect and a lack of L energy nurturing. He had wished someone away, and the backdraft of his wicked wish engulfed him. Once again, Midas's misery took its toll on another wicked wisher. The "me" wish error of coveting for the self what is rightfully someone else's, the "stuff" error of wanting more money and prestige, the "more" error of being unable to want what one already has, the "literal" error of thinking status means fulfillment, and the "wanting" error of thinking any one thing will forever and finally meet all needs combined to create another cold and lonely world for a wicked wisher.

How the Good Fairy Takes Revenge

When we swing a wish outward, it always swings back. The harder we swing it, the harder it comes right back at us. What comes back depends on what and how we wished and how we were when we made our wish. Our research subjects often reported what many wishing myths teach; beware of the revenge of the Good Fairy.

Writing about the impact of unwise wishing, anthropologist Catherine Bateson was the first to write about a wish's potential backlash as the "revenge of the good fairy."[2] She points out that many stories of granted wishes do not end with everyone living happily ever after. Many fables about wishing exist in cultures from Native America to China and from classical Greece to Australia. As physician Larry Dossey points out, "The fact that they [Good Fairy revenge fables] are spread through cultures worldwide suggests that maybe there is a generic wisdom here that we ought to ponder."[3] This generic wisdom is reflected in the list of common wishing mistakes discussed earlier.

Regaining Your Balance

A lot of anything is seldom good for us, but balance is always healthy. A little potassium and hemoglobin in the blood is healthy, a lot isn't. A little arsenic heals, a lot kills. A wish for an extraordinarily long life can result in years of artificially sustained vegetative life. The distinguishing characteristic of a wicked wish is that somewhere within it or its expression there rests the "me, stuff, more, literal, and wanting" characteristics of impaired wishful thinking.

When a group of people wish as one, they can create a "power wishing" effect. When several persons share the same wish, several tiny cosmic shoves can become a very big subtle energy push. An example of collective wicked wishing can be found in our society's wish to fly faster and faster, the dark "speed" side of the serenity wish realm. Consider the continuing rapid increase in numbers of persons flocking to airports. They push and shove (the me mistake), try every trick to exceed luggage limits (the stuff mistake), try to go more places more often (the more mistake), try to get places faster (the literal mistake), and act as if they really need to get where they're going at the speed of sound (the want mistake.) The result is a hurried, time-pressured, and often nightmarish air-travel industry functioning on the brink of disaster.

Dr. Bateson writes of the Good Fairy's revenge against the wishes of the frequent flyer: "After the engineers and technicians have taken some age-old human desire and made it come true, we find ourselves with something that doesn't correspond at all to the remembered vivid longing [the original wish] . . . the dream of flight is a far cry from the transport we experience in a sealed container, breathing stale air as we go, after endless delays, from one identical airport to another. The Good Fairy must laugh at our inept wishing."[4]

What "The Trickster" Teaches about Wishing

There is a universal corrective force that acts to keep all of life in a state of balance. Fighting this force or wishing against it results in the emergence of the dark wish domains. Wishing well is trying to flow in harmony and balance with this force and realizing that no matter how high you become you will end up feeling that low. When we wish "backward," or reactively and regressively on the wish star, the trickster appears to teach us to wish well.

The trickster phenomenon is found in almost every cultural mythology. It appears in our modern world as a flattened tire just when we are due at a major meeting or the breaking of our shoelace just when we are in our biggest rush. The trickster is constantly teaching us about the fundamental truth that we are not omnipotent.

The trickster is the counterforce for wishes that make the "me" mistake. Wishing well is first and foremost a humble, heartfelt act. It is the acknowledgment that we are not in charge of the world. The trickster is a kind of cosmic court jester and wishing's marshal of the reality of our interdependence with the whims and chaos of L energy. He (the trickster is usually a male figure in mythology) is in charge of being sure none of us delude ourselves for too long that we are totally in charge of our destiny.

In modern psychology, the trickster is seen as a universal cultural archetype left deep within our mind. When we mess up, we usually do it to ourselves; we are the ones who ultimately trick ourselves and unconsciously bring ourselves back to a humble realization that when we make plans, God laughs. Psychologist Carl Jung proposed that the trickster represents the irrational, chaotic, and unpredictable side of human thought that counterbalances our rational, controlled approach to life.[5]

Physician Larry Dossey writes, "At some deep inner level we may know that the omnipotence that is being exercised in this wild wishing is off base."[6] Our heart knows about balance and connection, but the brain is more concerned with doing and getting. Bateson writes, "If it is the case that not only is what you want not what you want, but also that, at some level, we already know this, what is the lesson to be learned?"[7] The lesson is that our own internal trickster comes out to tease us when we wish unwisely. He causes us to self-destruct when our wishes are too pushy and arrogant and when they stray too far from the way the world needs to be. As Bateson writes, ". . . we insert the worm into the apple and the weakness into the O-rings [referring to the Challenger space-shuttle disaster], building the faults into all we do."[8] In effect, when we make Midas-like wishes, it is not just the subtle energy rebound that strikes us down but our "foolish wit" within.

Transpersonal or depth psychology suggests that the trickster within us is the exact opposite of the "realist" and the values of order, precision, and control that come with our attempts to impose our will on the world. Just as healthy psychological adjustment requires a balance between the rational and irrational, healthy wishful thinking requires being constantly aware of the balance between these two vectors of our psyche and ready to have a good sense of humor when the trickster causes us to fall as we enter a boardroom full of executives ready to decide on our future.[9] Wishing well avoids the arrogant illusion of omnipotence, but wicked wishing often clings to the idea that wishing long and hard enough will allow us to assume total control of our life. To this, the trickster mocks, "Oh yeah? Watch this." Wise wishful thinking is aware of the comic troublemaking of the trickster. It is based on the awareness that wherever and whenever we think we are smart, the trickster will sow immediate confusion.[10]

Wish Lash

One of the most pervasive rules of wishing is the rule of retributive rebound. There is a long history to this aspect of wicked wishing. Author Shunryu Suzuki wrote, "The world is its own magic." He meant that nature has its own built-in immune system much older, sophisticated, and stronger than our own. The world will survive. It is our survival that is in question. Don't fool with Mother Nature is sound advice when it comes to making wishes.

Some collective or power wishes can have deadly and irreversible consequences. In Chapter 8, I mentioned the "sixth extinction" theory of anthropologist Richard Leakey. Leakey's devolution theory traces five great extinctions that have taken place since the earth began.[11] The most recent of these was 65 million years ago when the dinosaur species perished in the blink of an archaeologist's eye. Now, Leakey suggests, the sixth extinction is already well under way and we are wishing it upon ourselves. Thirty thousand species are wiped out every year by the effects of human selfish, impulsive, consumerist wishes, a rate that parallels the pattern of the first five extinctions. It is the wicked, rapacious wishing of the species most responsible for this process, Homo sapiens, that may ultimately bounce back to destroy the wishers. The trickster can make saps of us sapiens.

Of the approximately 30 billion species that have lived on our planet, more than 99.9 percent are gone. Forces beyond our control obviously played a role in the extinction process, but the increasingly wicked wishing by Homo sapiens (a name ironically meaning "thinking man") is having a growing negative impact. Although Darwin's theory of evolution is often used to explain the development of life on earth, wicked wishing and the extinction it has wrought has also played an important role. Until we relearn the skill of ecologically sound wishing compatible with nature, the earth will live on. It is we who will have wished ourselves into extinction.

Third-Wish Wisdom

The third- wish factor I discussed in Chapter 9 as a key lesson in teaching children how to wish well is also a factor in avoiding the wicked wish. This wish factor refers to trying to be aware of what we already have before we wish for more. In a famous tale by W. W. Jacobs, a couple first makes the "more," "stuff," and "want" errors of a wicked wish. They wished for more money and ended up receiving hundreds of dollars as compensation for the accidental death of their son. They begin to wish even more impulsively and make the "me" and "literal" wicked second wish that their son come back to life. When their second wish is literally granted, the parents are greeted at their door by the grotesque body of their decaying son. Terrified, the couple makes the mythologically traditional third wish, this time intentionally wishing the death of their own son. Their power wish in the form of a mutual Midas mistake had brought them wealth at the cost of unrelenting grief.

Do We Really Want to Let the Genie out of the Bottle?

We're in store for a magnificent adventure when we decide to let the genie out of the bottle. Before we deal with him, however, we are wise to consider the risks of the dark wish star. To avoid making wicked wishes, we need to test the L or subtle energy waters before diving in. It is wise to do a little prewish resonance rehearsal.

Identifying what might end up being your third wish well before you make your first may show you that you should make the third wish first. Had the couple not wished for more money and instead wished only that they enjoy the loving presence of their son, their agony may have been averted.

Like pushing a child on a swing, once a wish is sent outward it is difficult to control the swing back. The mythological wisdom that "you can't get the genie back in the bottle" pertains to knowing how to wish well. Wise wishing is dealing with the genie by giving up two of the wishes and making a wise, loving, gentle wish the first and only wish.

The third-wish phenomenon can be seen in many aspects of our life. For example, we often wish for long life, but this can lead to years sustained in failing health, pain, and even a vegetative state. We seem to be constantly wishing for an elusive sexual fulfillment, often ending up sensually and romantically anesthetized in our search for magic spots and seductive secret romantic rules. The latest example of a wicked wish is the new impotence drug Viagra—a wish apparently come true for millions of men that now appears to cause sudden death in some of those who take it and genital trauma and bruising in their female partners who become innocent victims of an unwise wish. Even in the privacy of our own bedroom, the trickster tricks us and the Good Fairy laughs at us.

The Heart for Wishing

Again, to minimize the dark side of wishing is to wish more from the heart than the brain. In the wishing realm of serenity and something to live on, a wicked wish of the brain focuses on "stuff" and "speed." The trickster often sees to it that we pay a price for these kinds of wishes by bogging us down in the effort to protect our stuff and letting us know that we will never have enough of it. When we make the Midas mistake, the trickster crashes our computer, disables our car, or chips our tooth.

In the wishing realm of delight and something to live for, the brain's wicked wish is based on getting more and constantly pursuing the new and improved versions of what we already have. For the brain, there is no glory in maintenance. The trickster sees to it that the wicked wishes for more and newness results in the feeling that we no longer have a life but that life has us. The third-wish phenomenon will eventually teach us, often the hard way, that we already have what we're trying so hard to wish for. The brain's wishes are based on the constant search for more and more intense excitement, but the heart desires only the joy of the comforting sameness that comes with life's simple pleasures.

In the wishing realm of purpose and something worth dying for, the brain often mistakes status and compensation for fulfilling work. The Good Fairy takes her revenge against our brain's wicked wishing to have power by giving us many responsibilities without the sufficient control to meet them. The brain's wishes are typically based on wanting a different "better" job, but then we may find ourselves "wasting" our valuable work time in a job that makes us feel stagnant and uncreative. The brain compulsively wishes to live to work, but the heart wishes only to work to live and enhance the living of others.

In the wishing realm of meaning and something to transcend life, the brain fears death. For the brain, there is nothing worse than its own demise, so it approaches life on a literal, concrete basis. The ultimate revenge of the Good Fairy may be the kind referred to by Thoreau when he wrote that he wished that when he came to die, he did not discover that he had never lived. Before the thanaphobic brain is willing to believe that there is a vital force that transcends death, it seeks factual proof. The heart has faith and loves life more than it fears death.

In the compassion wishing domain, which deals with finding someone with whom to share wishes in the first four realms, the brain mistakes passion for intimacy. It wickedly wishes to find a partner it can use to make itself feel better, safer, and more in control. Wishing for someone who can grant your every wish rather than share in making them leads to the ultimate wish backlash of loneliness and isolation. The brain wishes to find the right partner who will give it adoration, but it will never feel there is enough. The heart wishes only to be the right partner worthy of the loving from another heart.

Our Brain's Insistence or Our Heart's Desires?

When our heart's needs are neglected by our brain's wishes, the effects go beyond emotional and spiritual disappointment and strife. One of the leading causes of heart disease is the making of wicked wishes. The Good Fairy often takes revenge for our angry and selfish wicked wishes by turning our heart to stone. A "heart attack" is the heart fighting to get its brain to pay attention to its desires.

Hostility kills. When the brain drives the heart to serve its selfish needs for stuff, getting more, and doing it now, the heart's desires for security, delight, purpose, meaning, and compassion are neglected. Wishes that have elements of the brain's innate irritability and hostility are wicked and can result in negative health consequences. Such "heartfelt" hostility conveyed by the brain to its heart makes the heart beat faster than it desires.[12] As a result, blood cells are propelled through our vessels like microcosmic bullets ricocheting off the walls of our arteries. The platelet bullets leave tiny scrapes and nicks along the artery walls that make perfect fat-deposit catchers. Vessel-blocking plaque builds up, the supply lines to the heart are blocked, and it begins to starve to death. Over time, the heart and arteries become calcified or turned to stone. Wishing well can help open the arteries and allow the heart to live again.

Wishing Well as Anger Management

There are many helpful methods for reducing the anger and aggression that can lead to heart disease.[13] Learning to wish well is one of the easiest, simplest, and most user-friendly approaches to promoting a healthy heart. Based on our research on wishing and the heart, here's a heart-smart wishing-well program you can begin today to help reduce hostility in your life. In the same ritualistic fashion used throughout this book to model the magic ways of wishing, I've again used letters to represent the anger management formula. They are an antidote to anger—L O V E.

1. Learn: When people do you wrong, wish them well.
What we nurture in ourselves will grow. This
is nature's eternal law.

—JOHANN WOLFGANG VON GOETHE

Don't make wishes intended to "teach someone a lesson." The heat of the negative energy of an angry wish will ultimately only consume you. When you feel angry, wish the source of your anger well. Following the steps of making a wise wish slows down your cardiovascular system, decreases blood pressure and respiration rate, and calms the body's entire system. After making forgiving wishes many times, your body learns to react to challenges in a calmer manner and to be free of its lethal alliance with your irritable brain.[14] Remember the statement of Pittacus in 600 B.C. when he set his adversary free after having finally captured him, "Forgiveness is better than revenge."

2. Observe: When you see red, look for rainbows.
A person who can remember what he has seen can never be lonely or be without food for thought.

—VINCENT VAN GOGH

Many of us experience the "AIAI" (pronounced as in the angry and desperate statement "I y-eye y-eye" feeling). The letters stand for anger, impatience, aggravation, and irritability.[15] When you feel the AIAI response to a frustrating person or event, think of a natural object or event you have wished on in the past. When you have wished on something for a long time, the positive physical, emotional, and spiritual state induced by that wish is left as an imprint and cellular memory within your entire system. That response is stored within you in your own self-constructed neural architecture and is a prewired response system you have established over your life experiences. Recalling that image calms you down and returns you to that wonderful state. When I feel like I'm becoming angry, I close my eyes and see a rainbow. In Hawai'i, the island of Maui has a daily living code stated as "no rain, no rainbows." I make wishes almost every day on the many rainbows that arch over the Koholau Mountains behind my home. The image works well for me, but you should select your own natural tranquilizer. Your heart will thank you if you have an "anti-anger" natural image ready for what your brain sees as threatening emergencies.

3. Value: Don't use ten dollars' worth of energy on a ten cent problem.
It is because we don't know Who we are, because we are unaware that the Kingdom of Heaven is within us, that we behave in the generally silly, the often insane, the sometimes criminal ways that are so characteristically human.

—ALDOUS HUXLEY

In anger-inducing situations, remember what really matters to you.[16] You have read about the dangers of quick, impulsive, brain-driven wishing. Wishing well is based on the idea that the urgent things are seldom important and the important things are seldom urgent. One of the greatest wastes of time is to spend it succumbing to our innate irritability and by acting the fool that we say someone else is trying to make out of us. When you start down the slippery slope of frustration/aggression/regression, recall one of your fondest well wishes. The stature of a person can be measured by the size of the events with which that person allows himself to become preoccupied.

If you want to wish well in your life, remember to ask yourself this question: "When all the clocks and calendars have stopped their counting for you, what then has your life added up to?" Remember the words of artist Charles Ephraim Burchfield, "God's greatest gift to me is the ability to be astonished anew by the almost incredible beauty of a dandelion plant in full bloom." Who can be angry with such an image held in the heart?

4. Energize: Save your energy.
Do not say things. What you are thunders so, that I cannot hear what you say to the contrary.

—RALPH WALDO EMERSON

To deal less toxically with anger and angry people, you have to break the brain's habit of expending a lot of energy in self-defense. Author Marcel Proust wrote, "Habit is the hardiest of all the plants in human growth." Our habitual anger response exhausts our body and spirit, so when you feel yourself getting angry, ask, "Is this really worth dying for and wasting my wishes on?"[17]

You have probably been around people who seem to energize you and others who seem to drain your energy. Hawaiians refer to the subtle energy of wishing as *mana,* and persons who seem to drain us of this spiritual vigor as *mana* suckers. Wicked wishers can sap our spiritual energy. When we ourselves waste our wishes on the little problems and aggravations of everyday living, we do as one of our wish-research subjects described it, "spring our own spiritual energy leak."[18] Winston Churchill pointed out, "When a man cannot distinguish a great from a small event, he is of no use."

When we react with anger, we are turning our wish power over to the aggressor. Whenever your brain tells your heart to get ready for a fight, do "CPR." Make a cardio-pleasing response. Make a well or healing wish by placing your relaxed left hand (not a fist) over your heart, push it gently against your chest with your right hand, and take a very deep breath. It's better to gently hold your chest now than grip it in life-threatening pain later.

Here's an example of one of my own energizing wishes that I use when I feel that I am getting myself upset. It's a form of sympathetic magic based on the idea that like brings like and love leads to love. It can also serve as countermagic against those who wish you evil. Hand over my heart, I use these eight words when my brain tells me it's getting irritated with someone: "Energize my own and others' hearts with love."

Your Right to Wish

While you have no right to tell the universe what to do, you do have a right to make subtle sixth-sense suggestions to help find more harmony and love in your life. The following words were found by one of our wish-research group members while she was touring through Old Saint Paul's Church in Baltimore. An old woman was sitting alone in one of the pews with head bowed. As the tour group passed by, the woman slowly raised her hand and placed a torn and yellowed piece of paper in our subject's hand. On the bus back to the hotel after the tour, our participant opened the wrinkled paper and read it. On the bottom of the paper was the phrase "Found in Old Saint Paul's Church, Baltimore, Dated 1693." The words that my colleagues tell me are those of the seventeenth-century philosopher Desiderata capture the simple grandeur of well wishing and the importance of avoiding the wicked wish: "You are a child of the universe, no less than the trees and the stars; you have a right to be here. And whether or not it is clear to you, no doubt the universe is unfolding as it should. With all its sham, drudgery, and broken dreams, it is still a beautiful world. Be careful. Strive to be happy."

II

Practicing Wishcraft

I've had a wonderful life.
I only wish I'd been there for it.

—EXECUTIVE SUBJECT IN WISH STUDY PROJECT

.... *✐* ....

Eleven

How to Wish
for a Serene Life

If you haven't got all the things you want,
be grateful for the things you don't have that you don't want.

—ANONYMOUS

Way of the Well Wisher: Wish about "you," not about "it." Wish for gratitude even when you suffer and composure especially when you thrive.

Mr. Spock's Wish

One of the best-known wishers in the world is the Vulcan Mr. Spock in the popular television and motion picture series *Star Trek*. With a "V" formed between his middle and ring finger, his gesture expressed a wish that perfectly reflects wishing in the serenity realm of the wish star. He wishes, "Live long and prosper." Spock's wish was stated by one of our wish-project participants as "I wish for enough health and wealth not to be constantly trying to stay healthy and get rich." Another participant's wishing in domain one of the wish star expressed our need for a blissful life when she said, "Now that I'm an adult, I find myself wishing for the same thing I heard my parents wishing for. I wish for a little peace and quiet."

Serenity

Something to Live On
Doing
Attending
Knowing What Can and Can Not Be Changed
"Health and Wealth"
Grateful

A wish for serenity is a wish for something to live on—sufficient physical and financial well-being to do what one desires in one's life without worrying too much about staying alive (see the figure above). It is based on trying to employ the sympathetic or countermagic of wishing not only to survive but to thrive. Based on our interviews of the wish-research sample, domain one is the "antistress" area of wish making. It's the most basic category of wishful thinking because how we wish in this domain influences the other four domains of delight, purpose, meaning, and compassion.

The Solace of Accepting Suffering

Here are some bits of good news. You're going to suffer from severe stress, never live up to your own expectations, few will live up to your expectations, you're going to feel that life is not fair, you'll think many others are more fortunate and happy than you are, you'll never have enough money, you'll get sick and die, and you'll worry about all of this most of your life. This is good news because all of these experiences mean you are alive and fully absorbed in life. Achieving serenity is not changing any of these facts; it's wishing for the spiritual resiliency to be able to accept life's side effects with grace and a peaceful gratitude for the gift of life. It's not wishing for more things in order to find serenity but wishing for a different way of seeing things that allows you to feel more serene.

Wishing well for serenity is based not on wishes coming true but on being able to wish for the strength to accept the basic truths of life and the spiritual grit to accept life on its terms. To paraphrase Robert Louis Stevenson, wishing well for serenity is not wishing to be dealt a good hand but wishing to be able to play any hand, particularly a poor one, well. It's wishing to be able to enjoy just being in the game and with the knowledge that you are going to suffer but that you don't have to be miserable in the process.

The Problem of "Event Density"

How many things happened to you today? How many phone calls, e-mail or voice mail messages, pages, memos, meetings, letters, requests, and other forms of PDEs—personally demanding events—have you experienced since you woke up this morning? None of these events may have been big deals demanding a lot of your attention or time, but they may have been the serial little hassles that seem to create a dense fog of constant things to do, places to go, and obligations to meet. The way you reacted to these demands was carving out the internal neural pathways that become your automatic way of adapting to the world. By being the architect of your own neural structure, you wished upon yourself the life of serenity or stress you feel you are leading.

Your body fulfills your wishes. It exists to express your every command, attitude, and mood. It is made to react for you and to publicize your point of view about the world. It says, "Hey, if you're angry, I'll express it for you. I'll yell, scream, and even kill somebody for you if that's what I sense you wish. I don't censor wishes, I just try to make them physically come true. I don't even care what happens to me. I react and let everyone know the mood you're in." Your body is a wish expression machine, and wishing well means wishing in a way that acknowledges that you and you alone create the reality to which your body is constantly trying to react. Wishing well requires realizing that nothing upsets you—you get yourself upset. Your body is just doing what it thinks you are wishing it to do, even if it must die trying.

By wishing to be able to cope better than to somehow be a constant beneficiary of bliss, you become the architect of your neural-hormonal reaction system, in effect a spiritual body builder. By wishing for the spiritual patience to be able to remember at the terrible times that you always have a choice as to how to react to your world, your body will learn to be an expressor of that well-wishing attitude.

In a Jam

Consider the example of a traffic jam. Traffic jams don't cause stress, they cause stopping. They create the perfect ecology for making wishes for serenity because they force us to stop and offer the opportunity to wish slowly and wisely rather than impulsively and selfishly. Unless we make it so, snarled traffic doesn't make us snarl.

A traffic jam causes cars to stop moving, not your heart to race, your blood pressure to go up, or stress hormones to flood destructively into every organ of your body. You do that by simply reacting to leftover wish imprints in the form of prewired "stress structures"—nasty neural pathways just waiting to fire. When you wish, "Get me the hell out of here," you cause the stress. When you wish, "Help me settle down and enjoy this stopping," you cause serenity.

Wishing well for serenity is wishing to be able to remember when you most need to that you always have a choice. When traffic jams, you don't have to get yourself in an emotional jam. You could say, "Oh boy, a traffic jam! This is exactly what I've been waiting for all day long. Finally, here's my chance to sit quietly, turn up the radio, listen to some relaxing music, and make some well wishes for my family." Or you could say, "Oh no. Yet another frustration to add to the others that have been screwing up my whole day." Your intent makes possibilities into realities and your wishes tend to come true. How and what you wish in a traffic jam is one example of your wishing ways.

The Fleeting Fifth

When you make your wishes, remember that your brain is always one-fifth of a second behind "reality." Whatever you think you are seeing, feeling, hearing, smelling, or tasting is already over by the time your nervous system has been able to process the event. Because what you react to happened a fifth of a second before your brain could register it, you are never really dealing with immediate reality at all. You're dealing with the brain's creation of reality. If you allow your prewired neuronal networks to create the reality in which you live, the results can be fatal. If, however, you remain aware that you can create your own reality and not let your brain dictate its one-fifth-second delayed reality, you can calm down and make some time and allow your calmer heart to be a part of your perceptions.

Stanford physicist William Tiller writes, "Establishment science has failed to make a reality check on its mindset."[1] He points out that what we see as reality and the world in which we struggle to find our serenity is but a very small part of the many realities all around us. In the split one-fifth-second delay between what happens and what we sense happening, our reality takes form. It's not so much what happens to us but what we make of what happens to us that counts. Wishing well is making wishes based on the realization that nature may have provided the one-fifth-second delay to allow us the time to be participants and creators and not just reactors to and victims of the necessary stresses of being alive.

What we perceive is a tiny selected part of a broad spectrum of energies humming all around us. When you make a wish for serenity, remember that we are just dabbing our toe into the cosmic ocean of experiences. By the time we sense the temperature of that ocean, the moment is gone and the temperature has changed. We are always reacting to a past event and not to what is happening to us at this specific moment. Wish to be able to remember that you can choose to see things differently and from a different perspective than what your tardy brain seems to prefer.

Give Me Some Relief

At one time or another, we all wish for the same sense of relief wished for by our ancestors. We seek relief from the tribulations and aggravations of surviving in a constantly challenging world. Feeling overwhelmed by the constant bad news about threats to our health, disappointed in our failures to exercise enough or eat the right foods, and frustrated by the challenges of securing our own and our loved ones' financial futures, we tire of facing what psychologist David Kundtz calls "the mountain of too much."[2] This is a mountain that we ourselves are making through the granting of our own unwise wishes for more stuff.

We know in our heart that we are dying from the moment we are born and that no vitamin or aerobics videotape will avert the inevitability of our mortality. We know that no amount of money can buy the certainty we seek, yet we continue to make wishes related to the denial of the necessity of sickness and the limits of wealth. Wishing well for serenity is wishing to be able to more joyfully and calmly accept all of these challenges and realizing that mountains don't have to be climbed; they can also be appreciated. As author Ken Wilbur writes, ". . . to recoil from the death and impermanence of each moment is to recoil from the life of each moment."[3]

Although they don't seem to know or care much about it, every day is "too much" for our animal relatives. Their life is dominated by being constantly engaged in trying to get enough to eat and, unless elevated to pet status, avoiding being eaten. If they are capable of wishing, their wishes are simply and directly related to getting enough food, comfort, and maybe a little love. Free of our burden of the illusion of boundaries and beginnings and endings in time that block our sense of serenity, they are not troubled by concerns about when or even how they will die. As Wilbur writes, ". . . there is life and death in the world of nature, but . . . it doesn't seem to hold the terrifying dimensions ascribed to it in the world of humans. A very old cat isn't swept with torrents of terror over its impending death. It just calmly walks out to the woods, curls up under a tree, and dies."[4] How different this is from our human wish to not go gently into that good night and to rage against death. A wise wish for serenity is related to philosopher Ippen's statement, "Every moment is the last moment and every moment is a rebirth."

Cerebrally Malcontent

We humans are a dissatisfied lot. Unlike other animals, we seem to wallow in our malcontent. Dogs have pain, too, but they don't seem to worry about it. Although some scientists say that dogs and other pets don't really have a consciousness with which to experience subjective pain, we still use anesthesia when we operate on the family dog and we still watch them kicking, crying, and barking as they dream. Accidentally step on your pet's paw and she yelps, walks it off, and then comes running back with tail wagging. They feel pain; they just don't worry and ruminate about it. Even if they do put their tail between their legs, it doesn't stay there very long. One unfair or angry word from our boss at work and we may sulk off with our emotional tail between our legs and sink into a weeklong funk.

Neurologist and anthropologist Melvin Konner writes, "The motivational portions of the brain . . . have function characteristics relevant to the apparent chronicity of human dissatisfaction. . . . the organism's chronic internal state will be a vague mixture of anxiety and desire—best described perhaps by the phrase 'I want', spoken with or without an object for the verb."[5] The brain is the source of our malcontent. It is made to know what it wants and thinks our body needs, but unless reminded, it seldom knows what our heart desires. The generally contented heart is where our modest spiritual needs are monitored and expressed, and wishing well in the serenity domain requires calming our brain down and tuning in to what the heart thinks about our situation.

By wishing well, we can provide a heart- rather than brain-oriented object for the verb of "want." However, it is first necessary to know that no object will completely dismiss the verb. We will forever want. All physical needs are ultimately insatiable. Knowing and remembering our precoded discontent can help us accept rather than try to feed it.

Domain one wishes are made to allow us to feel totally absorbed in life rather than controlled by our fear of its consequences. There are big and small birds and even birds that can't fly at all, but they seem to have achieved a serenity with their "birdness" that we humans might envy. When they see an eagle, sparrows do not go into paroxysms of anxiety about their size or begin a bird body-building program. There aren't a lot of inferiority complexes in birds. Serenity requires self-acceptance and avoiding comparisons to what ought to or could be. It requires wishing well for enough health and wealth to live on, doing what you can do before wishing when you feel you can do nothing, and attending fully to the gift of life.

Resisting the Pull

A particularly strong force is pulling at us when we make our wishes in the serenity domain. When we don't use our wishing intuition to feel when our wish for serenity is in the process of being granted, we are drawn immediately backward on the wish star in desperate hope that we might find serenity faster by wishing for a lover or religion that might calm us down. Remember, the state of the wisher as well as the wish is at work, so failing to be at least serene enough to stick with our wish for more serenity usually brings us more agitation and impulsive regressive wishing (see the figure on page 210). Wishing well is a process of planting and waiting rather than demanding and expecting. Just follow the steps of wishing well and getting your heart in sync with your brain, and serenity will begin to come.

What's Your Stress Style?

To wish for serenity by physically approximating the state you wish for, remember that just by the act of wishing well, your blood pressure reduces, your heart and respiration rate slows, and your immune system strengthens. You come to feel as you are intentionally behaving, and in effect, the wisher begins to grant his own wish. Psychologist William James wrote, "I don't sing because I'm happy. I'm happy because I sing."

One of our wish group members trying to learn the art of wishcraft in domain one asked, "How do you 'act' serene when that's what you're trying to wish for in the first place? If I was already safe and secure and had no stress, I wouldn't have to wish for it." My answer was, "Remember the sympathetic magic principle of 'like produces like' involved in wishing well? You don't always come to act as you feel,

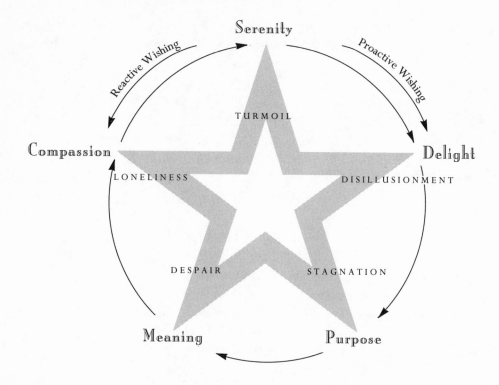

but it's automatic that your body feels as you act. If you act serene, that state can become how you are."

To enter a more serene state for wishing, it helps to know your "stress profile," how you act when you're not serene. This is your "stress default mode." Psychologists have shown that there are four states called "stress response styles." Most of us tend to "default" or automatically turn to one of these styles when we experience a situation for which our current mental, physical, or spiritual adaptive skills seem insufficient.[6]

◆ *Body Reactor:* Here are some questions to ask yourself to see if you tend to be a "body reactor" when you are stressed. When you are under stress, do you:

> Feel a little shaky and jittery?
>
> Feel tenseness in your muscles, particularly in your upper shoulders and neck?
>
> Get an upset stomach or bowels?
>
> Feel your heart racing and perhaps skipping beats?
>
> Get headaches?

◆ *Mind Reactor:* Here are some questions to ask yourself to see if you tend to be a "mind reactor" to stress. When you're under stress, do you

> Worry so much you can't sleep?

> Start making "stupid mistakes" you ordinarily would never make?

> Have anxiety-provoking images pop into your mind?

> Experience your mind as racing from one worry to another and have people tell you that you "just are not paying attention"?

> Ruminate or "go over and over" in your mind possible and past problems?

◆ *Spiritual Reactor:* Ask yourself these questions regarding spiritual reaction to stress. When you're under stress, do you

> "Catastrophize" and foresee the absolute worst scenario?

> Think you are "being paid back" for a past indiscretion?

> Become impatient and even angry with God?

> Question your belief system and wonder "why go on?"

> Think you're "under a dark cloud" and that everything always goes other persons' ways and against you?

◆ *Relationship Reactor:* Ask yourself the following questions to see if you react interpersonally to stress. When you're under stress, do you

> Treat your family more impolitely than you would a complete stranger?

> Throw "temper tantrums" at home that you would never throw at work or in public?

> Sulk and try to elicit a "pity party"?

> Think your family members are afraid to go near you when you're in PMS—a "pretty mean state?"

> Dominate the mood of the entire family?

While we all have characteristics from each of these categories, almost all of us tend to fall more often in one of the stress reaction categories. Some of our respondents, however, said "yes" to all twenty of the questions. We called them "the total tensors," and they were usually the unwise wishers who circled counterclockwise around the wish star and ended up firmly entrenched in the dark wish star's domains.

Once you have identified your "stress response style," you can select the behavioral approach to acting serene that is best suited to you. If you're more of a body reactor, a warm bath might be the place to start your wish making. If you're more of a mind reactor, one of the mindful meditations might be a better fit for you. These approaches involve simply keeping your attention in the present moment without making judgments or interpretations. Basically, these are ways of just sitting down and shutting up. If you're a spiritual reactor, seeking the counsel of a spiritual adviser or clergy person might be a good first step before making wishes. If you're more of a relationship reactor, addressing the health of your relationship or even seeking preventive counseling to soothe your family system might be a wise thing to do before making your own wishes. There are many helpful books that discuss various stress management and relaxation techniques, so I won't go into detail here about these procedures. The key point is to enter the wish state that is the prototype of the state in which you hope to find yourself when your wish comes true.[7]

Lowering Your Expectations

Once you have selected and assumed the right "wishing state" for you, the next step in wishing well in the serenity domain is to clarify your wishful thinking about your expectations. You have to know what you can change by doing something and what you can't change that requires the help of a subtle sixth-sense suggestion to get things moving the right way on the wish star.[8] Knowing when to "just do it" versus when to "wish for it" is related to the three aspects of the well-known "serenity prayer."[9] It's having the poise and self-control to accept what can't be changed, the courage to try to change those things we might be able to change if we are persistent enough, and the patient wisdom to wish wisely when we clearly see that we are in a situation where serene acceptance and willpower do not seem to soothe our soul.[10]

The primary characteristic of wishing well in the realm of serenity is having appropriately lowered expectations of the world. Because we were born irritable into an irritating world, wishing for complete serenity is unrealistic and reflects the brain's need to direct life's flow more than the heart's desire to go with it. As poet Alexander Pope wrote, "Blessed is he who expects nothing, for he shall never be disappointed."

Because our ancestors could never be sure where their next meal would come from or if they might not become a meal themselves, no amount of food in storage could ever be thought of as enough. Despite their best efforts, any primitive who did feel "totally secure" didn't live very long. Today's moderns are still driven by that same primal insufficiency motive that "nothing is enough." That's why wishing in the domain of serenity is so difficult. Learning to accept our innate dissatisfaction as a part of our humanness instead of trying to wish it away is a difficult challenge when the brain keeps trying to achieve satisfaction.

We can't realistically expect perfect health and sufficient wealth. By definition, if "more" is our destination, we can never actually get there but are forever in the process of trying to be there. "There are two things you can't have enough of," said one of our research subjects. "Money and good looks." His statement is an expression of the serenity domain's "wealth and health" orientation, which reflects our brain's need to make us "glow with health" and "smell of money." The "never enough" principle applies particularly to our financial wishes. No matter how wealthy, every person wants more of it. As King Midas learned the hard way, constantly wishing for more wealth can be an isolating and even deadly wasted effort. It's just a fact that you are not made to feel you have enough of anything, especially money. *Harper's* magazine editor Lewis Lapham asked people how much money they would need to be happy. He reports, "No matter what their income, a depressing number of Americans believe that if only they had twice as much, they would inherit the estate of happiness promised them in the Declaration of Independence. The man who receives $15,000 a year is sure that he could relieve his sorrow if he had only $30,000 a year; the man with 1 million dollars a year knows that all would be well if he had 2 million a year . . . Nobody ever has enough."[11]

Wishing wisely for serenity can help us soothe some of our irritability, but nothing we do or wish will ever cause us to lose our dissatisfaction. There's no way around it; few of us ever get what we expect, particularly when we our expectations are set very high. To wish wisely, we have to know our stress reacting style and wish based on realistically placed expectations in keeping with our heart's "just enough" desires rather than our brain's "never enough" demands. One of our wish-research subjects summarized the "just enough" concept when she said, "I've learned to wish to be satisfied that I'm never going to be satisfied."

A wish paradox in the serenity domain is that sometimes the only way we think we can be satisfied is by getting more of what we already have, which is already failing to give us the serenity we wish for. Upon reflection and clear wishful thinking, we learn that it's usually what we've got now that has left us feeling so malcontent. In effect, wishing for more stuff to reduce our dissatisfaction is actually wishing for more dissatisfaction.

Being Sick as a Sign of Health

The same dissatisfaction principle applies to our physical well-being. No matter how much and how fast we jog or how much tofu we have in our diet, we can't outrun or undereat our way to immortality. To wish not to die is to wish away our life. One of our respondents said, "I guess the only ones who don't die are those who have never lived. I no longer wish I won't die. I wish I'll learn to live more completely before I do." Once we get past what philosopher Aurobindo called the "vital shock" of the vulnerability and mortality of our flesh, we are free to be more fully alive,

Everyone gets sick. Saints and sinners and health fanatics and health reprobates all become ill. Mother Teresa and Albert Schweitzer both suffered serious illness at various times throughout their lives, and many of the most loving, giving people in the world have died young. The most fit among us suffer from colds, get cancer, and have heart attacks. In fact, there are two places where I've seen some of the sickest looking people: at holistic health conferences and in vitamin stores. Perhaps because these places tend to attract those who are looking for cures and ways to alleviate their suffering, many persons I see buying the latest miracle herb or attending a seminar on vegetarian cooking appear gaunt, drawn, and even tired. They seem to lack the robust glow of the joyfully eating herds of overweight carnivores huddled around the tables at McDonald's. Of course, looks can be deceiving and over-indulgence is clearly a health risk, but despite all the crystal pyramids, herbs, chanting, and bells, and despite all the aerobics videos and exercise contraptions, sickness is as natural and necessary as sleep and just as important to our health.

Darwin's Medicine

To wish wisely for serenity, never wish away illness or symptoms. They are essential for saving your life. The new science called Darwinian medicine suggests that the natural flaws and frailties that cause us to feel sick are actually built-in evolutionary advantages.[12] Sometimes we need a fever in order to get well. The slight elevation of our body temperature helps us fight off infection. We get sick to our stomach because what's in there doesn't belong there. To seek the serenity of no cold symptoms is to wish away our body's defense system. As the principle behind inoculations teaches, surviving a bout of disease can make us less vulnerable to future diseases. The pain we feel from an infection or injury is essential to our ultimate well-being because it prevents us from using damaged tissue when it needs time off to heal and regenerate. The same is true for emotional states such as anxiety and depression. Without these feelings, we cannot sense the impact of how we relate to and think about the world.

The aches and pains and just feeling "under the weather" that we often try to wish away are our evolutionary gifts. Any of our ancestors who lacked a sense of pain and suffering likely died before they could rest, heal, or do anything to get well. Sickness causes us to stop, sit, sleep, rest, and stay home, all behaviors that are healing to our heart even if they absolutely frustrate the brain so eager to "get back to work."

In another classic example of the revenge of the Good Fairy that results from unwise wishing for perfect health, our wish for magic elixirs capable of curing illness was granted. In the early 1940s, a pharmaceutical revolution took place that resulted in the thousands of magical potions that line the shelves of our pharmacies. The Good Fairy has seen to it that not only are many of them dangerous and addictive, but the related costs are strangling our economy and the bacteria some of them were designed to kill are already outsmarting them. Another wicked wish backlash is that these drugs can block the pain and natural body reactions essential for understanding the meaning of our suffering and the origins of our illness. Sneezing, coughing, nausea, and vomiting are not pleasant to experience, but they are essential for expelling the remnants of our immune systems' victory over an invader. Even if you eventually found serenity from freedom of hacking and wheezing, you may have caused the Good Fairy to strangle you to death by not being able to free yourself from congestion. To wish away our necessary suffering is to wish away our natural healing capacity.

The Worry Signal

The best wishers are worriers. One of the signals you can use to tell you when a wish is called for is worrying. If you don't worry you can't wish well, because worrying is an essential precursor of a well-made wish. What is called for, however, is to try to be a wise worrywart. Despite the popular psychology of "don't worry, be happy," worry is essential to our happiness and health. If we never worried, we would probably never need to wish. However, if we delude ourselves by thinking that any wish will ever free us from worry and make us feel completely safe and secure, we're wrong. If our wishes for serenity center around "never having to worry again" and having the feeling that we can be in complete charge of our destiny, we wish in vain.

No wish can completely convert the universe to an entirely safe place. Worry is distress and agitation resulting from the concern for something that might happen. It's our prewired stress surveillance monitoring system. Like our instinct to wish, we are also natural born worriers. Wishing and worrying both survived because our ancestors who wished unwisely or never worried did not. The worried wishers were those who coped best with their world because they were on the lookout for trouble and developed and relied on the essential countercomponent of wishing—their intuition—to sense it.

Our ability to think about consequences, reflect on them, try to sense them, and even ruminate a little about what "might be" is one of our most important adaptive skills. It's a means of rehearsing "what ifs" and "what will I do if" and running over and over again in our mind the worst-case scenarios without having to actually experience them. The key is to know you're worrying and when to stop worrying and do something or wish for something. Worry can be a tip-off that a wish in the domain of your worrying may be in order, but only after you follow the steps of wishing well for serenity described earlier.

Here's the worrywart test we employed in our wish research. We used it to help our participants become more comfortable with their worrying and to help teach them to use it to enhance their intuition rather than allow it to abuse them by dominating their lives.

Worrywart Test

4 = ALWAYS 3 = OFTEN 2 = JUST SOMETIMES 1 = ALMOST NEVER 0 = NEVER

1. _____ I immediately think "what if" before I do anything.

2. _____ When I see someone doing something risky like bungee jumping, I think "doesn't she know she could kill herself?"

3. _____ After I've left home, I wonder if I turned off the iron or the lights or if I locked the door.

4. _____ I never take my good luck for granted.

5. _____ I worry that I will outlive my money.

6. _____ I think about the possibility of getting seriously ill.

7. _____ I think people are "too foolhardy."

8. _____ I look before I leap.

9. _____ I take only calculated risks.

10. _____ I feel that many people don't realize how lucky they are.

11. _____ When approaching a green light, I keep my foot over the brake pedal of my car.

12. _____ As a child, I was called a "fraidycat" and did not take "double dares."

13. _____ When there is an announcement at a public event, I get a little nervous at first that it might apply to me.

14. _____ I don't take anything or anyone for granted.

15. _____ I think something can be "too good to last."

16. _____ I've never been a risk taker.

17. _____ When I see someone in a crisis, I easily imagine it happening to me.

18. _____ I worry if I'm not worrying.

19. _____ I'm a hypochondriac.

20. _____ I come to complete and lingering stops at traffic stop signs.

21. _____ Before I enter, I check to see if the elevator floor is level with my floor.

22. _____ I push elevator buttons that are already lit "just in case."

23. _____ I take preliminary test bites of my food.

24. _____ I check and recheck to see if I've stamped an envelope before dropping it in the box.

25. _____ I keep every single receipt as an IRS defense strategy.

_____ TOTAL WORRYWART SCORE

In our 2,166-person wish study, those who wished frequently averaged a score of 60 on the Worrywart Test. They were worrywarts who relied on wishing as one of their strategies for dealing with life's threatening nature. Those who did not wish often scored 30 or below on the test. While the worriers were more likely to say optimistically, "I wish," the nonworriers were more likely to say sarcastically and cynically, "You wish."

If you scored above 80, you are leaning toward becoming an unwise worrywart. You worry too much and probably either do not make wishes or make regressive, unwise wishes if you do. Our data shows that you probably have not adequately differentiated between what you can change and what you can't and tend to be such a "total tensor" in terms of your style of dealing with stress that you can't be temporarily serene enough to make a good wish for serenity.

Wise worriers are selective worriers. They worry just enough to filter out what should be wished for from what should not and to find the realm on the wish star that is the most productive place for them to begin wishing. The wise worrywart also benefits from another characteristic of wise wishful thinking, the belief in miracles.

Believing in White Crows

Wishing for serenity does not require giving up on the miracles that violate the known possibilities of what can, should, or has always happened. Making a wish is not an act of surrender; it's an act of belief. Once we have clarified in our mind what we are willing to try to change, know what we cannot change, and have worried our way into the right wishful state, a well wish for serenity and all the areas of the wish star requires that we take the well wisher's leap of faith. After going through the well-wishing steps outlined earlier, the way is cleared for our choice to believe that the impossible can happen.

Between 1858 and 1984, more than 2 million sick pilgrims visited Lourdes.[13] Approximately 6,000 of these people (3 percent) made official or recorded claims of miracle cures. They were examined by the doctors at Lourdes, and following rigorous evaluation, almost every claim was dismissed. Sixty-four (.003 percent of the total number of sick pilgrims) "impossible healings" were confirmed by the committee. These rare cases may be manifestations of the symbolic bird of the wisher, the white crow. Many of our 2,166 wish-project participants began wearing a small white pin in the shape of a crow to signify their belief in the power of wishing to create miracles. These pins started showing up on the hospital gowns of several of my patients. One little boy suffering from leukemia has a white crow pinned to the front of the bandanna covering his bald head. When I asked him about it, he answered, "It's neat. People always ask me about it, and when I tell them it's for wishing, they always start talking about their wishes."

Psychologist William James wrote, "If you wish to upset the law that all crows are black, it is enough if you prove one single crow to be white."[14] The fact that so few persons experience "documented" miracles does not diminish their reality. Each healing wish come true adds another "white crow" to the flock. Wishes are requests for an exception to the expectation. Certainly, prayers and other of the six ways we deal with our world are involved in miracles, but wishing can be a major contributor. As the little girl I discussed in Chapter 9 who believed in Santa Claus said, "That's why they're miracles. They're not supposed to happen. They're impossible. If they always happened and weren't impossible, they wouldn't be miracles. You have to wish for them just in case." Wishing well is asking for an exemption from the rule of the black crow, and sometimes, if we are patient and wish in the right direction, we see a white crow.

Our most regular wishers began to call themselves "possibilites" because they said they knew that the preposterous is extremely rare but not beyond the range of a gentle, well-motivated wish. They didn't necessarily see wishing as creating miracles so much as they used them to increase the odds in their favor. They often prayed for a miracle and then kept wishing for it to happen.

The criteria for a miracle, or in the brain's view an impossible cure, were established in 1735 by Cardinal Lambertini, who later became Pope Benedict XIV. He established that to be declared a miracle, the disease had to be incurable by any known medical treatments. It had to have disappeared completely or at least reached a stage at the time of its consideration by the committee to which it would clearly be resolved in the near future. No medications could have been given and the "impossible cure" had to be sudden and instantaneous—meaning that it took place in a few days' time. Finally, the cure had to be complete and total.[15] Unfortunately, these are the brain's kind of criteria for miracles.

Wishing well for a miracle healing deals with a more subtle, gentle, timeless approach to miracles. No modern treatment is held to the standard of "a few days," and wished-for miracles certainly cannot be. They deal with the invisible and timeless L energy and are matters of little nudges and not "big breakthroughs." Impossibilities know that the preposterous occurs in its own time and in its own way. The sense of comfort, loving, strengthened faith, and sacredness experienced by the Lourdes pilgrims is also a miracle. A room full of desperately ill and dying Lourdes pilgrims who had lost their way and ended up by mistake in a hospital waiting room would not likely leave with these "little miracles." No one has yet studied the pilgrims leaving Lourdes to ask them if they felt blessed with such little miracles even if they didn't receive their big one. I would guess that many of them did. That's a miracle, and that's what wishes are for.

A Wisher's Touch

Three of the women in our wish-research project were nurses trained in therapeutic or healing touch. I asked them if I could do an informal study of their healing approach and its relationship to wishing and they all happily agreed. I wondered if the wishes of the healing touch practitioner and the client would enter into their relationship. I interviewed three of their patients immediately before the healing touch procedure. I asked each of them, "What do you wish will happen because of your session?" All three patients were suffering from cancer. Two were women with breast cancer and one was a man with prostatic cancer. The two women wished, "To be rid of this cursed pain" and to ". . . become cancer-free." The man wished, "To not have pain." I asked the therapeutic touch practitioners the same question. Their three answers were, "To help her relax and focus on that part of her that is not diseased," "To help her balance her energy and feel a loving, healing energy within her," and "To facilitate his own healing powers and free up the flow of his healing energy."

Several hours after the healing touch sessions, I returned to the rooms of the patients. All were resting and seemed much calmer and relaxed than when I had first questioned them. I asked each of them, "What do you wish for now?" The first woman answered, "To stay as relaxed and settled as I feel right this moment." The second woman answered, "To feel this great all over my body when they give me my chemotherapy tonight." The man answered, "To wake up tomorrow just feeling like I do right now." While there seems little doubt that the relaxing nature of therapeutic touch and the gentle caring of the practitioner relaxed these three patients, it is interesting that the wishes of the healer seemed to somehow filter through to the patients. None of the patients was clinically any better than hours before, but all three were noticeably more serene. The healers' wish for their serenity seemed to have come true.

The Serenity of Depression

Another warning about wishing well for serenity is to refrain from wishing away depression and sadness. Like worrying, a little depression is necessary to our health, and it can also lead to wishing well. Depression slows us down and makes us pause to reflect. Looking sad can attract helpful attention from those who truly care about us. While unrelenting depression can be a serious health risk, a little dose of depression now and then is essential to the serene acceptance of life's challenges and disappointments. Life is so grand because it is often so sad. As day cannot exist without night, life elation loses all meaning if there is not sadness.

Depressed people don't have to learn to face reality because that's usually why they're depressed in the first place. Their intuition is working and reacting to the dark side of life. Unfortunately, some people become depressed about their depression. They get more down because they think only they can feel as sad as they do and that most others live in constant gleeful bliss. They literally lose heart and allow their brain to become so focused on the bitter realities of life that their heart loses its sense of life's magic.

To wish well for serenity, don't let depression get you down. People who have developed their potential to know and experience the joys of how the heart thinks and feels are also vulnerable to the dark side of life. Their heart is very sensitive to all sources and types of energy. If you're very sad, you have a very good heart. Your brain may be annoying you with its persistent pessimism and its tendency to take things personally and see problems as pervasive and permanent, but your heart knows better. Your brain fears sadness, but your heart knows it is a necessary part of being alive.

Learning to wish well allows sad people to experience what author David Goleman calls "the illusory glow of positivity."[16] That's the glow that confidence in the subtle but magnificent power of wishing well can provide even when we are feeling hopeless. If you're depressed as you read these words, try the steps of wishing well. Don't wish for things or for "it" to change, but wish for a new and more hopeful way to be able to see things in a new light. Another of our wish respondents said, "I know wishing is a kind of denial, but it's good denial. I'm proud I'm in it sometimes. In fact, I don't know what I'd do without it. Sometimes I pity people who don't know depression. I'm not sure they're fully alive in their heart."

Some Even Better News

This chapter began with some good news to consider in wishing for serenity. Here's some even better news about wishing for serenity based on what you've just read.

◆ **You'll probably live a long time.** Few people living in the early 1900s would have thought that life expectancy would increase almost a decade and a half by the turn of century. While considerable brainpower has contributed to these extra years with new medicines and techniques, wiser wishing for a calmer, balanced, serene, and more connected and compassionate life has played a major role in decreasing the diseases of civilization that are so related to the lack of serenity. Life expectancy in the United States has gone up from living into one's early sixties in the early 1940s to one's late seventies now. We still worry about our health and the length of our life, and there is much we will never change in terms of how long we can ultimately live, but our collective power wish to maximize our given time and its quality seems to be coming true. There are now more than 50,000 people in the United States who are over 100 years old. The outside range of life is now double that of our great-grandparents. In 1994, the last year data was collected on the overall death rate in America, the number of deaths in relation to the total population was the lowest ever recorded. Of course, as author David Shaw points out, ". . . the per capita death rate for all causes combined is, ultimately, 100 percent."[17] We will all die, but likely much later than anyone could have anticipated or wished for 100 years ago.

◆ **Your children or grandchildren will probably be healthy.** The serenity of a better start to life for our children can be found in the fact that since 1979, infant mortality in the United States has been cut in half. Procedures for caring for newborns and premature babies save the lives of thousands of children who would have died just a decade ago.

◆ **Your heart is probably getting healthier.** The serenity of a healthier heart is found in the fact that after decades of dire warnings about the poor health of our hearts, death from heart disease has dropped more than 25 percent and stroke is down by almost half. The brain's brilliance helped this happen by providing new surgical and medical procedures, but wishing well and its gentle effects on how we live has also played a significant role in decreasing heart abuse.

◆ **Cancer is not a death sentence.** I was cured of stage IV lymphoma. Of course, not all forms of cancer can be cured, but death rates from many forms of cancer and survival rates from many others have been vastly improved. The serenity of more freedom from a large part of the cancer curse is likely to be achieved in this millennium. Despite cancer's terrible viciousness, we are much better able to diagnose, treat, and even prevent many forms of the disease than we were even ten years ago. As ghastly as the death rate from breast cancer in women is, about 1 in 43 women (not the 1 in 5 number we often hear about) will develop breast cancer and 1 in 250 (not the 1 in 10 we see in the media) will die from it. Ninety-five percent of women die of other causes than breast cancer. A woman is nine times more likely to die of heart disease than breast cancer, and there is much she can do to reduce her risks of this disease.[18]

Wishing well for serenity begins by first embracing the truths about life. The challenge is not so much in trying to make your wishes come true but in wishing based on the truth. Life is certainly not always easy, peaceful, and painless, but as one of my fellow cancer patients said, "Just as long as you're breathing, you can still wish. No matter how sick you are and how hard it is to pay attention, you still have your intention. I find a lot of solace in the truth that I can just lie in my bed and wish. I need my worries because they're the guides for where I should be doing my wishing."

A Mother's Wish

As an illustration of the careful process involved in making a wish in the serenity domain, here's a verbatim example of a wish made from a woman in our wish-research group.

"I knew right away what I had to wish for in the serenity domain. I had to wish for peace with my teenage daughter. She was breaking my heart and I was breaking hers. When you asked what I worried about the most, that was it. When you asked what kind of stress reactor I was, I knew I was a body reactor. Just ask my husband. He says he can see me tense up, so I knew I'd have to relax if I was going to make a good wish. It really got to me when I faced the fact that if I would ever have peace with her, I had to face that I could never really change her. I had to raise her as she was, not as I wanted her to be. It really helped when you said I had to lower my expectations of both her and of myself as a parent.

"It took weeks to think this through with my husband and talking with my daughter. Just the whole process of putting it in the context of wishing for all of our serenity and not just my own peace of mind really helped. And, oh yeah, the actual wish. Now that took some time to get it into the eight-word form, but when I finally sat down in our backyard, touched my heart, and took a deep breath, I wished to "love Tina now, not the Tina I want." When I told her my wish, she hugged me. She hadn't done that since she was a very little girl. She actually hugged me, and we both started to cry. It was a kind of miracle."

The serenity granted this mother came from her clear wishful thinking about how she dealt with the stress of her parenting, realizing what she could change and what she could not, and learning to experience some of the same wonder and awe for her daughter that she had felt at her daughter's birth. The word "miracle" is derived from the Latin verb *mirari,* meaning to wonder or marvel. The suffix *cle* turns *mirari* into a noun, so a miracle becomes very similar to the act of wishing. Both wishing and miracles involve the state of wonder and awe, so wishing well for serenity is ultimately wishing to be able to more fully experience all the good news about being alive. When we wish well in this way, we are more likely to finally experience what millions wish for every day, a little more peace and quiet.

·················· ✒ ··················

Twelve

How to Wish for a Delight-Filled Life

If there is a sin against life, it consists perhaps not so much in despairing of life as in hoping for another life and in eluding the implacable grandeur of this life.

—ALBERT CAMUS

Way of the Well Wisher: Wish for a joyful way of seeing things, not for more things. Wish for the strength to say "no" and for gladness in the doing more than success through a goal.

Have a Nice Day

How many times in the last few days have you wished someone a nice day? What did you mean by "nice"? It's one of the most popular wishes in the world and one that, if we really meant it, could make life in the world a much more pleasant place to live for all of us. From the cashier at the grocery checkout line to police officers handing us a traffic ticket, "have a nice day" has become one of the most common social wishes. An important step in learning to wish well is to recognize that what we wish most often for others is usually what we most urgently wish for ourselves. The more "have a nice day" wishes you're sending, the more likely that these wishes are tugging at your own heart.

What would a nice or delight-filled day be for you? Those who wish well know that the heart holds the answer. A key first step in wishing well for delight is to do the "heart warming" exercise. Here's how it works:

The Heart Warming Exercise

1. Sit down quietly and temporarily clear your brain of its immediate concerns and worries. Take a deep breath, relax, and put your left hand over your heart.

2. Ask your heart this question: "Has this day warmed you so far? How are you enjoying our day to this point?" Try to "feel" or sense your heart's answer. If you completely relax, you will sense a warm feeling coming from your heart associated with something you did. That's your heart's answer as to its delight with the day.

3. Now ask your heart another question: "What has happened today that has made you feel cold?" Again, try to feel or sense your heart's answer. It may come at first in the form of an image, but if you are patient and keep your hand on your chest, you will sense a cool feeling associated with something you did.

4. Finally, ask your heart, "Do you have any suggestions for things we can do that will bring you warmth?" If you wait, your heart will warm and provide an image that can provide a wish target.

This whole exercise will take only a few minutes, but you will be surprised how wise the heart is and how many wishing hints it will provide not only for what to wish for but also for what not to wish for. Reflect on the characteristics of what your heart considers warming and delightful. What you sense is the menu for a wish for delight.

Have a Nice Life

Wishes in domain one of the wish star are wishes to "have" a life. Wishing in domain two is to have a life worth living (see the figure on page 226). Serenity is related to having sufficient health and wealth to "go and do." Delight is related to achieving the life balance to "flow and be." The fact that the "nice day" wish is so spontaneous and instinctive reflects that our heart knows what a delight it can be to be alive even when the brain is so busy making a living.

Wishing for a delight-filled life is a luxury only those who have found enough health and wealth to live on can afford. If you are starving, you care little about

Serenity
Something to Live On
Doing
Attending
Knowing What Can and Can Not Be Changed
"Health and Wealth"
Grateful

Delight

Something to Live For
Being
Feeling
Knowing What to do With Life
"Balance and Bliss"
Fulfilled

wishing for pleasurable, enjoyable, tasty food; you wish for food. Being granted the gift of being able to wish further clockwise around the wish star toward delight is not only an opportunity, it is a responsibility, an obligation to treasure and take full advantage of that gift and to share it with others.

Enjoyment or Pleasure?

Another important step in wishing well for delight is to understand the difference between enjoyment and pleasure.[1] Pleasure has more to do with domain one of the wish star. It's related to achieving satisfaction of basic physiological imbalances and trying to return the body to a state of "nonthreat" and less agitation. It has to do with being grateful for what we already have and is associated with trying to comply with our preprogrammed genetic imperatives such as eating, drinking, resting, and raising our young in a healthy and safe manner. It's trying to "have" enough to be at least temporarily satisfied and being satisfied with having just enough.[2] Enjoyment is what we feel when we find a good match between our abilities and our challenges. It's what we experience when we use our life skills to match a perceived opportunity for action. It's much more than just doing what our genes tell us to do or allowing, as social biologist E. O. Wilson suggests, our genes to wear us.[3]

Wishing well in the delight domain requires making wishes in keeping with the principle that enjoyment generally lasts much longer than pleasure. Wishing in domain two requires a longer-term perspective than wishing for domain one's more short-lived, transitory, and easily sated pleasure. Enjoyment is a matter of the heart because it requires appreciation of the variety and depth of the natural world and being sensitive to its subtle L energy. Pleasure is more the business of the brain as it tunes in to our body's energetic signals and directs us to whatever seems to respond and gratify them. To enjoy life and wish well in the delight domain, we have to get our brain to pay more attention to our heart so it can realize, as the characters in the classic movie *It's a Wonderful Life* learned, it's a delightful life if we wish it to be.

It is comparatively easier to wish for pleasure because the wish may feel as if it is granted quickly. This is because it is immediately pleasurable to have a physical need met over and over again. We feel pleasure when a need is met, but we feel delighted when the way we meet our needs brings us and those we love great enjoyment. Although both phrases have become socially automatic, there is a difference between "It's a pleasure to meet you" and "I'm very delighted to meet you." Quickly saying "It's a pleasure to meet you" reflects our relief that we have fulfilled our need to meet someone or that we have met and acknowledged a social obligation. It feels "nice" not only to meet them, but because of our social need, to meet almost anyone. If you look into the eyes of a person and really mean it when you say, "I'm very delighted to meet you," it conveys that you feel enjoyment that this new relationship has the potential to last longer than a glancing greeting. It feels "very nice" to make their acquaintance.

Another distinction between pleasure and enjoyment is the concept of refraction. Refraction refers to a primarily physiological state of satisfaction during which one of our body's systems rests and enters a state of greatly reduced responsivity. It's a brief neurological respite that prevents us from suffering from stimulus overload. Without refraction, the brain would stimulate itself to death; we would make love all day and night until we collapsed in erotic exhaustion. As pleasurable a possibility as "status orgasmus" may sound, it would be lethal. Refraction sees to it that we don't pleasure ourselves to death. Enjoyment has no refractory period.

Enjoyment involves activities from which we have to be reluctantly pulled away. When we are having a delightful or enjoyable experience, it seems we could go on doing it forever. Time, place, and basic biological functions are forgotten until they become urgent demands or someone else reminds us about them. When we are delighted, we have found our match between the state of our intellectual and spiritual development and the challenges the world has to offer. We are in a state of balance and bliss and "into the flow," precisely the state many of us are wishing for in the delight domain.

One of our research subjects, a retired real estate agent who had been married for sixty-one years, summed up the difference between pleasure and enjoyment in these words: "If we want a little pleasure out of life, we go out to eat. We can go to the same restaurant and order almost the same meal every few weeks. After we're stuffed, we always say we won't come back for months, but we always do. It's a real pleasure for us. But if we really want to fully enjoy our life, we work together in our garden. We don't talk much there, but we seem more connected there than almost anywhere else. We sometimes don't go inside until it's so dark we can't see. We lose all sense of time. It's new for us every time and our garden seems to change and grow with us. Don't get me wrong. We still have pleasure in our bedroom and we have enjoyment in our garden."

Just Messing Around

How much time during the day do you spend in the simple delight of non-goal-directed behavior? In other words, how much time do you spend just messing or playing around? An important step in wishing well for delight is to allow yourself the enjoyment of the heart's desire for goal-free, simple pleasures rather than trying to fulfill the brain's insatiable desire for intense arousal and goal achievement. The brain fears the state of calmness that comes with playing around without a direct goal in mind. It says, "Hey. It seems awfully quiet around here. I don't think we're getting anywhere. We're not achieving a thing. Let's get going and do and accomplish something. Somebody, something, stimulate me right now or I'll start creating my own arousal by stirring up trouble in my body." The brain mistakes tranquillity for looming danger and sameness for monotony. It constantly spurs us on to do more, get something done, move faster, and try more dangerously stimulating things. The heart sees things much differently.

As you may have noticed when you did the heart warming exercise, wishing well for delight comes from the heart's preference for the simple, quiet, comforting pleasures of life. Researchers in happiness have shown that contentment depends much more on a continuing series of little bursts of joy than on big intense booms of ecstasy.[4] You have read that wishing well in all the wish star domains is a matter of making a little cosmic nudge and not trying to change the world with one big shove. This same rule applies to wishing in the delight domain. The prescription for delight is tiny, regular doses of happiness PRN—the doctors' prescription designation for "taken as needed."

Many baby boomers seem to have become "big boomers." They seek the existing, new, fast, and intense as sources of happiness. Even what they call play is goal-directed and competitive and therefore not really play at all. Jet-skis often replace canoes and snowmobiles replace cross-country skis. Races replace journeys and someone who is meandering is maddening to the person with places to go and things to do.

An example of wicked wishing in the delight domain is the recent experience of several billionaire "big boomers" from around the world. They set out on their respective journeys to try to be the first to ride a hot-air balloon around the world. While a balloon ride can be a wonderfully peaceful and a goal-free way to play, these men turned their balloons into racing baskets. The brain is big on being first. These men had more than enough health and wealth to live on, but they sought the delight of intense stimulation and the challenge of, as one of them put it, "Doing something really big that nobody else has done." Brains understand that statement, but hearts ask "why?" One of the balloons containing three rich thrill seekers crash-landed just off the Hawaiian Islands. The occupants were rescued from certain death and, in a hurry to get started on another big project, forgot to close the door on the capsule of their balloon. In the echo of the laughing of the Good Fairy, the multimillion-dollar apparatus sank to the bottom of the sea.

When the three rich men returned to shore, they were met by their large staffs, champagne, and a stretch limousine. In a hurried interview as they rushed to their car, one of them said, "It's a big challenge, but we'll achieve our goal." The assembled crowd cheered and clapped, but one of the Hawaiians who had assisted in the rescue shook his head and said, "For what? Why?"

An example of a well-made wish in the delight realm came from the same Hawaiian firefighter who had just risked his life to save the "boomers" so they could live again to seek their delight in their goal of being first. As the limousine drove off, a young girl yelled, "I wish you well in your goal!" The young paramedic turned to me and said, "You know that wish research you're asking everyone about? Put down my wish, will you? I don't wish to fly fast on a balloon so I can be first around the world. My wish is to sit on the beach with our new baby when he's a little older. My wish is to make castles with him. The castles will always be washed away and it would not really be a big deal, but I wish I'll make it through these rescues so I can just play around with my family. Just play and mess around and not accomplish a damn thing." When he noticed that I saw tears glistening down his brown cheek, he quickly wiped them away with his wrist. Looking down to gather his gear, he said shyly, "I'm still all wet from the rescue. It's just salt water, that's all." Whether what I saw was the salt water of the ocean or of a well wisher's tears, it seemed to symbolize the simple goal-free nature of a well-made wish in the second domain of the wish star.

A Test for Delight

To help you make wishes for a more enjoyable life, here's the "realm two delight wish" test we designed based on our work with the wish-research group. I've included tips on how to identify the difference between head and heart wishing in each of the items on the test.

Delight Survey

Answer yes or no to the following questions. Take your time with each question. Stop and reflect on the point about the differences between how the heart and the brain see each point. Enjoy the test one item at a time rather than focusing on your score.

When doing what you enjoy most,

1. _____ Do you spend at least as much time engaging in goal-free behavior as you do goal-directed behavior? (As stated earlier, good health depends on a match between the amount of time you dream and the amount of time you engage in non-goal-directed play behavior.) The brain has its objectives, but the heart knows and treasures "just playing around."

2. _____ Do you enjoy the process (i.e., painting, mowing the lawn) more than the product (the finished painting or the best lawn in the neighborhood)? The brain wants to complete the best painting fast; the heart desires to have fun painting.

3. _____ Do you derive immediate, intangible personal rewards from doing what you are doing? The brain desires extrinsic rewards, but the heart knows that extrinsic rewards can ultimately diminish the initial sense of personal reward derived simply from the act of doing something. For the heart, just doing what it loves is reward enough.

4. _____ Do many of your activities seem to warm and relax your heart rather than stress it? The brain desires intense and extensive public feedback; the heart desires feedback from the subtle energy of the hearts around it and the people who matter in its life.

5. _____ Do you feel your skills are well matched for your challenges? The brain is constantly moving the goalposts farther out and seeking challenges that bring intense arousal; the heart seeks a comfortable match between what it wants to do, what its body can do, and what its spirit needs to do.

6. _____ Do you become fully absorbed and "lost" in an activity without regard for "getting it done"? The brain tends to become "totally" absorbed for only a little while and then sets out for new goals; the heart adores redundancy, simplicity, ritual, predictability, and being fully connected with the activity at hand even if it never gets finished.

7. _____ Do you lose all sense of time? The brain is ever alert for time and wants to "use" it; the heart has little sense of clock time and easily loses track of it.

8. _____ Does everything else around you seem to disappear as you become involved in your task? The brain is naturally paranoid and on the lookout for threats or new and different sources of stimulation; the heart is easily drawn into those tasks it loves to do and becomes unaware of its physical environment.

9. _____ Do you experience an almost complete sense of loss of self-awareness when you do what you love to do? The brain seldom is unaware of itself and its needs and monitors the degree of self-accomplishment; the heart is selfless and loves activities that allow it to be free of the insistent brain's demands.

10. _____ Does the activity you're engaged in seem to be worth doing for its own sake and more like a redundant enjoyable habit than something to be accomplished? The brain functions as a battery watch constantly humming with energy. It deplores "wasting its time" on activities it views as nonproductive by its criteria of intensity and extrinsic reward. The heart functions more like a pendulum clock and easily falls into the enjoyable rhythm of an activity regardless of an end objective.

_____ TOTAL YES RESPONSES

If you scored more than seven yes responses, you are more likely to fall easily into the enjoyable state of delight. The lower your score is below 7, the more likely you are under the influence of your demanding brain. You can learn to make better wishes for delight in your life by studying the characteristics listed on the test and trying to apply them in your own life. Remember again the sympathetic wish magic of "like produces like." The more you try to enjoy the simple things of life and get into the flow of life, the more likely your wish for delight will come true.

Better or Bliss

Unless we've sensed some discomfort or distress, we seldom wish someone a "better day." Usually, nice is good enough. If most of our days are congenial, at least mildly joyful, peaceful, and seem to flow, we feel that we are leading a life anyone would wish for. Having a delightful life is based less on having a "better" life than having one that's "good enough for now." There's an evolutionary wishful thinking wisdom hidden beneath the common "have a nice day" wish that can guide our wishing for bliss and joy in our daily living.

Ralph Waldo Emerson pointed out, "Life consists of what a man is thinking of all day." I would add that life becomes what we are wishing for most of the day every day. Thorough examination of what we wish for requires learning from what and how our wishes are granted. If we are wishing for a much better life, we miss out on the opportunity to fully relish the one we have.[5] To wish wisely in the second domain, one has to understand the statement by Mme de la Fayette in a letter to Gilles Menage. It stated, "If one thinks that one is happy, that is enough to be happy." Her statement is another example of the sympathetic wish magic of like induces like.

Another step in wishing well for delight is to wish to be better able to delight in what we have rather than wishing for more and new things to have to bring us delight. In a search for a sense of balance and bliss, wicked wishing for intensity, newness, and variety can cause us to wish-regress. We can end up wishing for more time, more money, and more stuff to bring us the daily delight that eludes us. Mistaking excitement for enjoyment and feeling our wishes are not coming true, we see the serenity domain's health and wealth as sources of the delight we cannot seem to find. We think that "more stuff" or "more stimulation" might fill the bill that keeps mounting on our bliss account. We forget the wisdom in the words of author Kin Hubbardat, "It's pretty hard to tell what does bring happiness. Poverty an' wealth have both failed."

Making a wise wish for bliss is wishing for better and fuller awareness of just how good we have it even at those times when things don't really seem all that good. As you saw on the test earlier, it's a way of connecting with our world on the level of the heart instead of our constantly needy brain. It's a way of being granted the gift of knowing how happy our heart is even when our brain can be so annoyingly ungrateful.

Are You Too Happy?

How many times a day do you wish for a better life? Compare your answer with the number of times you wish your life could stay just as happy as it is right now. How many times a day do you say to yourself, "My life is just wonderful!" If your need for better exceeds your sense of "just fine," you will benefit greatly from wishing more wisely to be able to see the bliss all around you just waiting to be experienced.

Our brain acts much like a surly security guard protecting what it sees as our turf. It's constantly agitated and desirous of more of whatever it already has. The heart is a gentle resonating organ that has only the briefest of refractory periods that occur between each of its beats. The quiet times between heartbeats make good relaxation times for wishing. The brain adapts quickly to whatever pleasure it finds, has longer refraction periods that it finds obstructive to its "constantly on the go" style, and quickly sets us off in search of more pleasure. Our heart prefers a more gentle, subtle, regular kind of joy. It doesn't need intense joy and in fact can be set off beat with too much joy too soon.

George Engle, professor of medicine and psychiatry at the University of Rochester School of Medicine, has collected evidence that intense happiness is not necessarily compatible with health. He collected 170 cases of sudden death over a six-year period and then analyzed the general emotional state of the individuals before their deaths.[6] While most of the deaths were accompanied by unhappy states such as fear or depression, 6 percent were immediately preceded by sudden and intense happiness. The brain may enjoy intense and very, very happy surprises, but the heart does not. It prefers a nice day over one full of happy shocks, and it delights in mild, blissful doses. It's what one of our cardiologist wish-study participants described as ". . . governed by WAM or 'wise and mellow,' while the brain is directed by 'BAM,' or 'big and massive.' I've told my patients that to keep their hearts healthy, they'd better help them with their wishes and avoid letting their brain have its way with them."

Your Happiness Set Point

You've probably noticed that some people seem to be naturally upbeat. They seem genetically predisposed to be happy. Knowing how to wish to enjoy life requires awareness of your "delight default mode" or your general temperament. How do you look at life when things are going just "okay" instead of spectacularly and when you're just sitting around doing nothing in particular? When you're not very high, what is your general mood? Wishing wisely in the delight domain is wishing to find delight in how you are rather than comparing yourself with other people's delight default mode.

Psychiatrist Thomas Szasz writes, "Happiness is an imaginary condition, formerly attributed by the living to the dead, now usually attributed by adults to children, and by children to adults."[7] He meant that no amount of effort on our part will do much to bring us happiness because it will always remain elusive. This may be because, contrary to popular self-help psychology, there's little we can do about how happy we can be. Research on happiness now shows that we all have a "happiness temperament," a kind of cheer quotient pretty much established at birth. No matter what happens to you, you're probably as happy right now as you're ever going to be. Whether you inherit millions of dollars or experience the loss of your most cherished pet, research shows you will return to your happiness set point within a few months to a year.[8]

Whether we are happy even in hardship and cranky even in good fortune is to a large measure genetically "set" within us. Wishing well for happiness requires knowing our set point and knowing that we can make subtle sixth-sense suggestions to adjust that set point up a bit by identifying what leads our heart to its sense of flow. If gardening results in a sense of flow, wishing to become more involved and absorbed in gardening and doing so regularly can nudge up your set point. Researchers now estimate that about 50 percent of the happiness you feel is due to your genetic set point, and the other half is modifiable within limits.[9] As you have read, wishing is perfect for asking for little adjustments in life, so it is a good way to nudge up your happiness set point. Part of the definition of the little boom of wishing well is trying to modify the quality of your life within limits. Wishing for delight won't make your happiness set point go up by much, but it just might tilt life's playing field a little more in your direction.

Wishing well for delight requires the further step of finding your happiness set point and accepting the fact that none of us will vary too much from that point no matter what wishes we make. Circle the number on the following scale that best reflects how happy you are at this moment. The farthest number to the left on this scale is the unhappiest you could possibly imagine being. The farthest number to the right represents the happiest you have ever been.[10]

Not at all happy   1 2 3 4 5 6 7 8 9   Very, very happy

When the studies on reports of happiness are combined, the average rating of people in our society is 6.5 on this scale. Where did you score? Now, imagine that you just received news that you hit it big on the lottery and made a million dollars. What number on the scale would you circle in that case? Next, imagine that you just received the news that your recent medical tests revealed that you would never walk again. Where would your score fall now?

Most people assume that becoming a sudden millionaire would move one's score far up the happiness scale and that becoming a paraplegic would significantly lower their score. When lottery winners were surveyed near the time of their winning, their scores did in fact move quickly to the right on the scale. However, after one year, their score dropped back to an average of 6.5 to 6.8, just about where most of us lottery losers fall.[11] When paraplegics were asked about their happiness one year after their injury, their happiness score had dropped about a half point to 6, just slightly below that of those running through traffic against the "don't walk" signs.[12] The subtle gravity of one's happiness set point tugs at our heart no matter what happens to us.

Wishing for circumstances we think will permanently alter our happiness quotient is wasted energy and may cause more pain than pleasure. It can lead to counterclockwise regressive wishing for more money, more stuff, a love partner who will bring the happiness we lack, some spiritual guarantee of happiness in a later life, or a new job or promotion guaranteed to finally bring us the happiness for which we keep wishing. We become drawn into the dark wish star of disillusionment with what we do have, stagnation in what we are doing, despair that we will never be happy, and loneliness when searching for our own happiness when we realize that no one can make us any happier than we allow ourselves to be.

Necessary Misery

Another step in wishing for delight is to learn that we have to be very careful not to try to wish unhappiness away. Just as worry and depression are essential aspects of the wishful thinking behind well wishing for something to live on, unhappiness is essential to making wise wishes about happiness.

George Orwell wrote, "Men can only be happy when they do not assume that the object of life is happiness."[13] If we wish to get all the unhappiness out of our life, we are wishing away an essential aspect of our living. Just as anxiety and depression are essential adaptive emotions, the more general state of feeling unhappy is the required counterforce against which we develop our spiritual, emotional, and cognitive strength.[14] Healing and dealing with life's challenges is not always a matter of feeling good. Feeling unhappy is not being dysfunctional. We all need a little unhappiness to balance our happiness. Without it, our happiness has no reference point. Ask those who have experienced terrible sorrow and they will tell you how that pain seems to add a depth to their joy. If we wish for happiness to try to cancel our unhappiness, we miss the point that one does not cancel out the other. When Sri Ramana Maharishi was dying from stomach cancer, he cried out in pain. His screams caused his followers to try to dismiss their teacher's experience of pain by saying that he was not actually in pain but was wisely using a unique form of "yogic control" expressed through his screaming. The Maharishi protested this rationalization by saying, "There is pain, but there is no suffering." He meant that pain, serenity, and a sense of delight can coexist on some level and are not required to eradicate each another.[15]

When I was dying of cancer, I, too, was in excruciating pain. I screamed and cried regularly. As was true for almost every one of my fellow cancer patients, I still felt delighted to be alive. I was in agony, but I was never miserable for too long. Something kept tugging me back to the same state of happiness and unhappiness I had felt through most of my life. Although I read about how cancer survivors report feeling born anew after their cure, I was not. Like most of my fellow patients I have spoken with over the years since our recovery, I'm as happy and unhappy as I have ever been. For better or worse, I'm still me. I'm still loving and arguing with my family. I'm as up and down as often as before my cancer. I know that others who have escaped death may disagree, but my wish miracle was not that I became an entirely new person because of my cancer. It was that I was allowed to "remain me."

If we wish to obliterate all unhappiness and suffering, we ultimately lose one of the most vital ways in which we can find more enlightenment and wisdom in our life. Mythologist Joseph Campbell suggests that we become wise in two ways.[16] We may experience a spontaneous epiphany or vision or we can learn through unhappiness and pain. If we wish away all of our unhappiness, we have closed one door to a more blissfully aware life.

Rejoicing in the Ordinary

The last two components of a well-made delight wish are rejoicing and renouncing. To wish well for happiness, you must learn to rejoice in the ordinary and not seek the magnificent. If we would only pay more attention to our heart instead of the implacable brain, we would realize the fact that research has shown: No matter what happens, 90 percent of us say we are happy most of the time.[17] We wish unwisely when we try to wish away our bald spot instead of wishing we could be happier that we have a head. If we wish too hard and too much from our brain instead of our heart, we miss the key point about happiness: we already have it! Happiness is learning to wish to able to enjoy what we have and not wishing to have what we want so we can be happier.

I learned when I was dying from cancer that one of my biggest mistakes when I was healthy was to miss out on the ordinary. I often became angry with the doctors, nurses, and visitors who seemed to complain so much about the little things and so infrequently relished the ordinary things I was too sick to be able to take part in. They wished there was better parking, but I wished I could enjoy going anywhere again. They wished for better weather while I wished to walk again in the rain. One of my unhappy doctors complaining about his lost cellular phone seemed shocked by the bluntness of the quote I handed him by author David Shaw. It tersely summarizes the importance of making the best of the hand we are dealt. It states, "Many people seem to forget that life, ultimately, is much like a penis: how long it is matters far less than what you do with it."[18]

The Joy of Renouncing

The Bible presents a guide for wishing well for delight. It states, "Rejoice in all that God has given you." We already have enough stuff. Now we need to learn to wish to enjoy it. Helen Keller had every reason to be unhappy, yet she wrote, "Life is a daring adventure or it is nothing." As a cancer survivor and as someone who has talked with hundreds of skilled wishers, I know the truth of the phrase "less is more."

Sir Walter Raleigh's poem about wishing well for happiness in the ordinary summarizes the "rejoice" and "renunciation" step in making a wise wish for delight. It is a wish for the simple pleasure of enjoying the presence of the human spirit more than tangible things.

> I wish I loved the human race;
> I wish I loved its silly face;
> I wish I loved the way it walks;
> I wish I loved the way it talks;
> And when I'm introduced to one,
> I wish I thought What Jolly Fun.

Five Facts of Delight

Well-made wishes for delight always involve trying to become more absorbed in the precious present and to experience gratitude for the moments of our life.[19] They are more about making moments than getting more of them. Before wishing in domain two, consider the following five "facts of delight" that summarize some of the things we know to date about the true nature of delight.

1. Wish for a more joyful outlook, not more stuff and status. Research shows clearly that objective life circumstances have a negligible role to play in how happy we are.[20] We are now five times richer and have five times the amount of stuff our grandparents did. Do you think you are five times happier than they were?[21]

2. Wish to be just as happy as other people, not happier than other people. Research shows that we usually assume that most people are much happier than they really are.[22]

3. Wish to be as happy as you're supposed to be, not happier than you are. The psychological theory of adaption teaches that we calibrate our happiness level based on our previous experiences. Fifty degrees in winter feels warm, but the same temperature in July feels cold. Don't compare yourself with yourself or you will end up wishing backward on the wish star. Physically impaired Cambridge physicist Stephen Hawking said, "When one's expectations are reduced to zero, one really appreciates everything that one does have."[23]

4. Wish to see the world from just a tad more joyful perspective, but not to be extremely happy. Psychologist Richard Solomon's "opponent process theory" indicates that any emotional state triggers the exact opposite and degree of its opposing emotional state.[24] There is a cost for intense pleasure and a benefit to a little pain.

5. Wish to be happy now, not for permanent happiness. Philosopher Seneca wrote, "No happiness lasts for long." A Chinese proverb states, "Happiness is fleeting. We are never happy for a thousand days." Psychologists have shown that every desirable experience is transitory.[25] Wishing against the way the world and its L energy works results in a wasted wish. Your every wish comes true when you wish for what is true.

A Pilot's Pleasure

To illustrate the process of wishing well in the delight domain, here's another verbatim example from a forty-two-year-old airline pilot in our wish project.

"I had it all. Because I did, I thought I could get more. I'm embarrassed by it now, but I compared what I had to my pilot friends. The size of my house, the jewelry my wife wore, all of it. I just wasn't as happy as I thought everyone I compared myself to was. When we talked about wishing to be able to appreciate what I already had instead of wishing for more, I thought it was ridiculous. I wanted more excitement. I thought happiness should be a high, not the balance you talked about. I was rappelling down mountains, rafting alone down the most dangerous rivers, and hang-gliding off cliffs. I'm an excitement and thrill junkie. When my wife [also in our wish project] said that nothing ever seemed to make me happy except trying to stop from being unhappy, it really hit me. I had taken her for granted in all of this. I finally sat down by our big oak tree in our backyard and just looked at it for almost an hour. I thought about the ideas of the second domain you talked about. You know what? In all the years we lived there, I never really sat by that tree and never really looked at it. Then I closed my eyes, put my hand here [to his heart], and wished. Here it is. I keep it in my wallet. My wish was 'share with Sylvia the happiness we have right now.' I told my wife my wish and I know she was getting ready to cry. She usually makes a joke when she's going to cry, so she asked me if I wanted to know her wish. She said it was that she wished I would have wished this way a long time ago. It looks like we both got our wish."

When making a wish for delight, remember you are wishing for a way to be and another more joyful way to look at what you already have, not for more things. Psychiatrist Milton Erikson pointed out, "Life will bring you pain all by itself. Your responsibility is to create joy." Wish for a more delightful outlook and disposition and your chances for a life of happiness are greatly enhanced. Remember the words of philosopher La Rochefoucauld, "Happiness and misery depend as much on temperament as on fortune."

·····················🖋·····················

Thirteen

How to Wish for the Job of Your Life

The highest reward for man's toil is not what he gets for it but what he becomes by it.

—JOHN RUSKIN

Way of the Well Wisher: Wish for work that creates rather than consumes. Wish for a power that matches your responsibilities and an objective that matches your values.

Why We Do What We Do

Following "How do you do?" the question "What do you do?" is something we ask very early in our conversation with a new acquaintance. When we ask, "What do you do for living?" we are really inquiring as to what a person is living for and how and what they are wishing in the third domain of the wish star. To get to know a person, we want to know not only how that person "is" but also about the person's social purpose in life. When we ask about the kind of work a person does, we are really asking about a person's mission in life and what she does as her contribution to the world.

Wishing in the third domain of the wish star has to do with finding our niche in

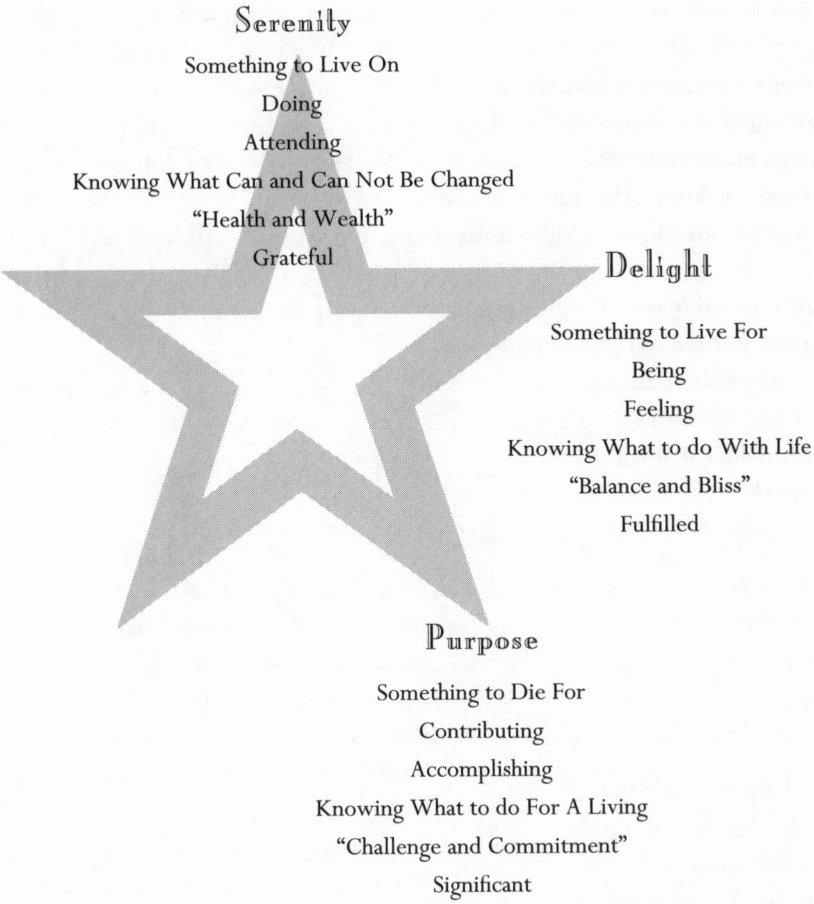

Serenity

Something to Live On

Doing

Attending

Knowing What Can and Can Not Be Changed

"Health and Wealth"

Grateful

Delight

Something to Live For

Being

Feeling

Knowing What to do With Life

"Balance and Bliss"

Fulfilled

Purpose

Something to Die For

Contributing

Accomplishing

Knowing What to do For A Living

"Challenge and Commitment"

Significant

life. A well wish in this realm results in a job that energizes you and leaves time to truly "be" with family and friends (see the figure above). Wishing here is about how we decide to invest and spend ourselves in life. Sarah Bernhardt wrote, "It is by spending oneself that one becomes rich." Wishing for purpose relates to feeling that we are spending ourselves wisely and that we are good workers doing good work that good people appreciate. It's a matter of identifying and fulfilling our mission in life and where, how, and with what objectives in mind we will spend the time of our lives. Aside from sleep, we spend more time doing whatever it is we see as our job than in any other activity. To wish well for purpose, it is essential to have our heart fully involved in our work. If not, the stress of our work will find its way into our heart.

Here are two job wish hints derived from our wish-project group. First, it seems that a heartfelt job is one that leaves you with a sense of plenty of AT&T—appreciation, time, and tenderness. A brain-dominated job results in aggravation, tenseness, and chronic tiredness. Working hard is good for you if you're working smart by balancing your emotional commitment to your work with commitment to your loving. You're working dumb if your job leaves you emotionally numb. Second, are you having time every day for play? This is play in the sense of purposeless, goal-free, noncompetitive activities engaged in for their own sake without pressure to do well, win, or score. Competitive sports, exercise on the treadmill, or pressured efforts to get basic household chores done don't count. About two hours a day of MAT, or "messing around time," seems crucial to a healthy work/life balance. Remember, wishing well for purpose is wishing to love your work while still having plenty of time for loving your life.

Psychological Absenteeism

The results of wrongful wishing in the purpose domain is a condition called "psychological absenteeism." Its direct and indirect effects cost corporate America more than $200 billion a year. It's trying to lead two lives by being mentally and spiritually "home" when we should be at "work" and at "work" when we should be "home." As a result, both our home and work wishes go unfulfilled, physical and mental health suffer, and one's heart is not in work or at home. This pervasive condition is caused by a lack of balance between working, living, loving, and playing that could lead to finding a mutual and unifying purpose among all of these areas of our life.

Wishing well in the purpose domain is learning to wish for a sense of balance in our life between what our brain knows we must do and what our heart tells us we love to do. Failed wishing in the purpose domain results in true workaholism, characterized not by working hard and many hours but by a busy state of mind that results in being emotionally unavailable to the persons in our life who matter most. Ultimately, the corporate bottom line will never exceed the worker's sense of meaningful work and purpose that augments his or her personal, family, and spiritual life. Our heart flourishes when we have a job we love but is tortured when our job has us. The books of corporate America will not balance if workers' lives are in a state of imbalance.

A Warning from Wall Street

Writer Sue Shellenbarger reported in *The Wall Street Journal* about the issue of purpose and balance between work and other life activities.[1] She reported the answers of several business leaders to the following question: "If you could change one thing about the way you balanced your career, personal, family, and community activity over the years, what would it be?" Every answer reflected to some degree a remorse over not having wished well for balance. Here were some examples of responses to the balance question. I suggest you answer it first as a step in learning to wish well in the third domain of the wish star.

- Laurel Cutler, vice chairperson of Foote, Cone, and Belding, answered, "I wish I had known sooner that if you miss a child's play or performance or sporting event, you will have forgotten a year later the work emergency that caused you to miss it—but your child will not have forgotten that you weren't there."
- Ilene Dolins, senior vice president and founding partner of Windham International Relocation Consultants, answered, "The most creative thing I've ever done is being a parent."
- Muriel Siebert, president of Muriel Siebert and Company, answered, "Maybe I should have spread the message [about balance] better. Those of us who are fortunate enough to have been successful have an obligation to do that."
- J. Michael Cook, CEO of Deloitte and Touche, answered, "I wish that over the years I had had more control over my time and more opportunity to be involved in family things. I wish I'd understood the importance of that Thursday afternoon soccer game."
- Randall Tobias, chairman and CEO of Eli Lilly, answered, "I can remember some blurry choices when my children were younger, when I may not have attended a play or a soccer game because I had some conflicting business commitment. It's ironic that twenty-five years later I can remember I didn't go to that event, but I can't remember what business thing I did. I want to be defined as the father of my children, as someone who made my community a better place."

Reflected in these statements is each executive's discovery of the importance of work/life balance and its relevance to their ultimate success. Those persons who do cut back on working to achieve balance still move ahead to success. They are highly rewarded not only by spiritual joy and well-being but by continued advancement in the workplace. Wishing for purpose is wishing to know what to do with one's time and how, where, and why "to spend one's self." It's wishing not for work rewards but to be able to feel productive and contributing in all that we do, not just at a "workplace" but everyplace with everyone.

What Do You Do for a Living and What Do You Live for Doing?

A key step in learning to wish well in the purpose domain is to ask your heart if what you "do for a living" is what you love to do and an activity you might do even without pay. If the answer is yes, you are wishing well in the purpose domain of the wish star. Pause before reading on to check back now with the wish card you have written and been using as a bookmark. Read the last wish you wrote. How does it relate to your wish for purpose and your daily work? How does it support, interfere with, or become disrupted by your wish for purpose in your working?

How do you spend Sunday morning? For most people in Western society, the most nonproductive part of their week is Sunday morning between ten and noon.[2] Particularly for those who don't go to church on a regular basis or have an enjoyable and delightful hobby that helps them find Sunday morning serenity, it is often the least structured time of their entire week.[3] When what we do for a living does not match what we live to do and when we feel we don't have to "get to work," we often seem to be at a loss for what to get to. Here's an example of Sunday morning malaise from one of our research subjects.

"When I do have time to myself, I don't seem to know what to do with myself. On Sunday mornings, I'm less sleepy but I sleep in later. In fact, I usually just lay there in a post–work week coma. When I do finally drag myself up, I sort of slouch and drag out to get the Sunday paper. I don't even get dressed. I just go out in my robe even when it's freezing. Then, I eat breakfast, read the paper, and that's about it. You'd think I'd enjoy taking the time to just sit there and read and eat, but it feels more like I'm stuck on idle. I wouldn't say it's a day of rest because I don't feel like I'm resting as much as restless and down. They're not real bad blues, but I do have the Sunday morning blues almost every Sunday."

As this woman's statement reflects, without the sense of purpose that "going to work" seems to provide in our life and without a balance between how we work and how we live our life, we can become lethargic, directionless, and feel blue when we are "off" work. When we have no purpose, our brain does not return to some pleasant mental state but instead seems to either stumble through its repertoire of leftover worries or unresolved problems or go into neutral gear until sparked back into action on Monday morning.

If our brain's drive and our heart's content are not in balance, we can feel bored and without a sense of direction. If we're only motivated by the brain's wants, we are not accustomed to tuning into our heart's desires even when we do have the time. As one of our research subjects put it, "I'm like a horse in harness waiting with no place to go." When we do have a sense of balance and dedication to the higher goals of our working, all of our days are filled with purpose. Reading the Sunday paper while sipping a glass of orange juice is not "down" time; it is "up" time as we restfully scan for news to discuss with our family and friends that may be related to the goals of what we do for a living.

Soul Work

Author Thomas Moore writes, "Finding the right work is like discovering your own soul in the world."[4] To wish well in the domain of purpose, it is necessary to think of working not as what you do to get something but as what you do so your life means something. "Dying" to work is a metaphor for the fact that our work is not just what we do but who we are. If we have found purposeful work, our Sunday and Monday mornings blend into a more peaceful and continuous life flow. If we are dedicated to what our work provides to the world, we are in effect giving our life for the world. Henry David Thoreau wrote, "The price of anything is the amount of life you pay for it." Next to sleeping, we spend the largest amount of the years we are given involved in working, so in effect our work is costing us our life. For that price, we should reap the most profoundly fulfilling rewards.

Once we have learned to wish well for enough to live on and the enjoyment that comes from delighting in what we have, what we do as work becomes an expression of our wishing. Our work conveys what we wish for ourselves, our family, and the world. Certainly most of us would be willing to give our life for those we love, but those we love seldom want that gift. Giving them the gift of sharing in our sense of contribution, challenge, and commitment in our work and bringing a sense of flow to our relationship with them is a most welcome and treasured gift.

The Principle of Diminishing Returns

When I say "something to die for" when it comes to purposeful work, I'm not talking about a fanatic, obsessive, and compulsive approach to work. Wishing in the purpose domain is wishing for spiritual fulfillment through involvement in a daily task that has meaning beyond tangible reward. Most of our greatest scientists and Nobel laureates report that they are surprised to be paid so much to do what they enjoy doing so much.[5] What they do to live and live to do is in good balance.

Ask the spouse or child of a highly successful person, "Why does she work so hard?" If the answer implies in some way the response, "Because she loves what she does and feels it's important in the overall scheme of things," chances are you are speaking to the family of someone who has had her wish granted for purposeful work. If the answer reveals a sense of family pride in the worker and a sharing in her joy of working, the wish for purpose is being granted for everyone. If the answer in any way implies, "Because she has to" or implies a personal drive to compete with and be better or more successful than others, you are probably speaking to a worker and family being harmed rather than healed by the worker.

After one of my lectures to a large group of business leaders on the purpose wishing domain, one executive approached me after my talk. She said, "It sounds very romantic to speak of your work as an expressing of your wish for purpose and helping the world and all that, but in reality you work to stay alive. Whether we like it or not, the hardest worker reaps the most rewards and gets the biggest piece of the pie." She held up her daily calendar book stuffed full with papers and laughed, "See this. This is my life, but notice that I only really work half days. Remember, that's what twelve hours are, a half of twenty-four. I tell my family I'll only work half a day from now on."

Hard or Heart Work?

This high-ranking executive was mistaking hard work for heart work. If your work expresses your heart's wishes, you don't really feel you are working hard at all. In fact, our clinic had a sign in one of the physical exam rooms that read, "Hard work hardens the heart." When you work from the heart instead of on the heart, no work feels all that hard. Finding such work is a wish come true.

When we work for significance, we feel so spiritually compelled by our work that our Sunday mornings still reflect our work's purpose and our Monday mornings are continuations of that purpose. We are not distracted by our work but so absorbed in its purpose that when we read the Sunday paper, we read with that purpose directing our attention. Our working purpose influences what stories catch our eye and causes us to reflect on some new idea about even more purposeful work.

When we do heart work, we invite and welcome our family to share our purpose. They know what and why we do what we do and are proud of the product or service we provide. They seem aware that we really have our heart in our work, resonate or are in "sympathy" with it and its objectives, and that it's our heartfelt purpose that leads us to live to work. The purpose of the brain leads us to work only to live. As you have read, living to work does not mean that we become so absorbed in our working that we neglect our family, fun, fitness, and loving. It means being so committed to our work's purpose that we can't help but share our excitement and pride in what we do for a living.

When we wish for purpose, we wish for a sense that no matter how small, we are making our mark on the universe. When our wish to find what we need to do and be able to do it is granted, we experience a deep and pervasive sense that we were meant to do what we do and the world needs us to do it. No matter if we garden, jog, or read the Sunday morning paper, we do so with our sense of purpose involved in the activity. We are invigorated by the smell of fresh-cut flowers as we work in our garden and stimulated in our creative thoughts about what we do for a living that, however indirectly, helps preserve the flowers. Some new idea of how we can make a creative contribution may come to mind as we jog along the road thinking about ways to enjoy our work more and not about the latest work war story and what we "should have said" or "how could they do that to me?"

Is Time Your Friend?

If it has purpose, meaning, and connection with our full life, being busy is healthy. Being busy without purpose and meaning is mentally, spiritually, and physically destructive. Having a busy body without an occupied heart and spirit can be lethal. For the busy body, there is never enough time. Being busy is not a behavior but a state of mind that is living in unfriendly terms with time. Ask someone at work, "Is time your friend?" If they laugh, sigh, and answer, "There's never enough of it," time is certainly not on their side. For the occupied heart, time doesn't seem to exist. Another aspect of wishing wisely in the domain of purpose is to develop a healthy sense of timelessness.

"Hey," laughed a young single mother of three daughters who was a member of our wish-research group. "What do you mean what do I do with my Sunday mornings? I don't have mornings anymore. I'm always getting my daughters ready, me ready, food ready, the house ready. I mean, I'm the most ready person you've ever seen. When you ask about wishing about purpose, I don't have time to think about purpose. I only have time for preparation." Harvard researcher Juliet Schor reports that wage earners in the United States work an extra month of time on the job each year compared with workers two decades ago.[6] With all of the technological wonders our brain has created for us, we still don't seem to have the time to do what we say we really want to do.

Economist E. F. Schumacher proposed his own law of working economics that reflects our modern problem with time. He wrote, "The amount of genuine leisure available in a society is generally in inverse proportion to the amount of labor-saving machinery it employs."[7] Today we seem to have more timesaving devices yet increasingly less time. We seem so busy that we lose sight of why we're busy. As if afraid of being exposed as lazy, we automatically answer "busy" when asked how we are. Wishing well for purpose requires that we stop being what one frustrated wife called her husband, a ". . . hyper-chroniac with a clock for a brain."

Busy Bodies or Involved Hearts

If we have purpose in life, we feel that we have plenty of time. If we are still trying to find our purpose, time always seems to be running out. If you find yourself constantly wishing for more time, the wise wishful thinking questions to be asked are "to do what" and "where." We already have all the time there is. We can't make more of it, we can only enjoy the time we have.

To help our wish-research group understand the pressure of time in their own lives and to illustrate that time is a product of thought and not clock, we used the following Test of Time.

The Test of Time

Circle A or B for each item that follows. Pick the item that most closely seems to describe you even if it is not a perfect characterization of your own view of time. We found it enlightening to ask the spouse or close associate of the wish-research subject to do the scoring for the respondent.

1. A. There never seems to be enough time.
   B. I always seem to have too much time on my hands.
2. A. I get very angry and take it personally when people are late.
   B. I'm not that concerned with being exactly on time to the minute.

3. A. It's not the quantity but the quality of time with your family that really matters.
   B. I think spending a lot of time with your family is more important than spending just a little quality time with them.

4. A. Time seems to be racing by.
   B. Time seems to stand still.

5. A. I don't want to waste a minute if I can help it.
   B. I enjoy sitting for several minutes doing nothing at all.

6. A. I'm impatient with slow talkers.
   B. People are in too much of a hurry.

7. A. Most people seem to take forever to make a decision.
   B. I prefer to take my own sweet time.

8. A. This test is taking too much of my time.
   B. I'm thinking about each of the items on this test.

9. A. Time is my enemy and often works against me.
   B. I always have plenty of time.

10. A. I like to do several things at once.
    B. I can only do one thing at a time.

11. A. Time is money.
    B. Money doesn't matter nearly as much as having more time.

12. A. I feel rushed much of the time.
    B. I'm sort of poky.

13. A. I hate shopping.
    B. I love shopping.

14. A. I look at my watch several times a day.
    B. I often do not wear a watch.

15. A. If I sit still for long, I get sleepy.
    B. When I sit still, I start thinking.

16. A. I drive fast.
    B. I drive slow.

17. A. I love to channel surf and keep changing channels.
    B. I find one channel and stick with it.

18. A. I say "thirteen minutes past the hour" or "twenty-eight minutes past one."
    B. I say "quarter past" or "half past."

19. A. I think "don't just sit there, do something."
    B. I think "don't just do something, sit there."

20. A. I hate waiting in lines.
    B. I don't mind waiting in lines.

TOTAL A RESPONSES _____ TOTAL B RESPONSES _____

The more A responses you had, the more likely you are the "alpha-T" or time-oriented person. Even though you think you are driven by purpose, it is more likely that you are just driven. You are likely to be cynical, hostile, anxious, and impatient and in the process of getting ready to live rather than living.

The more B responses you had, the more likely you are the "beta-T" time-oriented person. You tend more toward feelings of inadequacy, pessimism, and rumination. It is difficult for you to find a sense of purpose because you feel stuck or trapped in your present situation. The "best" score in terms of wishing well for purpose in your life would be an even split between alpha and beta time types. This allows for sufficient motivation to get going and enough reflection to be clear as to where.

Wishing for Ordinary Work

Have you done your chores today? A chore is an obligatory recurrent task, and when we say our work is a "chore," we often mean it is not something we want to do. Wishing in the purpose domain is wishing that our work cease to be a chore and become a challenge, but wise wishful thinking recognizes that a challenge can be found in the redundancy of a simple task that heals rather than hurts the world.

Work that is done over and over again to maintain the world as a beautiful, safe, and healthy place is often the lowest on the job hierarchy. The jobs most essential to and that contribute most to the quality of our daily existence and that leave the least lasting impact on the ecology are often those that receive the least pay.[8] The high-flying "brainpower" jobs are highly compensated, tend to create very lasting marks on the face of the earth, and disrupt our world's natural ecological balance. Skyscrapers and nuclear warheads are produced by high-pay, high-status "professionals." Well-maintained, clean parks and clean septic tanks are the responsibility of low-paid "workers."

Ordinary, purposeful work is associated with those tasks that can be done over and over again and that help us recognize the natural cycles of growth and decay in the world. This kind of work is in sync with an "order" and means doing things within the cycle of the dynamic order of the universe. As its root word indicates, "ordinary" work is doing things that are in harmony and balance with L energy and the natural ebb and flow of the universe. When we work at the ordinary and enjoy our chores, we are working within and for the order of things. It is at these times that our wish for purpose comes true.

Whether we are aware of it or not, our home is a place of daily work whether or not we have an "outside" job.[9] In most spiritual traditions, work is not separate from spiritual life. In monasteries, working is a key part of a monk's "ordinary" day. The rhythm of work and its connective sacred purpose are fundamental to the monastery day. Work is a rhythmic spiritual ritual. The word "occupation" means to be taken or seized. We can have an occupation without having a purposeful job. If our job has us, we end up fooling ourselves into thinking that we can divide our personal life from our professional or work life. This divisive effort always fails, however, because what we wish to accomplish through our work is no different from what we wish to accomplish for our life.

A Working Woman's Wish

Earlier in this chapter, I mentioned a young morningless mother trying to balance parenting with a sense of productivity. After our tests and interviews, she provided us with an example of a wise wish in the purpose domain. Here's what she said:

"I know one thing for sure. I will work. I must work. I want to work. What I don't want to feel is overworked and doing things with no reward or sense of fulfillment. I really thought about this third domain of purpose a lot. I could see that I'd done some pretty regressive wishing in my time. Like a lot of young women, I'd wished for purpose by trying to find a man who would give me that sense. Of course, that doesn't work. I tried to find a hobby, but of course I didn't have time for it and it never gave me a sense of the purpose I was looking for. Then I realized what I think many women have realized. I never thought about purpose for me. I was too busy trying to live up to other people's view of superwoman. When I was at lunch one day, I sat on the cement steps outside the law building where I clerk. I got to thinking about the wish project. Something drew my eye to the huge waterfall they have there and I could feel the spray. I'd never really thought much about that waterfall before, but now it seemed suddenly to be the world's loudest wishing well screaming at me to just make a wish. I took a penny out of my purse, held it in my hand, and closed my eyes. I remembered what you said about putting my hand on my heart and taking a deep breath. This wish just sort of came out of me and I think I even got it in the eight magic words. I wished "to do something that makes me feel whole." Last month, about five months after that wish, the lawyer I work for got me a scholarship to law school. I told her I had wished for it, but she just laughed. I'm still busy as hell. Maybe I'm even busier, but it feels like good busy. I love books. They've always been my avocation. I guess they were my hobby and I didn't know it. I'm going into civil rights law. I do want to make a difference. I stopped wishing backwards for happiness, a little peace and quiet, and even for a good man. I focused on the wish I think I needed to make, my own wish right from my heart. I do think I've found it. If not, I'll wait and make another one."

Poet Robert Frost wrote, "But yield who will to their separation, My object in living is to unite my avocation and my vocation as my two eyes become one sight."[10] Wishing well in the domain of purpose is developing the "in sight" to know what to do to live fully and feel fulfilled.

·········· ❧ ··········

Fourteen

How to Wish for Meaning in Your Life

I believe deeply that we must find, all of us together, a new spirituality. This new concept ought to be elaborated alongside the religions, in such a way that all people of good will could adhere to it.

—THE DALAI LAMA[1]

Way of the Well Wisher: Wish that the spirit in which you live is more important than the results of your living. Wish to live so that God can believe in you.

"The Question"

"What does it all mean?" We all ask ourselves this question at some time in our life. We all wish in some way to find relevance for ourselves in the overall scheme of things above and beyond the five-sense world. We wish for some form of personal immortality, survival in some way of ourselves as experiencing and thinking beings who transcend death. We wish to believe that the fact that we were born means something more than a brief cellular existence as a genetic transmitter. Wishing in the fourth domain of the wish star relates to wanting to experience a reverence for what we can't know for sure, a sense of faith, devotion, and coherence that makes all of our wishes for serenity, delight, and purpose in our physical existence infinite (see the figure on page 254). Put simply, we don't want to die.

Serenity

Something to Live On
Doing
Attending
Knowing What Can and Can Not Be Changed
"Health and Wealth"
Grateful

Delight

Something to Live For
Being
Feeling
Knowing What to do With Life
"Balance and Bliss"
Fulfilled

Meaning

Something After Life
Believing
Revering
Knowing What We Can't Know
"Faith and Coherence"
Devoted

Purpose

Something to Die For
Contributing
Accomplishing
Knowing What to do For A Living
"Challenge and Commitment"
Significant

While our heart's wish is that it never be a separate self, our brain's most urgent wish is that its sense of individuality never vanish. It spends its every waking and sleeping moment engaged in maintaining physical life and trying to delay the inevitability of the physical dying process that began at our birth. It works its entire life protecting and trying to perpetuate the ego, its five-sense version of who we are. It wishes that the self will be immortal and transcend the boundaries of the time it uses to measure life. Death prevention is the brain's lifelong occupation. As the *Mahabharata* says, "Of all the world's wonders, which is the most wonderful? That no man, though he sees others dying all around him, believes that he himself will die."[2]

Even in the physical sense, we are to some extent immortal. Twenty-five percent of a child's genes come from each parent, about 6 percent come from each grandparent, 1.4 percent from each great-grandparent, and so on. Evolutionary biologist

Richard Dawkins suggests that once we've passed reproductive age, our genes have no further use for us. Our body has served its genetic purpose and is free to go.[3] He considers death to be nature's way of disposing of those who are no longer genetically useful but are taking up valuable resources needed by those still sexual enough to be players in the genetic game. But are we merely the expression of our genes' wishes? Are we here to be sexual biogenetic servants passing on a little of our own genetic code to the overall pool? Can the brain wish us to transcend death? Of course, the answer to these questions is no, but the brain only knows and devises ways to keep its physical body alive for as long as possible. It has no idea of how to help who we are exist forever, but the heart does.

Heartfelt Immortality

The heart wishes for the immortality of its spiritual essence, not the physical body in which it beats. The heart knows the answer to "the question": we are all connected on a level beyond our brain's cerebrally selfish point of view. Wishing well in the fourth domain of the wish star requires tuning into the heart's version of immortality, one in which our sixth sense is really our first and is in keeping with who we really are "deep in our heart." Our heart has the innate sense of the subtle energy it shares with the universe and is free of the brain's illusions of time and boundaries that create what it calls death.

The heart knows and therefore bases its wishing upon the fact that your real self, the timeless and invisible L-energy shaman that healers call the "transcendent self," is in fact immortal, timeless, and nonhistorical. Although the phrase "transcendent self" has been bandied about in the New Age movement for decades and sounds arcane and even ridiculous to the brain, it is one of our oldest spiritual concepts. As the true center of who we are and can be, it's at the core of most of our wishes. As has happened to many of the ancients' best ideas, modern science is now claiming the idea of the transcended self as one of its own.

The Death-Defying Self

When we go beyond wishing for something to live on, something to live for, and something to die for, we finally wish to transcend death. When the five-sense-oriented brain asks, "Is this all there is?" the answer is yes. Its physical and selfish view is tied to the body rather than the spirit and what it sees as matter rather than senses as subtle energy dooms it to a certain end. When the sixth-sense-oriented heart asks the same question, the answer is, "Certainly not."[4] We are energy, and energy changes form but can never be destroyed. Wishing well for meaning after death requires wishing for a clearer vision of who and how we are deep in our heart.

The concept of a death-defying self has a long and illustrious history. It's been described by ancient priests and medicine men as the "you" inside that seems to be untouched by the passage of time.[5] Your body changes, your sensations are different now from what they were years ago, and the memories you have today are much different from those you had a decade ago. The you who has lived through these changes, however, is still and always will in some form be "you." It has not substantially changed and you "feel" pretty much the same as you have always felt. The you that is forever is the same you that felt the fear of the first day of kindergarten, the thrill of your first kiss, and the spiritual pain of your first loss. Your five senses change as you age, but your sixth sense is constant, always there waiting to help you find meaning beyond the physical world.

When I turned fifty, my young medical students would often ask me how it felt to "be that old." I answered that I really felt no different than when I was their age. My body did, but not me. When I was dying of cancer, my body was deteriorating and racked with pain, but "I" had changed little. I had lost more than fifty pounds and shrunk nearly four inches in height. I was literally falling apart, but I felt like author William Saroyan when he wrote, "I'm growing old! I'm falling apart! And it's very interesting!" A bone marrow transplant can age the body, and when my hair grew back after my chemotherapy, it was much finer and pure white. I now look older than my years, but I still feel just as "young at heart" as I did before my cancer. My three "deaths" during my cancer taught me that our sense of "I-ness" never changes. Physicist Ken Wilbur describes the "immortal I" that is the heart's version of the self by writing, "There is something within us—that deeply inward sense of I-ness—that is not memory, thoughts, mind, experience, surroundings, conflicts, sensations, or moods. For all of these have changed and can change and are changing now without substantially affecting that inner I-ness. That is what remains untouched by the flight of time—and that is the transpersonal witness and self."[6] It is this "transpersonal" or timeless witness-self that we must wish to find if we are to live forever. Instead of wishing to live forever, wishing well in the meaning domain of the wish star is wishing for the wisdom to see that on a spiritually energetic level, we all do.

Poet T. S. Eliot wrote in his poem *Four Quartets,* "In my end is my beginning." He was referring to the fact that our wish to find meaning in life by knowing we can transcend physical life requires that we surrender our dependence on our five-sense self. To wish well in the domain of meaning is to acknowledge that wishes based on the fear of physical death are wasted. The Zen paradox, "If you die before you die, then when you die you won't die," refers to wishing to "kill off" the brain's illusion of a separate physical self somehow perpetuated in some form in an afterlife. The Zen saying, "While alive, Be a dead man, Thoroughly dead," expresses the idea of going beyond a version of a life led by the five senses and clock time to an L-energy-system-connected self. This is the "I-witness" I experienced when I was dying of cancer.

Laughing and Loving

There are two special times when we experience this L-energy-based immortal self in our daily life: when we laugh and when we experience sexual orgasm. "Dying" to live and wishing for something beyond physical life is captured in one of our most common statements. We say, "Stop it, you're killing me," when we are laughing so hard we lose all sense of who, where, what, and how we are. We "die laughing" as we become totally unaware of the boundaries of time and space. When we "lose our self" in sexual orgasm, we often say things like "Oh God," or something more secular like "I'm coming." The implication is that by losing ourselves in the intense intimate pleasure of sexual delight, we at last find ourselves, and by coming, finally arrive.

Creative Fidelity

Silencing the self to wish lovingly with another person helps us fulfill our heart's desire not only for compassion but also for the realization of its form of meaning. The French Christian existentialist Gabriel Marcel wrote of "creative fidelity" through which a loving relationship with another person forever perpetuates the consciousness of the sixth-sense connection we share with that person.[7] He wrote, "It seems to me that we should begin by observing that there can be no question of treating the absolute cessation of consciousness as a fact."[8] Marcel thought that immortality was derived from our ongoing relations with the dead made possible as a consequence of the close loving bond and intimacy we establish with a loved one while we are both physically alive. To him, what is immortal is our heart-to-heart connections, not our physical bodies.

The kind of heart-energy connection Marcel referred to is the object of our heart's desires and the object of a wise wish in the meaning domain of the wish star. It's the kind of connection we experience when our relationship with a lover, parent, child, or friend gets inside our heart and self to influence and help define who we are from within. In the wishing well sense of meaning, we become our relationship. As Midas learned, without our relationships, we become nothing. Death is the end of physical relationship, but by every mystical, romantic, and quantum physics principle, the L energy of the heart cannot be destroyed.

A key step in learning to wish well in the fourth domain of the wish star is to remember that when we wish for meaning, we are also wishing to love and be loved forever. When we wish to be able to love deeply in our heart and be loved in that same way, we are making a subtle sixth-sense suggestion to the L-energy system that we are ready and willing to live forever with and through another person. If we wish well for this kind of meaning in our life, even when we or our lover is physically "dead," we can remain energetically bonded. We can still hope, plan, and worry together because we are forever together. Our own and a loved one's life is reincarnated through a quantum love-energy imprint of a loving heart-to-heart connection established while we are still in our five-sense physical form.

It is within the meaning domain of the wish star that science and the spiritual most profoundly meet. The mystical-sounding language of a transcendent self and the L or subtle "fifth" energy you have been reading about throughout this book derives from both explanatory systems, and they are not less meaningful despite the fact that they have been co-opted by "folk" or New Age psychology. To wish well for a meaning that allows for an immortal loving relationship with our spouse, parent, friends, or even pets, we have to think in terms of Marcel's words, which so clearly express the lessons of quantum physics and the ancient cultural magic of wishing. He wrote, "I must think of myself not merely as somebody thrust into the world at a moment of time that can be historically located, but also as bound to those who have gone before me in some fashion that cannot be brought down to the mere linkage of cause and effect."[9]

An Oceanic Feeling

When you read about the domains of serenity, delight, and purpose, you learned that wishing well in each of these domains results in a sense of flow, connection, and significance. The same is true of wishing in the meaning domain. When we do it well, we end up feeling "in sync," sympathetic, energized, unafraid. Instead of feeling stressed and driven through life, we feel as if we are sailing through it. When I asked one of the kahuna, or healers, on the Big Island in my home in Hawai'i about the wish star and particularly about the meaning domain, he took my hand and sat with me on the beach. I asked if I could at least turn on my tape recorder to save his words. He smiled at my spiritual naivete but reluctantly agreed. He said, "We have a word for what you are trying to describe about meaning and connecting forever. We say 'holoholo' or to 'just go sailing around.' It means that we should not try to impose our will on the 'aina' [the world]. We are an ocean people. We have motors on some of our boats now, but in our hearts we will always be sailors. If you want to wish well, you have to think like a sailor connecting with the ocean. You have to think of yourself as the ocean. You are made of salt and water. Like the ocean, you exist in many forms, but you are timeless. You are mist, water, waves, and stillness, and other life systems are a part of you and you are a part of them. When you make a wish, try to get the ocean feeling. Think that way and you will find the meaning you are wishing for."

Wishing well for meaning results in what the kahuna described and what Sigmund Freud called an "oceanic feeling."[10] If you have ever sailed on the ocean, you may have felt a sense of its infinite energy and your heart-to-heart connection with it. We feel it every time we paddle our canoe on Maunalua Bay behind our home. Your sixth sense may have led you to become contemplative about your life and your connection and responsibilities to all life. You may have thought about the seething life in the sea that only on rare occasions shows itself and the millions of species deep within the sea that we have never seen. You may have thought about how the sea rages and calms in a rhythmic cycle of its own that ultimately influences the entire planet. You may have thought that you came from that sea, and even though you cannot drink from it and live, your life depends upon it. If you sit by the sea, place your hand on your heart, and take a deep breath to inhale its salty air, you can experience the oceanic feeling of your immortal self. When I go "holoholo," I feel that I have the heart of a sailor and, despite my many bouts with cancer, feel that I can live forever.

Wish Life Crisis

Are you in a wish life crisis? At about age thirty or so, many persons start wishing less in the areas of something to live on, something to live for, and something to die for. Their wishes usually begin to relate to what life means and how it might survive physical death. They start wondering about their prior wishes and what they meant as they wish for meaning now. Authors Judy Jones and William Wilson write, "Have you ever noticed how prophetic revelation seems to give some people a new lease on life at about the same time others their age are gearing up for midlife crisis?"[11]

Whether we end up with more faith or more frustration as we get older is in part a function of how we wish and what we wish for in the meaning domain of the wish star. Buddha, Jesus, Zoroaster, and Muhammad were approaching what would have been middle age at the time they lived, and their wishing centered around the meaning of a spiritual life.

Midlife crisis is often a whole life wishing crisis finally recognized. Learning to wish well for meaning can help us through it. Seeking a sense of coherence and developing a deeper sense of reverence for the moments of this life as a means of realizing the true nature of immortality are all components of wishing well in the meaning domain. Wishing well here is a matter of living our life not so much by believing in God but so that God or the Absolute can believe in us. It's less wishing that there is a heaven than living every moment so that we deserve to be there.

Psychologist Carl Jung observed that anyone coming to a psychotherapist in mid-life comes not so much with a psychological crisis as a spiritual one.[12] When we wish unwisely in the meaning domain, we wish from the despair that our ego or physical self might not last forever. When the literal, five-sense proof of immortality never comes, we begin to regress in our wishes. We may seek to find meaning in life exclusively through our work rather than in a blissful balance between contributing work, shared delight, and the peace and calmness of knowing that "what" we are ends but "who we've been" lasts forever; an L energy imprint in the hearts and souls left by those who knew and loved us.

Healing as Finding Meaning

Psychologist Jean Achterberg writes, "Medicine, as it has been practiced throughout history, is invariably linked to the divine . . . Healing work is a spiritual process— it always has been and it always should be."[13] Wishing well in the realm of meaning is an act of healing. It is one way we find what psychologist Aaron Antonovsky calls the "sense of coherence" when we need it the most—at those times when we are suffering.[14] Antonovsky's research showed that meaningfulness depended on seeing the world as comprehensible and making sense, exactly what we need when we are in trouble. His work showed that those persons who did find meaning in their life had established some sense of order, constancy, structure, and clarity in their life.

When we wish for meaning, we are wishing that things will work out in the long run and that we are not helpless victims of a chaotic, meaningless, random, accidental, inexplicable cosmic mess. Healing derives from the Greek *halen,* meaning to make whole. Understanding that physical death is not spiritual death helps us find that sense of wholeness even when our body is in distress. When I was dying of cancer, I felt that wholeness even when toxic cells were killing my healthy body cells at the rate of thousands per second. Wishing for meaning helped me stay together even as my body was coming apart.

We wisely go for regular physical exams but often neglect regular examination of our spiritual health. Most physicians ask us about our diet but seldom ask if we are nurturing our soul. They put us on a scale to see how strongly the invisible energy force of gravity is pulling on our physical body but seem insensitive to the pull of subtle L energy upon our spiritual life. They measure the pressure of our blood as our heart pumps it through our veins and arteries but fail to ask what is really in our heart. However, disregarding the soul in the attempt to heal the body is spiritual malpractice.

There is one group of healers that has historically led the way to spiritual healing and helping patients find meaning through their suffering. Since 1983, the North American Nursing Diagnosis Association has had a diagnostic category they call "spiritual distress."[15] Especially when I was dying of cancer, I have always found that the nursing profession played a leading role in the practice of the art of meaningful medicine. Because nurses spend hours a day with those of us who are sick and dying, they are more likely than "rounding" physicians periodically "attending" to us to be attentive and absorbed in our spiritual health and well-being. One of my nurses expressed this spiritual sensitivity when she told me, "Just view your time on the bone marrow transplant unit as attending a spiritual university. The curriculum is extremely difficult and challenging, but we're here to learn with you. There will be a lot of visiting adjunct faculty, but we nurses are in residence."

Spiritual Distress Syndrome

When I left the bone marrow transplant unit, I looked up the "spiritual distress syndrome" in nursing texts. When I began to study wishing, I noticed that our wish group often made most of their wishes in the meaning domain when they were sick or focusing on their advancing age. They seemed to experience a deepening homesickness for heaven but were often unable to clarify their feelings about their search for connection beyond the physical body. I noticed that many of them seemed to be wishing from a point of spiritual distress and that having some secular way of assessing their general state of spiritual health could be helpful in their wishing. Being "spiritual" was clearly defined by author William Starke when he wrote, "When the spirit in which you live is more important to you than the results of your living, you are spiritual."[16]

To help focus this area of wishing, I designed the following "Spiritual Distress Syndrome Survey" based on the professional nurses' diagnostic category.

Spiritual Distress Syndrome Survey

Use this scale to indicate the frequency with which the following thoughts go through your mind:

5 = EVERY DAY 4 = TWO OR THREE TIMES A WEEK 3 = QUITE OFTEN
2 = ONCE IN A WHILE 1 = ONLY ON VERY RARE OCCASIONS 0 = NEVER

1. _____ I think about what death is and what will happen to me when I die.

2. _____ I express and discuss my concerns about the meaning of life.

3. _____ I think about my fear of death.

4. _____ I think about and fear the death of someone I love.

5. _____ I worry that I don't have any "religion" or deep convictions about the meaning of life and death.

6. _____ I think people who regularly go to church, synagogue, or other institutions of worship do so simply for social support.

7. _____ I say how stupid or silly most religious rules, rituals, and practices are.

8. _____ I verbalize my anger toward God.

9. _____ I think that the terrible things that happen in the world prove that God does not exist.

10. _____ I use God's name in vain.

11. _____ I think about life as "you're born, you live, you die, you rot."

12. _____ I spend time thinking "what if there really is a hell."

13. _____ I feel conflict or guilt associated with my childhood religion.

14. _____ I feel a conflict between my religious or spiritual beliefs and how I lead my daily life.

15. _____ I feel in conflict between what it takes to be successful and what it takes to be a spiritually pure person.

16. _____ I think of prayer as a superstitious act.

17. _____ I break one or more of the Ten Commandments.

18. _____ I cannot forgive people who do bad things to me.

19. _____ I'm uncomfortable talking about spiritual things.

20. _____ I think "I wish I could believe in God."

_____ TOTAL SPIRITUAL DISTRESS SCORE

In our 2,166-member wish-research group, the average (mean) score of the frequent wisher group was 28. The average score of those who wished less frequently was 63. At least in terms of this survey, those who wished were those who seemed to experience what the nurses' diagnostic system would see as less spiritual distress.

Of all the tests administered to our research group, the members considered this one to be extremely personal. More often than for any of the several tests we used that you have read about in this book, our research sample closely guarded their scores on this test and repeatedly reminded us about our commitment to protect their privacy. No matter what our brain says, there seems to be something in our heart that considers our spirituality to be a most personal part of our life.

Spirituality goes beyond religious conviction. Physician Neome Remen writes, "The spiritual is inclusive . . . one might say that the spiritual is that realm of human experience which religion attempts to connect us to through religion and dogma. Sometimes it succeeds and sometimes it fails. Religion is a bridge to the spiritual—but the spiritual lies beyond religion."[17] Wishing well for meaning in life is a spiritual act that goes beyond learned religious practices and rules. It is ultimately our own personal answer to the question asked in the first sentence of this chapter, "What does it all mean?"

You have read that spirituality does not have to be in conflict with science. It can give meaning to the health that science seeks to enhance. Psychologists Steven Krippner and Peter Welch write, "Scientific data and spiritual perspectives can be quite compatible when one's convictions about the 'highest' and 'deepest' human potentials and values are based on both reason and intuition, both intellect and feeling. . . ."[18]

Wishing Away the Ghastly

Without a belief in the power of wishing's subtle energy, the five-sense orientation of the brain is appallingly dreadful. It says that death means that how we lived and loved made no difference other than to perhaps make a few years on earth somewhat comfortable physically. To limit what we wish for from life to the brain's literal view of our existence is to see ourselves as only gene-carrying mortal creatures trapped in a decaying body as the clock counts off our days. Unfortunately, this is still the view of many scientists, psychologists, and physicians.

When I lecture on the fourth domain of wishing and the nonlocal or subtle L energetic nature of life, I often encounter what physician Larry Dossey calls "spiritual agoraphobia."[19] The five-sense scientists in my audiences fear the openness and vastness of the heart's vistas and the possibility that the ultimate wisdom is knowing what can't be known by the brain alone. They balk at what physicist and philosopher Henry Margenau called "primitives," those things and processes in the world that are indefinable in terms of empirical facts.[20] Wishing and the energy with which it deals, however, is basically a primitive process. It derives from ancient cultural practices and, as you have read, deals with a kind of energy that rigorous scientific studies have shown plays its role in every event.

The energy of wishing is not energy in the way modern science has always understood it. It isn't a force "sent" somewhere by someone. By wishing, we try to connect with this energy and become absorbed in its pervasive presence. Wishing in the meaning domain is wishing on the quantum "well of being" described by physicist Dana Zohar. We find the Absolute or universal energy in everything and everywhere. We find meaning by wishing to be more aware of our being as it is constituted by the L energy that operates by the principle physicists call "nonlocality." Nonlocality as modern physics defines it refers to everything being linked to everything else beyond the artificial barriers of time and space.[21] As you have read, some spectacular demonstrations of nonlocality have taken place in laboratories in prestigious universities. Physicists Harold Puthoff and Rusell Targ at the Stanford Research Institute have done fascinating work to show the time- and space-free effects of our intentions.[22] The nonlocality and total connectedness upon which the limitless power of wishing is based is not a matter of conjecture; it is a scientific and spiritual fact.

The Perennial Philosophy

Wishing well in the meaning domain is enhanced by the recognition of what is called the perennial or the "universal" philosophy. This is the philosophy that is at the base of most of the world's religious systems. The name was borrowed from Gottfried Leibniz, the seventeenth-century philosopher and mathematician who first wrote about the idea that all religions seem to contain the same fundamental concepts and deal with the same basic issues. It also appears that despite their respective claims to exclusive connection with the Almighty, all religions ascribe meaning to life in about the same way. Aldous Huxley wrote about these concepts of the meaning of life in his famous *The Perennial Philosophy*.[23] There he outlined three fundamental "faith factors" that can serve as a basis for structuring a wise wish in the meaning realm. They all reveal the theme in Huxley's quotation from the *Theologia Germanica*, "Goodness needeth not to enter the soul, for it is there already, only it is unperceived."[24] Wishing well for meaning is wishing for the privilege of knowing more fully what is in our soul.

Based on the perennial philosophy, here are three additional guidelines for wishing well for meaning:

1. Wish for tiny miracles, not a major miracle of faith.
Well wishing is based on finding the miraculous in the ordinary and simple. It's a matter of being "sympathetic" and getting into the gentle swing of the subtle energy of our existence. In wish star domain one, wishing for "just enough" is the key to wishing well for serenity. In domain two, wishing for "just a little joy" and a slightly different way to see and appreciate what we have is the key. In domain three, wishing for the privilege of enjoying doing ordinary and simple work is likely to provide the sense of purpose we seek. In each case, wishing well is really wishing more for a slightly different point of view than for a major miracle.

The perennial philosophy teaches that ordinary things, ordinary lives, and ordinary minds are made of "divine stuff"—the L energy that connects everything. This faith factor relates to the presence of subtle L or love energy in everything everywhere, and it is most obvious in the simple things. We feel the subtle energy more when we take the time to study a lovely rock than when we attend a loud rock concert. Every major religion teaches about the sacred to be found in the ordinary and the idea that the true prophet is more likely to be found sweeping the street than standing at the podium at a New Age seminar. Wishing well for meaning requires wishing to be blessed with more awareness for the common, alertness for the everyday miracles that come with being alive, and the ability to find God in the simplest things and events. The poet Yung-chai Ta-shih stated this wishing principle when he wrote, "One nature, perfect and pervading, circulates in all nature."[25] Scientist Francis Bacon wrote that God never wrought miracles to convince atheism, because His ordinary works convince it.

2. Wish to know how to live so the Divine or Absolute can believe in you, not for signs of proof so you can believe in the Absolute.
Wishing well for meaning requires that we be willing to believe so we can see rather than see before we believe. The perennial philosophy

teaches that there is an aspect of "divine reality" or subtle L energy that resonates within the core of every living thing. Wishing well for life meaning is wishing for the high honor of deserving the sixth-sense experience of the sacred in everything, not the personal privilege of being presented with the proof of a big-time miracle that confirms a literal belief. It's wishing to be able to see and feel God in everything now rather than for a free pass into heaven for a personal meeting with God later. Almost 2000 years ago, philosopher Plotinus said, "Each being contains in itself the whole intelligible world."[26] If you wish to find God or the Absolute, don't look out or up, look in.

3. Wish to be available for God's appearances, not to be able to see God somewhere "up there." One minister in our wish-research group told me, "When I make my wishes in the fourth domain of our wish star, I think of my glasses. I annoy my wife by constantly asking her where I left my glasses. Usually she just smile and points to my face. I almost always already have them on. It's like that with God. If you wish to see Him, He's here. Before you can see him, you have to stop looking for Him so hard and wish to live a life that allows Him to let you know He sees you."

The perennial philosophy teaches that a spiritual person's most important task is not only to discover the divinity of ordinary things, lives, and minds now, instead of later, but also to experience one's identity as the created trying to be one with the Creator in the present moment. A wise wish for meaning and a "life after life" requires wise wishful thinking about one's place in the world and relationship with the sacred. Christian philosopher Meister Eckhart clearly referred to this aspect of the nonlocal nature of the subtle energy that is life when he wrote, "The knower and the known are one. Simple people imagine that they should see God, as if He stood there and they here. This is not so. God and I, we are one in knowledge."[27] A priest who was a member of our wish project summarized the above three faith factors of wishing when he said, "Wishing for meaning is trying to wish for what you sense God wishes. You should be much less concerned about whether or not you can believe in God and concern yourself with, as He looks in your heart, if He still believes in you."

Wishing to Know the Numinous

Numinous refers to those aspects of human experience that are ascribed to a deity or force that transcends life. Psychologist Carl Jung wrote, "The approach to the numinous is the real therapy and in as much as you attain to the numinous experiences you are released from the curses of pathology. Even the very disease takes on a numinous character."[28] Wishing for meaning, then, is ultimately wishing to bring the numinous into your daily life. It's about not searching for the meaning of life but being open-hearted enough to experience a life of meaning.[29] As one of our wish-research subjects put it, "Wishing for meaning in life is really more a matter of wishing to be able to live life like you really mean it and in a way that means something."

When we come around the wish star to the domain of meaning, we have usually gained wishing experience in the realms of seeking safety, security, joy, and a sense of making a difference in the world. Wishing for meaning is the most difficult realm of wishing up to this point because it requires wishful thinking that embraces a different view of eternity, immortality, death, and the self than is typically embraced by modern establishment or "impossibilite" thinking. One reason there may be so much soul-sickness in our world is our tendency to wish more for personal salvation later than for sacred connection now.

Jung summarized the nature of a wise wish for meaning and immortality when he wrote, "If, from the needs of his own heart, or in accordance with the ancient lessons of human wisdom, anyone should [believe in] what is inadequately and symbolically described as 'eternity'—then critical reason could counter no other argument than the most eloquent of science. Deviation from the truths of the blood begets neurotic meaninglessness, and the lack of meaning is a soul-sickness whose full extent and full import our age has not as yet begun to comprehend."[30]

A Minister's Wish

An example of a wish in the meaning realm was offered by one of our research subjects. He is another minister in our research group and the pastor of a small church in rural Ohio. He was a member of the "infrequent" wishers and often thought of wishing as at least silly and maybe even sacrilegious. He was going through his own soul-sickness and considering leaving the clergy. We met him when he happened upon our star wishing seminar in Hawai'i when the comet passed so close to the earth. He recognized me and said he had read some of my books and heard about my current research on wishing. He said, "I don't know if it all has any meaning. I think I've ruined my faith by all my reading about science, new science, new physics, new age, new this, and new that. None of it has any meaning to me anymore. I just came up here to see a few shooting stars." He may have come to see the stars, but he left a recommitted minister wishing upon them.

When we met, he didn't know about the principles of well wishing that were evolving from our wish research, including making contact with nature and his heart and trying to form his wish into eight words for clarity, specificity, and later recall. Nonetheless, here's his wishing process in exact words:

"There was something majestic about it all. All those stars dancing around up there. I'd had a really bad day. I couldn't come up with another sermon and quite frankly I didn't care to. I felt like a spiritual hypocrite. I had just officiated at my third child's funeral in two months and I was angry with God. I was ready to quit and go back to teaching school. Then I saw something or should I say I sensed something that changed all that. It wasn't the stars, but they sort of set the stage for what happened. It was an old golden retriever lying off to the side of the crowd that caused me to wish. Her face was white and she must have been at least fifteen years old. She seemed weak and clearly didn't have long to live. She was looking at a small puddle just in front of her paws. Her head kept darting around and every so often she'd take her paw and slap the water. At first I thought she was catching bugs or something. Her tail would wag, she would watch the puddle, and she would slap it again. She was acting like a young puppy. I went over quietly and noticed that she was watching reflections of the shooting stars in the little puddle. When the light from one shot by, she was trying to catch it. Everyone else was looking up at the stars, but this old dog was catching them. She wasn't worrying about dying, and if it wasn't for her appearance, you would have thought she was a young dog from the way she was playing. All of a sudden, I found myself standing there holding my chest and taking a deep breath. Then I made what you guys call a meaning realm wish right there on the spot. I didn't wish on a star. I wished on that young old dog. Ironically, I think the wish ended up having eight words in it, but that was by accident. What I wished for was to 'learn, feel, and teach a dog's simple sacredness.' She became a part of my sermon and I still use her every few Sundays. I tell my congregation to find meaning in the new Golden Rule, the golden retriever rule. I tell them to find meaning in the simplest and most ordinary miracles and to be free of their fear of their own mortality. That dog will live forever in my heart."

Dying to Live

As you have read, Buddha taught that we are not fully alive until we die. He meant that through surrendering our sense of a separate self and our focus on its perpetuation, we become more fully aware of the full energy of the gift of life. We lose all fear of the end of the self because self becomes an illusion. As a result, our wish for meaning is a wish to be less selfish, less time-dominated, and more loving of this moment with these people now.

In formulating your wish for a meaning in your life, consider the words of those who find the meaning death gives to life.

- Rabbi Joshua L. Liebman writes, "I often feel that death is not the enemy of life, but its friend, for it is the knowledge that our years are limited which makes them so precious."[31]
- Poet Emily Dickinson writes, "That it will never come again is what makes life so sweet."
- Author Stephen Levine writes, "When you start using death as a means of focusing on life, then everything becomes as it is just at this moment, an extraordinary opportunity to be really alive."
- Physicist Ken Wilbur writes, "To find real meaning in life is also to accept death in life, to befriend the impermanence of all this is to release the entire bodymind into emptiness with each exhalation. To yield unconditionally to death on each exhalation is to be reborn and regenerated with each inhalation."[32]

Perhaps we wish so often in the meaning domain because we're all a little homesick for heaven, pining for a sense of coherence and consistency that seems to elude the cruel randomness of our earthly life. We all long for the "something more" and a deeper connection with forces beyond the five-sense world. Scientists have looked to deep space for answers but as yet have found none. They have looked at deep time and studied our evolution, but again the meaning of life remained a mystery. Recently, they have looked to "deep structure" and the paradoxical and mysterious quantum world for where heaven and the meaning of life might be, but they have been left with only more tantalizing questions and some interesting metaphors. Wishing well for meaning is looking deeply into our heart for where the traces of heaven are stored. It's allowing the death of the secular egotistical self in favor of the birth of the sacred sense of self that transcends time and space. If you wish to live forever, start wishing to live more in the now than for it.

Once we have learned to wish well to stay alive, enjoy life, to do something with our life, and find meaning that transcends life, our wishing turns to finding someone with whom to share our life. Once the serenity, delight, and purpose domains are coalesced by wishing well for meaning, there is only one realm of wishing left to master: to be able to wish in concert and in Marcel's "creative fidelity" with someone with whom we can share the first four realms.

.... ✒ ....

Fifteen

How to Wish for
a Loving Life

No one has ever loved anyone the way everyone wants to be loved.

—MIGNON MCLAUGHLIN

Way of the Well Wisher: Wish to be the right lover, not to find a right lover. Wish to be more forgiving and to live so you require less forgiveness.

The Magic of Love

The magic has gone out of our marriage," said the tearful wife. "It just seems to have lost its spark." In a statement we often heard in our marital therapy program, this wife was intuitively expressing the need for a wish in the compassion domain of the wish star. She had accurately identified the importance of the magical nature of a loving bond, but her husband was love-blind, unable to sense the wish incompatibility that was robbing his relationship of the loving energy that bonded it together.

"I really don't get it," he responded as his eyes appealed to me for support. "I give her everything. Her every wish is my command. She has a fantastic house, a maid, her own car, and enough clothes to stock a department store. I've never cheated on her. We take vacations most people would dream of. And now she says the magic is gone. I just don't understand her."

"That's just the problem," I answered. "You think you're granting her wishes, but her real wish is that you would start making and sharing wishes with her." He looked at his wife, and before he could ask her wishes, she said, "Yes, I just wish your wishing included me. I know you're faithful to me, but I really wish you'd be more faithful to our relationship. I don't need a big house, I just need you to be more with me—I mean really with me—than you are."

Therapy for mutual wishing is the topic for another book, but the central tenet of compassionate wishing is its vulnerable disclosure of our most personal wishes and the need to wish with and not just for another person. It is adoring not only our partner but the bond we have with her and giving most of our time and attention to our relationship. The compassion domain combines with the realms of serenity, delight, purpose, and meaning to complete the wish star and provide its energy to keep wishers wishing around and around the star (see the figure on page 272).

Wishing as the "Third Thing"

Finding someone with whom we can make and share wishes for life relates to philosopher Gabriel Marcel's "creative fidelity" discussed in Chapter 14. Marcel wrote that it is possible to get "so inside" our partner and to allow our partner to be so inside us that we come to share every wish with our lover. A compassionately wishing couple has the type of relationship that permeates the heart of each partner to such a degree that the relationship ultimately defines their respective "selves." Psychologist Carl Jung wrote, "The meeting of two personalities is like the contact of two chemical substances, if there is any reaction, both are transformed."[1]

Within a compassionately wishing couple, each partner energetically becomes the relationship. Just as a mother feels her baby is an extension of herself, and as research is now showing, babies "feel" the same way, a compassionately wishing couple ultimately erases any distinctions between its individual partners. They enter a healthy kind of conative codependence within which both partners' wishes depend on one another's wishful thinking. Love lasts when we learn how to wish away our narcissism and wish with someone else for the good of the relationship. Wishing well for love is wishing less to "do our thing" than to do loving things with another person.

Wishing is the magic, the "third thing" that holds two persons together in a loving bond. It's the "and" that joins our two selves. Author Arthur Eddington described the magical "and" of subtle L energy wish connection when he wrote, "We often

Serenity

Something to Live On

Doing

Attending

Knowing What Can and Can Not Be Changed

"Health and Wealth"

Grateful

Compassion

Something to Share Life

Loving

Connected

Knowing How to be Vulnerable

"Kind and Tender"

Adoring

Delight

Something to Live For

Being

Feeling

Knowing What to do With Li

"Balance and Bliss"

Fulfilled

Meaning

Something After Life

Believing

Revering

Knowing What We Can't Know

"Faith and Coherence"

Devoted

Purpose

Something to Die For

Contributing

Accomplishing

Knowing What to do For A Living

"Challenge and Commitment"

Significant

think that when we have completed our study of 'one' we know all about 'two,' because 'two' is 'one' and 'one.' We forget that we still have to make a study of 'and.' " The "and" factor in loving is hardly a new idea. Plato wrote, "Two things alone cannot be satisfactorily united without a third; for there must be some bond between them drawing them together."[2]

A Wedding of Wishes

Couples who have moved together to the fifth realm of wishing discover what philosopher Martin Buber calls "the between," the binding subtle L energy that draws and holds the I and the Thou into what Buber calls the "I-Thou."[3] Psychologist Walter

Tubbs writes, "We are fully ourselves only in relation to each other. The 'I' detached from a 'Thou' disintegrates."

The compassionate couple marries not to fulfill individual wishes but to assist one another in wishing to make the world a better place. This point was made by Leo Tolstoy when he wrote, "The goal of our life should not be to find joy in marriage, but to bring more love and truth into the world. We marry to assist each other in this task."[4] By creating a loving bond, we help each other move to the highest level of wishful thinking, wishing together for the welfare of the world.

When I speak of marriage, I am speaking of a decision to combine and share L or love energy. Whether or not there is a legal commitment, the kind of marriage I am referring to here is a wedding of wishes, a spiritual union that takes place when two people decide to commit to share their wishes for life. I'm referring to two persons who wish to create a kind of cardio-codependence through which their individual hearts literally beat as one. This kind of high monogamy is a mutual commitment to wish together to create the "and" factor—combined intentions to influence the world with the love of the union.[5]

Intending to Attune

Love is "couple coherence" in which two hearts entrain and fall into "sympathy" with one another, a shared resonance that connects us beyond our five senses. To wish well for love, wish for close attunement with another heart and an unqualified sympathy that endures all of the brain's brash selfishness. Wish from your heart and try to entrain or resonate with the energy of another heart. This process is far more than metaphor; it is a scientific reality. It is possible to hook up two persons and record their brain, heart, respiration, and other bodily measures of how their energy is resonating. If both persons "intend" or "wish" to resonate together, their hearts and therefore all of their other body organs fall into sync. They establish a mutual sympathy with one another in the form of what researchers in their brain language call an "electromagnetic and ethereal energetic sympathetic resonance" and what the heart calls "falling in love."[6]

You can do this same experiment. If you take someone's hand, your heart's energy will resonate immediately in that person's heart and brain. If you have someone you wish to love well, take her or his left hand with your right, close your eyes, take a deep breath, and as you exhale, say the eight words that seem to be the magic number of a well-made wish, "I wish to love you from my heart." Both of your hearts will feel warmed by this process, your hearts, brains, and entire bodies will feel "sympathy" for one another and fall into the measurable sympathetic resonance we experience as deep loving.

Little Things Mean a Lot

Author Thomas Moore writes, "Jung discussed the 'little people'—gnomes, dactyls, elves, Tom Thumbs—the ones who do the work of the soul. The soul of marriage is no exception."[7] If love is being in sympathy with the world, the core of all well wishes is love. Like a well-made wish, a well-bonded relationship is made by repeating a few kind words, a few gentle and kind acts, simple shared politeness and respect, and acts that reflect a simple mutual sympathy that in turn reflects love's sympathetic resonance. Moore's focus on the "little things" refers to the idea that lasting love is a matter of sharing everyday tiny wishes together. Wishing for compassion is wishing to share ("com") the glorious suffering of everyday life together ("passion"—referring to suffering in the divine sense).

In my more than thirty years of working with couples in my clinic at Sinai Hospital, I seldom saw a relationship end because of a major problem. It always seemed to be the little things that did in the loving. It was blindness to the little loving or unloving wishes expressed by the very small gestures or actions that ultimately—as all wishes do—have major consequences. You have read that wishing works by the principle of the "little boom" and causing tiny vibrations in the energy of a system that can eventually have major effects on that system. So it is with the wishes expressed in a relationship. Every word and deed is an expression of a little wish that strengthens or weakens the loving bond. Like the little girl pushing on a building who induced sympathetic resonations that could cause it to tumble, several little "ouches" experienced in a relationship can end up being one big hurt.

To wish well in the domain of compassion is to wish to find someone with whom to share wishes in all of the other four wishing realms. It requires knowing how to give the ultimate gift, the gift of self. It requires being vulnerable and completely open-hearted. It's being as kind and tender toward our lover as we wish they would always be toward us and being adoring more than wishing to be adored.

Thomas Moore writes, "Marriage is by nature miraculous and magical."[8] Couples often lose sight of the enchanted nature of loving by dividing up household chores, separating financial resources, and trying to come up with a sexual compromise that meets the busy schedules and biological needs of both partners. As one of the husbands in our clinic said after attending a "sex clinic" in another state, "I think we've finally found her G spot, but we sure aren't saying, 'Gee! What a great romance we have together.' We have the means but not the magic."

Intimate Intentions

Wishing is intentionally trying to make a possibility a reality, and compassionate wishing is trying to fulfill love's potential. To wish well in the compassion domain, you must intentionally try to make love happen, not wait to "fall in it." If you "find yourself in love," you're probably in lust. If you've wished together with someone for love, your behaviors match your wishes. You experience your lover with sympathy even when he seems "out of sync" with you. You're patient and forgiving and keep wishing together through the tough times. In effect, you and your lover become one another's human forms of what physicist William Tiller calls an "IIED"—an intention-imprinted electronic device that has been shown to be influenced by and to store the intentions of another person.[9] Just as parents' wishes "imprint" on their children, each person in a loving bond becomes a system imbued forever with the loving wishes or intentions of the other.

Loving is a commitment to sharing intimate intentions and reflects each partner's knowledge and understanding of what is truly in the other's heart. Wishing together gives little "love bond boosts" that keep the relationship's magic flowing. When wishing in this domain becomes more dark-wish-star oriented, the relationship is one of two selves trying to have their own way and to manipulate one another into the kind of loving each thinks is the right way to love. The result is always loneliness, which leads to reactive wishing back to search for individual meaning, purpose, delight, and serenity. Wishing backward leads us into wishing's dark star.

The fifth domain of the wish star's power is also the most challenging because "it takes two." It's a mutual process requiring two people learn to wish for the same things, in the same way, and at the same time. It requires surrendering selfish wishing in an attempt to practice love magic together. If one partner's wishing is selfishly involved in seeking his own version of meaning, purpose, delight, and serenity, the wish-deprived partner is left wishing alone in the compassion domain. She finds herself lovesick as she wishes desperately for someone who is willing to make wishes with her.

Love Lessons from a Maple Tree

Our couples' clinic at Sinai Hospital found it helpful to approach relationship problems from the perspective of learning to wish well together. Since wishing was often a concept both partners had forgotten about or at least left out of their idea of a way to express love, it was a safe, neutral, and productive starting point for rediscovering the magic of love.

We told our couples that compassionate wishes are not always expressed directly or verbally. They are subtle sympathetic vibrations that express a deep caring and symbiotic connection symbolized by what we called "maple tree magic." The sugar maple tree is unique. It appears to "care" and wish well for and with its fellow plants. During dry spells, sugar maple trees have been shown to sink their deep roots even further into the soil. They seem able to search for and find the slightest amount of groundwater far beyond the reach of other plants. Once they manage to find the water and pump it up, the sugar maple drinks some to survive the drought. Then something magical happens. The tree saves the rest of the water for its neighboring smaller plants, such as the goldenrod, that cannot find water on their own at severely dry times.[10] Sugar maple trees may not know it, but they display caring and wish well for their forest mates.

Of course the sugar maple doesn't, at least as we understand the term, make a "conscious" decision to share its water. It's acting purely in terms of its genetic code or perhaps a vegetative version of subtle wishing that reflects its floral sensitivity to the subtle energy of the universe that connects all things. Its altruistic action, however, illustrates the collaboration that can be found in nature and how its various systems end up caring for one another through unstated but actualized well wishes. When someone in a relationship says, "You don't care anymore," that person is expressing a sense of wish neglect and a feeling that her partner doesn't care enough to wish with her.

The Power of the "We Wish"

Are you and your lover making the same wishes? Do you share the same big or main wish about your life and love? Do you have secret wishes you never share with your lover, or do you suspect that your partner has such wishes? If you could make one wish for your relationship, what would it be? What do you think your lover would wish for you? Your answers to these questions determine to a large measure not only how long and well you will love but, because research shows that loving promotes health and healing, how long and well you and your partner will live.

Magical marriage or loving is not a matter of finding a lover who fulfills our every wish but of finding someone with whom we can learn to make and share more loving wishes. The key to lasting, adaptive, growing love is not finding our true love but finding a lover with whom we can learn to wish together to share the truths about life and love.

You have read about the work at the PEAR laboratory and other centers studying the processes involved in "distant intent" or wishing. You have read how research subjects could, by their intent, alter the functioning of machines and other systems. Findings from this research suggest the way in which even more miraculous subtle energy connections and sympathetic vibrations called wishes can be made when two persons who love each other wish together. This research shows clearly that two persons wishing together are much more powerful in their wishing effect than one person wishing alone. They show clearly that giving up selfishness and becoming more sensitive to the very subtle but powerful energy that bonds us heart to heart is the nature of the "power wish" you read about earlier in this book.

Male and Female Wish Bonds

While all kinds of loving bonds have wish power, laboratory studies show clearly that male/female loving bonds seem to manifest the strongest L energy or wish effect. This may be because they comprise an example of what PEAR researcher Arnold Lettieri calls "the primordial aspects" of L energy. He calls these "substantiality," our individualistic, singular, egotistical, "male" nature; and "relationality," our more "female" or interactive, connective, selfless nature.[11]

Physicist Dana Zohar refers to these factors, respectively, as our "particle and wave" energetic states. To achieve a lasting loving bond, it is first and foremost necessary to acknowledge the unique individual nature of each partner in the bond. That distinction being made, the next step is for each partner to be willing to at least partially surrender the self to a bonded state in order for the exchange and resonation of L energy to be activated. To wish well for love, there must be a blurring of who we are in favor of where we intend to go together. Whether or not Lettieri is correct in his hypothesis about the nature of a power of combined conscious intent, the data is clear. Two people wishing together had the most powerful effect on the systems within which they wished.[12]

Sex and Sympathy

Three of every four adults in the United States suffer from serious sex problems.[13] Lack of interest in sex, inability to have orgasm, difficulty with erections, premature ejaculation, and pain during sex are so common as to be an important public health concern. The damage to self-esteem, interpersonal relationships, and even physical health traceable to sexual problems is clear, and the destabilization of marriages to which these problems may relate has severe and lasting individual and societal consequences. Clearly, many persons' sexual wishes are not coming true.

When I ran a large sexual dysfunction treatment clinic at Sinai Hospital of Detroit, it was clear that behavioral techniques alone would not mend sexual distress. The problem was seldom technique or time. The problem usually seemed to be mistaking copulation for connection and having sex with having sympathy—true sympathetic resonance with another person. Sex often seemed to be a shortcut or surrogate for shared wishing and the vulnerability to connect heart to heart rather than body to body. It was something partners did to or for one another but less often with one another. Sex without love and copulating without resonating may be at the root of our national pandemic of sexual suffering.

Love as Resonance

You have read that wishing is a process of resonating with subtle L energy. Dr. Robert Jahn, director of the PEAR program, where more than 5 million trials have been made and billions of bits of information gathered about how a conscious intent can have effects on systems, writes, "The most common subjective report of our most successful human/machine experimental operators [wishers] is some sense of 'resonance' with the devices—some sacrifice of personal identity in the interaction— a 'merging' or bonding with the apparatus. As one operator [wisher] put it: 'I simply fall in love with the machine.' And indeed, the term 'love,' in connoting the very special resonance between two partners, is an apt metaphor. . . ."[14]

The language in this chapter and throughout this book has no doubt been off-putting to many skeptics who believe that terms such as subtle L or love energy, resonating together with love energy to share wishes, and sympathetic resonance or vibrations have absolutely no place in an objective science of clear, rational thinking. The careful scientist and engineer Dr. Jahn disagrees. He writes, "Allusions to love can be found in scientific literature."[15] One of the patriarchs of modern physics, Prince Louis de

Broglie, wrote, "Love . . . that force which directs all our actions, which is the source of all our delights and all our pursuits. Indissolubly linked with thought and with action, love is their common mainspring and, hence their common bond. The engineers of the future have an essential part to play in cementing this bond."[16]

If we have the courage to come out of science's imposed box to understand wishing to be, as many scientists themselves now suggest, sympathetic resonance with the subtle energy that engineer Dr. Jahn calls L or love energy, and if two persons together seem to amplify that resonance, compassionate wishing is arguably one of our most profoundly passionate and compassionate acts. It's the ultimate act of altruism because it requires being willing to surrender self-centered interest in favor of the pair.[17] It's a way to find the immortality of the fourth or meaning domain of the wish star because love offers a place where self matters less than the system and us means more than me.

Wishing well in the realm of compassion is realizing that wishing and loving are one and the same. As philosopher Rollo May stated, "For in every act of love and will [wishing]—and in the long run they are both present in each genuine act—we mold ourselves and our world simultaneously."[18] Wishing well in the fifth wish star domain is learning to convert our early infatuation and physical desire for one another into the commitment and capacity to share wishes for the same kind and degree of security, life purpose, and spiritual meaning. Unless you allow yourself to fall into a loving "wish sync" and are eventually wishing in the same way for the same things as the person you love, it is highly unlikely that your relationship will thrive or even survive.

Sigmund Freud's classic example of a couple's wish gone wrong involves a once loving couple in which selfishness and dark star wishing take over. A greedy wife wishes for sausages for herself and gets them. Her jealous husband becomes outraged and wishes the sausages attached to his wife's nose, and it is done. Finally, and as the Good Fairy again stands by laughing, the couple must learn to employ the wisdom of the third wish and wish together to get what they already had, a loving relationship free of petty jealousies and selfish motives.

Unless you decide to make your lover's wishes as important to you as your lover is, both you and your lover will end up wishing alone for security, purpose, and meaning in life. When the "me" wish is granted for each individual's desire for his or her version of these things, the relationship ends up weakened or even wished away. Unless you learn the art of intimate wishing, you will do as the people you read about in the fairy tales described earlier did and learn the hard way about the devastating dangers of selfish wishing. You will fail to realize that we must work as hard to be wish granters as we do at making our own wishes, and that as Midas learned the hard way through his omnipotent alchemy, we ultimately need one another to make our wishes come true.

The Midas Marriage

There is a profile of a relationship in which unwise wishing is taking place. In my clinic we called this "couple character" the "Midas marriage" because the individual partners' wishing eventually left them feeling isolated in a cold, uncaring relationship. This was a relationship in which the mutual dissolving of egos into one energetic shared unity did not take place. Wishing was drawing the partners apart instead of together. The seven characteristics of a Midas marriage are as follows:

1. Each partner has his/her own individually motivated, separate, private wish usually unshared with the partner.

2. One partner is consumed by his individual wish in one of the first four wishing domains, leaving the partner out of his wishful thinking.

3. One or both partners tend to be consumed by wrongful wishing in the "purpose" domain and reflect a narrow M and M (money and me) definition of success at work outside the home.

4. If only temporarily and closely associated with the dark side of wishing, one partner's "purpose" wish tends to be granted. This brings the wisher the "toxic success" of power and prestige in the workplace that she comes to expect and attempts to impose in the family setting.

5. One or both partners begin to feel, as King Midas ultimately did, that they are living the "golden" life for which they had wished but still feel lonely, sad, stagnant, and even clinically depressed. Because of the lack of compassion and shared love, the more one of the partners' wishes seem to come true, the more depressed and lethargic that wisher seems to become despite the apparent high level of success. Separating work and love life robs the marriage of its magic.

6. One partner typically feels like a "sex" or "wish" object being used in the sexual aspect of their relationship as more of a sex wish fantasy fulfiller than a partner in shared intimate loving.

7. One partner begins to feel more of a "means to the partner's wishes" than a partner in making wishes. Because of the toxicity of this role and the negative backspin along the domains of the bright wish star, the dark side of wishing emerges in the relationship. There is no sense of shared life meaning or pur-

pose, little shared delight, and eventually no serenity in the relationship's home.

The Magic Marriage

The profile of a well wishing bond is the exact opposite of the low-monogamy Midas Marriage. We called it the "magic marriage" because it constantly was going through transformations and seemed to have magical powers to deal with all sorts of problems that for less magical marriages would have been relationship-threatening stressors. The magic marriage relished the sharing of the little things such as politeness and simple acts of kindness and had learned the skill of intimate well wishing. Here are the seven characteristics of the magic marriage:

1. Each partner feels that the other fully and vulnerably shares his or her wishes with the other.

2. The couple work their way around the bright wish star together and make mutual wishes. They find their serenity, delight, purpose, and meaning in life together and they develop a marital momentum that continues to move them around and around the bright wish star together.

3. Partners share a common "working purpose." Work is a shared process in which each partner plays an important role and takes pride in the work done by the other.

4. Each partner's contribution to the relationship is highly valued by the other and there is no dominant member of the bond. All wishing generates from within the bond rather than from one of the individual partners.

5. Both partners value their relationship and its creations as primary in their lives. They take their greatest joy from within their relationship and find meaning, purpose, delight, and healing support from their relationship above and beyond all other sources.

6. Both partners derive fulfillment from their sexual relationship and feel comfortable and secure in the expression of their personal sexual wishes in their intimacy.

7. Both partners feel comforted by and healed through their participation in their relationship. They both seek solace and relief from the pressures of daily living together in their relationship more than from any other source.

The Six Skills of "We Wishing"

Wishing well together is a key to avoiding the Midas marriage and developing a magical or wish-fulfilling loving bond. When we power wish, we stop trying to control our own or our partner's life and recognize and acknowledge that we are one with each other. Like every well wisher, we are not only fully personally absorbed in life but also totally absorbed in our relationship. We realize that we belong to our relationship but do not control it. Intimate wishing is relinquishing the illusion of the sole ownership of our partner or the relationship. Intimate wishing in the compassion domain does not result in a perfect relationship without problems, but it does allow us to join hearts and wishing to dance together in what the character Zorba the Greek called "the full catastrophe" of being alive.

Based on our interviews and wish-research data, wise intimate wishing (or as one of our wish-research subjects called it, "we wishing") requires mastery of six basic skills: identifying the degree of wish compatibility in your relationship; learning how to make "androgynous" wishes (a combination of our "substantiality" and "relation-ality" natures); learning the difference between wishing for "true love" or "love's truths"; avoiding the dangers of making your or your lover's wish into a command; waiting and giving plenty of time for an intimately made wish to work its loving miracle within the relationship; and recognizing, understanding, recasting, and healing the scars of latent "leftover love wishes" from familial or other loving relationships.

"We Wishing" Skill One: Determine Your Relationship's Wish Compatibility

We administered the Wish Compatibility Inventory (WCI) to some of the couples whose members were both a part of our wish-research group. We also gave the WCI to 1,000 couples in our marital and sexual dysfunction clinic at Sinai Hospital of Detroit. The scoring and interpretation of the results is based on our work with both the wish and clinic couples. If you're interested in learning to power or "we" wish, take the WCI yourself and with your partner.

Wish Compatibility Inventory

One of the most neglected relationship skills is learning how to make and share wishes together. The following inventory is a starting point for communicating about the role of wishing in your own relationship. Both you and your partner should take the test, remembering that beginning to talk about intimate wishing is more important than a single score.

Using the following scale, how true is each of the statements in your life?

4 = ABSOLUTELY TRUE   3 = OFTEN TRUE   2 = SOMETIMES TRUE
1 = ALMOST NEVER TRUE   0 = NEVER TRUE

1. _____ I'm getting the kind of love I've always wished for.

2. _____ I think my partner feels that he/she is getting the kind of love he/she always wished for.

3. _____ My partner knows precisely what my most important wishes about love and life really are.

4. _____ I know what my partner's most private wishes about life really are.

5. _____ There isn't any wish I have that my partner doesn't know about.

6. _____ There isn't any wish my partner has that he/she has not shared with me.

7. _____ I get the kind of love I wish for *when* I need it.

8. _____ I think my *partner feels* that he/she is getting the kind of love her/she wishes for *when* he/she needs it.

9. _____ I get the kind of love I wish for *as often* as I wish for it.

10. _____ My *partner* is getting the kind of love he/she wishes for as often as he/she wishes for it.

11. _____ I'm getting the love I wish for *in the way* I wished for it.

12. _____ My *partner* is getting the love he/she wished for in the way he/she wishes for it.

13. _____ My partner knows the details of my most intimate "sex wish" (fantasy, act, way of making love).

14. _____ I know the details of my *partner's* most intimate sex wish (fantasy, act, way of making love).

15. _____ I feel that my every "sex wish" (fantasy, act, way of making love) has been or will be fulfilled in our relationship.

16. _____ My *partner* feels that his/her "sex wish" (fantasy, act, way of making love) has been or will be fulfilled.

17. _____ My relationship is the relationship I have always wished for.

18. _____ Our relationship is the relationship my partner has always wished for.

19. _____ My partner and I share the same wishes for our future life together.

20. _____ My *partner thinks* we share the same wishes for our future life together.

21. _____ My partner would say that he/she thinks that my most important *wish about life has or will come true.*

22. _____ My *partner* feels that his/her own most important wish about life has or will come true.

23. _____ When it comes to religious or spiritual beliefs, my partner shares my most sacred wish about our destiny at life's end.

24. _____ My partner shares my wishes when it comes to money.

25. _____ My partner and I are free from wishing that either of us would have found a different partner.

_____ TOTAL SCORE

Interpreting Your Wish Compatibility Inventory Score

There are two steps in interpreting your WCI score. First, compare your own score and, if possible, your partner's individual score, with the scores from some of our 2,166 members of the wish-research group and the over 1000 clinic couples' scores.

90–100 = High Wish Compatibility—Likelihood of relationship survival extremely high.

80–89 = Wish Compatibility—Likelihood of relationship survival high.

70–79 = Wish Incompatibility—Likelihood of relationship survival uncertain.

60–69 = Severe Wish Incompatibility—Relationship survival at high risk.

59 and below = Extreme Wish Incompatibility—Relationship at serious risk.

Next, calculate the difference between your score and your partner's score. It doesn't matter whose score is highest, just determine the difference between your two scores. Compare your "D" or wish difference score with the "D" scores of the 1,000 clinic couples who took the WCI.

5 or fewer points' difference—Hardy, adaptive, bonded relationship with statistically (less than 1 in 1,000) no chance of separation or divorce.

6–10 points' difference—Strong relationship with almost no chance of separation or divorce but likelihood that one partner is to at least some degree "putting up" with or tolerating the relationship.

11–15 points' difference—Relationship vulnerable, one partner not very happy but tolerating relationship. Need for open communication regarding relationship's "wish compatibility."

16 or more points' difference—Extremely fragile relationship requiring immediate vulnerable and mutual disclosure of wishes.

"We Wishing" Skill Two: Make an Androgynous Wish

Now that you have an idea about your relationship's wish compatibility, the next step in learning to wish intimately is to learn how to make an androgynous wish. The process itself is very time-consuming, but the lessons and the process both help teach the principles of patient loving that are essential to wishing well for and with compassion.

First, take ten 3-by-5-inch index cards and write the following ten phrases in large letters, one phrase per card. The phrases are taken from interviews of our wish-research subjects regarding various aspects of the five realms of the wish star.

- Love
- Money/Unearned Riches
- Special Object Labor Saver/Latest Technical Toy
- Power/Control
- Sex/Fantasy Love Object or Act
- Self-Health/Healing

- Independence/Autonomy
- Another's Welfare/Healing/Well-Being
- Special Place/Escape
- Fame/Glory/Recognition

Now, shuffle the ten cards several times and spread them out. Next, arrange them in order of what you wish for most in your life. On the back of each card, number it in order from your highest-priority wish to your lowest. Even though you may not have a wish that relates to some of the general areas, do your best to put the cards in the closest order to your wishful thinking. If you have a wish you think does not fit the ten categories, write one on an eleventh "wild" card.

This approach is a simplified version of what researchers call the "Q-sort" technique for assessing psychological variables. By assigning values and frequencies to each card as placed by the men and women doing the Wish-Sort test and then counting the number of times that each wish appeared in each place on the list, the following "average" wish-priority lists emerged for 200 men and 200 women ages 17 to 92 who had either attended one of my lectures or had come to our clinic. Because of the averaging and the small, nonrandomized sample, this is only a very general list, but it provides a starting point for discussing the degree of androgynous wishing in your own relationship. I've included a sample wish from one of our research sample members as illustrative of each wish category.

Respondents were asked to close their eyes, touch their chest, take a deep breath, and make a wish softly by beginning, "I wish . . ." Based on the approach just outlined, the men's wish list reads as follows.

Men's Wishes

1. **Love** ". . . to really feel loved for who I am and that my wife would love me for who I am and not what she expects me to be."

2. **Money/Unearned Riches** ". . . I'd win the lottery."

3. **Special Object/Labor Saver/Latest Technical Toy** ". . . I had a red 980 Porsche."

4. **Power/Control** ". . . I could get people to do what I want them to do."

5. **Sex/Fantasy Love Object or Act** ". . . I could have sex with two women at once."

6. *Self-Health/Healing* ". . . I'd never get sick or die of a heart attack."

7. *Independence/Autonomy* ". . . my life was really my own."

8. *Another's Welfare/Healing/Well-Being* ". . . my daughter would be happier."

9. *Special Place/Escape* ". . . I could run away to a desert island paradise somewhere."

10. *Fame/Glory/Recognition* ". . . could be like Mike." [Michael Jordan, the basketball star]

Women's Wishes

1. *Sex/Fantasy Love Object or Act* ". . . I could have easy and multiple orgasms and be touched, hugged, and held all night long."

2. *Another's Welfare/Healing/Well-Being* ". . . my son could be successful."

3. *Power/Control* ". . . I could have more time just for me and not have to take care of everyone else."

4. *Love* ". . . someone would fall madly in love with me."

5. *Self-Health/Healing* ". . . I would never have another migraine headache."

6. *Special Place/Escape* ". . . I could just have a little peace and quiet."

7. *Fame/Glory/Recognition* ". . . people would say they appreciate what I do and that people would really know all I do."

8. *Money/Unearned Riches* ". . . I could hit it so big at slot poker that I could do whatever I wanted to do when I wanted to do it."

9. *Special Object/Labor Saver/Latest Technical Toy* ". . . I could have a maid and a butler."

10. *Independence/Autonomy* ". . . I could have more time just for me."

Putting both lists together for comparison and for learning the art of androgynous wishing, the following comparison exists.

MALE	FEMALE
1. Love	1. Sex/Fantasy Love Object or Act
2. Money/Unearned Riches	2. Another's Welfare/Healing/ Well-Being
3. Special Object/Labor Saver/ Latest Technical Toy	3. Power/Control
4. Power/Control	4. Love
5. Sex/Fantasy Love Object or Act	5. Self-Health/Healing
6. Self-Health/Healing	6. Special Place/Escape
7. Independence/Autonomy	7. Fame/Glory/Recognition
8. Another's Welfare/Healing/ Well-Being	8. Money/Unearned Riches
9. Special Place/Escape	9. Special Object/Labor Saver/ Technical Toy
10. Fame/Glory/Recognition	10. Independence/Autonomy

To help them learn more about making androgynous wishes, we asked couples to discuss their own Q-sorted wish lists and compare them with the lists presented here. For example, in the sample parallel wish lists here, it appeared that male and female wishing were highly weighted toward unmet needs for love (men rated it number one and women number 4), but there was a difference between males' wishes for money and things (ranked 2 for men but 8 for women) and the comparatively low priority they gave to sex (1 for women and 5 for men). Female wishes related more to the welfare of others than did those of men (ranked 2 for women but only 8 for men). Both genders' wishes reflected a need for more power and control (men rated it 4 and women 3).

To wish androgynously, it helps to recognize differences and similarities in the wishful thinking of men and women. Discussing the ways and objects of male- and female-oriented wishes promotes better understanding of a process that is always going on in relationships whether or not we are aware of it.

"We Wishing" Skill Three: Wish for "True Love" or "Love's Truths"

Intimate wishing does not only involve recognizing the wish compatibility and gender-based aspects of your relationship, it also involves learning to make loving wishes based on the fundamental truths about love rather than on a romanticized, personalized, passionate view of loving. Here are some of the truths of love as determined by researchers who have turned their attention to affairs of the heart.

1. *Love is not a feeling, it is a choice.* If you wish to "fall in love" or "feel intense love," you are not wishing well because you are not letting the truth be your wish. The romantic version of loving asserts that we involuntarily "fall in love" or are spontaneously attracted to someone almost against our will. Although relationships may begin with such infatuation, lasting love transcends romance and grows from a mental decision to behave lovingly toward and with another person.[19] You wish unwisely when you seek popular but unresearched psychology's idea of romantic love rather than deciding together to wish as one for a mutually created and creative new loving together.

2. *Learn to love others, not yourself.* If as folk or popular psychology teaches, you wish to learn to love yourself before you love someone else, you are wishing against the nature of L energy as a connective force rather than an individual experience.

3. *Wait for love.* Our consumerist, hurried hyperculture tends to use and then dispose of almost everything, including our relationships. Mutual wishing is one way of constantly regenerating the subtle energy that helps solidify a loving bond. Our clinical advice to couples was "if in doubt, work it out."

4. *Love is diachronic.* Diachronic means adaptable, changeable, adjusting, and constantly accommodating. Synchronic refers to stable, unchanging, and fixed. A wish for love or a lover to never change leads to regressive wishing that can petrify a relationship and render it less adaptable.

5. *Quantity time, not quality time, is crucial to lasting love.* Wishing for "a little quality time together" is less productive to growing love than wishing for a larger quantity of time for loving. Spending more of the time we do have together actually loving is more important to a lasting love than hurriedly

fitting in time periods for high effort at loving. Even though sympathetic resonation transcends time and space, it's easier to resonate together when we are together.

6. *Love at first sight results in love blindness.* Lust rushes you, but you can't rush love. Heated passion is easy, but heartfelt compassion takes time and patience. Our lover loves a fool and so do we, so wishing for the "perfect lover" to flash quickly into our heart can be the wish that breaks our heart.

If we are going to wish for lasting love, we must know the difference between attraction, infatuation, attachment, and loving bonding. Attraction and infatuation are always short-lived, attachment results when you become dependent on "the one," but a loving bond evolves over time as hearts become one.

"We Wishing" Skill Four: Avoid Making Wishes into Commands

A wish can often be perceived as a command. Because our partner may love us so intensely and become attached rather than bonded to us, he can view our wish not as an invitation to join in mutually refining that wish but as a directive to prove love. In our clinic, we called this the "genie syndrome." One partner may play the role of the genie constantly committed to granting a lover's wish rather than lovingly joining with a lover to make wiser and more compassionate wishes.

"We Wishing" Skill Five: Wait for a Loving Wish

As the popular Motown song says, you can't hurry love. A key skill in intimate wishing is learning the power of what one of our wish-research subjects called "wish and wait" and what physician Larry Dossey calls "the great wait."[20] To wish wisely for compassion or shared loving in our life, we have to be extremely patient. Researchers know that it takes at least four years or so for a loving bond to form.[21] To allow intimate wishing to coalesce, we have to have the imagination to see what our life could look and feel like several years down the line from lust. As Oscar Wilde wrote, "The basis of action is lack of imagination. It is the last resource of those who know not how to dream."[22] It is also the lack of thinking wishfully together.

Most premature divorces and failed relationships occur not because of differences over sex, money, and children but because of lack of imagination. They happen because one or both partners are unable or unwilling to be a believer in the "four-year hitch" and that you can't hurry love. They happen because we are often unwilling to allow a wish for love to work its magic.

"We Wishing" Skill Six: Overcome Wish Wounds

The last of the six intimate wish skills is to recognize the scrapes and scars on our love map left by our own and others' wicked wishes. To wish compassionately, we have to be aware of our love style and how it affects others. We have to be alert for when our resentment from a prior hurt is causing us to pull away, be angry, test our partner's love, or try to wish away something rather than wish with someone else for it.

We can't wish our love wounds away. We can, however, wish to love again and to be vulnerable enough to allow someone else to join us in wishing for a better, healthier love. As one young wife in our clinical sample said, "I want our wishes to be our wishes. I don't want them to be his mother's angry wishes or his dad's selfish ones. I want them to be only ours."

Ten Love Lessons from Successful Wishers

The research on wishing and the power of a loving wish conducted at the PEAR lab and other centers as well as our own clinical and wish-research subject interviews indicates that the most successful wishing couples showed ten compassionate characteristics. As a review of what it takes to wish not only in the fifth but in all the domains of the wish star, I am listing here the ten characteristics of power wishing couples.[23] These characteristics incorporate most of the lessons of wishing well you have read in this part of the book. In keeping with the method employed in presenting material in previous chapters, I've summarized the research into ten questions. Remember, the "magic marriage" or loving bond I'm talking about is not just one between a man and woman. It could be between two men or women, two friends, or between a parent and child.

1. *Are both you and your partner excited about loving and do you show that excitement to one another every day?* Being fully absorbed and believing unequivocally in the power of L energy is essential to a couple if they want to be good at wish teamwork. Both partners have to be enthusiastic about the privilege of loving and being loved and about the power of a loving bond to make wishes come true.

2. *Do you pay intense attention to and give consideration to your lover?* To make wishes together, you have to really know one another. You have to establish a "creative fidelity" that goes beyond being self-absorbed to being immersed in the relationship.

3. *Do you give immediate loving feedback to your partner?* Saying things like "great job, I love that, you were just great" and saying them with feeling, immediately, and often help increase your relationship's wishing quotient. Marriage researcher John Gottman has shown that for love to survive and grow, the "5 for 1" rule must be followed.[24] You should provide at least five compliments for every one of your criticisms of your partner.

4. *Do you give and receive complete trust with no hidden agendas?* Secret wishing destroys intimacy. What you don't know or your partner doesn't know will hurt your relationship in some way some time. The best wishing teams were always those who had complete, unqualified trust in one another and their relationship's integrity.

5. *Are you in a loving partnership rather than a master/slave relationship?* The teams at the PEAR laboratory that had two equal, mutually respectful members were those who wished the best. The necessary balance of wishing energy is disrupted when the relationship is not androgynously balanced as to power and responsibility for the relationship. When it comes to wishing, it is not only true that two minds are better than one. It also seems true that the best wishing takes place when two hearts become one.

6. *Are you deadly serious about and completely committed to your relationship?* The most effective wishing teams were those who put their relationship first above all else. Their relationship was not just a source of individual support, it was their reason for being. One of my research subjects illustrated the issue of commitment when she said, "If you're going to have more husbands than you do children, something isn't right. It's hard to be committed to a relationship if you're mostly devoted to yourself."

7. *Is your relationship living in and creating together a beautiful, calm, peaceful place?* You have read about the importance of the ecology of your wishes. The peaceful, serene energy of nature helps us wish well. There is also a "love ecology" within relationships. A mutual effort to create a home of graceful serenity helps promote more effective intimate wishing. One of my research subjects said, "It's not easy making love in a war and boardroom. You have to make your home a place where love lives. It can't be 'my' house. It has to be 'our' home."

8. *Are you trying to lead a very simple life together?* Wishing well is a simple, easy, gentle, energetic swinging. The best wish teams didn't "try hard" to make their wishes or their loving come true. They wished gently together, waited, and allowed plenty of time to let love happen to them. You've read about the "decline" effect in wishing when we push our wishes too hard and make them into big bangs instead of little booms. One of our most successful well wishers, a music teacher, said, "I'm not interested in bending spoons and levitating. I just wish to love and be loved forever."

9. *Do you have more than enough time together?* You can't wish well together if you are hardly ever together. The best wishing teams were those who spent sufficient time together to allow for the development of a mutual resonation of their respective energies. As a physics teacher who was one of our wish-research subjects said, "It's not as easy to cause one tuning fork to vibrate or resonate with another one if the other one is far away. It may vibrate sometime and in some small way and no matter where it is, but it's a lot easier if you bring the two forks to the same table."

10. *Do you regularly act, speak, and exchange "looks of love" with your partner every day?* We noticed that there is indeed a "look of love." We could identify those couples who wished well together by looking at how they looked at each other. We even noticed that many of the most effective wishing teams actually fell into a "breathing resonance" and breathed in sync with one another. Our instruments also indicated that their electrocardiograms fell into the same patterns.

One Couple's Wish

There was a husband and wife in our sample who seemed to take to heart the lessons of "we" or intimate wishing. The husband, now retired, had been a carpenter and his wife had taken care of the business's records and billing. Everyone who knew them said they seemed to be one of the most loving couples they had ever encountered.

"It was really unusual at first for us to talk about our wishes," said the sixty-three-year-old wife. "We've been married for forty-two years and I don't ever recall us talking about wishing unless it was with the kids. We started when we got into the wish-study group. We talk about it a lot now. We've taken the tests and done the sorting of our wishes several times."

"I was kind of surprised," said her seventy-one-year-old husband. "When we started to try to make our eight-word wish together, something very, very strange happened. We were out in our garden. It was cold. There were no flowers, but we could kind of feel them there under the ground just itching to come up and grow again. You could sense them there. Like you told us, I put my left hand on her heart and she put her hand on my heart. We took a deep breath and said at exactly the same time that we wished "to share everything now and be together forever." I think you guys would say that we were really on the same L energy wavelength. We felt this profound sympathy in our hearts. I think that sympathy has been developing for decades."

Wishing compassionately as this couple did is harnessing L energy together. The warm glow of wishing well together makes wishing well the ultimate act of love.

Sixteen

Putting Your
Sixth Sense First

The most beautiful experience we can have is the mysterious.
It is the fundamental emotion which stands at the cradle
of true art and true science.

—ALBERT EINSTEIN

Our Sixth Senses

To learn to wish well in any of the five domains of the wish star, you have to be willing to be a little "paranormal" by coming to your sixth senses. As you have read, wishing is one of the most common ways in which we put our sixth sense into action, one form of which is often called "extrasensory perception" (ESP). It's studied by parapsychologists working in the paranormal, meaning that wishing is a way of dealing with life that, although everyone does it, many scientists still regard as belonging in the category of "beyond the normal." However, what we call our sixth sense is really very "normal" in that we all have it, use it, and rely on it at key times in our lives.

What we call our sixth sense is really our first and most basic sense. It's the way we experience, connect with, and try to influence those aspects of our world that are beyond the reach of our other five senses. Since we appeared on this earth, we have used this sense much more than our brain knows. We probably began using it long before we stood up on our own two feet and could effectively deal with our physical senses. It's the process involved when our intention affects things around us and our intuition detects the subtle influence of everything going on around us, even the impact of another person's wishes.

There is not one "sixth sense" but many dimensions and manifestations of our ability to tune into the nonlocal or "everywhere-all-the-time" L energy that relates to wishing and that most physicists are now willing to acknowledge. Just as our seeing, touching, feeling, smelling, and hearing senses are themselves made up of many complex subsystems, research is showing that our sixth sense is similarly complex and multifaceted. Precognition, psychokinesis, telepathy, and remote viewing are samples of other manifestations of our sixth sense, and they, too, are subtle processes extremely difficult to study with our current five-sense-extending instruments. Researchers into our "super sense-abilities" are learning every day about new and varying ways in which our sixth sense operates. If, rather than being inspired to look further into the mysterious nature of our sixth sense, establishment thinking refuses to come out of the box that excludes "psi" or so-called psychic phenomenon like wishing, it will neglect an important part of our humanness left by default to the pseudoauthorities, charlatans, and fakes who abuse it for their own profit.

Studying Scientific Leftovers

When scientists working "within the box" of establishment thinking encounter weird, unusual, and unexplainable results, they usually throw them "out of the box." This is the box whose walls exclude the before-life, afterlife, outer space, and inner-space phenomena with which most of us are fascinated and in which we place much of our trust. All scientists encounter the effects of sixth-sense phenomena like wishing in their work. Many try to ignore them as artifacts, label them away as *just* "placebo effects," or write about them as anomalies, unexplained variables, mere chance, or spontaneous remissions, precisely the "stuff" that parapsychologists, quantum physicists, and other outside-the-box researchers love to dig through. The mysterious, pervasive effects of intentionality or wishing have long been scientific throwaways, tossed out of the box so as not to shake up its comfortable system. As you have read, however, the power of wishing cannot be denied. Researchers who comfortably work both in and outside the box have proved that wishing works.

Contrary to some scientific opinion, most sixth-sense research is at least if not more carefully done than other scientific research. Because of often exaggerated skepticism turned cynicism, and the willingness of those scientists who operate exclusively "within the box" to attack any findings, psi researchers have had to be extremely careful in the setup, conduct, and reporting of their work. In fact, they have often been so careful that they may have refined and limited psi processes too far and defined them so narrowly as to diminish their actual effect. This may be one reason that studies of intentionally altering the world yield significant but typically small results. As if we were studying one heart cell to learn about the whole heart, we can often see one tiny pulsating event but not fully detect or understand its cumulative power.

The statistical protocols of those studying wishing and other psi phenomena often go well beyond most scientists' statistical sophistication. Remember, wishing and the energy with which it deals is an extremely subtle and sensitive process. Because of its fragility, the "wishes" of the experimenter and even those of the critics may have even more influence in sixth-sense studies than in more traditional psychological experiments.

The first detailed scientific report on ESP was published in 1934 by psychologist J. B. Rhine of Duke University. It was favorably received by the science editor of *The New York Times* and several other science writers.[1] At first, ESP, or the "sixth sense," encountered only the usual and appropriate scientific skepticism. Many scientists attempted to replicate ESP studies done in laboratories at places such as Duke, Harvard, Princeton, Cambridge, and the University of Groningen in Germany. Because psi or sixth-sense phenomena are not as controllable as many of the other phenomena psychologists were used to studying and because of the subtle nature of L energy makes it vulnerable to being altered when we "try too hard" to connect with it, negative results began to be reported as more psi studies were completed. These results were immediately and extensively publicized, and "ESP heresy" hearings were conducted by some of the boxed-in scientists whose skepticism seems to escalate to cynicism whenever they are forced to deal with out-of-the-box issues. Fortunately, the publication of *Extrasensory Perception after Sixty Years*, a book summarizing much of the careful psi research, quelled much of the hostile reaction and turned the subject back to more appropriate scientific scrutiny.[2] *The Journal of Parapsychology*, which publishes research dealing with sixth-sense phenomena such as wishing, appointed a statistical editor to its board and employs unusually high standards of statistical analysis.

The Maharishi Effect

Some of the most rigorous scientific analyses of sixth-sense phenomena have been applied to the result of power, or shared, wishing, called the Maharishi Effect. This effect was named after Maharishi Mahesh Yogi, the founder of transcendental meditation (TM). TM is similar to wishing in that it involves a "pure consciousness" freed of the urgent, selfish brain. Although TM practitioners do not use the term "wishing" when they describe their "pure contemplation" or "pure love" attempts to improve the world, their L-energy-oriented "passive volition" approach parallels many of the aspects of wishing well that you have read about in this book. It's possible that including wishing as I have described it in pure-consciousness approaches such as TM could enhance the Maharishi Effect.

At a scientific meeting held in Arosa, Switzerland, in 1974, the Maharishi suggested that if only 1 percent of a population "wished" together in the heartfelt, brain-silencing ways described in this book, the other 99 percent of the population could be positively affected. After careful scientific study, even the most doubting critics declared the Maharishi Effect "a discovery that is going to change the world."[3] Unfortunately, establishment thinking's discomfort with psi phenomena has slowed that change.

The Maharishi Effect is caused by "power wishing," the attempt by a small group of people to combine wishing forces for the good of their community and to transform the social environment into a more harmonious and loving system. It's creating a small but powerful L energy resonation that vibrates through the entire world system. Studies have shown that the Maharishi Effect decreases a community's rate of traffic fatalities, deaths from alcoholic cirrhosis, rape, larceny, unemployment, and even problems due to the weather.[4] Power wishing is a kind of gentle gang rebellion against the increasing viciousness of the world.

Despite the mystical descriptions and amazing implications of the Maharishi Effect and "power wishing," this subtle energy approach should not be dismissed as a quirky Eastern or far-out New Age idea. Wishing together is quintessentially human and, as you have read in this book, an important aspect of our species' legacy. It is one of the oldest cultural practices for rendering the world a more friendly place. You have read in the previous chapters that there is now good strong evidence that a small group of well wishers can change the world. I hope this book has convinced you to join us.

Psychologist Garland Landrith compared cities with 1 percent or more of their population practicing what he called "pure consciousness" free of the demanding brain with cities with fewer than 1 percent of these "well wishers." Landrith documented that cities with the well wishing 1 percent experienced a more than 8 percent decrease in crime, whereas the "nonwishing" cities reported a more than 8 percent increase.[5] Landrith's findings have since been confirmed by a score of other studies. Researchers concluded that the chances of the Maharishi Effect (the power of a shared wish) being due to chance were less than 1 in 5 billion.[6]

In-the-box establishment science cannot explain the Maharishi Effect or the power behind a loving group wish. Some "possibilite" scientists, however, are suggesting that an entire physical system such as a society can be changed by a small sympathetic resonation "swung out" by an "in sync" group of well wishers. They point to the well-established scientific principles of "phase transition" through which a small energetic change converts steam to water and water to ice. They also describe a magical-sounding "superfluid" brought into being through lowering of the temperature of liquid helium by a few degrees, a fluid fourth state of matter entirely different from gaseous, liquid, or solid states.[7] Power wishing and the Maharishi Effect may cause a "phase transition" in the L energy and collective consciousness that can reduce crime and make a society more loving.

If we come to our sixth sense, we can accept that wishing well not only can help change our individual life for the better but may even, through the force of a combined kind of "Maharishi Effect" power wishing, make the world a better place. The fact that ideas such as L energy, a Maharishi Effect, power wishing, and other sixth-sense psi phenomena seem to offend many of us may be one reason our world is teetering on its sixth extinction. Physician Larry Dossey writes, "It would be foolish to ignore the possibility that the voluntary entry by a group of persons into a specific state of consciousness [wishing well together] can literally change the world for the better."[8] This book has been an appeal for a consideration of a return to the delightfully simple act of making a wish to help heal the world.

The Choice Is Yours

You have a choice to make. You can stay on the edge of the box and elect to see wishing as a curious cultural custom based on superstitious mythology. If you so choose, you are still tapping into a very ancient process that has persisted over the millennia precisely because it works well in the mystical and mythological domains of our cultural life. You can, however, also choose to consider wishing as an often forgotten but extremely powerful way of making your own, your family's, and the world's life a more loving and connected energetic system of shared creative fidelity. You can consider including wishing in both your secular and spiritual adaptive repertoire and try to listen to what your heart needs rather than just what your brain wants. If you wish, you can try a little ancient magic to live well in the new millennium.

For those who choose to become more absorbed and aware of the L energy of life and to wish their way into it, there are the serenity, delight, purpose, meaning, and compassion realms of the bright star to lighten your own life and the lives of those you love. If you feel turmoil, disillusionment, stagnation, despair, and loneliness in your life, it might be because you are wishing in the realms of the dark side of the wish star or have become exclusively dependent on your five senses and the four forms of energy with which they have become increasingly comfortable. You may have chosen to depend on your intellect, cognition, and rational thinking and never on intuition and wishful thinking. Those of us who trust in wishing wish you would trust your heart and try a little wishing well in your life. As Adlai Stevenson wrote, ". . . what a man knows at fifty that he did not know at twenty is that he had too little faith and too little reverence for things you cannot see."[9]

The "WOW" Test

As a review of the concepts presented throughout this book, here's the Way of Wishing (WOW) test we used with our wish-research subjects. It provides a way to review the basic tenets of wishing well.

The WOW Test (Way of Wishing)

The following twenty-five questions were used to assess the way people around the world make their wishes. How true is each statement regarding your own way of wishing? After taking the WOW test, compare your total score with the wishing well research subjects' scores. After you have scored yourself, go over each of the twenty-five items and compare them with the twenty-five "Wishing Wisdom" points related to each item and based on the scientific research, mythology, and spiritual lessons presented and documented in the previous chapters of this book.

4 = ABSOLUTELY TRUE   3 = MOSTLY TRUE   2 = MOSTLY NOT TRUE

1 = JUST A LITTLE TRUE   0 = COMPLETELY UNTRUE

1. _____ If all of my wishes would come true, I wouldn't have to make any more wishes.

2. _____ If most of my wishes had already come true, I'd be much more content than I am now.

3. _____ If my wish to win $10 million came true, I'd be very happy.

4. _____ I wish I could "have it all."

5. _____ I wish I felt a lot happier a lot more often than I do.

6. _____ I wish for a much better future.

7. _____ I wish I could be as happy as other people.

8. _____ I wish I could just have the good luck other people always seem to have a lot more often than I do.

9. _____ I wish I could be happy almost all the time.

10. _____ I wish I didn't have negative feelings.

11. _____ I wish I could be "high" or content almost all the time.

12. _____ I wish I would never have to experience severe suffering.

13. _____ I wish I would never get low or depressed.

14. _____ I only wish my most basic desires would be fulfilled.

15. _____ I wish a lot for wealth and health.

16. _____ I know what I want and wish I could have it.

17. _____ My wishes are usually about things or events for me.

18. _____ I wish evil to some people.

19. _____ Most of my wishes have not come true.

20. _____ I wish I would find and fall in true love.

21. _____ If I could stay healthy and feel good, I wish I would never get old.

22. _____ I have wished out loud that something bad would happen to another person.

23. _____ I wish people would just do things my way.

24. _____ Even though I do it myself, I think wishing is probably just a silly superstition.

25. _____ I wish for things I never had.

_____ TOTAL WOW SCORE

Scoring

The lower your score on the WOW, the more likely you are practicing the art of well wishing. The mean or average WOW score for 500 indigenous people, including several Native American Indians, Hawaiians, Alaskan Indians, and various indigenous people in New Zealand and Australia was 18. The mean score of our wish-research sample was 23. Where does your WOW score place you on the following scale?

0–20 = WELL WISHING   21–40 = WORRIED WISHING

41–60 = WRONGFUL WISHING   61 AND ABOVE = WICKED WISHING

A Twenty-Five-Step Guide to Wishing Well

Here's a review of the principles of wishing well. Each point is related to the corresponding WOW test item and is based on the latest psychological research related to the principle identified. You will note that there are many "repeat" points about well wishing scattered through the test items and well wishing principles listed here. This redundancy, as with the redundancy intentionally included throughout this book, is illustrative of the contemplative, slower, Pooh Bear–style of learning that fits well with the ways of making wishes. This book is written in a modern version of the incantational and ritualistic style of magical thinking. The redundant items in the following list were included in the WOW as a cross-check of validity and consistency in test responses. The central points of altruistic, balanced, kind wishing can be found recycling through all of the twenty-five points. As one of our wish-research subjects said, "If I didn't quite get the point the first time, it came around again."

Also included here are quotes from philosophers, poets, and other authors brought to us by our wish-project participants that they found helpful as contemplative points related to each wishing concept.[10]

1. **Every desirable experience is transitory.** Wish in the precious present and not for a better tomorrow. Author Dan Millman wrote, "Keep in mind this daily notion: There are no ordinary moments." All true joy and deep suffering is only momentary.

2. **Objective life circumstances have very little impact on how happy a person says he or she is.** Booker T. Washington wrote, "Success is to be measured not so much by the position that one has reached in life as by the obstacles which he has overcome while trying to succeed. Wish to

enjoy what, where, who, and with whom you are, not to have more power and prestige."

3. **Well-being does not mean being well-off.** Author Hugh Black wrote, "Only God can fully satisfy the hungry heart of man." Wish to have just enough to feel safe. As King Midas learned the hard way and too late, wishing for more than enough is an eventually isolating process. Even multimillionaire John D. Rockefeller spoke of the Midas factor when he said to a Sunday school class, "It is wrong to assume that men of immense wealth are always happy."

4. **If you try to have it all, all you will have is trying.** No matter how smart or hard working, those who wish to have it all end up wishing in the realms of the dark wish star. None of us will ever be completely satisfied. Thomas A. Edison wrote, "Show me a thoroughly satisfied man, and I will show you a failure."

5. **You come to feel as you behave.** Going through the motions alters the emotions. Don't wish to be happy; wish for the strength to act happier. Happiness doesn't come to us, we bring it on by the state of our wishing. Author Storm Jameson wrote, "Happiness comes of the capacity to feel deeply, to enjoy simply, to think freely, to risk life, to be needed."

6. **Happiness and health require "being in" what many healers and poets call "the precious present."** Don't wish for "more time." You already have all the time you or any of us will ever have. Poet Pearl Yeadon McGinnis wrote, "I have no yesterdays, time took them away; tomorrow may not be—but I have today."

7. **Most people are not as happy as they tell you they are.** Don't wish to be as or more happy than other people. Philosopher Montesquieu wrote, "If one only wished to be happy, this could be easily accomplished; but we wish to be happier than other people, and this is always difficult, for we believe others to be happier than they are."

8. **Happiness and misery depend more on temperament and a general happiness "set point" than good or bad fortune.** In the statistical sense, we all have a "mean" mood, an average mood style. Don't wish to be what you can't be but to be all that you can be. Ralph Waldo Emerson wrote, "Make the most of yourself, for that is all there is of you."

9. **No emotional state lasts.** Don't wish to be very, very up or you will ultimately end up very, very down. An anonymous author wrote, "If you can't

be thankful for what you receive and how you are, be thankful at least for what you've managed to escape and who you'll always be."

10. *There is no negative emotion, only a "stuck emotion."* Don't wish to be "ideally happy" or to "never be depressed." After we are born and until we die, we only have the beginnings and approximations of total elation and deep despair. Unless we allow ourselves to become trapped at one emotional state, we are constantly in a state of emotional flux. A Spanish proverb states, "I don't want the cheese; I just want to get out of the trap."

11. *No matter how high you feel, you will ultimately feel that low.* Henry Wadsworth Longfellow wrote, "The lowest ebb is the turn of tide." Don't wish to stay high or to never be too low. Wish for balance. As Ralph Waldo Emerson wrote, "Keep cool. It will all be over 100 years hence."

12. *"Mild misery" tends to lead to feelings of isolation, but the agony of deep suffering tends to lead to profound feelings of connection.* Wishing away suffering wishes away the nature of our soul. Author Henry Ward Beecher wrote, "God asks no man whether he will accept life. This is not the choice. You must take it. The only choice is how."

13. *Life is as much suffering as celebration.* Don't wish to avoid the essential learning crises of life. Author C. S. Lewis wrote, "God allows us to experience low points of life in order to teach us lessons we could not learn in any other way."

14. *Again, remember Midas; don't wish for more stuff.* All desires are insatiable. Don't wish to feel fulfilled. All life is characterized by a little motivating irritability. Wish to live fully now. Ralph Waldo Emerson wrote, "We are always getting ready to live, but never living."

15. *A sense of coherence (a system of explanation for all of life's events) and flow (easy sense of direction), not great wealth and perfect health, is what predicts contentment.* Author Wilfred T. Grenfell wrote, "Real joy comes not from ease or riches or from the praise of men, but from doing something worthwhile."

16. *Wanting what one has makes one happier and healthier than trying to have what one wants.* Wish to be thankful, not for more things for which to be thankful. Author Edwin Percy Whipple wrote, "God is glorified, not by our groans, but by our thanksgivings."

17. Allocentrism (selflessness), not egocentrism, leads to health and happiness. Wish more for others than yourself. Winston Churchill wrote, "We make a living by what we get, we make a life by what we give."

18. What goes around always—sooner or later—comes around. Don't make angry, aggressive, vengeful wishes; they always come back to you. Author Thomas à Kempis wrote, "Be not angry that you cannot make others as you wish them to be, since you cannot make yourself as you wish to be."

19. Whether we ultimately wish them to or not, most of our wishes come true. The problem can be that our heart tends to attract what it secretly harbors. The state in which you wish, not just the object of the wish, is what is granted. Be careful not only what you wish for but how and when you make your wishes. Author Thomas Carlyle wrote, "The greatest fault, I should say, is to be conscious of none."

20. Love is volitional, not emotional, and depends much more on being than finding the right partner. Lasting love is a tolerant, forgiving, patient love that freely acknowledges one's own flaws and forgives the lover's faults. Don't wish to find the perfect lover but to be as close as possible to being one. Author Julius Gordon wrote, "Love is not blind—it sees more, not less. But because it sees more, it is willing to see less."

21. A wish to never get old is ultimately a death wish. It is the young who most fear death. Most older people have little fear of it, are in pretty good health, profoundly enjoy their later years, report being happier than young people report being, and say they would never wish to be young again. Don't wish to be or stay young; wish to love the changing processes and stages of life. Poet Henry Van Dyke wrote, "I shall grow old, but never lose life's zest, because the road's last turn will be the best."

22. Watch your mouth; words have power. A 2,000-year-old Hawaiian saying is "I ka 'olelo no ke ola, I ka 'olelo no ka make" (Words give life, words give death). Don't wish with anger; wish to get over it. Confucius said, "To be wronged is nothing unless you continue to remember it."

23. You can change yourself, but you'll never change people. Don't waste your wishes trying to make people what they are not. Psychologist William James wrote, "The art of being wise is the art of knowing what to overlook."

24. *Wish with cautious respect for the energetic system into which you are venturing when you make a wish.* A single wish causes vibrations that extend outward to the universe. Wishing can help create miracles, but wicked wishing can result in misery. Author Louis Adamic wrote, "My grandfather always said that living is like licking honey off a thorn."

25. *Never wish for what you never had.* Most of the grandeur of being alive is already present to some extent in your present situation. Wise wishing is realizing and appreciating fully what you already have and wishing for the ability to treasure in your heart the gift of life. Philosopher Cuang Tzu wrote, "My opinion is that you never find happiness until you stop looking for it." Wishing well is asking for a little help in seeing the joy already present in your everyday life.

The central premise of these Wishing Wisdom Points is that the best wish is one for a new way to see the world through your heart rather than your head. It is a wish in sympathy or resonation with the subtle energetic processes from which we all derive. Learning to wish well is learning to be supersensitive to the fact that by the simple act of focusing your intention and following your heart's intuition, you can change—if only a little bit—both your own life and the world.

Epilogue:
Getting a Well Wisher's
Perspective

⬩⬩⬩⬩⬩⬩⬩⬩⬩⬩⬩⬩⬩⬩⬩ 🖋 ⬩⬩⬩⬩⬩⬩⬩⬩⬩⬩⬩⬩⬩⬩⬩

One's destination is never a place but rather a new
way of looking at things.

—HENRY MILLER

From a Different Perspective

When it comes to the five realms of wishing, it all depends on your point of view. Learning to wish well is not just learning how to wish for more serenity, greater delight, grander purpose, deeper meaning, or more passionate love. It's learning how to wish for a more enlightened perspective on all of these things so that your wishes may come more from your heart than your head.

As you complete your reading of this book, look again at the "wish card" I suggested you make to use as a bookmark. Examine the wishes you've been writing on that card and consider whether or not they seem to have changed. Take another card and write down an eight-word wish in each of the five realms of the wish star. Reflect on how your wishes may have changed in their point of view and consider whether they reflect what your brain wants or what your heart really needs. Put your wish cards away and take a look at them again a month or two from now to see if and how your wishes may have come true.

Five Wishes Come True

To illustrate the effects of a well wisher's perspective based on the principles you have been reading about, here are five examples of wishes come true offered by our wish-project participants. I've selected an example from each of the five realms of the wish star.

1. *A young mother's wish for serenity:* "I wished and wished that sooner or later I would be able to be more relaxed and less stressed and have more time, even some time, to just sit down and find some peace and quiet. After I thought about my wish and asked my heart about it, here's the wish I came up with. I finally wished, 'to relish the moments I have right now.' It seems to have come true because I'm remembering that wish more and more and getting a little more joy in the simplest things. Making a sandwich for the kids' school lunch has stopped being a rushed, goal-oriented task and a chance to do something with the kids. I put little surprises in their lunches and they make suggestions for weird things to put in. It's become a game instead of a tribulation. It's a small thing, but it means a lot to us."

2. *A computer analyst's wish for delight.* "I was really into intensity. I thought fun was an adrenaline rush and winning at something. I really thought wishing was for those who lacked the courage to go after what they wanted. Everything I did was a competition. When my girlfriend convinced me to work on the wishing well thing, I really struggled. Finally, my wish was 'to be able to play without trying to win.' It must be working because there are a lot more people who want to play tennis and golf with me now. I never realized how many people hated playing with me before."

3. *An executive father's wish for purpose.* "I wished for more success at work. I got it and almost lost my family in the process. After weeks of trying, I learned to wish for a new definition of success. I just couldn't come up with one. Finally, I realized that the search for a new definition was my wish. My written wish was 'to develop a less selfish, more inclusive definition of success.' I keep that wish in my day planner and it helps me keep my perspective about why I work and for whom."

4. *A retired teacher's wish for meaning.* "I've tried every diet and exercise gimmick in the world. I've spent years trying to outrun death and delay aging. When my wife and I got into the wishing thing, it took about three months to get the hang of it. My wish was 'to be more fully alive before I die.' I've stopped

leading my life to delay death and I'm not wasting years now just to gain a few more years on the geriatric unit later. I watch my weight, I exercise, but mostly I'm on the lookout for living a lighter life than weighing fewer pounds. I've lost a lot of psychological weight but not too many physical pounds, but I feel much, much lighter somehow."

5. *A couple's wish for compassion.* "We've been married thirty-five years," said the husband. "I sort of pursued my wishes and she pursued mine too. When we tried the intimate wishing process, it was a shocker. I had been totally insensitive to my wife's wishes and she'd been a slave to mine. I thought I was fulfilling her wishes by working hard and giving her things, but she said she only wished that I would give her me. That made no sense at first and sounded like romantic soap opera or talk-show stuff, but looking at our contrasting wish lists and how men and women differ in wishing made it crystal clear. I was so into my own things that my wife said she often felt widowed by a living man. Forming a shared wish took weeks and weeks. We finally came up with wishing to 'become more sensitive to each other's loving style.' It's a wish in progress, but it's our and not just my or her wish."

These examples illustrate the importance of the process of wishing more than the exact object of the wish. They all illustrate a wish from the heart more than the brain and a change in wishing perspective conducive to wiser wish making.

Putting Wishing in Perspective

To help you as you begin to put into practice the ideas for wishing well you've read about, here are some mental exercises you can try to bring yourself out of the "brain's box" and broaden your own wishing beyond the brain's limits to the heart's horizons. Scientists dealing with quantum concepts cannot often do actual experiments in the laboratory. To help them deal with the out-of-the-box concepts that keep emerging from the world of the very big and very fast and the very small and timeless, they have to follow their hearts and use their imagination and intuition as much as their telescopes, microscopes, and particle accelerators. Scientists dealing with cosmic and quantum concepts have to be constantly aware of the impact of their wishes on those things they are studying. In order to try to understand more about the often bizarre paradoxes of the world of particles and waves, the mystery of photons, and how our intent enters into that world and shakes it up, they conduct what children call "let's pretend" and quantum physicists call "thought experiments." They imagine "what ifs" and try to look at things from an entirely new perspective, including the perspective that what they are looking at is somehow looking back at them and is responsive to their most subtle intentions.

I use the following five mental exercises to help me wish from a broader world and spiritual perspective in each of the five domains of the wish star. They help me remember where I really am in the world and they help me put my heart in my wishing. They work for me, but I hope they stimulate wish-horizon-expanding experiments that will work for you. I've noticed that my wishes seem more modest, humble, patient, gentle, and less self-centered when I try these thought experiments, and I wish that they do the same for you.

1. Find serenity in a horizon rising.

When my wife and I make our wishes for serenity, we often go to the beach and watch a horizon rising. Even though Copernicus altered forever our view of the "reality" of a sun moving around our earth, we really have not paid much attention to this major paradigm shift. Our five-sense-limited neuroarchitecture still sees its "reality" of the sun setting, but as it so often is, this five-sense system is wrong. It can't be trusted when it comes to wishing well. Another reality is one where you must use your sixth sense. To wish well, we have to spiritually "get on the ball" and feel in our heart the reality that we are riding around and around on a slowly spinning globe. To learn to wish from this cosmic perspective, try replacing watching a sunset with watching a horizon rising.

When we make our first wishes in the realm of the wish star, it seems to help when we realize that we are two among billions of people riding around together on a cosmic joyride. We sit down, relax, and feel the earth tilting backward as if we were riding a massive global Ferris wheel. We follow the steps in wishing well, take a very deep breath, and try to remember that even the horizon itself is an illusion that keeps extending on whenever we try to approach it. Then, we utter our eight-word wish. Something about this wishing perspective seems to make our wishes wiser, more in keeping with a cosmic rather than a clock view of the time of our life, and more connected than selfish. Perhaps this exercise will help you reshape your way of seeing your place in the universe and free you from what one of our wish subjects called "one reality wish making."

2. Find delight in an animals' restrained playfulness.

We are almost chimps and they are almost us. Mathematical cosmologist Brian Swimme points out that we share more than 99 percent of the same genetic material as chimpanzees. The one small part of our genetic difference is on a gene that regulates how fast we develop and mature. Chimps have the genetic advantage here because by about six months, they pretty much resemble an adult chimp. They have stopped much of their fooling around and carefree and often damaging playfulness. While they still play, they have lost much of their careless frolicking.

We humans are developmentally retarded when it comes to playfulness and imagination. We are fixated in both of these processes. Our lifelong curiosity, imagination, and playfulness results in wonderful ideas such as going to the moon and soon other planets, but it also results in the often rough play that is ruining our own planet. For example, fire was around long before we "discovered" it. Once we humans got our hands on it, we became carried away and couldn't stop playing around with it. We couldn't resist imagining for hundreds of uses for it. As a result, our entire planet is overheating, and like children playing with matches, we are in danger of burning down our own home. Our prolonged fixation at the imagination and playfulness stage has brought us great blessings, but it's also leading to great grief.

When I make wishes about delight, I sometimes imagine that I am a chimp, a dog, or a dolphin observing humans. I sometimes try to make a wish I think these animals or even a plant might make. I imagine that instead of going on a whale watch, I'm going on a human watch. I begin to wonder why these humans can't play more carefully in our home and be a little more aware of how their playing affects everything else. Sometimes I watch my golden retriever puppy named Liʻa (Hawaiian for a "playful spirit"), and I see that her boundless, irresponsible puppy play is diminishing while some of the adults I see are still recklessly playing around. Liʻa no longer destroys her toys or chews up her bed. She still finds great fun in the simple act of eating, the daily adventure of finding a place to defecate and urinate, and greeting us every morning as if we were never coming back. She stopped her destructive messing around all on her own, and at less than seven years old in human years, she now plays more carefully and with more awareness of her home and family.

By doing this wish perspective exercise, I find that my wishes for delight tend to be more moderate, socially responsible, and ecologically sound. Wishing for delight is fine, but wishing for a selfish and unrestrained amusement results in humans behaving like undisciplined, immature children running amuck in paradise. In doing so, our selfish delights are threatening the very survival of our Eden.

3. *Find purpose in a horizon setting.* I used to watch almost every sunrise. Now, to balance my horizon rising exercise, I try to be present for every horizon setting. The Copernican paradigm shift helps me remember that the beginning of my workday is the end of the day for millions of other people. I try to imagine the feeling of coming around again on the earth Ferris wheel for another chance to be of value to the planet and I sense more fully my cyclical planetary ride. I wonder what I can contribute to the world this time around. I remember that even the days of our week are named after mystical gods like the Greek god Thor (Thursday) and

the Germanic god Woden (Wednesday), and stars like our sun (Sunday). This mythological and planetary perspective helps me wish for a purpose that transcends the workaday world and to find work that helps the world.

Psychologists know about "black Monday." More people die of their heart attacking them at about 9 A.M. on Monday morning, the beginning of the workweek, than any other time. Several years after their retirement, their hearts seem to remember black Monday as retirees continue to die most often early Monday morning, even when they no longer physically go to work. These deaths are from a state of heart, not just hard work. They are due to the stress and pressure of a sense of high responsibility but little power and having to "get a job done" without "really accomplishing anything." There's nothing wrong with a busy body, but frustrated working leaves us disheartened. "Black Monday" victims suffer from a literally heavy heart clogged and hardened by neglect of its needs as it struggles to meet what the brain sees as obligations. Their heart suffers from unfilled wishes for the higher purpose in their working that acts as a buffer against the effects of the necessary stress of modern working. When I wish as I ride the planet upward, I feel invigorated and inspired to try to make my own work and writing contribute to making everyone's ride a little more healthy, happy, and safe. I remember why I'm working more than what work I must do. I remember the black Monday epitaph, "Got everything done, died anyway."

4. *Find meaning in the stars.* When the full moon glows, the sky is deep black, and the stars glitter from horizon to horizon over the ocean, I lie down on the ground and look down at the stars. I imagine I am looking down because, of course, there is really no up or down in the universe. I imagine that I'm lying on the bottom of the earth looking down at the stars. I try to feel them pulling me off the earth and remember that it is only the mild grip of the earth's gravity that is holding me on this tiny speck in the galaxy.

If I'm very still, breathe very deeply, and look with my heart and not just my eyes, I imagine I can feel the billions of stars drawing me to them with their own invisible force. I imagine that every element of these stars is also what makes up the elements that are my body, my temporary bio-suit for my stay here on earth. When I wish from this stargazer's perspective, I find that my wishes for meaning come more easily. Even when I'm terribly sad about something that happened that day or about a recalled loss, I find solace and sympathy resonating within me from the stars. When I remember that my own heart's energy is traveling at the speed of light, I also imagine that I am one with the stars and in resonating sympathy with them. The cultural myths and new science of wishing tells me I am right.

5. *Find love by looking at others with your heart.* When I wish for love, I always try to keep my heart clearly focused in my imagination. I try

to picture its combination of grit and grace and its unique blend of immense power and gentle nature as represented in its every systolic contraction and diastolic relaxation. I try to see my heart telling my brain to calm down and connect up.

Stanford physicist William Tiller writes, "This work [the research on the heart as the subtle energy center of the body] tends to suggest that the heart can be seen as the 'mainframe' of the body and that humans function best and most effectively when all the biological oscillators of the body take their lead from the heart."[1] Well wishing always comes from the heart because it is there that our fondest and most loving memories are stored. The heart is the most energetically powerful organ in our body, and as such, it is in a perfect position to handle the subtle L energy of wishing and not to coordinate our wishes within us but to send them outward to resonate with other hearts and even the stars.

If wishing connects us with the unique subtle L energy, what organ other than the heart has the robust energetic capacity and in-place trunk lines to handle this energetic connection? The heart nourishes all of our 75 trillion cells and sends packets of cells surging over a vessel system that, if extended, would wrap around the earth more than two times like a vast antenna radiating the heart's wishes. It's naturally made to be the organ that makes, resonates, and sends our best wishes through ourselves and others. My wish-enhancing image is to look at everyone around me with my heart and to try to resonate with their hearts.

When the brain looks at people with its five-sense orientation, it sees differences in gender, color, race, size, age, shape, and anything else that can help it distinguish one person from another and determine how another person is different from the body it is trying to protect. Remember, that's the brain's big wish—to stay alive and get all it can in the process. The heart's wish is to stay connected and get and give all the love it can. When the heart looks at strangers, it sees other hearts with which it can resonate and exchange "sympathies," the sympathetic resonances of a well-made wish.

When I wish for love after trying this heart imagination exercise, I usually end up wishing to be more loving. I begin to realize that those persons around me, even those my brain doesn't recognize or may see as potential threats, have more insights into my life and to what I should be wishing than I could ever have on my own. I feel the need to connect to these people heart to heart, to be in sympathetic resonation with them, in order to make wise wishes and for my wishes to come true.

Seeing through the Fog

The world seems pretty screwed up sometimes. So much seems to be happening, things change so fast, and so much is asked of us that it may seem a struggle just to make it through the day. Most of us are suffering from severe event overload. Our default cardiovascular and neurological state is one of edginess and readiness to take action. Whether we are aware of it or not, an immense amount of our physical and spiritual energy is expended just trying to keep quickly changing the focus of our attention several times from one event to another.

In this new millennium, the Event Density Dilemma I mentioned earlier has become the deepening fog of information overload and we have a nagging fear of lack of enough information. How is there time for loving when so much is asked of us just to make it through this dense haze of constant changes and demands in our life? One way out of this dilemma is to learn to wish our way through the fog.

Author Ursula K. LeGuin wrote, "It's good to have an end to journey toward; but it's the journey that matters in the end." Because wishing is the act of trying to connect with the energy of the universe by falling into "sympathy" or resonant vibration with it, wishing makes the trip through life a little less frightening. Because wishing well in all of the five domains begins with heartfelt gratitude for wishes already granted, wishing can help us find daily appreciation for being allowed to go along on the trip. Because it is the journey that matters, I hope this book has helped you find more joy, comfort, and empowerment in your voyage by relying a little more on the ancient magic and new science of wishing and by using your intentions to make possibilities into realities. Because it is the journey that holds the joy, because wishing well can be a unique and always available source of comfort no matter where your travels take you, and because your best wishes always come from your heart, keep on wishing to your heart's content!

Rabbi Harold Kushner writes, "When you have learned to live, life itself is the reward."[2] I would add that when you have learned to wish well, wishing itself can be reward enough. It can give us a little cosmic confidence just when we need it the most. It's a way we can feel empowered to connect with and control, even if ever so slightly, the mysterious magic of life. It's a way we can maintain a sense of faith that we are not just helpless victims in an uncaring and unresponsive random universe. Even if I haven't changed your mind about the power of wishing, I hope I have changed your heart. My wish is that when you attend your next horizon rising or setting, you will remember that wishing may not make the world go around, but it sure can help make the ride worthwhile.

Afterword:
Wishing and the Heart
of the Universe

Gary E. R. Schwartz, Ph.D., and Linda G.S. Russek, Ph.D.

.... 🖋 ....

When we are ready to listen with our heart, we are transformed.

—DR. JAMES LEVIN

When we were children in the early 1950s, we heard the words "when you wish upon a star" every Sunday evening as we faithfully watched the *Disney* show. Then, when we became serious scientists in the 1970s and '80s, we were essentially told to grow up about wishes and "stop being children." We remember being taught as graduate students in clinical psychology that although wishes did have psychological significance, they were neither physical nor spiritual. Wishes were an expression of wishful thinking. And wishful thinking was not real.

However, that was then, and this is now. It is the dawn of the twenty-first century, and as *Wishing Well* teaches us, it is becoming more than okay to be wishful about thinking. It may be scientifically necessary.

Contemporary scientific theory and research is leading all of us, professionals and laypersons alike, to return to the idea of wishing and view it with new eyes. The challenging work from Stanford, Princeton, the University of Arizona, and many other centers of higher education are leading to the conclusion that not only does the mind matter, but mind affects matter. Learning how to resonate with the world and the cosmos was a skill practiced by ancient cultures, including Paul's ancestors from Hawai'i. However, the power of wishing was temporarily forgotten during the "modern" age by a significant portion of the world's population.

In our Human Energy Systems laboratory at the University of Arizona, we have witnessed the power of wishing firsthand. We have replicated the Princeton random-event-generator studies with gifted individuals. We have made new discoveries that illustrate how wishing an "Egely" Wheel to move (a device that responds to subtle energy from the hands) can modify its movements from a distance. We have witnessed college student experimenters simply "imagine" staring at a subject's head or back, and have discovered that the subjects are able to detect, above chance, whether the imagined looking was focused on their heads or backs. The total set of experiments is sufficiently large that we can say, with some assurance, that wishing does operate beyond the body, at least beyond a few feet.

Why did Paul Pearsall invite us to share a few words about wishing at the end of his beautiful, wise, and inspiring book? The reason, we suspect, is because he knew that we would want to encourage you, the reader, to hold on to your wishes—not simply poetically, but scientifically as well. In our book *The Living Energy Universe: A Fundamental Discovery That Transforms Science and Medicine*, we write about a theory that not only encompasses wishing but encourages the belief in the possibility of what some consider the ultimate wish—survival of consciousness after death. This is the hypothesis that our loved one's energy and information, their spirits and souls, literally continue beyond physical death, and that their wishes and our wishes can continue to co-create better and more beautiful lives of sharing and evolving.

As Paul reminds us all, contemporary physics provides the conceptual bridge to a new vision of wishing. The proven lesson of the history of science is that the science fiction wishers of today can become the scientific facts of tomorrow.

But do wishes come only from the head, or are they of the heart as well? As Dr. James Levin said it, "When we are ready to listen with our heart, we are transformed." *Wishing Well* helps us find in our hearts the maturing wishes that we hope will transform us all.

Gary E.R. Schwartz, Ph.D., is professor of psychology, medicine, neurology, and psychiatry and director of the Human Energy Systems Laboratory at the University of Arizona. Linda G.S. Russek, Ph.D. is assistant clinical professor of medicine and codirector of the Human Energy Systems Laboratory at the University of Arizona. They are authors of *The Living Energy Universe*.

A Glossary of
Wishing Words

·····················••••·····················

Absorption: An established psychological characteristic manifested by high emotional and mental sensitivity and reactivity to and associations with the environment. Highly absorbed people seem supersensitive or sixth-sense-oriented and therefore are often frequent wishers.

Aleo-Biofeedback: Biofeedback is the process of using our intentionality to "wish" our autonomic nervous system (breathing, blood pressure, heartbeat, etc.) into a state of balanced relaxation. Alleo-biofeedback is wishing from a distance that causes this same state in another person. This may be one way that remote healing works, and it is a form of wishing wellness to another person across space and time.

Coherence: A balanced emotional and physiological state in which the heart "entrains" or resonates in gentle rhythmic "sympathy" or balance with the brain. The heart can also resonate and fall into coherence with another brain or heart.

Consciousness: Usually seen as the totality of all of our thoughts and feelings, consciousness is our personal awareness that we are aware. It's also the perception of our inward psychological or spiritual experience. Scientists have changed from looking for how consciousness could possibly emerge from everything else to studying how everything else might have emerged from consciousness. Focused consciousness is intent, and intention is wishing.

Conservation: The principle of permanence in the universe. Physicists know that energy and mass cannot be created or destroyed. The energy of a wish works the same way. We never really wish anything away; we only nudge it elsewhere and shift it around. Wishing is like moving furniture. No matter where you put it, it's still there. When we wish for something, it must come from somewhere else. To wish well, we must be careful where we put our wishes.

Countermagic: Doing some ritual to prevent a potential bad effect. Many superstitions are based on countermagic, such as knocking on wood to prevent the spirits from punishing you for your bragging.

Decline Effect: Refers to the effects of psi or psychic sixth-sense phenomena such as wishing that have been shown to decrease when the individual tries too hard to impose the effect.

Distant Intentionality: Scientists often use this term instead of wishing to refer to the power of our intent to alter systems anywhere and anytime. Remote healing is often seen as evidence of the effects of "distant intentionality."

DNA: Found in cell nuclei, particularly genetic cells, deoxyribonucleic acid is the genetic building block. Some scientists theorize that DNA's unique shape and resonance may serve as an "antenna" for the reception of the subtle energy of a wish. They also theorize that DNA can translate a wish's or intent's subtle energy into measurable electromagnetic energy in the body.

Entrainment: A falling "into sync" as when one tuning fork vibrates and sets off a similar vibration in another tuning fork. Entrainment happens when two systems "sympathize" with one another or fall into mutual resonation. Several pendulum clocks in proximity of one another will entrain and fall into one common "swinging." The heart and brain can entrain with one another.

Ethereal: From the Sanskrit *akash,* "ether" is not considered a factor in establishment science. It's another way of understanding "subtle energy" and has been referred to for millennia by most indigenous people. It's an as-yet immeasurable, unifying energy that transcends measuring devices but may be "picked up" with our sixth sense.

Fifth Force: Another name for "subtle energy" and energies beyond the known four accepted by science; gravity, electromagnetism, and strong and weak nuclear energy.

Heart: Physiologists now know that the heart literally thinks, feels, and sends messages to its own brain and other hearts and brains. In 1991, it was shown that the heart has its own "brain." It has its own intrinsic nervous system, including receiving, sending, and coordinating neurons and sensitive neurites scattered through the heart to receive messages from these neurons. In 1983, it was also shown that the heart is an endocrine or hormonal gland secreting ANF (atrial natriuretic factor), which affects our blood vessels and that it contains "intrinsic cardiac adrenergic" (ICA) cells which synthesize and secrete hormones priorly thought to be secreted only in the brain. The heart is a key to wishing well because it can calm the brain and express wishes in more coherence or balance with the world.

High Magic: An attempt to become superhuman and transcend all human limitations.

Intentionality: One's conscious attempt to turn a possibility into a reality. Researchers refer to the intentionality effect as being able to place a desired subtle energy imprint on a person, place, or thing simply by intending that imprint. Wishing is focused intentionality.

Intuition: A sudden insight gained without using any of the five physical senses. Intuition is our "wish-sensing mechanism" and seems particularly sensitive to subtle energy. Wishing is sending our intent; intuition is sensing a wish in progress.

L Energy: Yet another name for "subtle energy" or "the fifth force," some scientists use the letter "L" to refer to this energy's relationship to a "life force" and love. Researchers looking into the fifth force of subtle energy called it L or love energy because it seems to manifest itself most clearly when one surrenders the self, falls into "sympathy" with the world, "goes with the flow," and "allows" the connection with the nonlocality or timeless and boundary-free nature of the cosmos to "just happen."

Low Magic: An everyday magic practiced to gain a small worldly advantage. Wishing is a kind of low magic practiced for daily life survival. Prayer relates more to high magic and the pursuit of our divine nature.

Metaphysical: Not subject to empirical, five-sense verification.

Nocebo: The opposite of a placebo, which has positive effects, a nocebo is something that alters a system negatively simply by the power of someone's intentions or suggestions.

Noetic: Related to the highest and deepest form of knowledge, which is trying to understand those aspects of life that are beyond what is accepted as "fact" or "common sense." It is also related to the eternal forms of ideas and concepts, in contrast to "dianoetic," which refers to discursive thinking that flows from one thought to another without delving deeply into meaning.

Nonlocal: An established principle of physics, nonlocal refers to the ultimate connection of all systems beyond time and space. A difficult concept for the modern mind to embrace, nonlocality means that a wish doesn't really "go" anywhere because it doesn't have to. We are all connected energetically here and now and everywhere, so a wish happens everywhere all at once. Wishes do not weaken or diminish over distance and can be as potent when we stand next to someone as when we are a thousand miles away. Scientists say our intentions or wishes may travel "without decay and delay," meaning they nudge the universe everywhere, unlimited by the speed of light.

Occult: Present in some form but not measurable or detectable by our current instruments. While many people see the "occult" as evil, its real meaning refers to those aspects of our life that are beyond the range of our five senses. To not believe in the occult is to think that our five senses can sense all there is to sense, an assertion every scientist knows is false.

Passive Volition: Doing and accomplishing without trying too hard. This is the underlying tenet of biofeedback. Our five physical senses require "focus" to work at peak efficiency. Our sixth sense requires "flow" and "being" more than "doing." Passive volition is a state important to wishing well because of its gentle "swinging" of a suggestion rather than pushing one's own spiritual agenda.

Placebo: Derived from the Latin words meaning "I shall please," placebo refers to a system being altered simply by the power of a stated or unstated intention or suggestion. The power of a wish may relate to its placebo effect. It's usually a mild but positive and significant effect. Wishing is a way of using your innate power of suggestion. When you wish well, you are using your intent to induce a pleasing effect. When you wish wickedly or unwisely, you induce the nocebo, or negative power of intent. Well wishing can be seen as making wishes that "please" the cosmos with our good intentions.

Play: Activity without a goal or winner and designed for the perpetuation of pleasure rather than the end of a contest.

Prayer: Appeal to Absolute or High Power. Wishing is a more secular ritualistic process to the "powers that be" rather than source of the power.

Psi: The abbreviation used to refer to so-called psychic or extrasensory perceptions. Wishing is a psi phenomenon.

Quantum: The world of the very, very small moving very, very fast. Much of what quantum scientists "see" violates most of the "rules" of establishment science and the five-sense world of time and space limitations. In the quantum world, wishes have been documented to have profound effects. Whether something manifests as a particle or wave depends on what the observer "wishes" to see.

Sixth Sense: Our sense of subtle energy that goes beyond seeing with the eyes, smelling with the nose, tasting with the tongue, hearing with the ears, and feeling with the skin. In addition to processes such as telepathy, psychokinesis, and clairvoyance, wishing (intention) and intuition (sensing intentions) are examples of sixth senses.

Sorcerer: Someone who uses "black magic" or the power of evil spirits to gain advantage or control over another person, event, or thing.

Subtle Energy: A form of energy existing beyond the four known energies accepted by present-day science. Various instruments are sensitive to electromagnetic energy, gravity, and what scientists call strong and weak nuclear energy. The "fifth force," or subtle energy, is currently beyond the brain's measurement tools, but our heart senses it. There still may be physical forms of energy to be discovered, and it is likely that other forms and manifestations of subtle energy will be discovered.

Superstition: Often seen as a belief or act based on ignorance or unreasoning fear of the unknown. Superstition, however, is also our spiritual folklore teaching us to not entirely disregard the influence of the mysterious and magical in our own life. The metaphors and lessons of superstitions contain many long-standing adaptive cultural lessons.

Sympathetic Magic: Wishing based on "like brings like." Sympathetic magic is the basis of wishing well because it is a process of resonating our intentions "sympathetically" with the positive aspects of nature and trying to entrain or "be in sympathy" with things like rainbows, shooting stars, and other "wish elicitors."

Sympathetic Resonation: The tiniest amount of energy applied to any system vibrates or resonates within the system. It builds and accumulates in power. Making a wish is causing a little cosmic sympathetic resonation.

Talisman Effect: Applying the power of our wishing to an object or person so that it carries the energy of our wish.

Toroidal: A shape similar to the cloud that forms from an atomic blast. Energy goes up in the middle, down on the outside, and swings back up through the middle to go outward again. The appearance is that of a donut radiating energy. Human DNA sometimes exists in this form, and because of this shape it may act as a kind of subtle energy antenna capable of not only sensing the subtle energy of our intentions but also acting as a transducer or converter of subtle energy into the conventional and measurable electromagnetic energy that produces a variety of intracellular events in our body.

Wish: A focused intention that makes a possibility a reality. Wishing is ritualistically and gently focusing our consciousness to make a possibility reality. The effect of a wish is to cause a "sympathetic resonation" of the subtle energy that connects and is a part of all of us. A wish is less "something we send" than an intentional joining in the cosmic whole.

Wish Elicitor: A natural object or event such as a shooting star or a waterfall that seems to automatically invoke our need to resonate with it and elicits our wishing instinct to do so.

Wishful Thinking: Often seen as illusory or self-deluding thought, it is an important one of our many "intelligences." It's how we are thinking when we are thinking with our heart and using our intuition and sixth sense. In balance with our other intelligences, wishful thinking or "heartfelt" thinking can be a source of inspiration and insight.

Wizard: Someone who possesses the wisdom to use a special skill such as wishing well to do magical, mystical things beyond the five-sense world.

Notes

One: Mastering the Wizardry of Wishing

1. These characteristics often result in excessive stress hormones being released throughout the body, high cholesterol and calcification in the arteries which cause them to block, and lower the efficiency of the immune system. For a review of some of the issues related to disease-prone personality, see Blair Justice, *Who Gets Sick: How Beliefs, Moods, and Thoughts Affect Your Health* (Los Angeles: Jeremy P. Tarcher, Inc., 1988).

2. It is not the purpose of this book to document the power of intent to alter events beyond space and time. This is a book about how to wish well, not about the decades of research on the power of wishing. This evidence is presented in many sources usually under the title of "intentionality" or "intention at a distance." My book *The Heart's Code* presents one summary of the research of the power of our intentions to change the course of events beyond the limits of time and space and the nature of the subtle energy involved in this process (New York: Broadway Books, 1998). See also the work of Larry Dossey in his books *Recovering the Soul* (New York: Bantam, 1989) and *Healing Words* (San Francisco: HarperSanFrancisco, 1993). See also D. J. Benor, *Healing Research,* 4 vols (Munich: Helix Editions, Ltd., 1993).

3. For a description of this research, see R. G. Jahn and B. J. Dunne, *Margins of Reality: The Role of Consciousness in the Physical World* (New York: Harcourt Brace Jovanovich, 1987).

4. For example, almost two decades of research in the Princeton Engineering Anomalies Research program (PEAR) in the School of Engineering and Applied Science at Princeton University shows that, in their words, ". . . consciousness is a proactive agency in the establishment of reality." In less technical terms, PEAR has shown that what I am calling wishing alters reality. See R. G. Jahn and B. J. Dunne. "Science and the Subjective," *Journal of Scientific Exploration* 11, no. 2 (1997): 201–224.

5. For just one example of the careful way in which scientists study wishing or the capacity of conscious intent to alter various life systems, see E. Rauscher. "Human Volitional Effects on a Model Bacterial System," *Subtle Energies* 1, no. 1 (1990): 21–41.

6. Jahn and Dunne, "Science and the Subjective," p. 204.

7. For a thorough description of this research, see any of the work of Marilyn J. Schlitz, director of research for the Institute of Noetic Sciences. For one brief discussion of the role of intent, or what I am calling the power of wishing, see her "Intentionality and Intuition and Their Clinical Implications: A Challenge for Science and Medicine," *Advances: The Journal of Mind–Body Medicine* 12, no. 2 (1996): 58–66.

8. For a description of this fascinating research on intentional eye gaze (wishing) and subjects' abilities to detect it (intuition), see Gary E. R. Schwartz and Linda G. S. Russek, "Interpersonal Registration of Actual and Intended Eye Gaze: Relationship to Openness to Spiritual Beliefs and Experiences," *Journal of Scientific Exploration* 13, no. 2 (in press).

9. For a discussion of the making of a device that is imprinted with and carries the "power" of a wish, see W. A. Tiller, "A Gas Discharge Device for Investigating Focussed Human Attention," *Journal of Scientific Exploration* 2 (1990): 150–160.

10. Dr. William Tiller of Stanford University calls the "sacred space" effect of a wish imprinted device "conditioning the experimental site." See W. A. Tiller, et al., *Exploring Robust Interactions between Human Intention and Inanimate/Animate Systems*. Preprint. Presented at "Toward a Science of Consciousness—Fundamental Approaches," May 25–28, 1999. United Nations University, Tokyo, Japan.

11. For a complete technical description of the research documenting the effect of focusing a wish or intent to alter pH levels of water, human DNA, and liver enzymes, see W. A. Tiller, *Science and Human Transformation: Subtle Energies, Intentionality, and Consciousness* (Walnut Creek, Calif.: Pavior, 1997).

12. This research and theory is provided by Glen Rein of the Quantum Biology Research Labs. See his "DNA as a Detector of Subtle Energies," Proceedings of the Fourth International Society for the Study of Subtle Energy and Medicine, Monterey, Calif., October 1994. See also his "Effect of Conscious Intention on Human DNA," Proceedings of the International Forum on New Science, Denver, Colo., October 1996. Dr. Rein's research suggests that toroidal DNA (the mushroom-shaped kind) functions as an antenna to allow DNA to sense subtle energy and also acts as a transducer or converter of subtle energy to the electromagnetic energy that science can measure. This energy in turn affects all of the 75 trillion cells in our body. This may be one way that a wish is transduced or converted to biological reality and that our intention makes a biopossibility into a measurable reality.

13. W. A. Tiller, *Science and Human Transformation*, p. 21.

14. Ibid. Other findings regarding our ability to wish certain states upon various apparatus are reported by physicist W. A. Tiller in this same volume. Additional research on how our

wishes affect machines, clocks, drums, and various other devices to make them talismans or "subtle energy imprinted devices" can be found in Jahn and Dunne, *Margins of Reality.*

15. Reported in "The Power of Love," *First for Women,* April 19, 1999, p. 49.

16. F. Huxley, *The Way of the Sacred* (Garden City, NY: Doubleday, 1974), p. 56.

17. Again, I emphasize that this is a book more about how to wish well than about the science documenting the fact that wishing works. To illustrate the process of wishing and support the suggestions I offer about wishing well, I do present some of the many studies conducted on wishing and the power of our intent to act at a distance. Studies on the effect of intent or a wish on microorganisms such as body cells, bacteria, yeast, and fungus indicate that the power of "expectation" is not involved in the distant effect of intentionality and the power of a wish. For examples of such studies, see W. G. Braud, "On the Use of Living Target Systems in Distant Mental Influence Research," in *Research in Parapsychology,* ed. R. A. White and J. Solfvin (Metuchen, N.J.: Scarecrow Press, 1985), pp.149–188. See also J. Barry, "General and Comparative Study of the Psychokinetic Effect on a Fungus Culture," *Journal of Parapsychology* 32, no. 4, (1968): 237–243.

18. These and other scientists acknowledge the "nonlocal" or total connection of all minds and systems beyond space and time. See E. Schrödinger's *What Is Life? and Mind and Matter* (London: Cambridge University Press, 1969). See also A. Eddington, "Defense of Mysticism," in *Quantum Questions: The Mystical Writings of the World's Great Physicists,* ed. K. Wilber (Boston: Shambhala, 1984). See also J. Jeans, *Physics and Philosophy* (New York: Dover, 1981).

19. M. Murphy, *The Future of the Body* (Los Angeles: Jeremy P. Tarcher, 1992), p. 123.

20. Schlitz, "Internationality and Intuition," p. 65.

21. Dr. Candice Pert was an early pioneer in proving that the brain is not just in our head. If the brain is not just in the head, why should its processes and energy stop at the skin? The idea of what eminent astronomer-physicist Sir Arthur Eddington calls a "universal Mind or Logos" and what mathematician and physicist Sir James Jeans calls a collective "one body" follows from the most careful research on the brain itself. Dr. Pert discusses the implications of her work for human consciousness in *Molecules of Emotion* (New York: Scribner, 1997).

22. For a thorough review of the research on the effects of what I am calling sorcery, see L. Dossey, *Be Careful What You Pray For . . . You Just Might Get It* (San Francisco: HarperSanFrancisco, 1998).

23. Schlitz, "Intentionality and Intuition," p. 65.

24. R. Cavendish, *A History of Magic* (New York: Penguin, 1987), p. 12.

25. R. S. Broughton, "Glimpsing the Future," in *Parapsychology: The Controversial Science* (New York: Ballantine, 1991).

26. Almost a century ago, author Rudolph Steiner wrote about how we might develop our awareness of the vast information territories of the "supersensible domains," those aspects of our experience that are beyond current statistical consensus. See R. Steiner, *Occult Science: An Outline* (London: Rudolph Steiner Press, 1979).

27. Broughton, "Glimpsing the Future," p. 350.

28. Ibid.

29. E. Mitchell, *The Way of the Explorer* (New York: G. P. Putnam's Sons, 1996), pp. 85–87.

30. Dossey, *Recovering the Soul.*

31. E. Tenner, *Why Things Bite Back: Technology and the Revenge of Unintended Consequences* (New York: Knopf, 1996), pp.15–16.

32. Ibid., p. 16.

Two: Rediscovering the Miracle of Wishing

1. G. Zukav, *The Seat of the Soul* (New York: Simon and Schuster, 1990).

2. For an excellent discussion of the impact of the explosion of technology on our families, personal life, and health and how we have fallen into a "collective hyperactivity," see S. Bertman, *Hyperculture: The Human Cost of Speed* (Westport, Conn.: Praeger, 1998).

3. Physicist Gary Zukav writes, "What is a thought formed out of? A thought is energy, or Light, that has been shaped by consciousness," *The Seat of the Soul*, p. 105.

4. C. Darwin, *The Origins of Species* (New York: Modern Library, 1959).

5. J. White, *The Meeting of Science and Spirit* (New York: Paragon House, 1990), p. xviii.

6. For a witty discussion of the "showy incoherencies" of the pseudoscience to be found in many of the popular psychology movements, see Mark Twain's review of Mary Baker Eddy's *Science and Health*, the bible of Christian Science. M. Twain, *Christian Science* (Buffalo, N.Y.: Prometheus Books, 1986).

7. H. Benson, *Timeless Healing: The Power and Biology of Belief* (New York: Scribner, 1996).

8. Research in this area is summarized by physician Deale A. Matthews in *The Faith Factor* (New York: Viking, 1998).

9. For a review of the research on the positive effects of joyful states, see L. Dossey, "Now You Are Fit to Live: Humor and Health," *Alternative Therapies* 2, no. 5 (1996): 8–13, 98–100.

10. L. S. Berk, et al., "Humor-Associated Laughter Decreases Cortisol and Increases Spontaneous Lymphocyte-Blastogenesis," *Clinical Research* 36 (1988): 435A.

11. G. E. Schwartz, et al., "Cardiovascular Differentiation of Happiness, Sadness, Anger, and Fear Following Imagery and Exercise," *Psychosomatic Medicine* 43(1981): 343–364.

12. For a discussion of the health benefits of altruistic helping, see A. Luks, *The Healing Power of Doing Good* (New York: Fawcett Columbine, 1992).

13. The research on unconditional giving is presented in H. Andrews, "Helping and Health: The Relationship between Volunteer Activity and Health-Related Outcomes," *Advances* 7, no. 1 (1990): 25–34.

14. Ibid.

15. For a discussion of the state of "flow" and its psychophysiological manifestations, see M. Csikzentmihalyi, *Flow: The Psychology of Optimal Experience* (New York: Harper and Row, 1990).

16. For a discussion of the act of forgiveness and its psychophysiological potential to reduce and even reverse the damaging effects of anger on our body's systems, see B. H. Kaplan, "Social Health and the Forgiving Heart," *Journal of Behavioral Medicine* 14, no. 3 (1992): 3–14.

17. For research on the health benefits of a feeling of control, see S. R. Maddi and S. C. Kobasa, *The Hardy Executive: Health under Stress* (Homewood, Ill.: Dow Jones-Irwin, 1988).

18. R. J. Lifton, *The Protean Self: Human Resilience in an Age of Fragmentation* (New York: Basic Books, 1993).

19. H. Dreher, *The Immune Power Personality* (New York: Dutton, 1995).

20. P. W. Linville, "Self-Complexity and Affective Extremity: Don't Put All of Your Eggs in One Cognitive Basket," *Social Cognition* 3, no. 1 (1989): 94–120.

21. For a discussion of the crucial importance of social support and maintaining a feeling of connection at times of illness, see D. Spiegel, *Living Beyond Limits* (New York: Ballantine Books, 1993).

22. D. C. McClelland, "Motivational Factors in Health and Disease," *American Psychologist* 44, no. 4 (1989): 675–683.

23. This research is summarized in my book *The Heart's Code* (New York: Broadway Books, 1998).

24. This possibility was suggested to me by cardiologist Dr. H. C. Moolenburgh in Norway. He had read my book *The Heart's Code* and agreed with my thesis that the heart is a thinking, feeling organ. He wrote a letter about his research showing that the heart muscle could not actually be strong enough to pump blood as far as it does. His work suggests that the heart circulates tiny "blood rhythmic energy packets" and, in a variation of the "wag the dog" concept, that the circulatory system may actually "beat the heart." He added that his research is supported by the embryological finding that circulation evolves in the fetus first and that the heart muscle is generated and grows out of the vortex of the circulation.

25. T. Moore, *The Reenchantment of Everyday Life* (New York: HarperCollins, 1996), p. xiv.

Three: Harnessing the Power of a Little Boom

1. Nikola Tesla was the brilliant inventor of AC current and the AC generators that provide power throughout the world. He was the first to actually envision collapsing a building through the gentle cumulative power of what he called "sympathetic vibration." The far-reaching implications of the "sympathetic vibration" theory for life, memory, and the possibility of survival after death are addressed by Gary E. R. Schwartz and Linda E. S. Russek in their book *The Systemic Memory Hypothesis: Scientific Evidence for the Existence of God in an Eternally Evolving Universe* (in press).

2. An example of the cumulative power of "invisible energy" resonating through the universe occurred on August 27, 1998. An immense invisible wave of radiation smashed into Earth's upper atmosphere near the Hawaiian Islands. It was the most powerful burst of X and gamma rays from beyond the Sun ever recorded. By the time the resonation got to us, it contained enough energy to provide all of the planet Earth's energy needs for a billion billion years. It temporarily ionized Earth's entire outer atmosphere, but by the time it made it through our atmosphere, it became little more than the power of a dental X ray on the surface of Earth. It came from a little quiver of a neutron star unromantically called SQR1900@14 in the constellation Aquila 20,000 light-years away from us. A light-year is about 6 trillion miles, so a little energetic shove can make a very long trip. Considering the range and power of that one stellar shake, the possibility of the subtle energy of our consciousness in the form of a single wish having an impact on the energy of our own and others' lives seems at least a reasonable hypothesis.

3. A sixteen-year old boy in London received 33 million get-well cards after he was diagnosed with a brain tumor. Four years later, he was tumor-free, as reported in *The Orange Country Register* (Los Angeles), November 30, 1995.

4. The ancient concept of *ana ana,* or a death prayer, is described in M. F. Long, *The Secret Science behind Miracles. Unveiling the Huna Tradition of the Ancient Polynesians* (Marina Del Rey, Calif.: Devros and Company, 1976).

5. J. W. L. Gielding, et al., "An Interim Report of a Prospective, Randomized, Controlled

Study of Adjuvant Chemotherapy in Operable Gastric Cancer: British Stomach Cancer Group," *World Journal of Surgery* (1983): 390–399.

6. S. Wolf, "Effects of Suggestion and Conditioning on the Action of Chemical Agents in Human Subjects: The Pharmacology of Placebos," *Journal of Clinical Investigation* 29 (1950): 100–109.

7. T. W. Anderson, "Vitamin E in Angina Pectoris," *Canadian Medical Association Journal* 110 (1974): 401–406. See also R. Gillian, et al., "Quantitative Evaluation of Vitamin E in the Treatment of Angina Pectoris," *American Heart Journal* 93 (1977): 444–449.

8. E. H. Uhlenhuth, et al., "The Symptomatic Relief of Anxiety with Meprobamate, Phenobarbital, and Placebo," *American Journal of Psychiatry* 115 (1959): 905–910.

9. J. Solfvin, "Mental Healing," in *Advances in Parapsychological Research*, Vol. 4, ed. S. Krippner (Jefferson, N.C.: McFarland and Company, 1984): 55–56.

10. This story was reported to me by Dr. Bakken during a recent meeting at North Hawai'i Hospital, the First International Leadership Forum on Integrated Cardiovascular Health in the Twenty-first Century, March 14, 1999, The Big Island, Hawai'i.

11. See R. G. Jahn and B. J. Dunne, *Margins of Reality: The Role of Consciousness in the Physical World* (New York: Harcourt Brace Jovanovich, 1987).

12. Controlled laboratory experiments have shown that wishing affects plants. Whether the wisher is a few feet or several miles away from a microorganism, that organism's growth is influenced by the wisher. See C. B. Nash, "Test of Psychokinetic Control of Bacterial Mutation," *Journal of the American Society for Psychical Research* 78 (1984): 145–152.

13. The plant–human interaction is documented in J. Barry, "General and Comparative Study of the Psychokinetic Effect on a Fungus Culture," *Journal of Parapsychology* 32 (1968): 237–243.

14. L. Burbank, quoted in Robert Peel, *The Years of Authority* (New York: Holt, Rinehart, and Winston, 1977), p. 348.

15. For examples of cutting-edge research in subtle energy, see R. G. Jahn, "Information, Consciousness, and Health," *Alternative Therapies* 2 (1996): 32–38. See also G. E. Schwartz and L. G. Russek, "Do All Dynamical Systems Have Memory? Implications of the Systemic Memory Hypothesis for Science and Society," in *Brain and Values: Behavioral Neurodynamics,* vol. 5, ed. K. H. Pribam and J. S. King (Hillsdale, N.J.: Lawrence Erlbaum Associates, 1996).

16. Jahn, "Information, Consciousness, and Health."

17. R. G. Jahn and B. J. Dunne, "Science and the Subjective," in *Technical Notes* (Princeton, N.J.: Princeton University Press, 1997).

18. I described the work at Princeton in detail in my book *The Heart's Code* (New York: Broadway Books, 1998).

19. On November 3, 1998, U.S. Patent no. 5,830,064 was issued to MindSong, Inc. for a miniature version of the random number machines like those influenced by the "operators" or wishers in the PEAR program. This device is called "An Apparatus and Method for Distinguishing Events Which Collectively Exceed Chance Expectations and Thereby Controlling an Output. A "wish detector" seems an easier way to understand this apparatus.

20. This research is summarized in the patent acceptance. For example, see B. J. Dunne, et al., "Experiments in Remote Human/Machine Interaction," *Journal of Scientific Exploration* 6, no. 4 (1992): 311–322.

21. R. G. Jahn, "Information, Consciousness, and Health," pp. 32–38.

22. R. May, *Love and Will* (New York: Dell Publishing, 1969).

23. P. Teilhard de Chardin, "The Evolution of Chastity," in *On Love* (New York: Harper and Row, 1967), pp. 33– 34.

24. Jahn and Dunne, *Margins of Reality*.

25. Quoted in W. H. Auden and L. Kronenberger, eds., *The Viking Book of Aphorisms* (New York: Barnes and Noble, 1993), p. 329.

Four: Becoming Totally Absorbed

1. Wishing well's characteristics of being patient, open-minded, sensitive, and warm-heartedly connected with others are the same traits that lessen risk of heart disease and weakened immunity. They are the opposite of what is called type A behavior and its time urgency and self-protective hostility. See M. Friedman and D. Ulmer's classic *Treating Type A Behavior and Your Heart* (New York: Fawcett Crest, 1984).

2. See R. Moody, *Life after Life* (Covinda, Ga.: Mockingbird Press, 1975).

3. G. Gallup, *Adventures in Immortality* (New York: McGraw Hill, 1982).

4. My wish research indicated that "absorbed" and "less absorbed" people tend to marry one another. Perhaps in a subconscious balancing of L energy, many of the relationships among our wish-project subjects were between the wish-prone and the wish wary and the sensitive and the cynical.

5. G. Greene, quoted in "Quotus Profundus," *Pathways* (Riverside, Center for Contemplative Christianity) 5, no. 6 (1996): 22.

6. This concept is described in detail by Larry Dossey in "The Right Man Syndrome: Skepticism and Alternative Medicine," *Alternative Therapies* 4, no. 3 (1998): 12–20, 108–111.

7. S. M. Roche and K. M. McConkey, "Personality Processes and Individual Differences. Absorption: Nature, Assessment, and Correlates," *Journal of Personality and Social Psychology* 59 (1990): 91–101.

8. I. A. Wickramaskera, "A Model of People at High Risk to Develop Chronic Stress-Related Somatic Symptoms: Some Predictions," *American Journal of Clinical Hypnosis* (in press).

9. A. Tellegen, et al., "Personality Similarity in Twins Reared Apart and Together," *Journal of Personality and Social Psychology* 54 (1988): 1031–1039.

10. A. Tellegen and G. Atkinson, "Openness to Absorbing a Self-Altering Experience ('Absorption'): A Trait Related to Hypnotic Susceptibility," *Journal of Abnormal Psychology* 83 (1974): 268–277.

11. M. L. Glisky, et al., "Absorption, Openness to Experience, and Hypnotizability," *Journal of Personality and Social Psychology* 60 (1991): 263–272.

12. G. Reid, et al., "State, Emotionality, Belief, and Absorption in ESP Scoring," *Journal of the Association for the Study of Perception* 17 (1982): 28–39.

13. V. K. Kumar and R. J. Rekala, "Hypnotizability, Absorption, and Individual Differences in Phenomenological Experience," *International Journal of Clinical and Experimental Hypnosis* 36 (1988): 80–88.

14. J. D. C. Shea, "Effects of Absorption and Instruction on Heart Rate Control," *Journal of Mental Imagery* 9 (1985): 87–100.

15. J. Cohen and K. Sedlacek, "Attention and Autonomic Self-Regulation," *Psychosomatic Medicine* 45 (1983): 243–257.

16. P. J. Qualls and P. W. Sheehan, "Electromyograph Biofeedback as a Relaxation Technique: A Critical Appraisal and Reassessment," *Psychological Bulletin* 90 (1981): 21–42.

17. E. W. Mathes, "Mystical Experience, Romantic Love, and Hypnotic Susceptibility," *Psychological Review* 50 (1982): 701–702.

18. I. A. Wickramasekera, "Risk Factors for Parapsychological Verbal Reports, Hypnotizability, and Somatic Complaints," in *Parapsychology and Human Nature*, ed. B. Shapin and L. Coly (New York: Parapsychology Foundation, 1986), pp. 19–35.

19. O. Vassend, "Dimensions of Negative Affectivity, Self-Reported Somatic Complaints: Relevance to the Concept of Alexithymia," *Journal of Psychotherapy and Psychosomatic Illness* 47 (1987): 74–81.

20. A. R. Damasio, *Descartes' Error* (New York: Avon Books, 1994).

21. From William Faulkner's Nobel Prize acceptance speech, 1949. As quoted in Damasio, *Descartes' Error,* p. 254.

22. J. Frazer, *The Golden Bough* (New York: Simon and Schuster, 1996).

23. Ibid., p. 113.

24. See P. Pearsall, *Super Immunity: Master Your Emotions and Improve Your Health* (New York: McGraw Hill, 1987).

25. For a review of studies of the efficacy of prayer, see L. Dossey, *Healing Words: The Power of Prayer and the Practice of Medicine* (San Francisco: HarperSanFrancisco, 1993).

26. As discussed in my book *The Heart's Code* (New York: Broadway Books, 1998).

27. G. Easterbrook, *Beside Still Waters* (New York: Morrow, 1998), p. 61. This is the most thorough and evenhanded discussion of needed balance between science and religion.

28. For a discussion of the staggeringly improbable and theologically suggestive findings emerging from science, see G. Will, "The Gospel from Science," *Newsweek,* November 9, 1998, p. 88.

29. For a complete discussion of the anthropic principle, that the universe is not a random event but a preplanned, perfectly ordered system, see P. Glynn, *God: The Evidence* (Rocklin, Calif.: Forum Press, 1997).

30. M. Seligman, *Learned Optimism* (New York: Knopf, 1990).

31. E. Adler, "Gestures: Are You Talking to Yourself?" *The Honolulu Advertiser,* November 24, 1998, p. 1.

Five: Learning a Sixth Way to Get Your Way

1. Shooting stars, solar and lunar eclipses, rainbows, and other natural occurrences have always elicited the wishing response. The worldwide wishing response to the Leonid meteor system was described by J. B. Berrengia in "Scientists Grab Chance for Meteor Encounter," *Honolulu Star Bulletin*, November 16, 1998, p. 1.

2. This theory of needs derives from the field of psychobiology. See A. M. de la Pena, *The Psychobiology of Cancer* (South Hadley, Mass.: Bergin Publishers, 1983).

3. For a description of the three evolutional levels of the brain, see P. MacLean, "On the Evolution of Three Mentalities," in *New Dimensions in Psychiatry: A World View,* volume 2, ed. S. Arieti and G. Chrznowki (New York: Wiley, 1977).

4. D. Goleman, *Emotional Intelligence* (New York: Bantam Books, 1995), p. 61.

5. For a description of the complete neurophysiology of the "rage rush" when our needs

seem frustrated, see D. Zillman, in *Handbook of Mental Control*. Vol. 5, ed. D. Wegner and J. Pennebaker (Englewood Cliffs, N.J.: Prentice-Hall, 1993).

6. R. Dawkins, *River out of Eden* (New York: Basic Books, 1995), p. 43.

7. E. O. Wilson, *Sociobiology* (Cambridge, Mass.: Harvard University Press, 1980).

8. For a discussion of various aspects of the needs hierarchy theory, see A. Maslow, *The Farther Reaches of Human Nature* (New York: Penguin, 1971). Any of the works of Sigmund Freud refer to basic human needs, particularly infantile sexual needs, as primary motivational forces.

9. See H. A. Murray, "American Icarus," *Clinical Studies of Personality,* vol. 2 (New York: Harper, 1955). See also H. A. Murray, *Explorations in Personality* (New York: Oxford, 1938). For the first discussion contrasting the RAS, or relaxed affiliative syndrome, and the IPS, or inhibited power syndrome, see D. C. McClelland, *The Achieving Society* (Princeton, N.J.: Van Nostrand, 1971).

10. J. D. Mayer and A. Stevens, "An Emerging Understanding of the Reflective (Meta) Experience of Mood" (unpublished manuscript, 1993).

11. Goleman, *Emotional Intelligence*.

12. N. V. Peale, *The Power of Positive Thinking* (New York: Fawcett Books, 1952).

13. W. Kaminer, *I'm Dysfunctional, You're Dysfunctional* (Reading, Mass.: Addison-Wesley, 1992).

14. See F. Clancy and Heidi Yorkshire, "The Bandler Method," *Mother Jones* (February/March, 1989): 24–28, 63–64. A National Academy of Sciences task force examined NLP and concluded that it made no scientific sense. See D. Druckman and J. A. Swets, *Enhancing Human Performance: Issues, Theories, and Techniques* (Washington, D.C.: National Academy Press, 1988).

15. For a description of enlightened denial, see D. Goleman, *Vital Lies, Simple Truths* (New York: Simon and Schuster, 1985).

16. N. Cousins, *The Anatomy of an Illness* (New York: Bantam Books, 1981). See also B. Siegel, *Love, Medicine, and Miracles* (New York: Harper and Row, 1987).

Six: Wishing on a Star

1. Cyprian Norwid (1850) in W. Tatarkiewica, *Analysis of Happiness* (The Hague: Martinus Nijhoff, 1976), p. 176.

2. This term was used in an Associated Press article on the increasing speed of modern life, "Why Can't We Just Slow Down and Relax?" *The Honolulu Advertiser,* December 29, 1998, p. 1.

3. The issue of gratitude and "wanting what you have" is discussed by Timothy Miller in *How to Want What You Have* (New York: Henry Holt, 1995).

4. D. Yankelovic, *New Rules: Searching for Self-Fulfillment in a World Turned Upside Down* (New York: Random House, 1981).

5. As quoted in L. E. Boone, *Quotable Business* (New York: Random House, 1992), p. 57.

6. Quoted in C. L. Wallis, ed., *The Treasure Chest* (San Francisco: Harper and Row, 1965), p. 142.

7. A. Antonovsky, *Unraveling the Mystery of Health* (San Francisco: Jossey Bass, 1987), p. 16.

8. E. B.Tylor, *Primitive Culture,* vol. 1 (London: Oxford University Press, 1871), p. 387.

9. G. Zukav, *The Seat of the Soul* (New York: Simon and Schuster, 1990), p. 167.

10. The Sermon on the Mount is in Matthew 5:3 to 7:27 and Luke 6:20 to 6:49.

Seven: Recovering the Wisdom of Wishful Thinking

1. R. Dawkins, *The Selfish Gene* (Oxford: Oxford University Press, 1976).

2. R. Brodie, *Virus of the Mind* (Seattle, Wash.: Integral Press, 1996).

3. The concept of "nonlocality" as related to the power of wishful thinking is based on our "timeless and space-free connection" with everyone and everything. This theory was first formally introduced by Einstein et al. See A. Einstein, B. Podolsky, and N. Rosen, "Can Quantum Mechanical Description of Physical Reality Be Considered Complete?" *Physics Review* 47 (1935): 777. Many careful experiments have been conducted to show that individuals can influence systems simply by "wishing" them to change no matter where the wisher or wish target may be. For example, see H. Schmidt, "PK Effect on Pre-recorded Targets," *Journal of the American Society for Psychical Research* 70 (1976): 267–91. The odds that Schmidt's results in altering events through mental intent happened by chance are several million to one.

4. J. Piaget, *The Origins of Intelligence in Children* (New York: International University Press, 1952).

5. For a fascinating discussion of the value of slower and not such "quick rational ways" of thinking that embrace wishful thinking, or what is called the "undermind" and what I am calling wishful or heart-oriented thinking, see Guy Glaxton's *Hare Brain, Tortoise Mind* (Hopewell, N.J.: The Ecco Press, 1997).

6. Ibid., p. 6.

7. J. B. Rhine and S. R. Feather, "The Study of Cases of 'Psi Trailing' in Animals," *Journal of Parapsychology* 26, no. 1 (1962): 1–21.

8. There are many documented cases of animal psi trailing. For example, there is the documented case of Minosch, a German cat who traveled over 1,500 miles in sixty-one days to find his vacationing family. Some animals seem to "sense" the emotional needs of their owners at remarkable distances. An example is the case of Prince, a small dog left with the wife of an Irish soldier in World War I. After the soldier left for the battlefields of France, the dog refused to eat and became despondent. After ten days, Prince disappeared from his Hammersmith, London, home. When the soldier's wife wrote to her husband to break the bad news of the lost pet, she was amazed when her husband wrote back from the heavily bombarded trenches at Armentières that Prince had found him there! He had made his way through the streets of London, 70 miles of the English countryside, crossed the English Channel and 60 miles of French soil littered with bombs and tear gas to rest by his master's side. This and other similar cases are reported in A. H. Trapman, *The Dog, Man's Best Friend* (London: Hutchinson and Company, 1929).

9. C. De Lys, *A Treasury of American Superstitions* (New York: Philosophical Library, 1958), p. 65.

10. See V. Brelsford, *Superstitious Survivals* (London: Centaur Press, 1958).

11. See A. Storr, *Churchill's Black Dog, Kafka's Mice* (New York: Ballantine Books, 1988).

12. M. Lings, *Ancient Beliefs and Modern Superstitions* (London: Tomorrow Publications, 1964).

13. For a discussion of wishful thinking as related to alternative views of reality, see L. LeShan and H. Margenau, *Einstein's Space and Van Gogh's Sky* (New York: Collier Books, 1982).

14. As quoted in Willard A. Heaps, *Superstition* (New York: Thomas Nelson, Inc., 1972), p. 43.

15. *Webster's Third New World Dictionary* (Springfield, Mass.: Merriam-Webster, Inc., 1993).

Eight: Taking a Leap of Faith

1. S. Kierkegaard, *Either/Or* (1843; reprint, Princeton, N.J.: Princeton University Press, 1987).

2. This principle is discussed in modern psychological terms by M. Scott Peck in *The Road Less Traveled* (New York: Simon and Schuster, 1978).

3. Richard Leakey and Roger Lewin coined this phrase. See *The Sixth Extinction* (New York: Doubleday, 1995).

4. J. Gleick, *Chaos: Making a New Science* (New York: Penguin Books, 1987).

5. Edward Lorenz, a meteorologist at the Massachusetts Institute of Technology, used the name "butterfly effect" to refer to one tiny event changing everything forever. He used the description in his address at the annual meeting of the American Association for the Advance of Science, Washington, D.C., December 29, 1979. He had originally spoken about the image of the wind beneath a seagull's wings.

6. Ibid., p. 355.

7. J. C. Pearce, *Evolution's End: Claiming the Potential of Our Intelligence* (San Francisco: HarperSanFrancisco, 1992), p. 104–105.

8. Careful research on the heart's energy has been conducted by HeartMath in Boulder Creek, California. See S. Paddison, *The Hidden Power of the Heart* (Boulder Creek, Calif.: Planetary Publications, 1992).

9. W. A. Tiller, *Science and Human Transformation: Subtle Energies, Intentionality, and Consciousness* (Walnut Creek, Calif.: Pavior, 1997), p. 214.

10. For a discussion of the magical nature of numbers, see R. Cavendish, ed., *The Encyclopedia of the Unexplained: Magic, Occultism, and Parapsychology* (New York: Penguin Books, 1989).

Nine: How Wishers Are Made

1. One of the clearest discussions of the three major theories of child development is still H. W. Maier, *Three Theories of Child Development* (New York: Harper and Row, 1965). He compares and contrasts the theories of Erik H. Erikson, Jean Piaget, and Robert R. Sears.

2. Psychologists have typically focused on physiological, affective, and cognitive development, "Conation," or the skill of correctly identifying a wish and learning to make it in a socially appropriate, balanced, and healthy way, has largely been ignored. The focus is on being "smart" and "assertive" rather than being able to gently focus intention to make slight changes in the world that benefit the wisher and the world. For an early comprehensive discussion of conation as an important development task worthy of study, see H. Poulsen, *Conations: On Striving, Willing, and Wishing and Their Relationship with Cognition, Emotions, and Motives* (Aarhus, Denmark: Aarhus University Press, 1991).

3. L. LeShan, *The Dilemma of Psychology* (New York: Dutton, 1990), p. xiii. The issue of psychology's relevance to modern daily life and its most significant challenges is also discussed in M. L. Gross, *The Psychological Society* (New York: Simon and Schuster, 1978).

4. J. W. Meeker, *Comedy and Survival* (Tucson, Ariz.: Arizona University Press, 1997).

5. Russian psychologist A. Leontjev first proposed what he called "activity-theory." This theory stressed the importance of the transition from an elementary sensory psyche to a more

conative or intention-fulfilling capacity. His theories are just beginning to receive more attention in the United States. See his *Problemer I Det Psykiskes Udvikling.* (Copenhagen: University Press, 1977).

6. The issue of society's movement from a social code of self-restraint as a cardinal virtue to one in which self-gratification is a central theme is discussed by James L. Collier in *The Rise of Selfishness in America* (New York: Oxford University Press, 1991).

7. L. Kohlberg, "Stage and Sequence: The Cognitive Developmental Approach to Socialization," in *Handbook of Socialization Theory and Research,* ed. D. A. Goslin (Chicago: Rand McNally, 1969).

8. For a discussion of the emerging field of ecopsychology, which deals with a more inclusive and world-sensitive view of one's life purpose, see T. Roszak, et al., eds., *Ecopsychology: Restoring the Earth, Healing the Mind* (San Francisco: Sierra Club Books, 1995).

9. These findings are reported in W. T. Boyce, et al., "Permanence and Change: Psychosocial Factors in the Outcome of Adolescent Pregnancy," *Social Science and Medicine* 21 (1985): 1281. See also E. W. Jensen, "The Families Routine Inventory," *Social Science and Medicine* 7 (1983): 210–211.

10. The concept of an imprint of an infantile paradise as a motivation for wishing is described in R. Heinberg, *Memories and Visions of Paradise* (Los Angeles: Jeremy P. Tarcher, Inc., 1989).

11. For a discussion of the long-term impact of perceptions of parents on the health and happiness when the child becomes an adult, see Linda G. Russek and Gary E. Schwartz,"Narrative Descriptions of Parental Love and Caring Predict Health Status in Midlife: A 35-Year Follow-Up of the Harvard Mastery of Stress Study," *Alternative Therapies* 2 (1996): 55–66.

12. For a discussion of the impact of marital strife and divorce on several aspects of children's adjustment, see H. S. Freidman, et al., "Psychosocial and Behavioral Predictors of Longevity," *The American Psychologist* 50 (1994): 197–207.

Ten: How to Avoid the Wicked Wish

1. The Founder of Christian Science, Mary Baker Eddy, wrote about the danger of wishing and praying for others without their permission. She wrote that to do so ". . . is a breach of good manners and morals; it is nothing less than a mistaken kindness, a culpable ignorance, or a conscious trespass on the rights of mortals." M. B. Baker, "Obtrusive Mental Healing," in *Miscellaneous Writings* (Published by the trustees under the will of Mary Baker Eddy. Boston: 1986), p. 282.

2. M. C. Bateson, "The Revenge of the Good Fairy," *Whole Earth Review,* no. 55 (Summer 1987): 34–48.

3. One of the most insightful writers about the search for an enlightened and tolerant merging between science and spirituality is Dr. Larry Dossey. This quote is from a chapter about "the revenge of the good fairy" in his *Recovering the Soul* (New York: Bantam Books, 1989), p. 277.

4. Bateson, *Revenge of the Good Fairy,* p. 4.

5. C. Jung, "On the Psychology of the Trickster-Figure," in *The Archetypes and the Collective Unconscious,* 2nd ed. (Princeton, N.J.: Princeton University Press, 1968), pp. 472–473.

6. L. Dossey, *Recovering the Soul,* p. 279.

7. Bateson, *Revenge of the Good Fairy,* p. 35.

8. Ibid., pp. 35–36.

9. This issue of balance between the rational and irrational aspects of our psyche is discussed by Larry Dossey in "The Trickster: Medicine's Forgotten Character," *Alternative Therapies* 2 (1996): 6–14.

10. I live in Hawai'i, where trickster mythology plays a major role in everyday life. Maui was the trickster demigod constantly playing tricks on those of us here in Hawai'i. The concept of the "trickster" itself was first written about in 1878. For a discussion of the evolution of this idea, see S. D. Gill and I. F. Sullivan, *Dictionary of Native American Mythology* (New York: Oxford University Press, 1992).

11. R. Leakey and R. Lewin, *The Sixth Extinction* (New York: Doubleday, 1995).

12. For a clear discussion of the role of anger in heart disease, see R. Williams and V. Williams, *Anger Kills* (New York: Harper Perennial, 1993).

13. For a review of many effective clinical strategies for reducing emotional states that contribute to heart disease, see R. Allan and S. Scheidt, eds., *Heart and Mind* (Washington, D.C.: American Psychological Association, 1996).

14. See R. Friedman, et al., "The Relaxation Response: Use with Cardiac Patients," in Allan and Scheidt, eds., *Heart and Mind,* pp. 363–384.

15. This acronym was first suggested by Dr. Meyer Friedman and Diane Ulmer in their pioneering book about treating type A behavior, *Treating Type A Behavior and Your Heart* (New York: Fawcett Crest, 1984).

16. For a discussion of what mystics, psychologists, philosophers, physicians, and scientists thought "really matters in life," see T. Schwartz, *What Really Matters* (New York: Bantam, 1995).

17. An excellent book about anger management and "saving your energy" is by cardiologist Robert S. Eliot, *Is It Worth Dying For?* (New York: Bantam: 1984).

18. M. Friedman, et al., "Diagnosis of Type A Behavior Pattern," in Allan and Scheidt, eds., *Heart and Mind.*

Eleven: How to Wish for a Serene Life

1. W. A. Tiller, *Science and Human Transformation* (Walnut Creek, Calif.: Pavior, 1997), p. 2.

2. D. Kundtz, *Stopping: How to Be Still When You Have to Keep Going* (Berkeley, Calif.: Conari Press, 1998).

3. K. Wilbur, *No Boundaries* (Boston: New Science Library, 1979), p. 120.

4. Ibid., p. 16.

5. M. Konner, "Human Nature and Culture: Biology and the Residue of Uniqueness," in *The Boundaries of Humanity,* ed. J. J. Sheehan and M. Sosna (Berkeley, Calif.: University of California Press, 1990).

6. The unique ways people experience tension, anxiety, fear, and fatigue are discussed in D. Sobel and R. Ornstein, *Mind/Body Health* 7, no. 4 (1998): 1–7.

7. One of the most helpful books on mindfulness and coping with stress is by John Kabat-Zinn, *Full Catastrophe Living* (New York: Delta Books, 1991). He writes, "Simply put, mindfulness is moment-to-moment awareness. It is cultivated by purposefully paying attention to things we ordinarily never give a moment's thought to" (p. 2). Well wishing requires paying attention to how we are before asking for what we want and realizing that "we only have moments to live."

8. See M. E. P. Seligman, *What You Can Change and What You Can't* (New York: Knopf, 1994).

9. The serenity prayer was written by theologian Reinhold Niebuhr: "O God, give us grace to accept with serenity the things that cannot be changed, courage to change the things which should be changed, and the wisdom to distinguish one from the other."

10. The serenity prayer is also attributed to author Friedrich Oetinger (1702–1782). Reinhold Niebuhr is said to have written it in 1934.

11. As quoted in A. T. Durning, "Are We Happy Yet?" in *Ecopsychology* (San Francisco: Sierra Club Books, 1995), p. 70.

12. R. M. Nesse and G. C. Williams, *Why We Get Sick* (New York: Random House, 1994).

13. S. J. Dowling, "Lourdes Cures and Their Medical Assessment," *Journal of Research in Social Medicine* 77 (1984): 634–638.

14. W. James, *Psychology: Briefer Course* (New York: Holt, 1890).

15. Ibid., p. 634.

16. D. Goleman, *Vital Lies, Simple Truths* (New York: Simon and Schuster, 1985).

17. Shaw, D. *The Pleasure Police* (New York: Doubleday, 1996), p. 18.

18. These data are derived from Shaw, Ibid., and R. Ornstein and Sobel, *Mind/Body Health*.

Twelve: How to Wish for a Delight-Filled Life

1. For a discussion of pleasure and enjoyment, see R. W. Burhoe, "Pleasure and Reason as Adaptations to Nature's Requirements," *Zygon* 17, no. 2 (1982): 113–131.

2. M. Cabanac, "Physiological Role of Pleasure" *Science* 173 (1971): 1103–1107.

3. E. O. Wilson, *Sociobiology: The New Synthesis* (Cambridge, Mass.: Belknap Press, 1980).

4. E. Diener, et al., "Happiness Is the Frequency, Not the Intensity, of Positive versus Negative Affect," in *The Social Psychology of Subjective Well-Being,* ed. F. Strack, et al. (Oxford: Pergamon Press, 1990).

5. I addressed these issues in my book *Super Joy: Learning to Celebrate Everyday Life* (New York: Doubleday, 1988).

6. G. L. Engel, "Sudden and Rapid Death during Psychological Stress: Folk Lore or Folk Wisdom?" *Annals of Internal Medicine* 74 (1971): 771–782.

7. Quoted in J. Winokur, *The Portable Curmudgeon* (New York: New American Library, 1987).

8. T. Bouchard, et al., "Sources of Human Psychological Differences: The Minnesota Study of Twins Reared Apart," *Science* 250 (1990): 223–228. See a review of some of the findings about happiness in B. Condor, W. Hooer, and E. Infante, "Happy Pursuits," *Honolulu Advertiser,* January 3, 1999, pp. F2–F3.

9. E. Diener, "Subjective Well-Being," *Psychological Bulletin* 93 (1984): 542–575. See also Condor, et al., "Happy Pursuits," p. F3.

10. Drs. R. Ornstein and D. Sobel combined the findings of several studies on happiness and a sense of well-being in their book *Healthy Pleasures,* (Reading Massachusetts: Addison-Wesley, 1989). They used the 1 to 9 scale as a means of combining the different numbering scales used by a variety of researchers. This results in a rounding off of some of the numerical averages but allows for easier generalization of the results. Despite the minor inconsistencies this causes, the general trends remain unchanged. I've used the same approach here.

11. P. Brickman, "Adaption Level Determinant of Satisfaction with Equal and Unequal Outcome Distributions in Skill and Chance Situations," *Journal of Personality and Social Psychology* 32 (1975): 191–198.

12. For more information on the psychology of happiness, see M. Argyle and M. Henderson, *The Anatomy of Relationships* (New York: Penguin Books, 1985) and M. Argyle, *The Psychology of Happiness* (London: Methuen, 1987).

13. Quoted in T. Miller, *How to Want What You Have* (New York: Henry Holt, 1995), p. 226.

14. This concept is developed in L. Dossey, "In Praise of Unhappiness," *Alternative Therapies* 2 (1996): 7–10.

15. This example was reported by L. Dossey, Ibid. p. 10.

16. J. Campbell, *The Power of Myth* (New York: Doubleday, 1988).

17. F. M. Andrews and S. B. Withey, *Social Indicators of Well-Being: Americans' Perceptions of Life Quality,* (New York: Plenum, 1976).

18. D. Shaw, *The Pleasure Police* (New York: Doubleday, 1996), p. 48.

19. This point is elaborated upon by T. Miller in *How to Want What You Have.*

20. R. Kammann, "Objective Circumstances, Life Satisfactions, and Sense of Well-Being: Consistences across Time and Place," *New Zealand Journal of Psychology* 12 (1983): 14–22.

21. Reported in A. T. Durning, "Are We Happy Yet?" In *Ecopsychology,* ed. T. Roszak, et al. (San Francisco: Sierra Club Books, 1995).

22. See L. Festinger, "A Theory of Social Comparison Processes," *Human Relations,* 7 (1954): 117–140.

23. As quoted in A. E. Guinness, *ABC's of the Human Mind: A Family Answer Book* (Pleasantville, N.Y.: Reader's Digest, 1990), p. 89.

24. R. L. Solomon, "The Opponent Process Theory of Acquired Motivation: The Costs of Pleasure and the Benefits of Pain," *American Psychologist* 35 (1980): 691–712.

25. For a detailed discussion and research documentation of the points regarding the nature of wishing for delight raised here, see P. Brickman and D. T. Campbell, "Hedonic Relativism and Planning the Good Society," in *Adaption Level Theory,* ed. M. H. Appley (New York: Academic Press, 1971).

Thirteen: How to Wish for the Job of Your Life

1. S. Shellenbarger, *Wall Street Journal,* January 5, 1998.

2. For a discussion of the Sunday morning factor, see S. Ferenczi, "Sunday Neurosis," in *Further Contribution to the Theory and Technique of Psychoanalysis,* ed. S. Ferenczi (London: Hogarth Press, 1950), pp. 174–177.

3. For the paradox of being least able to find purpose when we seem to have the most freedom, see M. Csikszentmihalyi, *The Evolving Self* (New York: HarperCollins, 1993), pp. 33–34.

4. As quoted in J. Levey and M. Levey, *Living in Balance* (Berkeley, Calif.: Conari Press, 1998).

5. The simple joy of working at what one loves to do and think about is revealed in a survey of eighty-three Nobel laureates in physics, chemistry, and medicine. See P. Fensham and F. Marton, "What Has Happened to Intuition in Science Education," *Research in Science Education* 22 (1992): 114–122.

6. Reported in D. Sharp, "So Many Lists, So Little Time," *USA Today Weekend,* March 15–17, 1996, pp. 4–6.

7. Quoted in A. T. Durning, "Are We Happy Yet?" in *Ecopsychology,* ed T. Roszak, et al. (San Francisco: Sierra Club Books, 1995), p. 73.

8. H. Henderson, *Creating Alternative Futures* (New York: Putnam, 1978).

9. This point is developed in detail in T. Moore, *Care of the Soul* (New York: Harper Perennial, 1992), pp. 178–180.

10. As quoted in J. Kaplan, ed., *Bartlett's Familiar Quotations* (Boston: Little, Brown and Company, 1992), p. 624.

Fourteen: How to Wish for Meaning in Your Life

1. Dalai Lama, "Beyond Religion," *Shambala Sun,* 1995, p. 17.

2. As quoted in H. Smith, *Forgotten Trust* (New York: Harper, 1976).

3. R. Dawkins, *The Selfish Gene* (Oxford: Oxford University Press, 1976).

4. Physicist William A Tiller has formulated some of the mathematical proofs and theories of "another reality" and posits that we are far from "five sensing" all there is to sense. He writes, "Today, everyone knows that humans see only a small fragment of the electromagnetic (EM) spectrum and hear only a small fragment of the sound spectrum. Thus, it shouldn't seem too unreasonable to propose that, on average, humans currently perceive only a small fragment of the reality spectrum." "Towards a Predictive Model of Subtle Domain Connections to the Physical Domain of Reality: The Origins of Wave-Particle Duality, Electric-Magnetic Monopoles and the Mirror Principle," *Journal of Scientific Exploration* 13, no. 1 (1999): 42–67.

5. For a brilliant discussion of the concept of the illusion of boundaries, see physicist Ken Wilbur's *No Boundaries* (Boston: New Science Library, 1979).

6. K. Wilbur, "Where It Was, There I Shall Become: Human Potential and the Boundaries of the Soul," in *Beyond Health and Normality,* ed. R. Walsh and D. H. Shapiro (New York: Van Nostrand Reinhold Company, 1983).

7. G. Marcel, *Creative Fidelity* (London: Victor Gollanca, 1951).

8. Ibid., p. 148.

9. G. Marcel, *The Mystery of Being* (Chicago: Henry Regnery Company, 1960), p. 242.

10. S. Freud, *Instincts and Their Vicissitudes,* vol. 14 (London: Hogarth Press, 1915).

11. J. Jones and W. Wilson, *An Incomplete Education* (New York: Ballantine Books, 1987), p. 434.

12. C. Jung, *Memories, Dreams, Reflections,* trans. R. Winston and C. Winston (New York: Vintage Books, 1963).

13. J. Achterberg, "What is Medicine?" *Alternative Therapies* 2, no. 3 (1996): 59.

14. A. Antonovsky, *Unraveling the Mystery of Health* (San Francisco: Jossey Bass, 1987).

15. L. Carpenito, *Nursing Diagnosis: Application to Clinical Practice* (Philadelphia: J. P. Lippincott, 1983).

16. W. Starke, *Homesick for Heaven* (Buerne, Tex.: Guadalupe Press, 1988), p. 20.

17. N. Remen, "On Defining Spirit," *Noetic Sciences Review* 27 (1993): 41.

18. S. Krippner and P. Welch, *Spiritual Dimensions of Healing* (New York: Irvington Publishers, 1992), p. 237.

19. For one of the clearest and most sensitive discussions of the search for the soul, see L. Dossey, *Recovering the Soul* (New York: Bantam Books, 1989).

20. H. Margenau, *The Miracle of Existence* (Woodbridge, Conn.: Ox Bow Press, 1984), p. 72.

21. For a clear and concise definition and discussion of the new physics concept of nonlocality, see N. Herbert, *Quantum Reality* (New York: Anchor Books, 1987).

22. See H. E. Puthoff and R. Targ, *Mind-Reach* (New York: Delacorte Press, 1977). For information on how our own government has employed the principles of nonlocality to find missiles, hostages, and other military targets, see R. Targ and J. Katra, *Miracles of Mind* (Novato, Calif.: New World Library, 1998).

23. A. Huxley, *The Perennial Philosophy* (New York: Harper and Colophon Books, 1945).

24. Quoted in Ibid., p. 14.

25. Ibid., p. 9.

26. Ibid., p. 5.

27. Ibid., p. 12.

28. G. Adler and A. Jaffe, eds., *Jung's Letters,* vol. 1 (Princeton, N.J.: Princeton University Press, 1973), p. 377.

29. This point was made in Bill Moyers's interview with mythologist Joseph Campbell. J. Campbell, *The Power of Myth* (New York: Doubleday, 1988).

30. C. G. Jung, *Psychology of the Occult* (Princeton, N.J.: Princeton University Press, 1977), pp. 136–137.

31. J. L. Liebman, *Peace of Mind* (New York: Bantam Books, 1961), p. 106.

32. Wilbur, *No Boundaries,* p. 120.

Fifteen: How to Wish for a Loving Life

1. C. Jung, *Collected Works,* ed. M. Read Fordham and G. Adler, Bollingen Series (New York: Pantheon Books, 1953). A similar point is developed by S. M. Johnson in his *Humanizing the Narcissistic Style* (New York and London: W. W. Norton and Company, 1987).

2. Plato, *The Collected Dialogues,* ed. E. Hamilton and H. J. Cairns, Bollingen Series, 71 (New York: Pantheon Books, 1961).

3. M. Buber, *I and Thou* (Edinburgh: T. and T. Clark, 1937).

4. I discuss Tolstoy's concept of marriage in my book *The Ten Laws of Lasting Love* (New York: Avon Books, 1993).

5. Author George Leonard first used the term "high monogamy" in "The End of Sex" in *The Fireside Treasury of Light,* ed. M. O. Kelley (New York: Simon and Schuster, 1990), p. 168.

6. This work was first conducted more than thirty years ago by L. E. Eemans. See his *Co-operative Healing* (London: Frederick Muller Ltd., 1947). More recently, this same "couple coherence" effect was documented by Linda G. S. Russek and Gary E. Schwartz. See their "Interpersonal Heart–Brain Registration and the Perception of Parental Love: A 42-Year Follow-Up Study of the Harvard Mastery of Stress Study," *Subtle Energies* 2 (1996): 55–625.

7. T. Moore, *Soul Mates* (New York: Harper Perennial, 1995), p. 53.

8. Ibid., p. 69.

9. This is a tiny "gas discharge device" with gold electrodes that records and actually "stores"

the energy of the intents or wishes of those who attempt to impose their will upon it. For a complete description of this research, see W. A. Tiller, "A Gas Discharge Device for Investigating Focussed Human Attention," *Journal of Scientific Exploration* 2 (1990): 250–260.

10. T. Dawson, "Hydraulic Lift and Water Use by Plants," *Oceologia* (Spring 1993).

11. A. L. Lettiere, "Toward a Philosophy of Science in Women's Health Research," *Journal of Scientific Exploration* 10 (1996): 539.

12. The data supporting the power of shared wishing and intentionality or cognition is in R. G. Jahn, "Information, Consciousness, and Health," *Alternative Therapies* 2, no. 3 (May 1996): 32–38.

13. This data is reported in a 1994 study by psychologist Edward Laumann of the University of Chicago. See P. Gorner, "Historic Sex Study Gives Many Something to Talk About," *Honolulu Advertiser,* Sunday, April 18, 1999, pp. B 1–4.

14. R. G. Jahn, "Report on the Academy of Consciousness Studies," *Journal of Scientific Exploration* 9, no. 3 (1995): 402.

15. Ibid., p. 403.

16. L. de Broglie, "The Role of the Engineer in the Age of Science," in *New Perspectives in Physics,* trans. A. J. Pomerans (New York: Basic Books, 1962), p. 231.

17. This definition of love is offered in R. G. Jahn and B. J. Dunne, *Margins of Reality* (New York: Harcourt Brace Jovanovich, 1987).

18. R. May, *Love and Will* (New York: Dell Publishing, 1969), p. 325.

19. The sequence to lasting bonding is described by Helen Fischer in *Anatomy of Love* (New York: W. W. Norton and Company, 1992).

20. L. Dossey, "The Great Wait: In Praise of Doing Nothing," *Alternative Therapies* 2 (1966): 8–13.

21. This concept is discussed in detail by Helen E. Fisher in *Anatomy of Love.*

22. As quoted in *The Times, The Daily Telegraph, and The Daily Mail.* London, December 7, 1995.

23. For a fascinating discussion of "wishing teamwork," see R. Targ and J. Katra, *Miracles of Mind* (Novato, Calif.: New World Library, 1998). See in particular pp. 63–83.

24. J. Gottman, *Why Marriages Succeed or Fail* (New York: Simon and Schuster, 1994).

Sixteen: Putting Your Sixth Sense First

1. For a review of the history of research in ESP, see R. Cavendish, ed., *The Encyclopedia of the Unexplained* (New York, Penguin Books, 1989).

2. J. B. Rhine, et al., *Extrasensory Perception after Sixty Years* (Boston: Humphries, 1966).

3. E. Aron and A. Aron, *The Maharishi Effect: A Revolution through Meditation* (Walpole, N.H.: Stillpoint Publishing, 1980).

4. E. Aaron and A. Aron, "The Gentle Invasion of Rhode Island," in *The Maharishi Effect,* pp. 55–67.

5. C. Borland and G. Landrith, "Improved Quality of City Life through Transcendental Meditation Program: Decreased Crime Rate," in *Scientific Research of the Transcendental Meditation and TM-Siddhi Program: Collected Papers,* vol. 1 (Livingston Manor, N.Y.: Maharishi International University Press, 1978).

6. Aron and Aron, *The Maharishi Effect,* p. 50.

7. R. K. Wallace, J. B. Fagan, and D. S. Pasco, "Vedic Physiology," *Modern Science and Vedic Science* 1, no. 2 (1988): 3–59.

8. L. Dossey, *Recovering the Soul* (New York: Bantam Books, 1988), p. 262.

9. Quoted in W. Attwood, *Making It through Middle Age* (New York: Atheneum, 1972), p. 107.

10. Most of the quotes included in the twenty-five points were taken from various texts. Others were provided from members of our wish research team. Some of the texts consulted were G. W. Fenchuck, *Timeless Wisdom* (Midlothian, Va.: Cake Eaters, Inc., 1994); M. C. Hunter, *Guidewords* (Coshocton, Ohio: Shaw-Baraton, 1971); C. L. Wallis, ed., *The Treasure Chest* (San Francisco: Harper and Row, 1965); and R. Byrne, *1,911 Best Things Anybody Ever Said* (New York: Fawcett Columbine, 1988).

Epilogue: Getting a Well Wisher's Perspective

1. W. A. Tiller, *Science and Human Transformation: Subtle Energies, Intentionality, and Consciousness* (Walnut Creek, Calif.: Pavior, 1997), p. 227.

2. H. Kushner, *When All You've Ever Wanted Isn't Enough* (New York: Pocket Books, 1986), p. 152.

Bibliography

....💋..

Meister Eckhart wrote, "If the only prayer you say in your whole life is 'thank you,' that would suffice." I express my deepest gratitude to the many great minds and warm hearts of those persons listed here. Thank you for being willing to go "out of the box."

Achterberg, J. "Clearing the Air in the Therapeutic Touch Controversy." *Alternative Therapies* 4 (1998): 100–101.

———. "What Is Medicine?" *Alternative Therapies* 2, no. 3 (1996): 53–62.

Adler, E. "Gestures: Are You Talking to Yourself?" *The Honolulu Advertiser*. November 24, 1998, p. 1.

Adler, G., and A. Jaffe, eds. *Jung's Letters*. Vol. 1. Princeton, N.J.: Princeton University Press, 1973.

Alfredson, L., et al., "Myocardial Infarction Risk and Psychosocial Work Environment: An Analysis of the Male Swedish Work Force." *Social Science and Medicine* 16 (1982): 463–467.

Allan, R., and S. Scheidt, eds. *Heart and Mind*. Washington, D.C.: American Psychological Association, 1996.

Andrews, F. M., and S. B. Withey, *Social Indicators of Well-Being: Americans' Perceptions of Life Quality*. New York: Plenum, 1976.

Anderson, T. W. "Vitamin E in Angina Pectoris." *Canadian Medical Association Journal* 110 (1974): 401–406.

Andrews, H. "Helping and Health: The Relationship between Volunteer Activity and Health-Related Outcomes." *Advances* 7, no. 1 (1990): 25–34.

Antonovsky, A. *Unraveling the Mystery of Health.* San Francisco: Jossey Bass, 1987.

Appels, A., et al. "Fatigue and Heart Disease: The Association between 'Vital Exhaustion' and Past, Present, and Future Coronary Heart Disease." *Journal of Psychosomatic Research* 33 (1989): 727–738.

Argyle, M. *The Psychology of Happiness.* London: Methuen, 1987.

Argyle, M., and H. Henderson. *The Anatomy of Relationships.* New York: Penguin Books, 1985.

Arieti, S. and A. Chrznowki, eds. *New Dimensions in Psychiatry: A World View.* Vol. 2. New York: Wiley, 1977.

Aron, E. and A. Aron. *The Maharishi Effect: A Revolution through Meditation.* Walpole, N.H.: Stillpoint Publishing, 1980.

Attwood, W. *Making It through Middle Age.* New York: Atheneum, 1972.

Auden, W. H. J., and L. Kronenberger, eds. *The Viking Book of Aphorisms.* New York: Barnes and Noble, 1993.

Baker, M. B. "Obtrusive Mental Healing." *Miscellaneous Writings.* Published by the trustees under the will of Mary Baker G. Eddy. Boston, 1986.

Baron, R. A. *Psychology.* 2nd ed. Needham Heights, Mass.: Addison-Wesley, 1992.

Barry, J. "General and Comparative Study of Psychokinetic Effect on a Fungus Culture." *Journal of Parapsychology* 32, no. 4 (1968): 237–243.

Bateson, M. C. "The Revenge of the Good Fairy." *Whole Earth Review* no.55 (Summer 1987): 34–48.

Benor, D. J. *Healing Research.* 4 vol. Munich: Helix Editions, Ltd., 1993.

Benson, H. *Timeless Healing: The Power of Biology of Belief.* New York: Scribner, 1996.

Berk, L. S., et al. "Humor-Associated Laughter Decreases Cortisol and Increases Spontaneous Lymphocyte-Blastogenesis." *Clinical Research* 36 (1988): 435–438.

Berrengia, J. B. "Scientists Grab Chance for Meteor Encounter." *Honolulu Star Bulletin.* November 16, 1998, p. 1.

Bertman, S. *Hyperculture: The Human Cost of Speed.* Westport, Conn.: Praeger, 1998.

Boone, L. E. *Quotable Business.* New York: Random House, 1992.

Borland, C., and G. Landrith. "Improved Quality of City Life through Transcendental Meditation Program: Decreased Crime Rate." In *Scientific Research of the Transcendental Meditation and TM-Siddhi Program: Collected Papers.* Vol. 1. Livingston Manor, N.Y.: Maharishi International University Press, 1978.

Bouchard, T., et al. "Sources of Human Psychological Differences: The Minnesota Study of Twins Reared Apart." *Science* 250 (1990): 223–228.

Boyce, W. T., et al. "Permanence and Change: Psychosocial Factors in the Outcome of Adolescent Pregnancy." *Social Science and Medicine* 21 (1985): 2180–2183.

Braud, W. G. "On the Use of Living Target Systems in Distant Mental Influence Research." In *Research in Parapsychology,* edited by R. A. White and J. Solfvin. Metuchen, N.J.: Scarecrow Press, 1985.

Bretsford, V. *Superstitions and Survival.* London: Centaur Press, 1950.

Brickman, P. "Adaption Level Determinant of Satisfaction with Equal and Unequal Outcome

Distributions in Skill and Chance Situations." *Journal of Personality and Social Psychology* 32 (1975): 191–198.

Brickman, P., and D. T. Campbell. "Hedonic Relativism and Planning the Good Society." In *Adaption Level Theory,* edited by M. H. Appley. New York: Academic Press, 1971.

Brodie, R. *Virus of the Mind.* Seattle, Wash.: Integral Press, 1996.

Broughton, R. S. "Glimpsing the Future." In *Parapsychology: The Controversial Science.* New York: Ballantine, 1991.

Bruhn, J. G., et al. "Psychological Predictors of Sudden Death in Myocardial Infarction." *Journal of Psychosomatic Research* 18 (1974): 187–191.

Buber, M. *I and Thou.* Edinburgh: T. and T. Clark, 1937.

Burhoe, R. W. "Pleasure and Reason as Adaptations to Nature's Requirements." *Zygon* 17 no. 2 (1982): 113–131.

Burns, S. *Home Inc.* New York: Doubleday, 1975.

Butterfield, H. *The Origins of Modern Science.* London: Centaur Press, 1958.

Byrne, R. *1,911 Best Things Anybody Ever Said.* New York: Fawcett Columbine, 1988.

Cabanac, M. "Physiological Role of Pleasure." *Science* 173 (1971): 1103–1107.

Campbell, J. *The Power of Myth.* New York: Doubleday, 1988.

Capra, F. *The Turning Point.* Toronto: Bantam Books, 1982.

Carpenito, L. *Nursing Diagnosis: Application to Clinical Practice.* Philadelphia: J. P. Lippincott, 1983.

Cavendish, R. *A History of Magic.* New York: Penguin, 1987.

———, ed. *The Encyclopedia of the Unexplained: Magic, Occultism, and Parapsychology.* New York: Penguin Books, 1989.

Childre, D., and H. Martin. *The HeartMath Solution.* San Francisco: HarperSanFrancisco, 1991.

Clancy, F., and H. Yorkshire. "The Bandler Method." *Mother Jones* (February/March 1989): 24–28, 63–64.

Cohen, J., and K. Sedlacek. "Attention and Autonomic Self-Regulation." *Psychosomatic Medicine* 45 (1983): 243–257.

Collier, J. L. *The Rise of Selfishness in America.* New York: Oxford University Press, 1991.

Condor, B., W. Hooer, and E. Infante. "Happy Pursuits." *Honolulu Advertiser.* Sunday, January 3, 1999): F2–F3.

Conrad, P. *Television: The Medium and Its Manners.* Boston: Routledge and Kegan, 1982.

Cousins, N. *The Anatomy of an Illness.* New York: Bantam Books, 1981.

Csikszentmihalyi, M. *The Evolving Self.* New York: HarperCollins, 1993.

———. *Flow: The Psychology of Optimal Experience.* New York: Harper and Row, 1990.

Csikszentmihalyi, M., and J. LeFevre. "The Experience of Work and Leisure." *Third Canadian Leisure Research Conference.* Halifax, Nova Scotia, May 22–25, 1987.

Dalai Lama. "Beyond Religion." *Shambhala Sun,* 1995.

Damasio, A. R. *Descartes' Error.* New York: Avon Books, 1994.

Darwin, C. *The Origin of Species.* New York: Modern Library, 1959.

Dawkins, R. *River Out of Eden.* New York: Basic Books, 1995.

———. *The Selfish Gene.* Oxford: Oxford University Press, 1976.

Dawson, T. "Hydraulic Lift and Water Use by Plants." *Oceologia* (Spring 1993).

De Broglie, L. "The Role of the Engineer in the Age of Science." In *New Perspectives in Physics,* translated by A.J. Pomerans. New York: Basic Books, 1962.

de la Pena, A. M. *The Psychobiology of Cancer.* South Hadley, Mass.: Bergin Publishers, 1983.

De Lys, C. *A Treasury of American Superstitions.* New York: Philosophical Library, 1958.

Dibble, W. E., Jr., and W. A. Tiller. "Electronic Device-Mediated pH Changes in Water." *Journal of Scientific Exploration* 13, no. 2 (1999): 22–37.

———. "On Augmented Electromagnetic Wave Communication between Remote Vessels of Water Containing ANCo3 Crystallites. I. Initial Two Vessel Experiment." Submitted to *Journal of Scientific Exploration.*

———. "Toward Objectifying Intention via Electronic Devices." Submitted to *Subtle Energies and Energy Medicine.*

Diener, E., et al. "Happiness Is the Frequency, Not the Intensity, of Positive versus Negative Affect." In *The Social Psychology of Subjective Well-Being,* edited by F. Strack et al., Oxford: Pergamon Press, 1990.

———. "Subjective Well-Being." *Psychological Bulletin* 93 (1984): 542–575.

"Diets: What Works—What Doesn't." *Consumer Reports,* June 1993, pp. 347–357.

Dossey, L. *Be Careful What You Pray For . . . You Just Might Get It.* San Francisco: HarperSan-Francisco, 1998.

———. Cancelled Funerals: A Look at Miracle Cures." *Alternative Therapies* 4 (1998): 10–18, 116–119.

———. "The Great Wait: In Praise of Doing Nothing." *Alternative Therapies* 2 (1996): 8–13.

———. *Healing Words: The Power of Prayer and the Practice of Medicine.* San Francisco: Harper-SanFrancisco, 1993.

———. "In Praise of Unhappiness." *Alternative Therapies* 2 (1996): 7–10.

———. "Now You Are Fit to Live: Humor and Health." *Alternative Therapies* 2, no. 5 (1996): 8–13.

———. *Recovering the Soul.* New York: Bantam Books, 1989.

———. "The Right Man Syndrome: Skepticism and Alternative Medicine." *Alternative Therapies* 4, no. 3 (1998): 12–20, 108–111.

———. "The Trickster: Medicine's Forgotten Character." *Alternative Therapies* 2 (1996): 6–14.

———. "Work and Health: Of Isolation, Sisyphus, and Barbarian Beds." *Alternative Therapies* 3 (1997): 6–15.

Dowling, S. J. "Lourdes Cures and Their Medical Assessment." *Journal of Research in Social Medicine* 77 (1984): 634–638.

Dreher, H. *The Immune Power Personality.* New York: Dutton, 1995.

Druckman, D., and J. A. Swets. *Enhancing Human Performance: Issues, Theories, and Techniques.* Washington, D.C.: National Academy Press, 1988.

Dunne, B. J. "Experiments in Remote Human/Machine Interaction." *Journal of Scientific Exploration* 6, no. 4 (1992): 311–322.

Durning, A. T. "Are We Happy Yet?" In *Ecopsychology,* edited by T. Roszak et al. San Francisco: Sierra Club Books, 1995.

Easterbrook, G. *Beside Still Waters.* New York: William Morrow and Company, 1998.

Eddington, A. "Defense of Mysticism." In *Quantum Questions: Mystical Writings of the World's Great Physicists,* edited by K. Wilber. Boston: Shambhala, 1984.

Eemans, L. E. *Cooperative Healing.* London: Frederick Muller, Ltd., 1947.

Eliade, M. *The Sacred and the Profane.* New York: Harcourt, Brace, and World, 1959.

Elias, M. "Anger Can Inflate Body's Spare Tire, Heart Risk." *U. S. A. Today,* March 22, 1999, p. 2.

Eliot, R. S. *Is It Worth Dying For?* New York: Bantam, 1984.

Engel, G. L. "Sudden and Rapid Death during Psychological Stress: Folk Lore or Folk Wisdom?" *Annals of Internal Medicine* 74 (1971): 771–782.

Erikson, E. *Childhood and Society.* New York: Norton, 1963.

Fenchuck, G. W. *Timeless Wisdom.* Midlothian, Va.: Cake Eaters, Inc., 1994.

Fensham, P., and R. Marton. "What Has Happened to Intuition in Science Education." *Research in Science Education* 72 (1992): 114–122.

Ferenczi, S. "Sunday Neurosis." In *Further Contribution to the Theory and Technique of Psychoanalysis,* edited by S. Fenenczi. London: Hogarth Press, 1950.

Festinger, L. "A Theory of Social Comparison Processes." *Human Relations* 7 (1954): 117–140.

Fisher, H. E. *Anatomy of Love.* New York: W. W. Norton and Company, 1992.

Frazer, J. *The Golden Bough.* New York: Simon and Schuster, 1996.

Freidman, H. S., et al. "Psychosocial and Behavioral Predictors of Longevity." *The American Psychologist* 50 (1994): 197–207.

Freud, S. *Instincts and Their Vicissitudes,* vol. 14. London: Hogarth Press, 1915.

Friedman, M., et al. "Diagnosis of Type A Behavior Pattern." In *Heart and Mind,* edited by R. Allan, and S. Scheidt. Washington, D.C.: American Psychological Association, 1996.

Friedman, M., and D. Ulmer. *Treating Type A Behavior and Your Heart.* New York: Fawcett Crest, 1984.

Friedman, R., et al. "The Relaxation Response: Use with Cardiac Patients." In *Heart and Mind,* edited by R. Allan, and S. Scheidt. Washington, D.C.: American Psychological Association, 1996.

Gallup, G. *Adventures in Immortality.* New York: McGraw Hill, 1982.

Garner, D., and S. Wooley. "Confronting the Failure of Behavioral and Dietary Treatments for Obesity." *Clinical Psychology Review* 11 (1991): 729–780.

Gielding, J. W. L, et al. "An Interim Report of a Prospective, Randomized, Controlled Study of Adjuvant Chemotherapy in Operable Gastric Cancer: British Stomach Cancer Group." *World Journal of Surgery* 43 (1983): 390–399.

Gill, S. D., and I. F. Sullivan. *Dictionary of Native American Mythology.* New York: Oxford University Press, 1992.

Gillian, R., et al. "Quantitative Evaluation of Vitamin E in the Treatment of Angina Pectoris." *American Heart Journal* 93 (1977): 444–449.

Glaxton, G. *Hare Brain, Tortoise Mind.* Hopewell, N.J.: Ecco Press, 1997.

Gleick, J. *Chaos: Making a New Science.* New York: Penguin Books, 1987.

Glisky, M. L., et al. "Absorption, Openness to Experience, and Hypnotizability." *Journal of Personality and Social Psychology* 60 (1991): 263–272.

Glynn, P. *God: The Evidence.* Rocklin, Calif.: Forum Press, 1997.

Goldberger, A. L., et al. "Nonlinear Dynamics of the Heartbeat." *Physica* 17D (1985): 207–214.

Goleman, D. *Emotional Intelligence.* New York: Bantam Books, 1995.

———. *Vital Lies, Simple Truths.* New York: Simon and Schuster, 1985.

Gorner, P. "Historic Sex Study Gives Many Something to Talk About." *Honolulu Advertisers,* Sunday, April 18, 1999, pp. B1–4.

Gottman, J. *Why Marriages Succeed or Fail.* New York: Simon and Schuster, 1994.

Greene, G. "Quotus Profundus." *Pathways* 5, no. 6 (1996).

Gross, M. L. *The Psychological Society.* New York: Simon and Schuster, 1978.

Guinness, A. E. *ABC's of the Human Mind: A Family Answer Book.* Pleasantville, N.Y.: Reader's Digest, 1990.

Heaps, W. A. *Superstition.* New York: Thomas Nelson, Inc., 1972.

Heinberg, R. *Memories and Visions of Paradise.* Los Angeles: Jeremy P. Tarcher, Inc., 1989.

Henderson, H. *Creating Alternative Futures.* New York: Putnam, 1978.

Herbert, N. *Quantum Reality.* New York: Anchor Books, 1987.

Hocrine, C. *Nutrition Plan for High Blood Pressure.* San Francisco: Jove Publications, 1977.

Honorton, C. "Rhetoric Over Substance: The Impoverished State of Skepticism." *Journal of Parapsychology* 57, no. 2 (1933): 191–214.

Hunter, M. C. *Guidewords.* Coshocton, Ohio: Shaw-Baraton, 1971.

Huxley, A. *The Perennial Philosophy.* New York: Harper and Colophon Books, 1945.

Huxley, F. *The Way of the Sacred.* Garden City, N.Y.: Doubleday, 1974.

Jahn, R. G. "Information, Consciousness, and Health." *Alternative Therapies* 2, no. 3 (May 1996): 32–38.

———. "Report on the Academy of Consciousness Studies." *Journal of Scientific Exploration* 9 (1995): 389–410.

Jahn, R. G., and B. J. Dunne. *Margins of Reality: The Role of Consciousness in the Physical World.* New York: Harcourt Brace Jovanovich, 1987.

———. "Science and the Subjective." *Journal of Scientific Exploration* 11, no. 2 (1997): 201–224.

James, W. *The Principles of Psychology.* New York: Holt, 1890.

———. *Psychology: Briefer Course.* New York: Holt, 1890.

Jeans, J. *Physics and Philosophy.* New York: Dover, 1981.

Jensen, E. W. "The Families Routine Inventory." *Social Science and Medicine* 7 (1983): 210–211.

Johnson, S. M. *Humanizing the Narcissistic Style.* New York: W. W. Norton and Company, 1987.

Jones, J., and W. Wilson. *An Incomplete Education.* New York: Ballantine Books, 1987.

Jung, C. *Collected Works.* Edited by M. R. Fordham and G. Adler. Bollingen Series. New York: Pantheon Books, 1953.

———. *Memories, Dreams, Reflections.* Translated by R. Winston and C. Winston. New York: Vintage Books, 1963.

———. "On the Psychology of the Trickster-Figure." In *Archetypes and the Collective Unconscious.* 2nd ed. Princeton, N.J.: Princeton University Press, 1968.

———. *Psychology of the Occult.* Princeton, N.J.: Princeton University Press, 1977.

Justice, B. *Who Gets Sick: How Beliefs, Moods, and Thoughts Affect Your Health.* Los Angeles: J. P. Tarcher, Inc. 1988.

Kabat-Zinn, J. *Full Catastrophe Living.* New York: Delta Books, 1991.

Kaminer, W. *I'm Dysfunctional, You're Dysfunctional.* Reading, Mass.: Addison-Wesley, 1992.

Kammann, R. "Objective Circumstances, Life Satisfactions, and Sense of Well- Being: Consistencies across Time and Place." *New Zealand Journal of Psychology* 12 (1983): 14–22.

Kaplan, B. H. "Social Health and the Forgiving Heart." *Journal of Behavioral Medicine* 14, no. 3 (1992): 3–14.

Kaplan, J., ed. *Bartlett's Familiar Quotations.* Boston, Mass.: Little, Brown and Company, 1992.

Kelly, M. O., ed. *The Fireside Treasury of Light.* New York: Simon and Schuster, 1990.

Kertzer, D. "Secrets of the Vatican Archives." *New York Times,* February 1998.

Kierkegaard, S. *Either/Or.* Princeton, N.J.: Princeton University Press, 1987. (Original work published 1843)

Kinder, M. *Going Nowhere Fast.* New York: Prentice Hall, 1990.

Klerman, G., et al. *Interpersonal Psychotherapy of Depression.* New York: Basic Books, 1984.

Koestler, A. *The Act of Creation.* London: Pan Publishers, 1970.

Kohane, M. J., and W. A. Tiller. "Energy, Fitness, and Electromagnetic Fields in Drosophila Melanogaster." Submitted to *Journal of Scientific Exporation.*

———. "On Intention-Induced Increase of In Vitro Enzyme and Inanimate/Animate Systems." *Conference Proceedings of "Toward a Science of Consciousness—Fundamental Approaches.* May 25–28, 1999, United Nations University, Tokyo, Japan.

Kohlberg, L. "Stage and Sequence: The Cognitive Developmental Approach to Socialization." In *Handbook of Socialization Theory and Research,* edited by D. A. Goslin. Chicago: Rand McNally, 1969.

Konner, M. "Human Nature and Culture: Biology and the Residue of Uniqueness." In *The Boundaries of Humanity,* edited by J. J. Sheehan and M. Sosna. Berkeley, Calif.: University of California Press, 1990.

Krippner, S., and P. Welch, *Spiritual Dimensions of Healing.* New York: Irvington Publishers, 1992.

Kuhn, T. *The Structure of the Scientific Revolution.* New York: Scribner, 1962.

Kumar, V. K., and R. J. Rekala. "Hypnotizability, Absorption, and Individual Differences in Phenomenological Experience." *International Journal of Clinical and Experimental Hypnosis* 36 (1988): 80–88.

Kundtz, D. *Stopping: How to Be Still When You Have to Keep Going.* Berkeley, Calif.: Conari Press, 1998.

Kushner, H. *When All You've Ever Wanted Isn't Enough.* New York: Pocket Books, 1986.

Larson, E., and L. Witham. "Scientists Are Still Keeping the Faith." *Nature* 3 (1997): 18–24.

Leakey, R., and R. Lewin. *The Sixth Extinction.* New York: Doubleday, 1995.

LeFevre, J. "Flow and the Quality of Experience in Work and Leisure." In *Optimal Experience: Psychological Studies of Flow in Consciousness,* edited by M. Csikszentmihalyi and I. S. Csikszentmihalyi. New York: Cambridge University Press, 1988.

Leontjev, A. *Problemer I Det Psykiskes Udvikling.* Copenhagen: University Press, 1977.

LeShan, L. *The Dilemma of Psychology.* New York: Dutton, 1990.

LeShan, L., and H. Margenau. *Einstein's Space and Van Gogh's Sky.* New York: Collier Books, 1982.

Leskowitz, E. "Un-Debunking Therapeutic Touch." *Alternative Therapies* 4 (1998): 101–102.

Lettieri, A. L. "Toward a Philosophy of Science in Women's Health Research." *Journal of Scientific Exploration* 10 (1996): 535–545.

Levay, S. "A Difference in Hypothalamic Structure between Heterosexual and Homosexual Men." *Science* 253 (1991): 1034–1037.

Levey, J., and M. Levey. *Living in Balance.* Berkeley, Calif.: Conari Press, 1998.

Liebman, J. L. *Peace of Mind.* New York: Bantam Books, 1961.

Lifton, R. J. *The Protean Self: Human Resilience in an Age of Fragmentation.* New York: Basic Books, 1993.

Lings, M. *Ancient Beliefs and Modern Superstitions.* London: Tomorrow Publications, 1964.

Linville, P. W. "Self-Complexity and Affective Extremity: Don't Put All of Your Eggs in One Cognitive Basket." *Social Cognition* 3, no. 1 (1986): 94–120.

Long, M. F. *The Secret Science behind Miracles: Unveiling the Huna Tradition of the Ancient Polynesians.* Marina Del Rey, Calif.: Devros and Company, 1976.

Luks, A. *The Healing Power of Doing Good.* New York: Fawcett Columbine, 1992.

MacLean, P. "On the Evolution of Three Mentalities." In *New Dimensions in Psychiatry: A World View,* vol. 2, edited by S. Arieti and G. Chrnowki. New York: Wiley, 1977.

Maddi, S. R., and S. C. Kobasa. *The Hardy Executive: Health under Stress.* Homewood, Ill.: Dow Jones-Irwin, 1988.

Maier, H. W. *Three Theories of Child Development.* New York: Harper and Row, 1965.

Margenau, H. *The Miracle of Existence.* Woodbridge, Conn.: Ox Bow Press, 1984.

Marcel, G. *Creative Fidelity.* London: Victor Gollanca, 1957.

————. *The Mystery of Being.* Chicago: Henry Regnery Company, 1960.

Maslow, A. *The Farther Reaches of Human Nature.* New York: Penguin, 1971.

Mathes, E. W. "Mystical Experience, Romantic Love, and Hypnotic Susceptibility." *Psychological Review* 50 (1982): 701–702.

Matthews, D. A. *The Faith Factor.* New York: Viking, 1998.

May, R. *Love and Will.* New York: Dell Publishing, 1969.

Mayer, J. D., and A. Stevens. "An Emerging Understanding of the Reflective (Meta) Experience of Mood." Unpublished manuscript, 1993.

McClelland, D. C. *The Achieving Society.* Princeton, N.J.: Van Nostrand, 1971.

————. "Motivational Factors in Health and Disease." *American Psychologist* 44, no. 4 (1989): 675–683.

Mead, M. *Sex and Temperament in Three Primitive Societies.* New York: Morrow, 1935.

Meeker, J. W. *Comedy and Survival.* Tucson, Ariz.: Arizona University Press, 1997.

Miller, T. *How to Want What You Have.* New York: Henry Holt, 1995.

Mitchell, E. *The Way of the Explorer.* New York: G. P. Putnam's Sons, 1996.

Moody, R. *Life after Life.* Covinda, Ga.: Mockingbird Press, 1975.

Moore, T. *Care of the Soul.* New York: Harper Perennial, 1992.

————. *The Re-enchantment of Everyday Life.* New York: HarperCollins, 1996.

————. *Soul Mates.* New York: Harper Perennial, 1995.

Morowitz, H. *Cosmic Joy and Local Pain.* New York: Charles Scribner's Sons, 1987.

Muckley, M. *Wise Words: Perennial Wisdom from the New Dimensions Radio Series.* Carlsbad, Calif.: Hay House, 1997.

Murphy, M. *The Future of the Body.* Los Angeles: Jeremy P. Tarcher, 1992.

Murray, H. A. "American Icarus." *Clinical Studies of Personality.* Vol. 2. New York: Harper, 1955.

————. *Explorations in Personality.* New York: Oxford, 1938.

Nash, C. B. "Test of Psychokinetic Control of Bacterial Mutation." *Journal of the American Society of Psychical Research.* 78 (1984): 145–152.

Nesse, R. M. "Evolutionary Explanations of Emotions." *Human Nature* 1 (1990): 261–289.

Nesse, R. M. , and C. G. Williams. *Why We Get Sick.* New York: Random House, 1994.

North, J. *The Norton History of Astronomy and Cosmology.* New York: Norton, 1995).

Norwid, C. *Analysis of Happiness.* Edited by W. Tatarkiewica. The Hague: Martinus Nijhoff, 1976.

Nuland, S. B. *The Wisdom of the Body.* New York: Alfred A. Knopf, 1997.

Ornstein, R., and D. Sobel. *Healthy Pleasures.* Reading, Mass.: Addison-Wesley Publishing Company, 1989.

Paddison, S. *The Hidden Power of the Heart.* Boulder Creek, Calif.: Planetary Publications, 1992.

Peale, N. V. *The Power of Positive Thinking.* New York: Fawcett Books, 1952.

Pearsall, P. *The Heart's Code.* New York: Broadway Books, 1998.

————. *The Pleasure Prescription.* Armeda, Calif.: Hunter House, 1997.

———. *The Power of the Family.* New York: Doubleday, 1990.

———. *Super Immunity: Master Your Emotions and Improve Your Health.* New York: McGraw Hill, 1987.

———. *Super Joy: Learning to Celebrate Everyday Life.* New York: Doubleday, 1988.

———. *The Ten Laws of Lasting Love.* New York: Avon Books, 1993.

Peck, M. S. *The Road Less Traveled.* New York: Simon and Schuster, 1978.

Peel, R. *The Years of Authority.* New York: Holt, Rinehart, and Winston, 1977.

Pert, C. B. *Molecules of Emotion.* New York: Scribner, 1997.

———. "The Wisdom of the Receptors: Neuropeptides, the Emotions, and BodyMind." *Advances* 3 (1986): 6–14.

Piaget, J. *The Origins of Intelligence in Children.* New York: International Univeristy Press, 1952.

Pirsig, R. M. *Zen and the Art of Motorcycle Maintenance.* New York: Morrow, 1974.

Plato. *The Collected Dialogues,* ed. E. Hamilton and J. J. Carrins. Bollingen Series, 71. New York: Pantheon Books, 1961.

Polivy, J., and P. Herman. *Breaking the Diet Habit.* New York: Basic Books, 1983.

Poulsen, H. *Conations: On Striving, Willing, and Wishing and Their Relationship with Cognition, Emotions, and Motives.* Aarhus, Denmark: Aarhus University Press, 1991.

Pukui, M. K. *Olelo No' Eau. Hawaiian Proverbs and Poetical Sayings.* Honolulu, Hawai'i: Bishop Museum Press, 1983.

Puthoff, H. E., and R. Targ. *Mind-Reach.* New York: Delacorte Press, 1977.

Qualls, P. J., and P. W. Sheehan, "Electromyograph Biofeedback as a Relaxation Technique: A Critical Appraisal and Reassessment." *Psychological Bulletin* 90 (1981): 21–42.

Rabkin, S. W., et al, "Chronobiology of Cardiac Sudden Death in Men." *Journal of the American Medical Association* 244 (1980): 1357–1358.

Rauscher, E. "Human Volitional Effects on a Model Bacterial System." *Subtle Energies,* 1 (1990): 21–41.

Reid, G., et al. "State, Emotionality, Belief, and Absorption in ESP Scoring." *Journal of the Association for the Study of Perception* 17 (1982): 28–39.

Rein, G. "DNA as a Detector of Subtle Energies." Proceedings of the Fourth International Society for the Study of Subtle Energy and Medicine. Monterey, Calif., October 1994.

Remen, N. "On Defining Spirit." *Noetic Sciences Review* 27 (1993): 38–42.

Reston, J. *The Last Apocalypse: Europe in the Year 100.* Garden City, N.Y.: Doubleday, 1998.

Rhine, J. B., et al. *Extrasensory Perception After Sixty Years.* Boston: Humphries, 1966.

Rhine, J. B., and S. R. Feather. "The Study of Cases of 'Psi Trailing' in Animals." *Journal of Parapsychology* 26, no. 1 (1962): 2–21.

Roche, S. M., and K. M. McConkey. "Personality Processes and Individual Differences. Absorption: Nature, Assessment, and Correlates." *Journal of Personality and Social Psychology* 59 (1990): 91–101.

Rossa, L., et al. "A Close Look at Therapeutic Touch." *Journal of the American Medical Association* 279 (1998): 1005–1010.

Roszak, T. *The Making of a Counter Culture.* New York: Doubleday/Anchor, 1969.

Roszak, T., et al., eds. *Ecopsychology: Restoring the Earth, Healing the Mind.* San Francisco: Sierra Club Books, 1995.

Russek, L. G., and G. E. Schwartz. "Energy Cardiology: A Dynamical Energy Systems Approach for Integrating Conventional and Alternative Medicine." *Advances* 12, no. 4 (1996): 4–24.

————. "Narrative Descriptions of Parental Love and Caring Predict Health Status in Midlife: A 35-Year Follow-Up of the Harvard Mastery of Stress Study." *Alternative Medicine* 2 (1996): 55–66.

Schlitz, M. J. "Intentionality and Intuition and Their Clinical Implications: A Challenge for Science and Medicine." *Advances: The Journal of Mind-Body Medicine* 12, no. 2 (1996): 58–66.

Schor, J. B. *The Overspent American: Upscaling, Downshifting, and the New Consumer.* New York: Basic Books, 1998.

Schrödinger, E. *What Is Life? and Mind and Matter.* London: Cambridge University Press, 1969.

Schwartz, G. E. "Psychobiology of Health: A New Synthesis." In *Psychology and Health,* edited by B. L. Hammonds and D. J. Scheirer. Washington, D.C.: American Psychological Association, 1984.

Schwartz, G. E., et al. "Cardiovascular Differentiation of Happiness, Sadness, Anger, and Fear Following Imagery and Exercise." *Psychosomatic Medicine* 43 (1981): 343–364.

Schwartz, G. E., and L. G. Russek. "Do All Dynamical Systems Have Memory? Implications of the Systemic Memory Hypothesis for Science and Society." In *Brain and Values: Behavioral Neurodynamics.* Vol. 5, edited by K. H. Pribram and J. S. King. Hillsdale, N.J.: Lawrence Erlbaum Associates, 1996.

————. "Interpersonal Hand-Energy Registration: Evidence for Implicit Performance and Perception." *Subtle Energies* 6, no. 3 (1995): 180–187.

————. "Interpersonal Registration of Actual and Intended Eye Gaze: Relationship to Openness to Spriitual Beliefs and Experiences." *Journal of Scientific Exploration* 13, no. 2 (in press).

————. *The Systemic Memory Hypothesis: Scientific Evidence for the Existence of God in an Eternally Evolving Universe* (in press).

Schwartz, T. *What Really Matters.* New York: Bantam, 1995.

Seligman, M. *Learned Optimism.* New York: Knopf, 1990.

————. *What You Can Change and What You Can't.* New York: Knopf, 1994.

Sharp, D. "So Many Lists, So Little Time." *U.S.A. Today Weekend,* March 15–17, 1996, pp. 4–6.

Shaw, D. *The Pleasure Police.* New York: Doubleday, 1996.

Shea, J. D. C. "Effects of Absorption and Instruction on Heart Rate Control." *Journal of Mental Imagery* 9 (1985): 87–100.

Sheldrake, R. *A New Science of Life.* Los Angeles: J. P. Tarcher, 1981.

————. "The Past Is Present." In *At the Leading Edge,* edited by M. Toms. New York: Larson Publications, 1991.

Shellenbarger, S. *Wall Street Journal.* January 5, 1998.

Shermer, M. *Why People Believe Weird Things.* New York: Times Books, 1988.

Siegel, B. *Love, Medicine, and Miracles.* New York: Harper and Row, 1987.

Silverstein, S. *The Giving Tree.* New York: Harper and Row, 1964.

Smith, H. *Forgotten Trust.* New York: Harper, 1976.

Sobel, D., and R. Ornstein. *Mind/Body Health* 7 (1998): 1–7.

Solomon, R. L. "The Opponent Process Theory of Acquired Motivation: The Costs of Pleasure and the Benefits of Pain." *American Psychologist* 35 (1980): 691–712.

Solvin, J. "Mental Healing." In *Advances in Parapsychological Research.* Vol. 4, edited by S. Krippner. Jefferson, N.C.: McFarland and Company, 1984.

Spiegel, D. *Living Beyond Limits.* New York: Ballantine Books, 1993.

Spinoza, B. *The Philosophy of Spinoza*. New York: Random House, 1927.

Starke, W. *Homesick for Heaven*. Buerne, Tex.: Guadalupe Press, 1988.

Steiner, R. *Occult Science: An Outline*. London: Rudolph Steiner Press, 1979.

Storr, A. *Churchill's Black Dog, Kafka's Mice*. New York: Ballantine Books, 1988.

Syme, L. S. "Control and Health: A Personal Perspective." *Advances* 7 (1991): 16–27.

Targ, R., and J. Katra. *Miracles of Mind*. Novator, Calif.: New World Library, 1998.

Teilhard de Chardin, P. "The Evolution of Chastity." In *On Love*. New York: Harper and Row, 1967.

Tellegen, A., and G. Atkinson. "Openness to Absorbing a Self-Altering Experience ('absorption'): A Trait Related to Hypnotic Susceptibility." *Journal of Abnormal Psychology* 83 (1974): 268–277.

Tellegen, A., et al. "Personality Similarity in Twins Reared Apart and Together." *Journal of Personality and Social Psychology* 54 (1988): 1031–1039.

Tenner, E. *Why Things Bite Back: Technology and the Revenge of Unintended Consequences*. New York: Knopf, 1996.

Thomas, A., and S. Chess. *Temperament and Development*. New York: Brunner-Mazel, 1977.

Tiller, W. A. "Can an Aspect of Consciousness Be Imprinted into an Electronic Device?" *Journal of Consciousness Studies* (in press).

———. "A Gas Discharge Device for Investigating Focussed Human Attention." *Journal of Scientific Exploration* 2 (1990): 250–260.

———. *Science and Human Transformation: Subtle Energies, Intentionality, and Consciousness*. Walnut Creek, Calif.: Pavior, 1997.

———. "Towards a Predictive Model of Subtle Domain Connections to the Physical Domain Aspect of Reality: The Origins of Wave-Particle Duality, Electric-Magnetic Monopoles and the Mirror Principle." *Journal of Scientific Exploration* 13, no. 1 (1999): 41–67.

Tiller, W. A., et al. *Exploring Robust Interactions Between Human Intention and Inanimate/Animate Systems* [reprint]. Presented at "Toward a Science of Consciousness: Fundamental Approaches." May 25–28, 1999. United Nations University, Tokyo, Japan.

Trapman, A. H. *The Dog, Man's Best Friend*. London: Hutchinson and Company, 1929.

Twain, M. *Christian Science*. Buffalo, N.Y.: Prometheus Books, 1986.

Tylor, E. B. *Primitive Culture*. Vol. 1. London: Oxford University Press, 1871.

Uhlenhuth, E. H., et al. "The Symptomatic Relief of Anxiety with Meprobamate, Phenobarbital, and Placebo." *American Journal of Psychiatry* 115 (1959): 905–910.

Vassend, O. "Dimensions of Negative Affectivity, Self-Reported Somatic Complaints: Relevance to the Concept of Alexithymia." *Journal of Psychotherapy and Psychosomatic Illness* 47 (1987): 74–81.

Wakai, R. T., and C. B. Martin. "Spatio-Temporal Properties of the Fetal Magnetocardiogram." *American Journal of Obstetrics and Gynecology* (March 1994): 770–776.

Wallace, R. K., J. B. Fagan, and D. S. Pasco. "Vedic Physiology." *Modern Science and Vedic Science* 1, no. 2 (1988): 3–59.

Wallis, C. L., ed. *The Treasure Chest*. San Francisco: Harper and Row, 1965.

Webster's Third New World Dictionary. Springfield, Mass.: Merriam-Webster Publishers, Inc., 1993.

White, J. *The Meeting of Science and Spirit*. New York: Paragon House, 1990.

Wickramaskera, I. A. "A Model of People at High Risk to Develop Chronic Stress-Related Somatic Symptoms: Some Predictions." *American Journal of Clinical Hypnosis* (in press).

———. "Risk Factors for Parapsychological Verbal Reports, Hypnotizability, and Somatic Complaints." In *Parapsychology and Human Nature,* edited by B. Shapin, and L. Coly. New York: Parapsychology Foundation, 1986.

Wilbur, K. *No Boundaries.* Boston: New Science Library, 1979.

———. *Quantum Questions: The Mystical Writings of the World's Great Physicists.* Boston: Shambhala, 1984.

———. "Where it Was, There I Shall Become: Human Potential and the Boundaries of the Soul." In *Beyond Health and Normality,* edited by R. Walsh and D. H. Shapiro. New York: Van Nostrand Reinhold Company, 1983.

Will, G. "The Gospel from Science." *Newsweek,* November 9, 1998, p. 88.

Williams, R., and V. Williams. *Anger Kills.* New York: Harper Perennial, 1993.

Wilson, E. O. *Sociobiology: The New Synthesis.* Cambridge, Mass.: Harvard University Press, 1980.

Winokur, J. *The Portable Curmudgeon.* New York: New American Library, 1987.

Wolf, S. "Effects of Suggestion and Conditioning on the Action of Chemical Agents in Human Subjects: The Pharmacology of Placebos." *Journal of Clinical Investigation* 29 (1959): 100–109.

Wright, R. *Three Scientists and Their Gods: Looking for Meaning in an Age of Information.* New York: Times Books, 1988.

Yankelovic, D. *New Rules: Searching for Self-Fulfillment in a World Turned Upside Down.* New York: Random House, 1981.

Zillman, D. *Handbook of Mental Control.* Vol. 5. Edited by D. Wegner and J. Pennebaker. Englewood Cliffs, N.J.: Prentice Hall, 1997.

Zukav, G. *The Seat of the Soul.* New York: Simon and Schuster, 1990.

Index